THE ENCYCLOPEDIA OF BEATLES PEOPLE

Bill Harry

BLANDFORD

A BLANDFORD BOOK

First published in the UK 1997 by Blandford
A Cassell Imprint

CASSELL PLC
Wellington House
125 Strand
London WC2R 0BB

Distributed in the United States by Sterling Publishing Co., Inc.
387 Park Avenue South, New York, NY 10016–8810

British Library Cataloguing-in-Publication Data
A catalogue entry for this title is available from the British Library

ISBN 0–7137–2606–7

Typeset by York House Typographic Ltd, London
Printed and bound in Great Britain by
Creative Print and Design Wales, Ebbw Vale, Gwent

All photographs supplied by Bill Harry

Photographs on the front cover show (from left to right):
First row: Rory Storm, Chuck Berry, Roy Orbison, Brian Epstein
Second row: Buddy Holly, Julian Lennon, Billy Fury, Gene Vincent
Third row: Bill Harry, Elvis Presley, Cynthia Lennon, Dick James
Fourth row: Helen Shapiro, Jane Asher, Little Richard, Neil Aspinall

CONTENTS

Introduction
THE BIRTH OF MERSEY BEAT

THROUGHOUT THEIR LIVES and career, the Beatles were associated with literally thousands of people. In limiting this encyclopedia to approximately 500 entries, I have therefore had to be selective and have concentrated particularly on fellow musicians. Specifically, a large number of other Mersey Beatsters have found their way into the book, as this gives readers a flavour of the scene in which the Beatles grew and developed musically.

All too often, books about the Beatles intimate that they virtually created the Mersey scene, presuming that it was only in the wake of their success that groups in Liverpool began to emerge. Numerous authors have taken the line that it was only following the Beatles' national break-through that every youngster in Liverpool suddenly wanted to join a group.

In fact, the groups were already active in what was probably the most amazing nucleus of youth culture in the world between the years 1958 and 1964. Far from leading to an increase in the number of bands in Liverpool, the success of the Beatles possibly resulted in the local music scene diminishing.

At a time when the British music scene was firmly controlled from London, the Beatles forced a crack in the barrier through which groups from the provinces poured, until the powers that be in the capital closed it again. After 1964 groups from Liverpool, no matter how talented, were *personae non gratae*.

Talent in the city didn't dry up, as many presumed; it was simply condemned to isolation once more when London regained control of the music business. Yet whenever any enterprising recording manager or entrepreneur did take an interest in Liverpool, they discovered as much talent as they could handle. For example, in 1976 the British charts found themselves with a host of Liverpool bands in the Top 30 – Liverpool Express, Our Kid, The Real Thing, Supercharge, Buster – then a few years later there were Orchestral Manoeuvres in the Dark, Teardrop Explodes, Echo & the Bunnymen, China Crisis and Icicle Works; on 28 January 1984 a combination of Liverpool artists old and new dominated the Top 20:

1. *Relax*, Frankie Goes to Hollywood
2. *Pipes of Peace*, Paul McCartney
3. *That's Living Alright*, Joe Fagin
6. *Nobody Told Me*, John Lennon
9. *Wishful Thinking*, China Crisis
17. *The Killing Moon*, Echo & the Bunnymen
19. *Love is a Wonderful Colour*, Icicle Works

And it took Liverpool band Frankie Goes to Hollywood to repeat fellow Liverpudians Gerry & the Pacemakers' record of a hat trick of No. 1 hits with their first three releases.

The Mersey scene was unique for its time, yet an acknowledgement of its real contribution to the forging of the Beatles has not really been apparent in the many books which have been written about them.

In fact, the Hamburg scene has been given more prominence in the 'birth of the Beatles' story. But there was no Hamburg scene when the Beatles arrived there in 1960. It wasn't a city like Liverpool, where thousands of youngsters were pouring into venues to listen to hundreds of bands. Rock 'n' roll hardly existed in Germany at the time and the only two bands to precede the Beatles were the Jets and Derry & the Seniors.

It's true, as I've always pointed out, that their initial months in Hamburg, from August to December 1960, were a real baptism of fire and made them a better group than they'd been previously, but it was their battles with the other bands in Liverpool over the following two years which gave them their edge.

Basically, the Hamburg scene comprised of only three clubs, all within walking distance of each other: the Kaiserkeller, the Top Ten and the Star Club. As a rock venue the Kaiserkeller didn't last more than a year, leaving just two venues.

In contrast, Liverpool had far in excess of 300 venues where groups would play, including those like the Tower and Locarno Ballrooms which were large enough to accommodate thousands of youngsters. However, these were not where the Mersey sound was originally forged.

In the late 1950s groups began to thrive in Liverpool in 'jive hives', the ballrooms and town halls booked by enterprising local promoters such as Brian Kelly, Doug Martin, Wally Hill, Vic Anton, Dave Foreshaw, Sam Leach and Charlie McBain, who are among the unsung heroes of the Mersey scene. They promoted regularly at venues such as the Grosvenor Ballroom, Wilson Hall, Hambleton Hall, Aintree Institute, Blair Hall, Litherland Town Hall, St John's Hall, Alexandra Hall, Lathom Hall, Mossway Hall, Knotty Ash Village Hall and New Clubmoor Hall.

The three music venues in Hamburg were situated in the notorious red-light district of St Pauli, where audiences were generally composed of punters seeking 'adult entertainment' in clubs which actively encouraged their patrons to drink. In Liverpool it was the youth of Merseyside who crowded the venues, where only soft drinks were available. They went because they loved the music. The kids attended the venues throughout the area in their thousands in what was arguably the first major youth movement in the British Isles.

Between 1958 and 1964 there were probably around 500 different bands in the Merseyside area. The figure at any one time probably stood at 350. When Bob Wooler and I originally compiled a list of groups that we knew personally in 1961, it ran to almost 300 names.

Among the Mersey bands and artists during this period were:

The Aarons
Abraham & His Lot
Adam & the Sinners
The Agents
The Alamos
The Alaskans
Alby & the Sorrals
Steve Aldo
The Alibis
Tony Allen
The Alley Cats
The Almost Blues
The Alphas
The Ambassadors
The Anzacs
The Aristocrats
Arrow & the Archers
The Arrows
The Atlantas
The Aztecs
Babs and Joan
The Bachelors
The Backbeats
Bags Blue Beats
The Banshees
The Beat Boys
The Beatcombers
The Beathovens
The Beatles
The Beatwoods
Bertie Collins & the Sundowners
The Big Three
Billy Forde & the Phantoms
The Black Cats
The Black Diamonds

The Blackjacks
The Black Knights
The Black Velvets
The Blackwells
The Blak Katz
The Blue Beats
The Blue Chips
The Blue Country Boys
The Blue Diamonds
The Blue Mountain Boys
The Blue Notes
The Blues System
Bob Evans & the Five Shillings
Bobby & the Bachelors
Bobby & the Halers
The Bobby Bell Rockers
Bob's Vegas Five
The Boleros
Amos Bonny
The Boot Hill Billies
The Boys
The Breakaways
The Brokers
Irene Brown
Bruce & the Cavaliers
Buddy Dean & the Teachers
The Buffaloes
The Bumblies
Billy Butler
Cadillac & the Playboys
The Cadillacs
The Calderstones
Carl Vincent & the Counts
Carol & the Corvettes
Irene Carroll

The Carrolls
Cass & the Cassanovas
The Casuals
The Cavaliers
The Cavemen
The Caverners
The Centaurs
The Centremen
The Chain Gang
The Challengers
The Champions
The Chants
The Cheaters
The Cheetahs
Vicki Cheetham
The Chelseas
The Chessmen
Chick Graham & the Coasters
Christine Ching
Chris & the Diamonds
Tony Christian
The Cimarrons
The Cirques
The Citadels
The Citrons
The City Beats
The Clansmen
The Classics
Clay Ellis & the Raiders
The Clayton Squares
The Climbers
The Coins
Collage
The Collegians
The Columbians
The Comets
The Concords
The Connoisseurs
The Conquests
The Conspirators
The Contenders
The Contrasts
The Corals
The Cordelles
The Cordes
The Corsairs

The Corvettes
The Countdowns
The Country Four
The Creoles
The Crescendoes
The Crestas
The Crossbeats
The Croupiers
The Cruisers
The Crusaders
The Cryin' Shames
Cy & the Cimmarons
Cy Tucker's Friars
The Dakotas
The Daleks
Danny & the Asteroids
Danny & the Escorts
Danny & the Hi-Cats
Danny Lee & the Stalkers
The Darktown Skiffle Group
The Dateliners
Dave & the Corvettes
Dave & the Rave-Ons
Dave Bell & the Bell Boys
The Daybreakers
The Dealers
Dean Fleming & the Flamingos
The Deans
Barbara Dee
Dee & the Dynamites
Dee & the Pontiacs
The Dee Beats
Dee Fenton's Silhouettes
The Deepbeats
The Deerstalkers
The Defenders
The Defiants
The Del Renas
The Delecardoes
The Delemeres
The Delltones
The Delmont Four
The Demoiselles
The Demon Five
The Denems
Denis & the Newtowns

The Dennisons
Denny Seyton & the Sabres
The Deputies
Derry Wilkie & the Others
The Detonators
The Detours
The Diablos
The Diamonds
The Dimensions
Dino & the Wild Fires
The Diplomats
Dixie & the Daredevils
The Dominant Four
The Downbeats
The Drifting Cowboys
The Dynachords
The Dynamic Daybreakers
The Dynamos
Earl Preston & the Realms
Earl Preston & the TTs
Earl Royce & the Olympics
The Earthlings Blues Band
The Easybeats
Eddie Dean & the Onlookers
Eddy Falcon & the Vampires
The Elektones
The Elektrons
The Epics
The Escorts
The Everests
The Excelles
The Excheckers
The Executioners
The Explorers
The Expressions
The Eyes
The Factotums
The Falcons
The Fallons
Faron & the Burnettes
Faron & the Crossfires
Faron & the Tempest Tornadoes
Faron's Flamingos
The Fast Cats
The FBI
The Federal Five

The Feelgoods
The Few
The Fire-Flites
The Fix
The Flames
The Flintstones
The Flyaways
The Flyovers
The Foggy Mountain Ramblers
The Fontanas
The Four Aces
The Four Aristokats
The Four Clefs
The Four Dimensions
The Four Gents
Four Hits & A Miss
The Four Jays
The Four Just Men
The Fourmost
The Four Musketeers
The Four Originals
Frank Knight & the Barons
Freddie Starr & the Delmonts
Freddie Starr & the Flamingos
Freddie Starr & the Midnighters
Freddie Starr & the Ventures
The Fruit Eating Bears
The Futurists
The Galaxies with Doreen
The Galvanizers
Gary B Goode & the Hot Rods
The Gay Tones
Gee Gee & the Go Men
The Gems
Gene Day & the Django Beats
Geoff Stacey & the Wanderers
The George Nield Trio
The Georgians
Gerry & the Pacemakers
Gerry Bach & the Beathovens
Gerry De Ville & the City Kings
The Ghost Riders
The Gibsons
The Globetrotters
The Griff Parry Five
Barbara Grounds

Group One
Groups Inc,
Gus & the Thundercaps
Gus Travis & the Midnighters
The Hailers
The Hammers
Hank & the Drifters
Hank Walters & the Dusty Road
   Ramblers
The Harlems
The Heralds
The Heartbeats
The Hellions
The Hi Spots
The Hi-Cats
The Hideaways
The Hi-Fi Three
The Hi-Hats
The Hillsiders
Howie Casey & the Seniors
Rita Hughes
The Hustlers
The Hylites
Ian & the Zodiacs
The Illusions
The Impacts
The Incas
The Inmates
The Invaders
Irene & the Sante Fes
Jackie and Bridie
The Jackobeats
The Jaguars
The James Boys
The Jaybeats
The Jaywalkers
Jenny & the Tallboys
The Jensons
Jet & the Valients
The Jets
Jimmy & the Jokers
Jimmy & the Midnighters
J.J. & the Hi-Lites
Joan & the Demons
Johnny Apollo & the
   Spartans

Johnny Gold & the Country
   Cousins
Johnny Marlowe and the Whip
   Chords
Johnny Martin & the Martinis
Johnny Paul & the Dee Jays
Johnny President & the Senators
Johnny Ringo & the Colts
Johnny Rocco & the Jets
Johnny Saint & the Travellers
Johnny Sandon & the Remo Four
Johnny Sandon & the Searchers
Johnny Tempest & the Tornadoes
The Jokers
Tommy Jordan
The Kandies
The Kansas City Five
The Karacters
Karina
Karl Terry & the Cruisers
Ken Dallas & the Silhouettes
Keoki & the Hawaiianeers
The Kingpins
Kingsize Taylor & the Dominoes
The Kinsleys
The Kirkbys
Kliff Hilton & the Merseys
The Knutrockers
The Kobras
The Koobas
The Kordas
The Kruzads
The Landslides
The Lawmen
Lee Castle & the Barons
Lee Crombie & the Sundowners
Lee Curtis & the All Stars
Lee Curtis & the Detours
Lee Eddie & the Chevrons
The Lee Eddie Five
Lee Shondell & the Boys
Lee Shondell & the Capitols
The Leesiders
The Legends
Lenny & the Team Mates
Liam & the Invaders

The Li'l Three
Lilli Leyland
The Lincolns
The Liverbirds
The Lonely Ones
The Long & the Short
Lottie & the Weimars
L'Ringo's
The Mafia
The Mailman
The Mal Craig Three
Joan Malloy
The Managers
The Maracas
The Marescas
The Markfour
Mark Swain & the Tornadoes
The Marlins
Jackie Martin
Jill Martin
The Masqueraders
The Masterminds
The Mastersounds
The Mavericks
The Megatones
The Memphis R&B Combo
The Memphis Three
The Merchants
The Merseybeats
The Mersey Four
The Mersey Five
The Mersey Men
The Mersey Monsters
The Mersey Sounds
The Mersey Bluebeats
The Meteors
The Method
The MGs
The Michael Allen Group
The M.I.5
The Mikados
Mike & the Explorers
Mike Byrne & the Thunderbirds
Mike Dee & the Detours
Mike Savage & the Wildcats
The Miller Brothers

The Minibeats
The Minutes
The Missouri Drifters
The Mojos
The Moments
The Morockans
The Mosquitos
The Motifs
The Musicians
The Music Students
The Mustangs
The Mystery Men
The Mystics
The Nameless Ones
The Nashpool Four
The Night Boppers
The Nightriders
The Nocturnes
The Nomads
The Notions
The Onlookers
The Others
The Outkasts
The Pacifics
The Page Boys
The Paladins
The Panthers
The Paragons
The Pathfinders
Paul & the Diamonds
Paul Francis & the Wanderers
The Pawns
The Pegasus Four
Peter Demos & His Demons
Pete Picasso & the Rock
   Sculptors
The Phantoms
Phil Brady & the Ranchers
Phil's Feelgoods
The Pikkins
The Pilgrims
The Plebs
The Plims
The Pontiacs
The Poppies
The Premiers

The Press Gang
The Pressmen
The Principles
The Profiles
The Prowlers
The Pulsators
The Pyramids
The Quarry Men
Tommy Quickly
The Quiet Ones
The Quintones
The Rainchecks
The Rainmakers
The Ramrods
The Ranchers
The Ravens
The Rebel Rousers
Reds Incorporated
The Remo Four
The Renegades
The Renicks
The Rent Collectors
Rhythm Amalgamated
Rhythm & Blues Incorporated
The Rhythm Quintet
Rick & the Delmonts
Ricky & the Dominant Four
Ricky Gleason & the Top Spots
Rikki & the Red Streaks
The Riot Squad
Rip Van Winkle & the Rip-It-Ups
The Rivals
The Roadrunners
The Robettes
Robin & the Ravens
The Rockerfellers
The Rockin' Rivals
Rocky Stone & the Pebbles
Rogues Gallery
Rita Rogers
The Ron Pickard Combo
The Rondex
The Rontons
Rory & the Globe Trotters
Rory Storm & the Hurricanes
Roy & the Dions

Roy Montrose & the Midnights
The Runaways
St Louis Checks
The Sandgrounders
The Sandstorms
The Santones
The Sapphires
Savva & the Democrats
The Scaffold
The Schatz
The Screaming Skulls
The Searchers
The Secrets
The Seftons
The Seniors
The Senitors
The Sensations
The Sepias
The Set Up
The Shades
The Shakers
The Shimmy Shimmy Queens
The Silvertones
The Sinners
The Skeletons
The Skylarks
The Sneakers
The Sobells
Some People
The Sonnets
Sonny Kaye & the Reds
The Soul Agents
The Soul Seekers
Sounds Plus One
The Spectres
The Spidermen
The Spinners
The Sportsmen
The Squad
The Statesmen
The Stereos
Steve & the Syndicate
Steve Day & the Drifters
The Strangers
The Strettons
The Subterranes

The Sundowners
The Swaydes
The Swinging Bluejeans,
The Syndicate
The Tabs
Take Five
The Talismen
The Team-mates
The Teenbeats
The Templars
The Tempos
The Tenabeats
The Tennessee Four
The Terry Hines Sextet
The Texans
That Group
Them Grimbles
The Three Bells
The Three Deuces
The Three of Diamonds
The Thrillers
The Thunderbirds
Tiffany's Dimensions
The TJs
The Tokens
Tom and Bernie
Tommy & the Olympics
Tommy & the Metronomes
Tommy & the Satellites
Tony & the Checkers
Tony & the Quandros
Tony Carlton & the Mersey Four
The Topics
The Tornadoes
The Traders
The Travellers
The Tremas
The Trends
The Trents

The Tributes
The Tudor Four
The Tudors
The Tuxedos
The Two Tones
The Undertakers
The Vaders
The Valkyries
The Vampires
Vance Williams & the Rhythm
    Four
The Ventures
The Verbs
The Vernons Girls
Vic & the TTs
Vic Takes Four
The V.I.C.s
The Vigilantes
The Vikings
Vikki Lane & the Moonlighters
Vince Earl & the Talismen
Vince Earl & the Zeroes
Vince Reno & the Sabres
Vinny & the Dukes
The V.I.P.s
The Walter Corless Combo
Wayne Calvert & the Cimmarons
Wayne Stevens & the Vikings
The Weeverbeats
Wells Fargo
The Wheels
Lorraine White
The Wild Harkes
The Willows
The Wranglers
Wump & His Werbles
The Young Ones
The Zenith Six
The Zephyrs

The most popular line-up was a quartet with three guitarists – lead, rhythm and bass – plus a drummer. The three guitarists up front would engage in vocal harmony. The Beatles were particularly adept at this as Paul McCartney, being left-handed, could use the same microphone as John Lennon, when they sang together – also producing a visual effect which many of the other groups couldn't imitate.

This basic line-up was the one generally referred to when people later talked of the Liverpool Sound, and it was most apparent with groups such as the Beatles, the Searchers, Faron's Flamingos and the Swinging Bluejeans. However, this image tends to make people forget just how extensive the range of the music scene in Liverpool was: there were duos, trios, quintets, and groups with pianos and saxophones in their line-ups.

Comedy outfits such as the Fourmost were parodying other artists long before Duke D'Mond & the Barron Knights became famous for numbers such as 'Call Up the Groups'.

There were folk groups, country music bands, vocal groups, girl rock bands – even speciality bands such as the Mersey Monsters. I remember hearing that there was a Chinese rock 'n' roll group in Chinatown, but I was never able to track them down to interview them for *Mersey Beat*.

Liverpool had been called the Nashville of the North, because it had the largest country music scene in Europe. There were approximately 40 C&W bands contemporary with the Beatles. They had their own clubs, such as the Black Cat Club and Wells Fargo, their own Country Music Federation and they ran their 'Grand Ole Opry' annually at the Philharmonic Hall. Their attempt to revolutionize country music, just as the rock groups in Liverpool revolutionized rock 'n' roll, has never been properly acknowledged.

There were basically two forms of country bands in Liverpool – the purists, who played in the traditional manner, parroting the American records and wearing stetsons and cowboy clothes – and the new wave, such as the Hillsiders, young bands with a fresh approach to the music, who didn't dress in country style, but provided a new and exciting beat to country sounds.

Unfortunately, this movement tended to be overshadowed by the Beatles and the Mersey sound, and the new revolution in country music didn't occur until the late 1980s, with young Nashville artists who gave the music a fresh image – but it was happening on the banks of the Mersey in the late 1950s!

There were also several all-girl rock 'n' roll groups in Liverpool, the most noted being the Liverbirds. The girls became so popular in Hamburg that they remained in Germany for several years, missing out on the Mersey Beat boom. But the fact remains that there were girl rock bands in Liverpool a decade before groups such as Fanny.

In the field of folk music, Liverpool gave rise to the Spinners, who remained Britain's premier folk outfit for 30 years, until their retirement.

There was also a healthy black music scene on Merseyside. Apart from artists such as Derry Wilkie and Steve Aldo, there were several vocal outfits in the Liverpool 8 district, such as the Chants, the Sobells, the Challengers and the Poppies. Only the Chants were to have a limited degree of success. It seemed that when Britain eventually accepted black artists into the charts – with the Motown acts and soul music, the black hit artists were almost exclusively American. Few black British artists made it until the 1970s. Strangely enough, the group to make the breakthrough and hit the top of the charts was the Real Thing, who included some of the original members of the Chants. It had taken them 15 years to achieve their success!

Coexisting with the rock, folk, country and black music scenes was the poetry scene. Local poets used to hold readings at clubs such as Streates. I also organized and promoted a poetry-to-jazz concert at the Crane Theatre – the first concert of its kind to be held in the north of England. Three of the poets, Roger McGough, Adrian Henri and Brian Patten, established themselves as leading British poets of the decade.

Mersey Beat also reported on 'clubland', the thriving entertainment scene for an older generation. Over 300 clubs were affiliated to the Merseyside Clubs Association. There were social clubs for unions, stores and factories which provided entertainment for their members – in addition to drinks at prices far below the normal prices in pubs.

It was on the clubland scene that many local comics, such as Ken Dodd and Jimmy Tarbuck, developed. Liverpool has always had a reputation for providing more than its fair share of comedians, including Tommy Handley, Ted Ray, Arthur Askey and Norman Vaughan.

Liverpool had already provided chart acts from this background in the 1950s, with artists such as Frankie Vaughan, Lita Roza and Michael Halliday.

Although clubland was the training ground for comedians, speciality acts and country bands, there was also work for numerous rock groups in the various clubs. Early gigs for groups with Gerry Marsden and Ringo Starr took place at Pitt Street Labour club, and a Quarry Men gig was on behalf of the Speke Bus Depot Social Club.

Imagine groups taking the stage at cinemas in intervals between the films; performing in coffee bars; strutting their acts at swimming baths; performing at ice rinks; learning their craft in almost every youth club, church hall, synagogue and village hall in the Merseyside area; blasting their music from the stages of town halls; lugging their gear into the bandrooms of the numerous ballrooms; performing before audiences of varying ages at social clubs; playing in the city centre cellar clubs and pulling in the audiences by the thousand in the larger venues – no place in the world at that time had so many young groups performing virtually nightly in such a compact area. In 1961 I dubbed Liverpool 'the Rocking City'.

Liverpool's maritime heritage had resulted in the city becoming a melting pot of cosmopolitan influences. As the main port during the days of the slave trade, its black population became established centuries ago. Ironically, the large mansions built by the slave traders became the abodes in the twentieth century of the black population, who mainly dwelt in the Liverpool 8, or Toxteth, district.

The city was also a main destination for the Irish fleeing the potato famine in the mid-nineteenth century and Liverpool boasts a huge Irish population – it's often jokingly referred to as the capital of Ireland. There is also a substantial Welsh intake and Liverpool had a Chinatown before San Francisco.

Different cultural influences also led to the development of a wide range of musical tastes, and, from sea shanties to Irish folk songs, Liverpool danced to the music of the world for more than two centuries. Most specifically, pub sing-alongs were a standard form of Liverpool entertainment and the musical heritage was strong.

This is where the truth and myth part, for the maritime heritage had no direct influence on the development of Mersey Beat.

Writers in the 1970s began to suggest that the reason Liverpool groups were different from groups in other parts of the country was that 'Cunard Yanks' brought them records that couldn't be obtained elsewhere in Britain. 'Cunard Yanks' were the Liverpudlians who went to sea in the ocean liners and brought presents back to their families. The myth is that they brought American records for their younger brothers and sons, and this is how the Liverpool bands built up their repertoires.

Sounds nice, but it's not true.

In the 1950s Liverpool was still a seaport and a number of Liverpool men still sailed the seas, but it was a pathetic number compared to the pre-war days and the turn of the century. One or two members of groups, such as John McNally of the Searchers, had brothers who went to sea and brought them records. However, the most important records in the Searchers' collection came from drummer Chris Curtis, who gathered them in his trips around the record stores. Some of the country bands, such as Hank Walters & His Country Road Ramblers, were able to obtain rare country albums from merchant seamen, but the 'Cunard Yank' theory remains a myth.

A study of the Beatles repertoire from the time, laying aside the original Lennon and McCartney numbers, proves that every song they played was available on record in Britain through the normal channels.

Johnny Byrne, the noted Johnny Guitar of the legendary Rory Storm & the Hurricanes, confirmed to me: 'That's a myth about the groups receiving copies or having records from "Cunard Yanks". We certainly never got any material this way and I doubt that the Beatles did. Most group material was gleaned from the records (although some on limited release) that were issued at that particular time [1958–1961]. Chuck Berry, Jerry Lee, etc., were available and groups took their material from these and lesser-known artists with material that we were able to play and adapt that suited all the groups' limited styles.'

Chris Huston of the Undertakers added: 'When Johnny Byrne says that Liverpool groups didn't get their material from sailors he's right. But he's only partly right about the rest. We spent hours searching through piles of records on the stalls at the flea markets every time we went down to London. They were apparently records that had come, mostly, from the PX stores on the American Air Force bases. In fact I got my first James Brown, Lonnie Mack, Major Lance and Joey Dee albums from market stalls.'

Frankly, at the time when the Mersey scene began to flourish, the Cunard ships had long since been rerouted to Southampton. Cunard still retained offices in Liverpool, but the days of liners coming to the port had ended more than a decade previously. Liverpool had been the centre of Atlantic trade and at one time was the main European port and second city of the Empire. Between 1900 and 1914 one tenth of the world's tonnage passed through Liverpool and the era of the great passenger liners was Liverpool's greatest epoch. But between 1920 and 1980 Liverpool's dock-land steadily declined and, as ships got bigger, the docks became too small and the passenger liners no longer used the port.

The first major musical influence in Liverpool was a British artist, Lonnie Donegan, who sparked off the skiffle boom. When the boom began to wane, Liverpool groups turned to rock 'n' roll. Buddy Holly & the Crickets, Eddie Cochran, Elvis Presley, Chuck Berry, Little Richard, Ray Charles, the Everly Brothers, Gene Vincent, Carl Perkins, the Coasters, Arthur Alexander, Jerry Lee Lewis, the Olympics, Larry Williams, the Isley Brothers, Bobby Freeman, the Shirelles, Chan Romero, Lloyd Price, Bo Diddley, the Drifters and Fats Domino were their inspiration.

While rock 'n' roll bands were thriving in Liverpool, the music was encountering problems in America. Buddy Holly, the Big Bopper and Ritchie Valens were killed in an air crash 'the day the music died'; Little Richard got religion; Eddie Cochran died in a car crash, while Carl Perkins's career suffered following his road accident; Chuck Berry was in jail; Elvis had joined the army; Jerry Lee Lewis was 'disgraced' for marrying an under-age cousin. This was the opportunity media moguls had been waiting for – the chance to kill this devil's music! They titillated teenagers by saturating the airwaves with records by clean-cut handsome white youngsters who sanitized the sound – Pat Boone, Bobby Rydell, Fabian, Rickie Nelson (although he turned out to be more influential than first imagined), Dion, Tommy Roe, Tommy Sands, Frankie Avalon and Bobby Vinton.

Rock 'n' roll might literally have been safely caged in the States, but in Liverpool bands began to adapt the music to their own style. What was also different about the Mersey groups was their age: they were actually teenagers, whereas the American rock 'n' roll giants were almost a decade older.

My own involvement with the scene began in 1958, while I was attending Liverpool College of Art. I was asked to contribute to a magazine produced by the local music store Frank Hessy. Mr Hesselberg, the owner, insisted on the rather uncommercial title *Frank Comments*, but gave complete editorial freedom in all other respects. I designed the covers and produced interior illustrations, reviewed local events, wrote about jazz legends such as Bunk Johnson and even penned a science-fiction jazz serial.

In the meantime, Stuart Sutcliffe and John Lennon were among my closest friends and we used to spend a great deal of spare time together, mainly discussing the subjects young people discuss – what the future held, the latest books and films, art, academic life and so on.

John had a group and two of its members, Paul McCartney and George Harrison, were pupils of Liverpool Institute, which was situated next door to the college. They used to come to our canteen during lunch breaks and also rehearsed in the life rooms. Stu and I were members of the Students' Union committee and put forward the proposal that we use student funds to buy a PA system which John's group could use when they appeared at the college dances.

I referred to them as the 'college band' at the time and they were booked regularly for our dances as support to headliners such as the Merseysippi Jazz Band.

Skiffle music had been popular for the last couple of years and I used to study the history of American folk music and railway songs at Picton library, in addition to producing a duplicated magazine at the college, simply called *Jazz*.

With the experience of editing a number of fan magazines behind me, my involvement with *Frank Comments,* my association with their printers James E. James and studies in typography, printing and newspaper design and layout at the college, I had visions of producing a magazine called *Storyville & 52nd Street.*

One evening we all went along to Liverpool University to hear a poetry reading by Royston Ellis. Later, at Ye Cracke, in a discussion with John, Stu and Rod Murray, I pointed out that Ellis, in common with a lot of other poets, was simply copying the American Beat poets such as Lawrence Ferlinghetti, Allen Ginsberg and Gregory Corso. My feeling was that people were more likely to stretch themselves creatively by expressing their own environment and experience rather than by copying someone else's. I suggested that we should use our creative talents to express what we were personally involved in, that we should take a vow to make Liverpool famous: John with his music, Stu and Rod with their painting and myself by writing about the city. I even suggested that we should called ourselves the Dissenters.

At one time Stu and I were going to produce a book about Liverpool. I would write about interesting and unusual facets of the city and its people and he would illustrate it. We never did the book, but the seeds of *Mersey Beat* were sown.

In addition to Ye Cracke, the college canteen and various students' flats, we would also hang around the Jacaranda coffee bar, run by a gregarious Liverpool-Welshman, Allan Williams. It was here in May 1960 that I met Virginia. She was 16 years old, was wearing black barathea trousers and a green sweater and had flowing auburn hair.

The lads were playing downstairs in the 'coal hole', while their girlfriends held broom handles to which their mikes were attached. In those days we were all skint, yet managed to get by, even when we didn't have the proverbial 'two halfpennies to rattle together'.

Virginia became my girlfriend and the visions of creating a magazine grew. I'd initially begun thinking in terms of a jazz magazine because there was a huge trad jazz boom and Liverpool was a thriving centre. There were clubs such as the Cavern, the Liverpool Jazz Society and the Temple Jazz Club, and promoters such as Albert Kinder regularly booked artists of the calibre of Chris Barber and Lonnie Donegan at the Empire and Pavilion Theatres. A local promoter, Sam Leach, said he'd advance me the £25 I wanted to launch the magazine, but he never did.

By this time my thoughts were developing in a new direction. My experience writing for *Frank Comments* had taken me to places around Liverpool such as Wilson Hall, where local rock 'n' roll groups used to play. I began talking to members of groups who dropped by the Jacaranda and sensed that something unique was happening in Liverpool. The rock 'n' roll scene was larger than anyone – even the groups themselves – realized.

The little red pocket notebooks I carried around with me began to fill up with information on venues, promoters and groups.

I decided to write to national newspapers, such as the *Daily Mail*, to inform them that what was happening in Liverpool was as unique as what had happened in New Orleans at the turn of the century, but with rock 'n' roll groups instead of jazz.

No one took any notice. Liverpool, it seemed, was isolated. It didn't have any media which could reach out nationally. The two main local publications, the *Liverpool Echo* and the *Evening Express*, didn't cover the local music scene.

Historically, Liverpool had lost a great deal of power and prestige when the Manchester Ship Canal was built, allowing a lot of trade to bypass Liverpool and go straight to Manchester. Manchester became the capital of the North and was home to both Granada Television and the BBC TV studios, in addition to radio stations and the northern editions of the national newspapers. Most news on TV, radio and in the press had a Manchester bias. In comparison, Liverpool seemed to be almost a back-water. As a result, what was happening there developed without anyone realizing it and without any outside interference.

Having received no reaction to my appeals to the press to cover what was happening, I decided to do something about it myself. Instead of a jazz magazine, I'd write about the local rock 'n' roll scene.

Although I'd received my National Diploma in design, I was still at the art college, having become the first student on the new Graphic Design course and later winning the Senior City Art Scholarship. John had hoped to enter the Graphic Art department with me, but the lecturer, Roy Sharpe, wouldn't accept him.

Money was still a problem, but Dick Matthews, a friend from the Jac, introduced me to Jim Anderson, who offered to lend Virginia and me the £50 we needed to launch the project. By this time I'd decided on a fortnightly newspaper, completely devoted to the music on Merseyside, which would also be a 'What's On' of every musical event during the fortnight.

Virginia's support was what really kept me going and ensured that the visions in my head became a reality. She gave up her job to work full-time on the project and Jim found us an office above a wine merchant's shop in Renshaw Street. Jim, Dick, Virginia and I entered the tiny attic office room carrying a typewriter, a desk and a couple of chairs which Jim had provided for us. Dick also took out his camera and promised to cover the local music scene for the new paper.

Sitting in the Jac with John and Stu, I'd tell them of our progress. By that time they'd left the college and were about to go to Germany. I asked John if he could write a biography of the Beatles for the new paper which I could run in the first issue. When the Beatles returned from Germany, John gave me the biography, written in his own inimitable style, which I entitled 'On the Dubious Origins of Beatles. Translated from the John Lennon'.

By this time, of course, I was friendly with all members of the group. As well as knowing Paul and George from college days and attending their early gigs, I also got to know Pete Best, who joined them at the Jacaranda. They were the group I was closest to and were the ones I was obviously going to promote the most.

Sitting alone in the office at about two in the morning, I was attempting to think of a name for the new paper. Having decided that I'd cover the entire Merseyside region – Liverpool, the Wirral, Southport, Crosby, St Helens, Widnes, Warrington and so on – I suddenly visualized it as a policeman's beat. The image of a copper walking around a map of the surrounding area came into my head, along with the name *Mersey Beat*.

So the title which was to give its name to the Mersey sound, which led to bands being called Beat groups, was actually coined not from the 'beat' of the music but from a policeman's 'beat'.

The reaction to *Mersey Beat* was literally phenomenal locally and all 5,000 copies of the first issue sold out. The three main wholesalers, W. H. Smith, Blackburn's and Conlan's, took copies; I delivered copies personally to another two dozen newsagents, in addition to the main local venues and musical instruments and record stores.

At North End Music Stores (NEMS), when I asked to see their manager, Brian Epstein came down from his office. I showed him the publication and he agreed to take a dozen copies. He phoned me soon after to tell me how surprised he was that they had sold almost immediately. He ordered more – and more – and more. For the second issue he placed an advance order of 12 dozen copies, an incredible amount of copies for a single publication at one outlet.

That issue, published on 20 July 1961, devoted the entire front cover to the Beatles recent recordings in Hamburg under the headline 'Beatles Sign Recording Contract!'. There was also a photograph of the Beatles by Astrid Kirchherr which Paul had brought back from Germany, together with Astrid's permission for me to use any of the Beatles pics she'd taken as publicity for the group.

Brian Epstein invited me to his office for a sherry and wanted to discuss the groups he'd read about in *Mersey Beat*. He was incredulous that such a thriving music scene existed all around him which he'd been unaware of. He was also amazed at the number of young people who came into his store just to buy copies of the paper.

Brian asked me to describe the local scene and was particularly interested in the Beatles cover story and the fact that a local group had made a record. He immediately booked advertising space and asked if he could review records. I appointed him record reviewer, beginning with issue No. 3 and his column was headed 'Stop the World – and listen to everything in it. Brian Epstein of Nems'.

His advertisements and reviews shared the same pages as the articles and photographs about the Beatles and he was particularly impressed by Bob Wooler's article about the group in the 31 August 1961 issue. Over the months he liked to discuss the stories in *Mersey Beat* with me and then asked if I could arrange for him to visit the Cavern to see the Beatles. I did this and he visited the club, less than 100 yards from his store, during a lunchtime session on Thursday 9 November.

When he published his autobiography, *A Cellarful of Noise*, in 1964, he claimed that he first heard of the Beatles when a young man called Raymond Jones came into his store on 28 October 1961 and ordered a copy of the Beatles single. This is an apocryphal tale but it is so neat that writers who haven't really examined the facts chronologically love to cite it. It's the old story of having to choose between the truth and the legend and opting to go for the legend. I'm well aware that *Mersey Beat* readers went to NEMS to ask for copies of the Beatles single, but this was only after *Mersey Beat* printed the cover story in July.

It's possible that there might have been someone called Raymond Jones, but Epstein was fully aware of the Beatles months before the youth allegedly entered his store to order the disc. If Jones was a Beatles fan, he would have been known by the other hard-core fans. Freda Kelly, who ran the Beatles fan club and knew most of the local fans personally, said she'd never heard of him and didn't believe he existed. Pat Delaney, Cavern doorman, said he'd never heard of a Raymond Jones and believed he was a myth. In fact, Alistair Taylor, Brian Epstein's assistant, who accompanied him to the Cavern that first night, has finally admitted that Raymond Jones was a fabrication.

Whether he existed or not is beside the point. I had been discussing the group with Epstein for months and he had read all about them in *Mersey Beat* as they were the group I plugged most in the paper.

Sam Leach is another person who is puzzled by the Jones story. At the time he was promoting the Beatles for local gigs and his posters were displayed in NEMS, who also sold tickets and took a percentage of ticket sales. In fact, a poster in Brian's branch of NEMS was advertising his forthcoming 'Operation Big Beat' at the Tower Ballroom on 10 November. In large letters it announced:

> Rocking to Merseyside's TOP 5 GROUPS
>
> THE BEATLES
>
> RORY STORM & THE HURRICANES
>
> GERRY & THE PACEMAKERS
>
> THE REMO FOUR
>
> KINGSIZE TAYLOR & THE DOMINOES

On the group's return from Germany, Paul, in addition to the Astrid Kirchherr photographs, gave me a copy of the single in question. The only other spare copy he had he gave to Bob Wooler, who began playing it at the local venues. I still have the record, personally signed by them all (probably the first record the Beatles signed personally), but there is no indication that they are on it.

There is a photograph on the cover and the only words are:

Tony Sheridan
My Bonnie
The Saints (When the Saints Go Marching In)

There is no mention whatsoever about the Beatles and it would have been impossible for Epstein to have traced the record, as he said he did, on this information alone. Even if he had the catalogue number, he would have been told this related to a single by Sheridan only.

Mersey Beat became a catalyst for the scene and groups, managers and anyone connected with the music took to visiting the office. Initially the Beatles were the most frequent visitors, helping Virginia out on the typewriter or phone; even Ringo used to drop in when he was visiting the nearby dole office in Renshaw Street.

Soon, groups began calling themselves Beat groups instead of rock 'n' roll bands and venues which had been advertising 'Twist sessions' and 'jive sessions' began calling them 'Beat sessions', while the 'jive hives' were now being called Beat clubs. Once the Beatles had achieved their initial success on record and the papers were looking for a tag to identify the Liverpool sound, they adopted the name of the paper and 'Mersey Beat' became part of the English language.

As the world's first alternative music paper, the first 'What's On', it introduced many innovations which were later adopted by the national music press. It also created a wonderful range of early photographs of the Beatles for posterity. No other group achieving their initial success would have had such a large photographic record of their early career.

Initially Dick Matthews took all those wonderful shots of the Beatles at the Cavern for us. I made arrangements with various professional photographers and paid them with advertisements, publicity and recommendations in exchange for exclusive photographs for *Mersey Beat*. I did these deals with the professional studios of Peter Kaye, Harry Watmough and Graham Spencer.

As the policy of *Mersey Beat* was to introduce innovation, the photographers were encouraged to do what the London showbiz photographers didn't do – leave the studio and take shots on location or during performances on stage.

The Beatles had originally been portrayed brilliantly in Germany by Astrid and Jurgen Vollmer, and *Mersey Beat* created a whole range of unique photographs of them performing in Liverpool.

John, pleased with the fact that I'd printed his article in its entirety, gave me a huge bundle of approximately 250 stories, poems and drawings and I began to use some of them in a column which I called 'Beatcomber'. This was to form the basis of his book *In His Own Write*. Paul also used to write to me with all the personal information about their activities.

There was an undoubted editorial bias in their favour, and this caused Bob Wooler to come to the office one day to complain on behalf of the other groups. He said that *Mersey Beat* was plugging the Beatles to such an extent that we should rename the paper the *Mersey Beatle*, and in fact I later introduced a special section called just that.

When we decided to run a poll to establish the No. 1 group in Liverpool, we received a huge response. Virginia and I spent many hours sorting out the votes. When we'd finished, Rory Storm & the Hurricanes had more votes than anyone else. However, we noticed that a large bundle of their votes had been written in the same handwriting in green ink and posted at the same postbox at the same time, so we disqualified the green-ink batch, which made the Beatles No. 1 and Rory Storm & the Hurricanes No. 4.

Our famous cover of issue No. 13 with the headline 'Beatles Top Poll!' established them once and for all as the North's top group – a fact which Brian Epstein was quick to capitalize on.

The paper's circulation kept increasing issue by issue and began to stretch throughout the country, covering groups in Manchester, Birmingham, Sheffield and Newcastle. We were also to champion the Rolling Stones.

What gave *Mersey Beat* the edge was 'the bulge', which Americans refer to as the 'baby boom'. There were more babies born in the few years towards the end of and immediately following the Second World War than at any time in history, before or since. Those babies became teenagers in the 1950s.

In previous decades, there was no real awareness of 'teenagers' (a term which only emerged in the 1950s). In Liverpool, for instance, youngsters were mini-replicas of their parents. Fathers would look on with pleasure when their sons reached a certain age and started to accompany them to the local pub. Sons would also follow fathers into the business or union they belonged to, and youngsters would dress exactly like their parents.

Suddenly, there was an awareness of being young, and young people wanted their own styles and their own music, just at the time they were beginning to earn money, which gave them spending power. *Mersey Beat* was their voice. It was a paper for them, crammed with photos and information about their own groups, which is why it also began to appeal to youngsters throughout Britain as its coverage extended to other areas.

The newspapers, television, theatres and radio were all run by people of a different generation who had no idea what youngsters wanted. For decades they had manipulated and controlled them (see the scene with George Harrison and Kenneth Haig in *A Hard Day's Night*), but now the youngsters wanted to create their own fashions.

What existed on the banks of the Mersey between 1958 and 1964 was exciting, energetic and unique, a magical time when an entire city danced to the music of youth.

Bill Harry
London, 1996

A Chronology of the Beatles

THE FAB FOUR were most certainly John, Paul, George and Ringo, but earlier incarnations of the world's most famous rock band saw musicians come and go, starting with the group which originally began life in Liverpool as the Quarry Men.

When John Lennon started by forming his skiffle group, for the first week the only members were himself and his school mate Pete Shotton. John chose the name the Blackjacks. In March 1957 the name was changed to the Quarry Men, after the school John had been attending. They comprised John on guitar/vocals, Colin Hanton on drums, Rod Davis on banjo, Eric Griffiths on guitar, Pete Shotton on washboard and Bill Smith on tea-chest bass. This formation lasted until June of the same year, with two additional members alternating on tea-chest bass – Ivan Vaughan and Nigel Whalley.

Between June and July 1957, John, Colin, Eric, Rod and Pete were joined by Len Garry on tea-chest bass. From July until January the following year they had a new member on guitar/vocals who was to become one of the most important ingredients of their success: Paul McCartney.

From February 1958 until the middle of the year, the line-up was John Lowe on piano, George Harrison on guitar/vocals, Paul McCartney on guitar/vocals, John Lennon on guitar/vocals, Colin Hanton on drums, Eric Griffiths on guitar and Len Garry on tea-chest bass.

From the middle of the year until January 1959 the group was pruned down to a five-man line-up with John, Paul, George, John Lowe and Colin Hanton.

From August until October 1959 the Quarry Men were streamlined to a quartet: John, Paul, George and Ken Brown, all four on guitar/vocals, with no drummer. In October, for a period of two months, they became a trio under the name Johnny & the Moondogs, with John, Paul and George, and between January and April 1960 they were known as the Beatals, with a line-up of John, Paul, George and Stuart Sutcliffe on bass guitar.

The Silver Beetles emerged between May and June of the same year as a quintet with drummer Tommy Moore added to the line-up and between June and July they were back as a quartet, *sans* Moore, with the slightly adjusted title the Silver Beatles. In July 1960 the Silver Beatles added Norman Chapman on drums, but in August he had been replaced by Pete Best and they'd shortened their name to the Beatles.

John, Paul, George, Stuart and Pete performed as a quintet until November 1960, when Stuart left and was replaced by Chas Newby on bass guitar. In January 1961 Newby left and Stuart returned.

This line-up continued until June 1961, when Stuart remained in Hamburg to study art. The line-up was then John, Paul, George and Pete. Best was replaced by Ringo Starr, formerly with Rory Storm & the Hurricanes, in August 1962 and that famous line-up lasted until April 1970.

THE
ENCYCLOPEDIA

ABRAMS, Steve American student at Oxford who, in 1967, via Paul McCartney, arranged for the Beatles to pay for a controversial advertisement in *The Times* newspaper urging a more enlightened attitude towards marijuana. All four Beatles and Brian Epstein were among the 64 signatories supporting the proposal.

ADAMS, Beryl When North End Music Stores (NEMS) opened a second shop in Liverpool at 12–14 Whitechapel, with Brian Epstein as manager, Beryl, then 26 years old, became his secretary.

Once Brian had taken over management of the Beatles, she was involved in dealing with them at various levels – including preparing their pay packets.

She didn't join Brian once he moved offices to London, but began to manage a local group, the Kirkbys. She also married Bob Wooler, but it didn't last.

Beryl remarried, but the second marriage also broke down, and in the 1990s she became the woman in the life of Allan Williams. She also started appearing as a guest at conventions, reverting to her name from her first marriage, Beryl Wooler.

ADAMS, Bob Road manager who was hired by the Beatles for a time. The group called him 'Old Bob' and he called them 'the Beaters'. He retired in 1981.

ALBY & THE SORRALS A Liverpool group who appeared with the Beatles at the Cavern on Wednesday 20 June 1962.

They'd originally played on the Liverpool clubland circuit as the Cadillacs and comprised Keith Draper (lead), Albie Ellis (vocals), Dave Foley (bass), Pete Dobson (saxophone), Maurice Daniels (drums) and Brian Cox (rhythm).

They penned original material including numbers such as 'Why?' and 'Foolin'' and during 1962 appeared for 41 weeks at Barnabus Hall, Penny Lane. They were billed as 'the group with the saxy sound' until Pete Dobson left them at the end of 1963 to join a dance band. He was replaced by rhythm guitarist Brian Johnson, ex-member of the Blue Country Boys. They played mainly in Runcorn, Rochdale and St Helens, and performed, along with the Beatles, on the *Mersey Beat* Awards night.

ALDO, Steve One of Liverpool's leading black vocalists, Steve originally began singing at the age of 13 in 'The Backyard Kids' at the Pavilion, Lodge Lane. When he was 14 he sang at Holyoake Hall and on holiday in the Isle of Man he sang with the Ivy Benson Band. Later he appeared occasionally with Howie Casey & the Seniors, before moving to Cardiff to become a ladies' hairdresser. He worked at Raymonde's (Mr Teasy Weasy) in London, then went to sea for a year. He returned to Liverpool and fronted the Challengers, then moved to Germany and sang occasionally with the Dominoes. On his return to Liverpool he joined the

Noctures for a short while, before becoming a member of the Griff Parry Five.

At one time he was managed by Spencer Lloyd Mason and made his recording debut on Decca with 'Can I Get a Witness' in December 1964. He later recorded for Parlophone.

Steve appeared with the Beatles on their last British tour, in 1964, which, with only nine appearances, became their shortest theatre tour of Britain.

He later became a publican.

ALEXANDER, Arthur Influential black American R&B artist who had only one chart hit, 'You'd Better Move On', which reached No. 24 in the American charts in 1962. The Rolling Stones were to cover the number.

Born in Florence, Alabama, on 10 May 1940, Alexander was one of John Lennon's seminal influences and his use of the word 'girl' in his lyrics was adopted by John in a number of his compositions.

John also chose to include four of Alexander's songs in the Beatles repertoire in 1962: 'Anna (Go to Him)', 'A Shot of Rhythm and Blues', 'Soldier of Love (Lay Down Your Arms)' and 'Where Have You Been All My Life?'

The Beatles included 'A Shot of Rhythm and Blues' and 'Soldier of Love' in their BBC radio appearances and their version of 'Where Have You Been All My Life?' is found on the Star Club album.

'Anna', the haunting love song, was included on their debut album *Please Please Me*.

ALI, Muhammad Boxer who won the World Heavyweight Championship title three times. The Beatles visited him at his training camp on 18 February 1964, a few days before he won the title for the first time. He had changed his name from Cassius Clay on converting to Islam.

ALI, Tariq British-based, Pakistani-born political activist who was said to have sparked off John Lennon's political awareness when interviewing him for *Red Mole* magazine. Soon after the interview, John penned 'Power to the People'.

ALLEN, Dave Irish comedian who compered the Helen Shapiro/Beatles tour in 1963 and appeared with the Beatles on their Australian tour the following year. He also appeared with them on *Sunday Night at the London Palladium* on 12 January 1964.

ALLSOP, Kenneth A respected British journalist whose advice to John Lennon proved to have a positive effect on his songwriting.

Allsop, who wrote for the *Daily Mail*, was 44 years old at the time he first met John at BBC's Lime Grove Studio on Monday 23 March 1964, where he was conducting an interview with 'the literary Beatle' about his book *In His Own Write* for the television news programme *Tonight*. The actual interview lasted four minutes of screen time. In the green room, a hospitality suite, he had a chat with John and advised him not to hide his feelings when he wrote his songs. Having read *In His Own Write*, he suspected that John had the ability to produce lyrics of a more profound nature than the simple love songs associated with the Beatles at the time. He suggested that John used his own experiences as a basis for his lyrics.

John met him again at a Foyles Literary Luncheon at the Dorchester Hotel.

As a result of Allsop's advice, John began to write numbers such as 'I'm a Loser' and 'In My Life'.

John was also interviewed by Allsop on the last-ever edition of the *Tonight* programme on Friday 18 June 1965, when they discussed John's second book, *A Spaniard in the Works*.

Allsop went on to present another TV programme series, *24 Hours*. He was found dead at his home, a victim of an overdose of painkillers, in May 1973.

ALPIN, Kenny A classmate of Paul McCartney at Liverpool Institute, Kenny was once used by Paul as a scapegoat. Paul had drawn a rather vulgar sketch of a naked woman for the amusement of his classmates, then had put it in his shirt pocket and forgotten about it. His mother discovered it before washing the shirt and the embarrassed Paul told her that Kenny Alpin was the artistic culprit. His conscience got the better of him and two days later he confessed.

ANDERSON, Helen Former Merseyside art student, Helen first became friends with Cynthia Powell when she attended the Junior School of Art in Gambier Terrace. Later, the two girls entered the Liverpool College of Art and were both in the same class as John Lennon.

Helen had received publicity in the press because she'd painted a portrait of Lonnie Donegan and she and John became close friends, although the relationship was platonic.

Cynthia was jealous and realized that she loved John when she noticed Helen stroking his hair one day.

During the first year at college John fancied a baggy sweater Helen was wearing and asked if she'd give it to him. Helen was to say: 'Somebody knitted the jumper for me and John coveted it. I said I'd swap it for one of his drawings and he gave me the book and said, "Here, take the lot." '

The book was actually an exercise book from his Quarry Bank days with 22 caricatures of teachers and fellow pupils. She tried to sell it at Sotheby's, London, on 14 September 1995 for a sum in excess of £120,000, but there were no buyers.

ANN-MARGRET Following the Beatles' initial success in America, the media was literally 100 per cent behind them. However, the scandal magazine

Confidential, true to its image, produced an issue with the Beatles' picture on the cover and the cover-lines 'Psst! Who Hushed Up These Stories About the BEATLES? * Their Wild Antics in a Hamburg Sex Cellar. * The Nite Two Beatles Went to Jail. * How Ringo Flipped for Ann-Margret. * The Marriage Nobody Talks About. * Their Secret Love Life.'

The magazine hinted that Ringo and Ann-Margret were having a romance and commented that Ringo had 'bent her shell-pink ears with an hour of long-distance oggly-googling, all in a special type of Teddy Boy lingo that left little Annie limp'.

There were other reports that the two were linked romantically, which Ringo had to deny at press interviews during their second American tour.

Ann-Margret, a stunning singer-actress born in Stockholm, was to co-star with Elvis Presley in *Viva Las Vegas*, which brought her the nickname 'the female Elvis'.

She'd lived in America from the age of five and found success as both a singer and a film actress. In fact, the Beatles introduced her current hit 'I Just Don't Understand' into their repertoire in 1961, with John Lennon on lead vocal.

ANTHONY, Les Ex-Welsh Guardsman who acted as chauffeur-cum-bodyguard to John Lennon for seven years and wrote of his experiences for the tabloid press.

APPLE SCRUFFS Name used by 15 girls and two boys who kept vigil outside recording studios, offices and the homes of Beatles on a 24-hour basis. The most fanatical of fans, one of them, Carol Bedford, says they took the name Apple because they spent so much time outside the Savile Row offices and Scruffs 'because we were scruffy. Usually it was very cold, so we dressed in three layers of clothes.' The fans also produced their own fanzine, *Apple Scruffs*, and George Harrison wrote a number, 'Apple Scruffs', devoted to them.

APPLEBY, Ron Southport promoter and compere who had a residency at Litherland Town Hall and claimed to be the first person to announce the group on stage as the Beatles after they'd shortened their name from the Silver Beatles.

APPLEJACKS, The A group from the Solihull area of Birmingham whose introduction of a girl guitarist in their line-up was quite novel for the time. They comprised Al Jackson (vocals), Martin Baggott (lead), Phil Cash (rhythm), Don Gould (organ), Megan Davies (bass) and Gary Freeman (drums).

The group recorded for Decca and reached No. 7 in the British charts with their first record, 'Tell Me When'.

Their recording manager was Mike Smith, who'd recorded the original Beatles audition session at Decca studios, and for their second release he selected the Lennon and McCartney composition 'Like Dreamers Do', which had been included on the Decca session.

It was released in June 1964 and proved to be their final hit, reaching No. 20 in the charts.

ARCHER, Jeffrey Author of best-selling novels such as *Kane and Abel* and erstwhile MP. While at Oxford in 1963 he offered his services to Oxfam and suggested that the Beatles become involved in the charity's new campaign to raise £1 million.

Archer sent a telegram to Brian Epstein requesting an interview and signed it on behalf of 8,000 students at Oxford. However, Epstein was reluctant for the Beatles to become involved, as he believed it would result in requests from other charities.

Knowing that Epstein was unsure of how he should deal with the situation, Beatles press officer Brian Somerville suggested to Archer that he attend a Beatles concert in Liverpool. Together with Nicholas Lloyd, editor of the university magazine *Cherwell*, Archer travelled to Liverpool, armed with Oxfam posters and collecting tins, managed to get backstage and had photos taken of the Beatles putting money into the tins. The Beatles also liked the idea of associating their name with Oxfam.

Pat Davidson, Oxfam's press officer, phoned to apologize to Epstein over an announcement that had been made without his consent. She said that Epstein 'was spitting blood about it. He didn't want to speak to anybody from Oxfam. He was furious.'

A meeting was arranged between Epstein, Davidson and the *Daily Mail* and it was formally agreed that the Beatles would lend their name to the campaign, although they couldn't do much more than that.

Archer had pulled off the coup by explaining to Epstein and Somerville that it would look bad if the Beatles withdrew.

Archer also helped to organize a Beatles charity performance in aid of the NSPCC at the Grafton Ballrooms, Liverpool, on 12 June 1963.

He then organized a dinner at Brasenose College, Oxford, on 5 March 1964 to celebrate their fund-raising efforts.

ASHER, Jane Flame-haired British stage, screen and television actress who made her film debut at the age of five in *Mandy* (1952).

Her other screen appearances include *Third Party Risk* (1953); *Dance Little Lady, Adventure in the Hopfields* (1954); *The Quatermass Xperiment* (1955); *Charley Moon, The Greengage Summer* (1956); *The Prince and the Pauper* (1962); *Girl in the Headlines* (1963); *The Masque of the Red Death* (1964); *Alfie* (1966); *The Winter's Tale* (1967); *The Buttercup Chain, Deep End* (1970); *Henry VIII and His Six Wives* (1972); *Runners* (1983) and *Success is the Best Revenge* (1984).

Her television appearances are numerous and a brief selection includes 'The Cold Equations' episode of *Out of This World* (1962); Nigel Kneale's *The Stone Tape* (1972); *Brideshead Revisited* (1981); *A Voyage Round My Father* (1982); *The Mistress* (1987); *Wish Me Luck* (1990) and *Murder Most*

Horrid (1991). This is in addition to appearances in various series such as *The Adventures of Robin Hood*, *The Adventurer*, *The Saint* and *The Buccaneers*, plus prestigious productions including the part of Lise in *The Brothers Karamazov* and Maggie Tulliver in *The Mill on the Floss*.

She also made her stage debut at the age of 12 at the Oxford Playhouse, starring as Alice in *Alice in Wonderland*. At 14 she became the youngest actress to play Wendy in the London production of *Peter Pan*. She appeared in the Broadway production of *The Philanthropist*, played Perdita in *A Winter's Tale* and Cassandra in *The Trojan Women*. She also featured in various productions for the Bristol Old Vic, including the title role in *Cleo*, by Frank Marcus, the part of Ellen Terry in *Sixty Thousand Nights* and Eliza in *Pygmalion*.

Jane was born on 5 April 1946. She was the daughter of Dr Richard Asher, a consultant in blood and mental diseases at the Central Middlesex Hospital in Acton, London, in addition to being a writer and broadcaster, and Margaret Asher, Professor of Music at the Guildhall School of Music (where she'd taught George Martin to play the oboe; she was also to teach Paul McCartney to play the recorder).

Jane had a brother, Peter, who was two years older and a sister, Clare, two years younger. All three Asher children had the distinctive Titian-red hair.

At the time she first met the Beatles, Jane was also a frequent guest on *Juke Box Jury*.

She was 17 years old when, on 18 April 1963, she was asked by the *Radio Times* to cover the Beatles' appearance at the 'Swinging Sounds '63' concert at the Royal Albert Hall. In the article, which was published in May, she commented: 'Now these I could scream for!'

The Beatles were having coffee and sandwiches after the show at their hotel, the Royal Court in Chelsea's Sloane Square, when Jane joined them. Brian Epstein returned to his own hotel and Ringo stayed behind to have an early night, while singer Shane Fenton, who'd also been on the concert bill that day, drove Paul, John, George and Jane to journalist Chris Hutchins' flat, situated on the top floor of King's House on the King's Road.

Reports indicated that it was originally George who was taking an interest in Jane, but Paul soon began to occupy her attention and the others left him to talk to her alone. Chris Hutchins reported that at one point John embarrassed her by asking awkward questions of a sexual nature.

When they dropped her off that evening, Paul arranged to meet her again. The romance became public when they were snapped by a photographer as they left the Prince of Wales Theatre after seeing Neil Simon's play *Never Too Late*.

Paul moved into the Asher family home at 57 Wimpole Street, a five-storey terraced house. It happened shortly after Paul had missed his last train to Liverpool following a date with Jane and stayed the night. Margaret Asher suggested that he regard the house as his London home, thus saving on hotel bills. He moved into the top floor, where there were two rooms and a bathroom; the second room was Peter's bedroom. Jane and Clare had the two rooms below.

This relationship with an upper-middle-class family broadened his cultural horizons. There were stimulating discussions around the Asher family dinner table and the two of them attended musicals, classical concerts, plays and exhibitions and went on holidays together to exotic places. Paul even opened an account at Coutts, the Queen's bankers, and ordered Jane's birthday cake from Maxim's in Paris, while Jane helped Paul select his new car, a midnight-blue Aston Martin DB6.

The young actress became the inspiration for a number of his songs, initially purely love songs, which changed as the relationship entered stormy patches – primarily because she refused to give up her career. 'She Loves You' was written in the music room at Wimpole Street. Songs inspired by Jane included 'And I Love Her', 'Every Little Thing', 'We Can Work It Out', 'You Won't See Me', 'I'm Looking Through You' and 'Here, There and Everywhere'.

The crisis in their relationship arose from the fact that Jane had a successful career which she was determined to pursue. Paul wanted his girlfriend to dedicate herself to him in the type of relationship common between men and women in working-class Liverpool. However, Jane came from a different world and had her own strong opinions; extending her own horizons as an actress didn't include becoming a subservient woman and sacrificing her career for 'her man'. At one point she refused to answer his telephone calls, which inspired 'You Won't See Me'. Jane was appearing in *Great Expectations* at the Theatre Royal, Bristol, when he recorded the number.

He obviously tried to give messages to her through his songs and told Beatles' biographer Hunter Davies: 'I knew I was selfish. It caused a few rows. Jane went off and I said, "OK, then, leave. I'll find someone else." It was shattering to be without her. That was when I wrote "I'm Looking Through You".'

Jane was appearing at the Bristol Old Vic as Barbara Cahoun in John Dighton's *The Happiest Days of Your Life*, when Paul visited Bristol to see her. While there he noticed the name on a shop, 'Rigby & Evans Ltd, Wine & Spirit Shippers', which he says, gave him the surname for the song 'Eleanor Rigby'.

Jane helped Paul to find the five-storey Victorian house in Cavendish Avenue, St John's Wood, which they moved into in 1966. Jane decorated the house and always kept it in tip-top condition. Unfortunately, during a spring-cleaning session a number of original early Lennon and McCartney songs were lost for ever when she threw away a notebook full of lyrics while emptying out a cupboard.

It was Jane who, in June 1966, persuaded Paul to buy High Farm, a 183-acre farm in Machrihanish, Campbeltown, suggesting it would be a good idea for them to have a remote retreat to which they could escape from the pressures of being constantly in the public eye.

She embarked on a five-month tour of America in 1967, appearing with the Bristol Old Vic in *Romeo and Juliet* in Boston, Washington and Philadelphia. Paul flew over to America to celebrate her twenty-first birthday, which took place during the tour. It was during this trip that he conceived the idea of *Magical Mystery Tour*.

On her return, Jane said: 'Paul had changed so much. He was on LSD, which I knew nothing about. The house had changed and it was full of stuff I didn't know about.'

The two decided to get married and during an interview in the *Daily Express* in 1967 she said: 'I love Paul. I love him very deeply, and he feels the same. I don't think either of us has looked at anyone else since we first met.' She was to add: 'I want to get married, probably this year, and have lots and lots of babies. I certainly would be surprised indeed if I married anyone but Paul.'

On New Year's Day 1968 he proposed, gave her a diamond and emerald ring and they travelled up north to Rembrandt to tell Paul's father.

But the five-year romance came to an abrupt end, despite the fact that they obviously loved each other. Jane had been a virgin when they met and fidelity to a partner obviously meant a great deal to her. On the other hand, Paul had always been a womanizer. During her absences when touring, he had been dating other girls and began an affair with an American, Francie Schwartz.

Jane arrived home unexpectedly when Paul was in bed with Francie. She walked out on him and sent her mother to Cavendish Avenue to collect her belongings. On the 20 July edition of the BBC Television chat show *Dee Time*, she announced officially that their engagement was off.

The couple did meet once or twice after the Schwartz incident, but the split was final, although Jane was to say: 'I know it sounds corny, but we still see each other and love each other, but it hasn't worked out. Perhaps we'll be childhood sweethearts and meet again and get married when we're about 70.'

Jane fell in love with political cartoonist Gerald Scarfe in the 1970s and their first child, Kate, was born on 17 April 1974.

Jane appeared in further acting parts, including a TV production of *Romeo and Juliet*. After the birth of Kate, she curtailed her acting career for a while, but appeared in the stage version of *Whose Life is It Anyway?*.

Two more children were born and she and Gerald were eventually married in 1981 and have settled in Chelsea.

She returned to acting in the 1980s with many television appearances: with Jeremy Irons in *Brideshead Revisited*, with James Fox in *Love is Old, Love is New*, a drama about a couple obsessed with the 1960s which featured a lot of Beatles music; and with Laurence Olivier in John Mortimer's *A Voyage Round My Father*.

Other TV appearances included the costume drama *Hawkmoor* and an episode of *Tales of the Unexpected*. She teamed up with James Fox once again for the film *Runners*, and in 1985 with Ian Holm and Coral Browne for *Dreamchild*.

Jane has written ten books on entertaining, fancy dress and ornate cake decoration and in 1995 launched her own national publication, *Jane Asher's Magazine*, at a time when she was regularly featured on television commercials.

Tragically, her father died of an overdose of barbiturates and alcohol. His body was discovered on 26 April 1969.

Jane met Paul again in 1994 for the first time in more than 20 years.

ASHER, Peter Older brother of Jane Asher, Paul McCartney's erstwhile girl-friend, he became close friends with Gordon Waller when the two attended Westminster School. Both were the sons of doctors and they formed a duo.

Paul McCartney moved into the Ashers' Wimpole Street house in 1963 and was given a room on the fourth floor, where Peter also had his bedroom. The close association proved fruitful for the Peter & Gordon duo, as Peter asked for, and was given, a Paul McCartney song to record. The number, 'World Without Love', launched them to stardom, replaced 'Can't Buy Me Love' at the top of the British charts and established the duo in America.

Soon after playing for £40 a week at London's Pickwick Club, they began a chart run which brought them six more Top 30 singles before they split in 1967.

In the meantime, Peter had also launched a business, Indica Books, in partnership with John Dunbar and Barry Miles.

When Apple Records was formed, Peter was appointed the company's chief A&R (Artists & Repertoire) manager. He discovered the talented American singer/songwriter James Taylor and signed him to the company label.

On the TV show *Dee Time* on Saturday 20 July 1968, Jane had announced that her romance with Paul was over, following her discovery of his affair with Francie Schwartz. On the following Monday Paul stormed into the Apple offices, intending to sack Peter in retaliation for Jane's action, but Ron Kass, who was head of Apple Records at the time, talked him out of it.

However, Asher's productions received sparse promotion after the incident. James Taylor became disenchanted with Apple due to the lack of promotion for his records and returned to America. He asked Peter to become his manager. Peter was sacked when Allen Klein moved into Apple and he relocated to America, becoming manager to artists such as Taylor and Linda Ronstadt, in addition to producing their records. He was to become one of the top record producers in Los Angeles.

He now lives in Malibu and records many leading names, including Diana Ross, Cher and 10,000 Maniacs.

ASKEY, Arthur One of Liverpool's most famous comedians, born on 6 June 1900. From the age of 16 until 1924, he worked at the Liverpool Education Office and then became a singer and entertainer, spending years touring the provinces until he appeared on a new radio show *Band Waggon* in 1938. Numerous radio shows followed, including *Arthur's Inn*, *Hello Playmates* and *Askey Galore*. The five-foot-three comedian with the horn-rimmed spectacles became immensely popular and made a number of films, including *Charley's (Big Hearted Aunt)*, *The Ghost Train* and *King Arthur was a Gentleman*.

His first television series, *Before Your Very Eyes*, was transmitted in 1953 and he had a new series every year until the mid-1960s.

Arthur Askey was awarded an OBE in 1969 and was made a CBE in 1981.

Arthur met the Beatles on a number of occasions and claimed that he had originally noticed them in a demo studio in Liverpool where he had been recording one of his 'silly songs'. He said that he asked them what they called themselves and they told him 'Beatles', which resulted in him telling them: 'You'll never get anywhere with a name like that.'

He was possibly referring to Percy Phillips' studio at 53 Kensington, Liverpool, where the Quarry Men recorded in 1958 – and no doubt his memory played tricks on him as they were not known as the Beatles at that time. It is likely that he told them they would never get anywhere with a name like the Quarry Men!

Their success also provided him with comedy material, as in October 1966, when they received their MBEs and he was to comment: 'I'm not saying it's given them swollen heads, but now the boys think the initials on our pillar boxes stand for Eleanor Rigby.'

Despite suffering a severe heart attack, he topped the bill at the Royal Variety Performance in 1978. Arthur Askey died on 16 November 1982 at the age of 82.

ASPINALL, Neil The person who has remained closest to the Beatles and probably most deserves the tag 'the fifth Beatle'.

Neil Aspinall was born in Prestatyn, North Wales, on 13 December 1942 and his family then moved to Liverpool and settled in West Derby. Neil originally attended West Derby School before becoming a pupil at Liverpool Institute, where he shared the same Art and English classes as Paul McCartney. George Harrison was in a class one year behind them and Neil recalled: 'My first encounter with George was behind the school's air-raid shelters. This great mass of shaggy hair loomed up and an out-of-breath voice requested a quick drag of my Woodbine.'

On leaving the Institute in July 1959 with nine GCEs, he became a trainee accountant at a local firm for the next two years. He earned 50 shillings a week.

During those years Neil moved into the Best's house at 8 Haymans Green and formed a relationship with Mona Best. He also became a close friend of her son, Pete, who joined the Beatles in August 1960 prior to their first trip to Hamburg. On their return from Hamburg, Mrs Best asked Neil to make some posters promoting the group, using the phrase 'The Return of the Beatles'. Neil also saw them perform for the first time at Litherland Town Hall on 27 December 1960. Although he had known Paul and George from the Institute days, it was directly through the Bests that Neil became associated with the group.

As Pete was a member of the band, Mona began to take an interest in the Beatles' career, which included arranging bookings for them. By February 1961, it became obvious that they could no longer continue travelling to local gigs by corporation bus, so she arranged for the Casbah doorman, Frank Garner, to be their driver/road manager. This only lasted for a few months as he couldn't hold down the two jobs at once.

Pete then asked Neil if he could become the group's driver and suggested that he buy a van to drive them to their gigs. He recalled: 'He bought a battered old grey and maroon model for £15 [other sources say he bought a second-hand van for £80], but at least it went, which was the main consideration. So Neil entered enthusiastically the world of show business as our first roadie.' Neil decided to charge each member of the group five shillings for every gig he drove them to.

On their return from Germany in July 1961, Neil decided to pack in his job as an accountant to become the Beatles' official road manager. By that time he was earning more money as their driver than he was receiving as a trainee accountant. It also gave him more time to help Mona run the Casbah Club.

A major crisis occurred in August 1962. Neil drove Pete to meet Brian Epstein at NEMS. As far as Pete and Neil were concerned, it was the usual meeting at which Pete received information on future bookings. Neil remained downstairs at NEMS, while Pete saw Epstein.

A shocked Best came downstairs after the meeting to tell Neil that he had been sacked. Neil was furious and immediately called Mona to tell her what had happened.

Neil and Pete then went across to the Grapes pub to have a few drinks and commiserate. Neil was disgusted with what he saw as a completely underhand and unwarranted action and told Pete that he was going to quit his position as road manager. However, Pete insisted that he stay with the group as he was convinced that they were on the brink of success and didn't want Neil to also become a victim of what he considered to be an unjust decision.

So Neil remained with the Beatles, although initially there was some tension. When he turned up at the next booking and was asked by Epstein why Pete hadn't turned up, he told him: 'Well, what do you expect?' When he asked Paul and John to explain what had happened, they told him: 'It's got nothing to do with you. You're only the driver.'

However, a very close relationship was to develop between Neil and the Beatles over the coming years and decades. They affectionately referred to him as 'Nell' and placed their complete trust in him.

As their success grew, they employed Mal Evans to help Neil out and when their touring days were over, they appointed Neil as their personal assistant. This was prior to him becoming managing director of Apple Corps, the Beatles' new company.

Paul McCartney was present when Neil married Suzy Ornstein at Chelsea Registry Office on 30 August 1968.

When Allen Klein took over the Beatles' affairs and began his whole-sale sackings at Apple, the one person he was unable to sack was Neil.

These days Neil remains the managing director of Apple, although he and his American wife, Suzy, are also sole directors of Standby Films Ltd, which is based in their large house in Twickenham, Middlesex. In 1994 Apple paid Standby £408,000, from which Neil paid himself a salary of £62,000, and he and his wife are able to enjoy the trappings of a much-deserved success, including transportation by Rolls Royce.

Following a heart attack, Neil has had to restrict his attendances at the Apple offices in Ovington Square to three days a week. However, 1995 finally saw the release of *The Beatles Anthology*, a television series on the Beatles which Neil had first started working on in 1969, when he had called it *The Long and Winding Road*.

ASTAIRE, Fred Hollywood legend and the film world's most famous dance man. He was one of the figures on the *Sgt Pepper* tableau and made a guest appearance in John's *Imagine* film.

AULIN, Ewa Blonde starlet, formerly Miss Teen Sweden, who made her film debut in the title role of *Candy* in 1968. Ringo appeared as Emmanuel, a randy Mexican gardener, and received his first screen kiss from her.

AVEDON, Richard Innovative American photographer, born in 1923, who changed the face of fashion photography in the late 1940s. He was also a noted portraitist and one of his distinctive traits, of having a subject's face in half-shadow, inspired Astrid Kirchherr when she took her famous portraits of the Beatles in Hamburg. The style was also used to good effect by Robert Freeman on his famous *With the Beatles* cover.

Look magazine commissioned him to photograph the Beatles for their front cover. The picture was also published as a poster the same year and was later to be used on the cover and gatefold of *Love Songs*, a 1977 compilation, although the positions of Paul and Ringo were changed on the album sleeve.

Avedon's most famous pictures of the Beatles were a series of portraits in an almost psychedelic style, which he shot in January 1968.

During a trip to London, Avedon told how he was drawn to the Beatles and related an anecdote to journalist Pete Clark: 'Ringo loved photography. He said he would pose for me if he could photograph me at the same time. His idea was we'd do it like a Western movie. We'd each have a Scotch, then take a picture. Another drink, another picture ... until the last man took the last picture. We went on until we were both nearly unconscious. I took the last picture before he passed out, and that was of his toe – it looked like an interesting art photograph. Then Ringo slid off the chair. The next thing I remember was vomiting in the bathroom and the tiles felt nice and cold, and I looked out of the door and two women were carrying Ringo off into the night. I never saw him again.'

BACH, Barbara   Ringo Starr's second wife. Born in New York City in 1947 and raised with her sister, Margarite, in a predominantly Jewish area in Queens, she was educated at an all-girls school in Long Island. She left school at the age of 16 to become a model, shortening her surname from Goldbach. She married Italian industrialist Augusto Gregorini and moved to Rome, where her European origins (Romanian grandmother, Irish mother, Austrian father) helped her secure roles in several international films.

Her daughter, Francesca, was born in 1969 and her son, Gianni, four years later.

Barbara lived in Italy for ten years, appearing in TV commercials and movies. She starred as the sexy, beautiful Russian spy Anya Amasova with Roger Moore in the James Bond movie *The Spy Who Loved Me* and portrayed the evil Lady Agatha in the Italian sci-fi epic *The Humanoid*. Her other films include *Force Ten from Navarone, Black Belly of the Tarantula, Stateline Motel, Screamers, The Great Alligator, The Jaguar Lives, The Volcanic Island* and *The Unseen*.

She also appeared in a nude spread in *Playboy*.

Estranged from her husband, it was while filming *The Unseen* that her romance with cinematographer Roberto Quezada began.

She met Ringo when she co-starred with him as Lana, a prehistoric beauty, in the film *Caveman*.

Barbara was to say: 'It wasn't love at first sight. It began to grow within days of meeting each other.'

Ringo shed his current girlfriend, Nancy Andrews, and Barbara bade farewell to Roberto.

The couple were married on Monday 27 April 1981 at Marylebone Register Office in London. Wedding guests included George and Olivia Harrison and Paul and Linda McCartney. Sixty guests and their relatives then celebrated at the London club Rags. Barbara wore a cream satin suit, made by David and Elizabeth Emanuel, who designed the famous wedding dress for Diana, Princess of Wales. The ceremony was conducted by registrar Joseph Jevons, who had also performed the marriage ceremony for Paul and Linda at the same venue.

Ringo and Barbara had originally intended marrying in America, but the murder of John Lennon no doubt had an influence on their deciding to return to England to live. They settled at Tittenhurst Park.

In 1983 they were almost killed when their car collided with a lorry.

They appeared in the TV mini-series *Princess Daisy* as a jet-set couple and in *Give My Regards to Broad Street*, but by the mid-1980s their film careers seemed to be over.

During the decade there were rumours of fierce arguments and they both took to the bottle. Their alcoholism reached such a state that they checked into a rehabilitation centre in Arizona in October 1988 for five weeks.

BADFINGER Liverpool-Welsh group, formed from members of two Mersey Beat bands, the Masterminds and the Calderstones. As the Iveys they were managed by Bill Collins and for a while they provided backing for Liverpool singer David Garrick.

The group were spotted at the Marquee club in London by Mal Evans, who recommended them to Paul McCartney. Their line-up at the time comprised Pete Ham (lead), Tom Evans (rhythm), Mike Gibbons (bass) and Rob Griffiths (drums).

They were to become Apple's most successful group, apart from the Beatles themselves, and made their recording debut with 'Maybe To-morrow' in November 1968. It was Paul McCartney who suggested the name change from Iveys to Badfinger, recalling his working title for 'With a Little Help from My Friends', which was 'Badfinger Boogie'.

Gibbons left the band and Evans took over on bass guitar, with Liverpool guitarist Joey Molland taking over on rhythm.

Paul also penned their biggest hit, 'Come and Get It', which was used on the soundtrack of the Ringo Starr movie *The Magic Christian*. They had several other hits, including 'No Matter What', 'Day After Day' and 'Baby Blue'.

Ham and Evans wrote the number 'Without You', which provided a chart-topper for Harry Nilsson.

The group also appeared on *The Concert for Bangladesh*, and played on John Lennon's *Imagine* album and George Harrison's *All Things Must Pass*.

The group's career took an unfortunate turn and they became literally penniless when all their money was tied up in legal wrangles. In April 1975 Pete Ham hanged himself, leaving a note blaming the group's American manager. Joey Molland and Tom Evans worked for a couple of years as labourers until Evans also hanged himself in November 1983.

Molland formed another band, also called Badfinger, and they've been performing in America, with a mini-revival in 1995. An Apple CD, *The Best of Badfinger*, was released, there was an official Badfinger fan club and a Badfinger documentary went into production, produced by Gary Katz, which included interviews with Joey and Katie Molland, Mike Gibbons and Marianne Evans. In Los Angeles surviving members Mike Gibbons and Joey Molland, together with Marianne and Stephen Evans and manager Bill Collins, received an ASCAP (the American Society of Composers, Authors and Publishers) award for 'Without You'.

BAIN, Bob Compere who appeared with the Beatles on their autumn tour of Britain in October–November 1964.

BAKER, Barbara John's first steady girlfriend and the one he lost his virginity to. He was 15 and she was 16, and they were eventually forced to end the relationship because of parental pressure from Barbara's mum and John's Aunt Mimi.

BALLARD, Arthur Painter and teacher, born in Liverpool in 1915, who initially won a scholarship to Liverpool College of Art in 1930. He was to spend most of his life in the city and taught at the college from 1947 to 1980.

His paintings attracted great interest in the late 1950s and early 1960s and were bought by the likes of Aldous Huxley, J. B. Priestley and Sam Wanamaker. However, his changing style and determination to remain in Liverpool impeded his chances of major success.

As a teacher, he took a personal interest in the fortunes of his pupils and aided them when in difficulties. His most talented student was Stuart Sutcliffe, who was to share Arthur's passion for the works of Nicholas da Staël.

Due to Stuart's reluctance to attend various classes at college, Arthur took it on himself to provide him with one-to-one tuition at Stu's flat in nearby Percy Street. He also took an interest in John Lennon and at one time prevented his expulsion from the college. Arthur also used to meet students for discussions in the 'War Office' of Ye Cracke pub in Rice Street.

Arthur was married twice, the second time to Carol, one of his students. He had two sons and a daughter. On his retirement he moved to London for a while to live with his daughter, before settling down with one of his sons and his family in Wales. He died in Corwen Clyd on 25 November 1994.

Art critic Peter Davies prepared a touring exhibition of Arthur's work in 1996.

BALLOU, Donald Manager of a radio station in Ogdensburg, New York State, who banned Beatles records immediately after the publication of the Datebook feature in which John mentioned Christ.

BANKS, Jeremy Photographic director of Apple during 1968 and 1969, who also acted as photographic coordinator for the Beatles.

BARBER, Adrian A Yorkshire-born musician, based in Liverpool, and a founder member of Cass & the Cassanovas, who formed in December 1959. The group became the Big Three in January 1961.

Barber played lead guitar, Johnny 'Gus' Gustafson was on bass and Johnny 'Hutch' Hutchinson on drums.

Adrian was regarded as an electronics wizard and surprised friends at the Jacaranda club, one of his haunts, with his little gimmicks, such as putting a radio in a Coke can. His most impressive contribution to the local sound was his development of huge amplifiers, nicknamed 'coffins', which gave the trio a powerful stage sound. Other groups were impressed and Adrian was asked to make some 'coffins' for the Beatles.

Mersey Beat columnist 'Onlooker' wrote in the 30 November 1961 issue: 'A good night at the OPB last Saturday with the Big Three. I wonder who carried their coffins upstairs. The Undertakers probably – they were there as well. These enormous amplifiers on wheels always intrigue me. They must have quite a job getting them on some stages I've seen.'

Johnny Gustafson commented: 'Our speakers were five feet high by one and a half to two feet wide. Adrian Barber was a bit of an electronics wiz – he concocted these things. He got two Goodmans 15-inch speakers and made up this great big amp – it was only 50 watts, but he acoustically designed the cabinets to give it the most oomph, and they did sound very, very loud.'

When Brian Epstein showed an interest in the group, Adrian decided to leave and was replaced by Brian Griffiths in July 1962. Adrian then became stage manager of the Star Club in Hamburg.

Star Club owner Manfred Weissleder wanted to start a Star Club record label and record the acts on stage, so he engaged Adrian to develop a special sound system.

While Adrian was fitting in the system he was also testing it out by recording various groups, including the Beatles and Kingsize Taylor and the Dominoes.

He had been experimenting with a domestic tape recorder to check out the acoustics. With a single mike fixed in the right spot, he found he could get good results recording the Beatles on stage, complete with the dialogue between the group and the audience, the repartee, the jokes, and even a laugh and a bit of a song from Horst Fascher.

Adrian completed his recordings on 31 December 1962 and was approached by Taylor for the tapes of the Dominoes. As he'd been recording them for test purposes only Adrian told Taylor he could have them. The Beatles recordings from their third and final engagement at the Star Club were also on the tapes and these were the ones that eventually emerged as the double album *The Beatles Live! At the Star Club in Hamburg, Germany: 1962*, although the true story of their origin was never revealed.

When Joey Dee and the Starliters appeared at the Star Club, Dee was so impressed by the sound system Adrian had devised that he invited him to New York to design and install a sound system in the Peppermint Lounge.

Adrian went to live in America, fitted the Peppermint Lounge with the sound system, became a recording manager at Atlantic Records, managed a group called the New York Rock & Roll Ensemble and became a disc jockey.

Currently he lives in Hawaii.

BARDOT, Brigitte French actress known as 'the sex kitten' who is cited in early Beatles' biographies as their favourite film star. She once requested a meeting with all four Beatles at London's Mayfair Hotel, but only John Lennon turned up.

BARRON KNIGHTS, The A group who rose to fame following their appearance on the Beatles *Christmas Show*, which ran from December 1963 to January

1964 at the Gaumont, Bradford; the Empire, Liverpool and the Astoria, Finsbury Park, London.

Formed in Leighton Buzzard, they comprised Duke D'mond (vocals/rhythm), Butch Baker (guitar/banjo/vocals), P'nut Langford (guitar/vocals), Baron Anthony (bass/vocals) and Dave Ballinger (drums).

Their first hit, 'Call Up The Groups' in 1964, was a parody of recent record releases by groups such as the Searchers, the Rolling Stones and the Dave Clark Five. They specialized in lampooning the pop scene and other medleys included, 'Pop! Go The Workers' and 'Merrie Gentle Pops'.

The Barron Knights provided additional comedy relief in the show and, like the Beatles, were known for playing pranks on other acts. One spot in the show began with the Beatles standing on a blacked-out stage, while a small spotlight picked out each of their heads in turn, ending with John Lennon. One night, the Barron Knights grabbed John from the wings and held him back so that when the spotlight turned to where he should have been, there was nothing there.

The group continue to perform on the British cabaret circuit.

BARROW, Tony Liverpool-born former record review columnist for the *Liverpool Echo* and a full-time album-sleeve writer for Decca Records.

Brian Epstein contacted him about mentioning the Beatles in his column, 'Disker', which he couldn't do as he reviewed only record releases. However, he passed on a message through the Decca channels and Epstein was eventually given a recording audition date for the Beatles.

Once the Beatles made their debut disc, Epstein sought a press officer and initially approached Andrew Loog Oldham, who turned him down. He asked Barrow, who also turned down the post, having a secure job at Decca. When Epstein offered him twice the salary he was currently earning, Barrow then joined the NEMS staff.

He was mainly to concentrate on NEMS artists such as Cilla Black and Billy J. Kramer, as Epstein employed various other press agents, such as Brian Somerville and Derek Taylor, to handle the Beatles.

He did travel extensively with the group and taped their final concert at Candlestick Park, San Francisco, at Paul's request.

After leaving NEMS he established his own agency, Tony Barrow International, but left London due to ill-health and settled in Morecambe, where he lives in semi-retirement as a freelance journalist. He currently contributes to *Beatles Monthly*.

BART, Lionel Major British composer of hit songs and musicals, particularly in the 1960s. Born in London's East End on 1 August 1930, his songs helped launch the careers of Cliff Richard and Tommy Steele.

He began to write musicals and was intrigued by the Liverpool folk-song 'Maggie May' to such an extent that he decided to work on a 'folk opera set in Liverpool' based around the legendary Liverpool tart, asking writer Alun Owen to work on it with him. For a time Bart moved up to Liverpool to soak in the local atmosphere. In his book *Bart*, David Roper reports Lionel Bart as saying:

> At that time I was very thick with Brian Epstein and all of the Beatles. They really took off in a big way as I was writing 'Maggie May' and John Lennon phoned me once saying, 'Can I have a lend of your scriptwriter, we're going to do this film.' So I downed tools for a couple of months, and Alun went off and wrote the screenplay for *A Hard Day's Night*.

Bart became a very close friend of Brian Epstein and the Beatles regularly dropped by Bart's flat, where he held 'open house'.

A story he often relates concerns 'Eleanor Rigby'. He says that he helped Paul rethink the lyrics, recalling that Paul came to visit him to seek his approval for a song he'd written. The two of them were walking Bart's Alsatians Simon and Garfunkel in Wimbledon Common cemetery when they noticed a family headstone for Ann and Eleanor Bygraves. Bart says: 'But when he sat down at my clavichord and sang it, I wasn't too happy, because I wasn't too happy about Max Bygraves at the time – and made him change it to Rigby.'

Paul himself believes he used the name Eleanor because of Eleanor Bron and has said that Rigby came from the Bristol firm of wine and spirits shippers whose sign he saw when visiting Jane Asher once. Others claim that Paul may have subconsciously remembered the gravestone of Eleanor Rigby in St Peter's graveyard in Liverpool.

Bart's biggest success was the musical *Oliver!*

BASSEY, Shirley Internationally acclaimed singer who had chart hits with 'Something' and 'Fool on the Hill'. She visited the Beatles backstage at Carnegie Hall in February 1964.

BEACH BOYS, The Originally formed in 1961 by three brothers, a cousin and a schoolfriend, they performed under a variety of names – Carl and the Passions, the Pendletones and Kenny and the Cadets – before settling on the Beach Boys and becoming the most successful of all the American pop groups.

The Beach Boys were Brian, Carl and Dennis Wilson, Mike Love and Al Jardine.

Brian was the songwriter and undoubted genius of the band, who was frustrated with the success of the Beatles and continually sought to outdo them. The Beach Boys were, in fact, voted the world's No. 1 band in the British music press in 1966, pushing the Beatles into the No. 2 position.

Albums such as *Pet Sounds* and singles such as 'God Only Knows' and 'Good Vibrations' were masterpieces, but they didn't satisfy Brian's obsession with bettering the Beatles and he was eventually to suffer nervous breakdowns and retired from touring with the band.

He was depressed by the brilliance of *Sgt Pepper's Lonely Hearts Club*

Band and set out to counter it with an album called *Smile*. However, it was never completed, although tracks for it were to be included on the Beach Boys' next three albums.

The two groups established a friendship and Mike Love was one of the celebrities to join the Beatles at the Maharishi's ashram in India. On 15 March 1968, Love's twenty-fourth birthday, John, Paul, George and Donovan sang the songs 'Spiritual Rejuvenation' and 'Happy Birthday' to him.

Paul attended a Beach Boys recording session on 10 April 1967 and he was to say he considered 'God Only Knows' to be the best song ever written.

After Brian had ceased touring, he was replaced by various musicians, including Bruce Johnson, who in 1967, together with Mike Love, performed at the Beatles' 'Magical Mystery Tour' party.

BEAT BROTHERS, The Generic name created for the various musicians who backed Tony Sheridan on record and on stage.

The first group to actually back him on record were the Beatles, who cut the tracks 'My Bonnie', 'The Saints', 'Why (Can't You Love Me Again)?', 'Sweet Georgia Brown', 'Nobody's Child' and 'If You Love Me Baby' with him in Hamburg in May 1961.

They were paid a session fee rather than a royalty deal, and recording man Bert Kaempfert decided to use the name Beat Brothers on the actual record, although only Tony Sheridan is mentioned on the picture sleeve.

It's said that Kaempfert decided not to use the name Beatles because he thought it sounded like 'Peedles', a German slang word for the male sex organ.

The Beatles recorded no more tracks with Sheridan, although other musicians did. Since the name the Beat Brothers was consistent on a number of Sheridan's releases, people were originally confused, mistakenly believing the Beatles had recorded more tracks than they did.

The other musicians who recorded under the name the Beat Brothers included organist Roy Young, bass guitarist Colin Milander, tenor saxophonist Rikki Barnes and drummer Johnny Watson. In 1995 Tony Sheridan reformed the Beat Brothers with Howie Casey and Roy Young.

BEATMAKERS, The An unusual group who made a single appearance at Litherland Town Hall on 19 October 1961. Promoter Brian Kelly had booked the Beatles, Gerry & the Pacemakers and Karl Terry & the Cruisers.

As a bit of fun, both the Beatles and the Pacemakers decided to combine into one group called the Beatmakers. They joined forces on stage, with Gerry Marsden wearing George Harrison's leather outfit and George, who played lead, wearing a hood. Paul McCartney played bass and wore a nightie, and Freddie Marsden and Pete Best played one drum each.

The occasion seemed such fun that Karl Terry jumped on stage and joined them on the vocals. The one-off group performed four numbers: 'Whole Lotta Shakin'', 'What'd I Say?', 'Red Sails' and 'Hit the Road, Jack'.

BEATTY, Don Classmate of John Lennon at Quarry Bank School who first introduced John to the music of Elvis Presley.

BEDFORD, Carol Member of the Apple Scruffs, a small body of determined Beatles fans, mainly female, from Britain and America who devoted all their time to Beatles-watching. Carol wrote a book about her experiences, *Waiting for the Beatles*, which was published in 1988.

BEECHER-STEVENS, Sydney A Decca Records marketing manager who met with Brian Epstein to discuss the possibility of the label signing the Beatles. Together with Dick Rowe, he was to meet Epstein again in February 1962 to say the company wasn't interested. He died in 1987.

BEECHING, Dr Richard A former executive of ICI, born in Sheerness, Kent, on 21 April 1913. He was appointed by British Railways in 1961 to reorganize the nationalized company, which was a huge loss-maker. Within seven years he had streamlined the entire system, with a loss of 150,000 jobs, the axeing of 5,000 miles of track and the closing of 2,363 stations.

When the Beatles were having financial difficulties with the Apple organization and needed a tough businessman to sort out the mess, they reputedly approached him. He turned them down, but gave them a straightforward piece of advice: 'Get back to making records.'

He was knighted by the Queen.

BENNETT, Kim Assistant to Sid Coleman at Ardmore & Beechwood, EMI's publishing arm. He was responsible for getting radio plugs for the Beatles' debut disc, 'Love Me Do'.

BENNETT, Peter American record plugger, hired by the Beatles in 1967 to promote Apple Records in the States. He also worked for Allen Klein.

BENTON, Brook American singer, born Benjamin Franklin Peay in South Carolina on 19 September 1931. He had had a string of hits, including 'Baby (You've Got What It Takes)' and 'Good Way (to Mess Around and Fall in Love)', when he appeared as second on the bill to the Beatles on *Val Parnell's Sunday Night at the London Palladium* on 13 October 1963.

BERNSTEIN, Sid American promoter, the first to present the Beatles at US concerts.

At the age of 38 he was working for the theatrical agency General Artists Corporation (GAC) and taking evening courses in social research.

As a result he'd noticed the rise of Beatlemania in England through the British press cuttings he studied.

No one at GAC would accept his suggestion of booking the Beatles for the States, so he decided to take a chance himself, contacting Brian Epstein by phone in February 1963 and suggesting that he would like to book the Beatles for the Carnegie Hall. Epstein thought a Beatles American concert at that time would be premature.

Bernstein then suggested a fee of $6,500 for two concert appearances at Carnegie Hall, to take place the following year on 12 February. Epstein agreed on condition that the Beatles had reached the American charts by then.

The shows were completely sold out and Bernstein urged Epstein to let him have the Beatles for Madison Square Garden, but Brian told him: 'Sid, let's save it for the next time.'

Bernstein then had a brainwave. The biggest venue in New York was the 55,600-seater baseball arena, Shea Stadium, and the appearance was set for 15 August 1965. It was such a success that Sid was able to arrange a further Shea Stadium concert on 23 August 1966. However, when Sid proposed to Epstein that he would pay $1 million for the Beatles to appear again at the venue in 1967, he was turned down.

Sid attempted to book the Beatles on further occasions, but was unsuccessful. In 1981 he teamed up with Clive Epstein to manage a Liverpool band, Motion Pictures, but Clive died before the partnership developed.

BERRY, Chuck One of the seminal influences on the Beatles and one of their favourite musicians. Berry and artists like him should have featured on the cover of the *Sgt Pepper* album rather than the boxers, film stars and West Coast painters selected by Peter Blake and Robert Fraser, and would have reflected the Beatles idols and heroes more accurately.

During the period 1957–66, the Beatles were to perform more songs penned by Chuck Berry than by any other artist. Paul McCartney sang 'Little Queenie', but the other Berry numbers were mainly sung by John Lennon and included 'Roll Over Beethoven', 'Johnny B. Goode', 'Rock and Roll Music', 'Sweet Little Sixteen', 'Maybellene', 'Almost Grown', 'Carol', 'Memphis Tennessee', 'Reelin' and Rockin'', 'Too Much Monkee Business', 'I'm Talking About You', 'I Got to Find My Baby', 'Thirty Days' and 'Vacation Time'.

Their number 'Back in the USSR' was no doubt influenced by his 1959 hit 'Back in the USA' and Paul McCartney claimed that he borrowed the bass riff from Berry's 'I'm Talking About You' for 'I Saw Her Standing There'.

Born Charles Berry in San José, California, on 18 October 1926, he formed his first trio in 1952 while he worked by day as a hairdresser and beautician. He signed with Chess Records in 1955 and his first release was 'Maybellene'.

In 1962 he was convicted of violating the Mann Act by bringing an under-age girl over a state line (this was in 1959) and jailed for two years.

On his release in 1964, his career received a boost when the Beatles recorded 'Roll Over Beethoven' on their second album. He was so pleased at how rock 'n' roll had been revived in Liverpool that he recorded the album *St Louis to Liverpool* and penned 'Liverpool Drive'.

On 13 September 1969 he appeared at the Toronto Rock 'n' Roll Revival Concert on a bill which included John Lennon's Plastic Ono Band. John, the main Berry fan in the group, used to introduce a Berry song at the Cavern with the words: 'This is a record by Chuck Berry, a Liverpool-born white singer with bandy legs and no hair!'

In 1975 Berry's publisher Morris Levy claimed that John had plagiarized Berry's 'You Can't Catch Me' when writing 'Come Together'. John maintained that it was not a plagiarism, merely a tribute, and agreed to settle the matter by recording two Berry numbers for his album *Rock 'n' Roll*.

John eventually managed to perform with Berry when he was hosting *The Mike Douglas Show* on American TV in February 1962; he selected Berry as a guest and the two of them performed 'Johnny B. Goode' and 'Memphis Tennessee'.

Berry's autobiography was published in 1988 to coincide with a film of his 1988 birthday concert, *Hail! Hail! Rock 'n' Roll*.

BERRY, Mike Singer, real name Michael Bourne, born in Hackney, east London, in 1943. Independent record producer Joe Meek gave him his stage name and produced his hit 'Don't You Think It's Time?'.

Mike, who had established himself initially in Britain with his 'Tribute to Buddy Holly' single, was to appear regularly at the Cavern, initially with Mike Berry and the Outlaws for a week from Monday 21 to Friday 25 May 1962, during which he plugged his new record. Among the members of the Outlaws were two musicians who were later to find fame in their own right, Ritchie Blackmore and Chas Hodges (of Chas & Dave).

Brian Epstein and the Beatles saw him perform during that week and Epstein, who had watched Berry on the TV programme *Thank Your Lucky Stars* the previous week, invited him back to his flat, where he played him a tape of the Beatles. He told Berry that if he could arrange a television appearance for the group, he'd see to it that Berry was given a lot of work in the Merseyside area.

Three months later Mike was back again, leading Mike Berry and the Phantoms. They appeared on the same bill as the Beatles on Sunday 26 August. He returned to the Cavern the following year with Mike Berry & the Marauders.

He was booked to appear with the Beatles on their short tour of Scotland, which opened at the Concert Hall, Glasgow, on 6 October 1963 and he also joined the Beatles on their very first tour abroad, a five-date mini-tour of Sweden, commencing on 25 October 1963.

Berry's pop career fizzled out soon after and during the 1970s he found success as a TV actor in the series *Worzel Gummidge* and was later to appear as a regular cast member of the popular series *Are You Being Served?*.

Interestingly enough, his biggest hit was 'The Sunshine of Your Smile' in 1980, produced by Chas Hodges.

Berry was later to re-form the Outlaws for the many nostalgia shows of the late 1980s and early 1990s.

BERRY, Mike Music publisher who joined Apple Music as professional manager in January 1968.

BEST, Mona Merseyside promoter who did much to encourage the Beatles in the early stages of their career.

Born of English parents in India, she worked for the Red Cross in Delhi, where she met and married John Best, an army officer. The couple had two sons, Peter and Rory. In 1945 the family returned to England and settled in Haymans Green in the West Derby area of Liverpool.

The Victorian house had a number of cellars, which she decided to turn into a club. It became one of the first cellar clubs to present rock 'n' roll exclusively when it opened in August 1959 and 'Mo', as she was called, decided to call it the Casbah club. This was because her favourite film at the time was *Algiers*, which starred Charles Boyer, who, people asserted, said, 'Come with me to the Casbah,' although that line of dialogue isn't actually in the movie.

The resident group became the Quarry Men, who had re-formed specially for the club's opening on Saturday 29 August 1959. George Harrison, who was in another band, the Les Stewart Quartet, quit that outfit, along with Ken Brown, and sought out John and Paul to join them. The Quarry Men had been inactive for several months and had more or less disbanded. If Mo hadn't opened the Casbah, the Beatles might never have existed!

In some ways, the Casbah has more right to be called 'the birthplace of the Beatles' than the Cavern, which didn't book them until two years later, when they had already been established locally.

After her son Pete joined the group as drummer in August 1960, Mo began to take an active role in their career. For a time she arranged for the Casbah doorman to become the Beatles' road manager, and then presented them with a permanent roadie in the form of her lover, Neil Aspinall.

When the Beatles returned from their first trip to Hamburg they appeared at the Casbah and Mo, in an effort to keep them in work, began a series of independent promotions at St John's Hall, Tuebrook, and booked the Beatles for 11 gigs there. She also booked them on shows at Knotty Ash Village Hall, in addition to their Casbah work.

She wrote off to Granada Television in an attempt to get them on the *People and Places* show and was literally co-managing the group with Pete.

Once Brian Epstein entered the picture, he took over the reins of management, although Mrs Best was still obviously keen to promote the group in which her son was a member.

Mo was furious when Pete was sacked without explanation and set out to find the reason why. Epstein wouldn't answer her calls, but she managed to contact George Martin, who told her that he was completely surprised by the decision as he regarded Pete as a valuable member of the group.

It was felt by various people in Liverpool who were associated with the local scene that perhaps the Beatles resented Mo's efforts on their behalf – a situation which may have been one of the elements involved in Pete's dismissal.

Sadly, Mo died in hospital on 9 September 1988 following a heart attack.

BEST, Pete Drummer with the Beatles from 1960–62 and, at one point, the most popular member of the group among the majority of the Liverpool fans. In fact, in 1962, *Mersey Beat* was to observe that he was: 'a figure with mystique, darkly good-looking and seemingly the one likely to emerge as the most popular Beatle.'

He was born Peter Randolph Best in Madras on 24 November 1941. His English parents were stationed in India at the time, where his father, John, was an army physical training instructor and his mother, Mona, was a nurse in the Red Cross.

Following the birth of Pete's brother, Rory in 1944, the family sailed to England, moving to Liverpool and initially settling into a flat in Casey Street. Two years later they moved to 8 Haymans Green, a 15-room Victorian house in the West Derby district of the city.

When, at the age of 16, Pete began to take an interest in skiffle and rock 'n' roll music, he was encouraged by his parents. As so many friends were dropping in to see Pete and Rory, their mother suggested a novel idea – they could have a meeting place of their own by utilizing the seven adjoining basement rooms. The idea developed until they decided to turn the basement into a coffee bar-style venue, which was similar to Lowlands, a nearby club.

Mona (generally known to everyone as 'Mo') and her sons, together with about ten friends, began work on converting the basement. They had decided to open during the week as a coffee bar – where youngsters could dance to jukebox music – but would hire live groups for the weekend.

One of their helpers was Ruth Morrison, the girlfriend of George Harrison, who suggested that the Les Stewart Quartet, of which George was a member, could play at the club. They were currently appearing at the Lowlands club, which was situated on the opposite side of the street, 50 yards down from the Bests' home.

As a result, George and Ken Brown, another member of the quartet, came around to see Mo.

However, group leader Les Stewart didn't want to appear in the new coffee club, which Mo called the Casbah, and he had an argument with Brown. Brown left the group and George followed.

George then turned up with John Lennon and Paul McCartney and they teamed up with Brown as a quartet, assuming the former name of John's skiffle group, the Quarry Men, to begin their residency. The group didn't use a drummer at the time.

The club officially opened on Saturday 29 August 1959 and within a year they had enrolled 1,000 members.

On Saturday 10 October 1959 there was a dispute because Brown was unable to play, yet Mrs Best still paid him a share of the group's fee. As a result, John, George and Paul walked out on their residency and sacked Brown.

Ken then encouraged Pete to form a new outfit with him and to take over a residency at the club. They called themselves the Blackjacks (the original name of Lennon's first group). Brown played rhythm, Charles Newby played lead, Bill Barlow played bass and Pete became the group's drummer.

Mo bought Pete a drum kit from Blackler's store (where George Harrison was to work for a time) and the group repertoire comprised numbers from rock 'n' roll acts such as Little Richard, Jerry Lee Lewis, Chuck Berry and Carl Perkins.

In the meantime, the Quarry Men underwent a number of name changes ranging from Johnny & the Moondogs to the Beatals to the Silver Beetles, and enlisted the services of drummer Tommy Moore. As the Silver Beetles, they toured Scotland, backing Johnny Gentle and then began appearing in Liverpool, mainly at the Jacaranda Coffee Club, the Grosvenor Ballroom, Liscard and the Institute, Neston. By this time they had changed their name to the Beatles.

On 6 August 1959 their Grosvenor gig was cancelled when the Wallasey Corporation withdrew promoter Les Dodd's licence to operate there and that evening they dropped into the Casbah club, where they saw Pete perform with the Blackjacks. They were particularly impressed by his new blue mother-of-pearl drum kit.

At that time they had accepted their first Hamburg booking, which was to commence on 13 August. However, they were without a drummer as Tommy Moore had just left.

One afternoon, Paul phoned Pete at home and asked: 'How'd you like to come to Hamburg with the Beatles?'

Aware that the Blackjacks were on the point of disbanding and excited by the prospect of foreign climes, Pete accepted and successfully auditioned for the band at the Wyvern club. After playing together for 20 minutes on numbers such as 'Shakin' All Over', they told him: 'You're in!'

The line-up of the Beatles now comprised John Lennon (rhythm/ vocals), Paul McCartney (rhthym/vocals), George Harrison (lead/ vocals), Stuart Sutcliffe (bass/vocals) and Pete Best (drums).

Arriving in Hamburg, they discovered they were not playing at the Kaiserkeller as they had assumed, but at a smaller club called the Indra, which was further down, at the seedier end of the Grosse Freiheit.

After several weeks at the Indra, they then played at the Kaiserkeller and when their season was coming to an end, they had intended to move on to the Ten Ten Club in the nearby Reeperbahn.

The group's sleeping quarters were cramped ones at the rear of the Bambi Kino, owned by Bruno Koschmider, who ran the Kaiserkeller. Stu Sutcliffe moved out to live in Astrid Kirchherr's house and, when Koschmider found the group intended to move on to the rival Top Ten, George was deported for being under-age.

John, Paul and Pete moved into the dormitory of the Top Ten, intending to play for a season at the club as a quartet with Stuart.

As Pete and Paul needed to collect the rest of their belongings from the Bambi Kino, they crept along there one night to pack. In the windowless rooms, there was no light so some lateral thinking had them pinning condoms onto a frayed tapestry in the hall and then lighting them. The condoms singed the tapestry and that evening the police came and arrested the two of them for allegedly trying to set fire to the premises.

Pete and Paul left their equipment behind and John remained in Hamburg for a further week, while Stuart decided to stay on with Astrid. Mona Best phoned Peter Eckhorn, who sent their kit over by ship, and the group then intended to take up a residency at Williams' new club, the Top Ten. Unfortunately, it burned to the ground and the Beatles were left with few bookings. Mo got to work, offering them several gigs at the Casbah, setting up some promotions of her own to keep them in work, and Pete and Mo began to take over the bookings for the group. They were, in effect, managing the Beatles at the time.

Through Bob Wooler, the group were booked by Brian Kelly for Litherland Town Hall on 27 December 1960 – a highlight in their local career. Their baptism of fire in Hamburg had made them an exceptionally dynamic outfit.

When recalling this time to Beatles' biographer, Hunter Davies, Pete said:

> When we came back from Germany I was playing using my bass drum very loud and laying down a very solid beat. This was unheard of at the time in Liverpool as all the groups were playing in the Shadows' style. Even Ringo in Rory's group copied our beat and it wasn't long before most drummers in Liverpool were playing the same style. This way of drumming had a great deal to do with the big sound we were producing.

This style of playing (which Pete had developed in Germany) earned the tag 'the Atom Beat', and Pete was regarded as one of the 'Pool's leading drummers.

Issue No. 2 of *Mersey Beat*, published on 20 July 1961, devoted its entire front page to the story of the Beatles' Hamburg recording and Brian Epstein ordered 144 copies of that particular issue.

When Bob Wooler wrote his report on the Beatles' impact locally (in *Mersey Beat* on 31 August 1961), the only Beatle he mentioned by name was Pete, describing the group as: 'musically authoritative and physically magnetic, example the mean, moody magnificence of drummer Pete Best – a sort of teenage Jeff Chandler.'

It was due to pressure from Mo and Bob Wooler that Ray McFall eventually decided to book the Beatles at the Cavern and their rise to local fame continued at a meteoric pace. Pete and Mo continued to act as unofficial managers and agents for the group, arranging all their gigs and negotiating the fees.

Pete Best was emerging as the most popular Beatle among the fans. Bob Wooler considered him the Beatles' biggest asset and said that it was principally Best who was the attraction at the Aintree Institute and Litherland Town Hall gigs.

Due to his popularity, he was encouraged to introduce his own singing spot, 'Peppermint Twist' into the act. Next, Bob Wooler suggested something unprecedented – place Pete in front of the other three members of the group. This unusual line-up was presented only once – at the St Valentine's Dance on 14 February 1961 at Litherland Town Hall – because the stage was mobbed when the girls surged forward and almost pulled him off.

Reports in *Mersey Beat* and comments by people involved in the local scene confirm Best's huge local appeal. One story reported how girls slept in his garden overnight just to be near him!

Promoter, Ron Appleby, was to comment: 'He was definitely the big attraction with the group and did much to establish their popularity during their early career.'

In 1963, the Cavern doorman, Paddy Delaney, was to recall:

> Before the Beatles recorded, Pete was inclined to be more popular with the girls than any other member of the group. There were several reasons why I believe he was so popular. Girls were attracted by the fact that he wouldn't smile, even though they tried to make him. They also tried to attract his attention on stage, but he wouldn't look at them. When he left the Beatles there were exclamations of surprise. 'The Beatles will never be the same without him' ... 'He was the Beatles' ... 'They've taken away the vital part,' were comments I heard.

When Brian Epstein took over the management reins, it was Pete who discussed gigs and fees with him. The two men had an amicable relationship, although Pete was to point out that Brian once attempted to seduce him and had asked if he would come to a hotel and stay with him overnight. Pete politely told him to forget it – and nothing further was said.

1961 was an event-packed year, in which the group's Cavern bookings increased. They went on another trip to Hamburg, during which Stuart Sutcliffe left the band. The Beatles also recorded in Hamburg with Tony Sheridan and Bert Kaempfert, while Astrid Kirchherr developed the hair fashion which was to give them the 'moptops' identity a few years later – although Pete was the only member who didn't take on the hairstyle.

They began 1962 with a Decca recording audition and were confirmed as Liverpool's No. 1 group in a January issue of *Mersey Beat*. On 7 March 1962 they made their broadcasting debut on *Teenager's Turn* in Manchester. When they recorded their second radio appearance on 11 June, Pete was mobbed by the Manchester girls, while John, Paul and George managed to make their way to the coach. When Pete finally managed to break free and join the others, he was reprimanded by Paul's father, who accused him of hogging the limelight.

That month, Pete learned by accident that Decca had rejected the group. The other members knew about it, but no one had bothered to inform Pete. He said: 'I was hurt because I was the last to know about it. The others knew a couple of weeks earlier. They let it slip out in a casual conversation one day.'

Pete was also to comment: 'When I did eventually learn our fate, their lame excuse was that they had all thought I would take the result extremely badly.'

When news of the Parlophone deal came through, *Mersey Beat* ran the story on the front page, featuring a photograph of Pete Best with the caption: 'Congratulations to Pete, Paul, John and George.'

The Beatles were now on the brink of success, but a number of incidents hinted at a covert plan to get rid of Pete. Apart from the fact that the others had not immediately informed him of the Decca audition result, the same situation occurred regarding the Parlophone contract – they just didn't bother to tell him.

When Pete was chatting with Paul and mentioned he was considering buying a Ford Capri, Paul told him: 'If you take my advice you won't buy it, that's all. You'd be better saving your money.'

On Wednesday 15 August 1962, following their lunchtime gig at the Cavern, Pete asked John what time he and Neil Aspinall would collect him for the customary lift in the van the next day. John said: 'No, don't bother. I've got other arrangements.' and rushed away.

Brian was still in the Cavern and asked Pete if he could come and see him at the office the next morning. Pete saw nothing unusual in this – he was the one who met with Brian regularly to discuss forthcoming gigs. He arrived at NEMS the next day, driven by Neil, and went to meet Brian in his office.

The manager seemed unusually flustered and blurted out: 'The boys want you out and Ringo in. They don't think you're a good enough drummer, Pete. And George Martin doesn't think you're a good enough drummer.'

When Pete asked him: 'Does Ringo know yet?', Brian told him that he was joining the band that Saturday. Then the phone rang – it was someone asking if Pete had been given the news. Brian asked Pete if he could fulfil the remaining three bookings until Ringo replaced him.

Stunned, Pete said 'Yes,' then left, in somewhat of a daze.

When Pete rejoined Neil downstairs he told him the news and the two retreated to the Grapes to discuss it over a drink. Neil was furious and threatened to resign as the Beatles' road manager, but Pete told him to stay with the group as they were about to become successful.

When Neil phoned Mo, she was furious and spent the afternoon trying to contact Epstein by phone – in vain. She then managed to talk to George Martin on the phone and he denied that he had ever suggested sacking Pete. All he would say was that he would prefer having a session drummer that he was familiar with in a recording studio. In fact, this was confirmed when he used a session drummer even after Ringo had joined the group.

Martin actually told Mo:

I never suggested that Pete Best must go. All I said was that for the purposes of the Beatles' first record I would rather use a session man. I never thought that Brian Epstein would let him go. He seemed to be the most saleable commodity as far as looks went. It was a surprise when I learned that they had dropped Pete. The drums were important to me for a record, but they didn't matter much otherwise. Fans don't pay particular attention to the quality of the drumming.

At that point in time it was not uncommon for A&R men to use session drummers. Ringo was to experience something similar when he arrived at the recording studios on 11 September 1962. A session drummer, Andy White, was present. White also played drums on 'P.S. I Love You', while Ringo was handed a pair of maracas.

Martin told Beatles' biographer, Hunter Davies: 'He [Ringo] couldn't do a roll – and still can't – though he's improved a lot since. Andy was the kind of drummer I needed. Ringo was only used to ballrooms. It was obviously best to use someone with experience.'

Ringo himself was to tell Davies how shocked he was to arrive at the session and find another drummer there: 'I thought, "that's the end", they're doing a Pete Best on me.'

The decision to sack Pete was not a sudden one. It has been claimed that Paul and George had been overheard talking to Bob Wooler in the Grapes about sacking Pete, once they had John's approval. Their next step was to approach Epstein and tell him.

Epstein then considered Jimmy Hutchinson as the best replacement and contacted Hutchinson to offer him the job. Hutchinson turned him down – he didn't have a good opinion of the group.

On the evening of Best's sacking, Epstein was surprised to find that Pete didn't turn up for the gig at the Riverpark Ballroom. Neil told him: 'What do you expect?' Brian got Hutchinson to fill in the three bookings until Ringo was able to join. That evening when Neil questioned Paul and John about it all, he was told: 'It's got nothing to do with you. You're only the driver.'

The story in *Mersey Beat* read:

BEATLES CHANGE DRUMMER!

Ringo Starr (former drummer with Rory Storm & the Hurricanes) has joined the Beatles, replacing Pete Best on drums. Ringo has admired the Beatles for years and is delighted with his new engagement. Naturally he is tremendously excited about the future.

The Beatles comment, 'Pete left the group by mutual agreement. There were no arguments or difficulties, and this has been an entirely amicable decision.'

On Tuesday September 4th, the Beatles will fly to London to make recordings at EMI Studios. They will be recording numbers that have been specially written for the group, which they have received from their recording manager, George Martin.

The Beatles' comment, issued by Brian Epstein, was false. Pete was to tell *Mersey Beat*: 'The news came as a big surprise to me as I had had no hint that it could happen and didn't even have the opportunity of discussing it with the rest of the group.'

Local fans went wild with fury and hundreds of letters and petitions of protest were sent to *Mersey Beat*. When the Beatles were due to appear at the Cavern with Ringo on 19 August 1962, the Best fans were out in force. Ray McFall arranged for Brian Epstein to have a bodyguard and, during scuffles, George Harrison was given a black eye. Fans were chanting 'Pete for ever, Ringo never' and 'Pete is Best'.

However, the protests didn't last long. George was to write to a fan: 'Ringo is a much better drummer and he can smile – which is a bit more than Pete could do. It will seem different for a few weeks, but I think that the majority of our fans will soon be taking Ringo for granted.' To his credit, John Lennon was later to say: 'We were cowards when we sacked him.'

Added to the devastating news for Pete Best that after two years' unblemished service with the band, he was unceremoniously sacked when they were finally about to achieve success, was the fact that his name was tarnished.

Epstein attempted to soften the harshness of the group's decision by implying that Pete wasn't a good enough drummer. This will be disputed by the fellow Merseyside musicians and fans who actually heard him play. He genuinely contributed to the Beatles' success and was an integral part of them as they established themselves as the No. 1 band on Merseyside. There had never been a single complaint about his drumming and he had developed the 'Atom Beat', which other drummers had copied.

In 1984 Geoff Nugent of the Undertakers was to tell Spencer Leigh:

Pete Best put the Beatles on the map. You'd see two or three girls around Paul and George and John, but you'd see fifty round Pete. I very rarely saw him smile and yet he was always pleasant. If you look at any of the Beatles' photographs with Pete Best, the first face you're drawn to is Pete's. I don't care if you're a man or woman.

Instead of seeking to investigate the real motives behind the sacking of Best, writers have merely continued to perpetuate the lie that 'he was not a good enough drummer'. If a lie is repeated often enough, people will assume it is the truth.

Pete was to say: 'I wouldn't rate Ringo as a better drummer than me – I'm adamant about that – and when it happened I felt like putting a stone around my neck and jumping off the Pier Head.'

Mo told Epstein, quite frankly, that she believed the reason Pete was sacked was due to the fact that he was so popular locally and would probably have become the most popular Beatle when they achieved success. She put it down to jealousy by the other members of the group – particularly since a lot of people in Liverpool had been calling the group, 'Pete Best and the Beatles'.

She said to Hunter Davies:

They were jealous and wanted him out. Pete hadn't realized what a following he had till he left. He was always so very shy and quiet, never shot his mouth off, like some people I could mention.

He'd been their manager before Brian arrived, did the bookings and collected the money. I'd looked upon them as friends. I'd helped them so much, got them bookings, lending them money. I fed them when they were hungry. I was far more interested in them than their own parents.

In some quarters of Liverpool at the time, people suspected that the Beatles wanted to get rid of Pete because his mother was such a strong personality that she would continue to make her presence felt, even though Epstein was now managing the band.

Another reason was that Pete just never quite fitted in personality-wise with the other three members of the group. He was taciturn and didn't have the same wacky sense of humour. He didn't even adopt their hairstyle, although he says they never asked him to and he would have done so, if requested. The truth probably lies in a combination of these theories.

Still upset by the turn of events, Epstein, who had had a sleepless night prior to sacking Pete, then told him that he wanted to continue managing him and would place him with another band – the Mersey Beats. Pete didn't want to remain with Epstein after what had happened and certainly didn't want to start at the beginning again with an unknown group.

Behind the scenes, Epstein had Joe Flannery approach Pete about joining Lee Curtis & the All Stars. Pete had had numerous offers to join other bands, but decided to give the All Stars a shot and made his debut with them at the Majestic Ballroom, Birkenhead on Monday 10 September 1962. On 24 November, Pete was again appearing at the Majestic with the All Stars and was also celebrating his twenty-first birthday. Compèring the show, Bob Wooler read out a telegram that had arrived for

Pete: 'Congratulations. Many happy returns. All the best. John, Paul, George, Ringo and Brian.'

This was probably sent by Epstein as the relationship between Pete and his former colleagues was now a difficult one. Pete commented:

> We played on the same bill as the Beatles on two occasions. One was at the Cavern when we were second on the bill to the Beatles. The other was in the *Mersey Beat* Pollwinners' concert. On both occasions we were on just prior to the Beatles, and we had to pass one another face-to-face, yet nothing was ever said.

In fact, Lee Curtis & the All Stars were voted into second place in the second *Mersey Beat* Popularity Poll – and this was entirely due to the fact that Pete had joined them.

Lee Curtis & the All Stars comprised Lee Curtis (vocals), Tony Waddington (rhythm), Wayne Bickerton (bass), Frank Bowen (lead) and Pete Best (drums).

Pete began to pick up the pieces of his life and in August 1963 he married his girlfriend Kathy.

Lee Curtis signed with Decca, but recorded without the band. Decca then offered the group a separate deal. Pete said: 'Decca suggested we push my name, so we became the Pete Best Four.' Ironically, their debut record was produced by Mike Smith, who had recorded the Beatles' original audition for Decca.

The single, 'I'm Gonna Knock On Your Door' was released in June 1964, but it didn't register and Decca dropped the band.

On 30 March 1964 Pete appeared as a guest on the American TV show, *I've Got A Secret*.

Pete was to say: 'Magazines, both in Britain and across the Atlantic, have been printing far-fetched stories that I had quit the Beatles because of illness and that Ringo was called in only because I was too sick to play.'

In fact, this sort of falsification of the facts came to a head when a Beatles' interview in *Playboy* magazine in February 1965 had a quote from John saying: 'Ringo used to fill in sometimes if our drummer was ill, with his periodic illness.' Ringo commented: 'He took little pills to make him ill.' Pete sued and a few years later an out-of-court settlement was eventually reached.

Pete and his wife, Kathy, were living in Haymans Green, but one night when Kathy was visiting her mother, Pete became terribly depressed and attempted to gas himself. His brother, Rory, smelled the gas, battered down the door and, together with Mo, spent several hours reviving him.

Mo became manager of the group and they appeared in Hamburg and recorded with Joe Meek – although the Meek recordings were never released.

They were offered the opportunity of recording in the States by an independent A&R man, Bob Gallo. By this time, Bowen had been replaced by Tommy McGurk, but McGurk left before their American trip. The band added two sax players – Trevor and Bill – and, as a quintet known as the Pete Best Combo, they flew to the States, along with the Undertakers.

The Pete Best Combo appeared on television, toured Canada with Roy Orbison and cut almost 40 numbers in the recording studios. The American producers attempted to capitalize on the Beatles' connections and some of the releases included 'Best of the Beatles', 'The Beatle That Time Forgot' and 'My Three Years as a Beatle.'

Tony Waddington revealed to *Record Collector* magazine:

> In the summer of 1965, we were due to audition for the Monkees TV show – Pete Best could have been a Monkee! We'd been told what sort of show it was going to be and what it was all about, and we were going to fly out to Hollywood. By then, we'd split with the Gallo camp and we had a manager called Chuck Petri, who was wealthy and influential,

However, it wasn't to be. They had been in America so long that they either had to return to England and re-apply for a work permit, or become American citizens. If they became citizens, they would be eligible to be drafted for Vietnam, although it seemed an unlikely prospect. They returned home in July 1966 to appear at the Cavern and disbanded soon after that. By 1969, Pete had left the world of music and settled down to become a civil servant for the employment service in Liverpool.

In 1978, Dick Clark invited him to appear on a television reunion with various other veteran musicians. Then Clark invited him to be the technical adviser on a TV movie called *The Birth of the Beatles*, although the advice of Pete and other *Mersey Beat* veterans, such as Bob Wooler, was reportedly ignored by the producers.

In 1984 his autobiography, *Beatle!* was published. In 1990, together with Billy Kinsley, a former member of the Mersey Beats, he recorded a Rick Wakeman song, 'Heaven'. He also formed a new band and recorded a live album of their appearance at the Beatles' convention in Liverpool in 1991.

Pete was then invited to tour cities throughout Japan and became a guest at several international Beatles' conventions. He took early retirement in 1994 and resumed his musical career with his outfit, the Pete Best Band. His CD of rock 'n' roll favourites from the early Beatles' repertoire, released in 1995, was called *Back To The Beat* and the same year, he set out on a year-long world tour of 20 countries, which included Britain, America, Belgium, South Africa, Russia and Dubai.

Pete Best then received an unexpected piece of good fortune when it was revealed that the Beatles new 'Anthology' double CD, set for release in November, would contain several tracks on which Pete made an appearance. These included the Bert Kaempfert Hamburg recordings, tracks from the Decca audition and the initial Parlophone audition recordings.

BICKNELL, Alf Chauffeur who joined the Beatles during their British tour in 1964 and remained in their service until they finished touring in 1966. His book of reminiscences, *Baby, You Can Drive My Car*, was published in 1989.

BIG THREE, The Group who evolved from Cass & the Cassanovas, a four-piece band formed in the late 1950s and, for a time, regarded as the top group on Merseyside. They even ran their own club, the Cassanova Club, in Fraser Street. The group was led by Brian Casser, who used the names Casey Valence and Casey Jones. He was a dynamic personality, adept at organization.

They were a trio in 1959, comprising Casey Jones, Adrian Barber and Johnny Hutchinson, when Hutchinson brought Johnny Gustafson to see the group, as they needed a bass guitarist. He was asked to join them, but didn't have a guitar and couldn't play. Adrian converted a Hoyer Acoustic for him and put bass strings on it. He joined them and was commonly known as Johnny Bass, but later on was referred to as Johnny Gus.

Leader and rhythm guitarist Cass left for London at the end of 1960, missing out on the entire Mersey success scene, although it has been suggested that the others pushed him out.

The three remaining members of the Cassanovas stayed together and in January 1961 emerged as the Big Three. They were the first Merseyside group to play Ray Charles numbers and had a raw edge to their sound.

Despite the fact that they were a trio, they were one of the loudest bands on Merseyside, due to Adrian's electronic wizardry. He made giant amps, standing over five feet high, which were nicknamed 'coffins'. They were in big demand and the Beatles and other groups asked Adrian to make 'coffins' for them.

The Big Three's reputation locally was very high and, after the Beatles had signed to Epstein, Brian wanted the group in his 'stable'. He initially tried them out by putting them on a shared bill with the Beatles in Southport. When he signed the Big Three, he sent them over to Hamburg on 1 July 1962.

Adrian Barber had never been happy with the idea of Epstein managing the group and he decided to leave, remaining at the Star Club as stage manager. Brian Griffiths, one of the most acclaimed guitarists in Liverpool, replaced him.

Barber's suspicions about Epstein's capabilities proved correct. Brian arranged for them to audition for Decca and they recorded 'Some Other Guy'. Gus was to tell broadcaster Spencer Leigh: 'This was actually a demo tape for Decca. My voice was completely gone. We'd come back from Hamburg that very morning and were thrown into Decca's No. 2 studio in the basement. It was horrible. We were croaking like old frogs. Eppy wouldn't let us do it again and we went berserk. The bass sound was non-existent and the drum sound was awful.'

The group were appalled when they were told that Decca would be releasing their test recording and wouldn't allow them a proper recording session to perform 'Some Other Guy' the way they wished it to be played.

Instead of understanding why the Big Three were so popular – because of their aggressive sound, their wildness, their casual appearance on stage – Brian also forced them to wear uniform suits and began to dilute their sound, choosing lightweight pop numbers and insisting, against their wishes, that they record them.

He had them record Mitch Murray numbers, which were totally unsuitable for the group. Commenting to Leigh on the Decca recordings, Gus said: 'It was arms up the back, "Do it, boys, or it's all over." We didn't like it, but we tried our best. We hated "By the Way" and "I'm with You" because they were pop songs: poppy, horrible, three-chord Gerry-&-the-Pacemakers-type songs.'

In 1963 their A&R man Noel Walker recorded them live at the Cavern. Decca engineers had spent three days experimenting with microphone positions and the recording took ten hours because of technical problems.

The Big Three and Epstein officially came to a parting of the ways on 20 July 1963, but the damage had been done. Before their EP 'The Big Three at the Cavern' was released on 22 November 1963 there was dissension in the group. Johnny Hutch insisted he was leaving. Gus and Griff replaced him with Ian Broad, drummer with Rory Storm & the Hurricanes, and decided to call themselves the Seniors. They left for Germany, where they appeared at the Tanz Club, Hamburg.

Hutch approached Faron and Paddy Chambers of Faron's Flamingos and asked them to join him.

Letters poured into the *Mersey Beat* office from Flamingos and Big Three fans, upset at the split. Hutch was being so heavily criticized that he phoned *Mersey Beat* to comment: 'Because I now have two members of the Flamingos with me a number of people presume that I broke up the group. This is not the case. I'd known for some time that there were internal disagreements among the Flamingos and I heard they were breaking up, otherwise I would not have approached them.'

In the meantime, Billy Kinsley had left the Mersey Beats and their manager, Alan Cheetham, and members of the band flew to Germany to offer Johnny Gus the job. They also paid compensation to Griff and Broad.

The Big Three at the Cavern featured an introduction by Bob Wooler and the tracks 'What'd I Say?', 'Don't Start Running Around', 'Zip-a-Dee-Doo-Dah' and 'Reelin' and a Rockin''.

The Big Three had signed with Kennedy Street Enterprises but didn't find success on record again. They recorded an EP at the Oasis Club, Manchester. Titles were 'Money Honey', 'Cruel Cruel World', 'New Orleans' and 'Whole Lotta Shakin''. In June 1964 'If You Ever Change Your Mind' was issued.

The days of the Big Three were numbered. Paddy Chambers left, to be replaced by Paul Pilnick of the All Stars and the group recorded 'Bring It on Home to Me'. In August 1964 Paul was asked to join Tony Jackson's new band and Hutch had an offer to join Kingsize Taylor, although he decided to hang up his drumsticks.

In 1973 there was an attempt at reviving the band with Gus, Griff and Elton John's drummer Nigel Ollsen. Tony Bramwell produced an album called *Resurrection*, comprising numbers previously recorded by the band, which was issued by Polydor.

Adrian Barber now lives in Hawaii, Brian Griffiths in Canada, Johnny Gustafson in London and Johnny Hutchinson remains in Liverpool.

The Big Three appeared on numerous bills with the Beatles. In 1961 they included the Valentine's Night 'Rock Ball' at the Cassanova Club on Tuesday 14 February, St John's Hall, Tuebrook, in February and the 'Rock Around the Clock' all night session at the Liverpool Jazz Society on Saturday 11 March.

In 1962 they included the 'A Night to Remember' at the Tower Ballroom, New Brighton, on Friday 6 April, the 'Star Show' at the Tower on Thursday 21 June, the Plaza Ballroom, St Helens, on Monday 25 June, Heswall Jazz Club on Saturday 30 June, the Tower Ballroom on Friday 27 July, 'The Beatles Show' at the Rialto Ballroom on Thursday 6 September, the Cavern on Wednesday 19 September and the 'Little Richard Show' at the Tower on Friday 12 October.

During 1963 Brian Epstein had the idea of presenting a series of shows featuring his stable of acts: the Beatles, Gerry & the Pacemakers, Billy J. Kramer with the Dakotas and the Big Three. With permission from me, he called the series of concerts '*Mersey Beat* Showcase'. The first one took place on Thursday 7 March at the Elizabethan Ballroom in Nottingham. Other dates included the King's Hall, Stoke-on-Trent, on Friday 29 March, the Majestic Ballroom, Finsbury Park, London, on Wednesday 24 April, the Fairfield Hall, Croydon, on Thursday 25 April, the Tower Ballroom, New Brighton, on Friday 14 June and the Odeon, Romford, on Sunday 16 June.

There are three tracks by the classic Big Three line-up which have never been released: 'Fortune Teller', 'Long Tall Sally' and 'Walkin' the Dog'.

BILK, Acker   One of the three leading British jazzmen of the late 1950s and early 1960s, along with Kenny Ball and Chris Barber. Born Bernard Stanley Bilk in Somerset on 28 January 1929, he adopted the name 'Acker', which is slang for 'mate'. Acker formed an outfit called the Paramount Jazz Band, adopting a uniform of bowler hats and striped waistcoats. His biggest hit was 'Stranger on the Shore', which topped the American chart in May 1962.

His band was booked regularly on Liverpool's Cavern bills and the club booked him to appear on a 'Riverboat Shuffle' on the *Royal Iris*, travelling on the Mersey on Friday 25 August 1961, with the Beatles as support. The Beatles also appeared with Bilk at the Queen's Hall, Leeds, on 28 June 1963.

BILL BLACK COMBO, The Born in Memphis on 17 September 1926, Bill Black was the bass player on most of Elvis Presley's early records. When Elvis went into the army, Black formed his own band with Carl McVay (piano) Martin Willis (sax), Reggie Young (guitar) and Jerry Arnold (drums).

With his new group he had eight American chart hits between 1959 and 1962, his biggest being the No. 9 chart entry 'White Silver Sands'.

When the Beatles arranged their first American tour, which was to be 31 concerts in 24 cities, Nat Weiss of the General Artists Corporation drew up a list of possible acts who would be available to tour. The Bill Black Combo was one of the acts which the Beatles and Brian Epstein chose to appear with them.

Possibly they decided on Black because of his association with Presley, although only the combo and not Black himself were to appear on the tour.

The musicians were booked on a weekly basis. The Bill Black Combo were the opening act and were paid $1,500 per week.

Bill Black suffered from a brain tumour and died during the operation to remove it on 21 October 1965.

BIRD, Margo A member of the Apple Scruffs, a group of fans who hung around the Apple offices and Abbey Road studios. George Harrison devoted the number 'Apple Scruffs' to them.

BLACK, Cilla Liverpool's most famous female vocalist, born Priscilla Maria Veronica White on 27 May 1943.

She was working as a dictaphone typist at BICC, the cable company, when she first started singing with local groups. It all began when she went to the Iron Door club with her friend Pauline Behan, who was going steady with George Harrison at the time and was later to marry Gerry Marsden of Gerry & the Pacemakers.

The group on stage were Rory Storm & the Hurricanes and Pauline asked them if Cilla could get up with them and sing 'Fever'. As a result she made several further appearances with the band.

Rory's drummer was Ritchie Starkey, whom Rory had dubbed Ringo Starr. Rory had also given him his own five-minute spot in the show called 'Starrtime' and he generally sang one song per performance.

'Boys', the song popularized by the Shirelles, was the number he usually performed, but when Cilla began to sing with the band it was also the number she preferred. There was a bit of a dispute about this, which was resolved when they performed it as a duet.

Commenting on the compromise, Cilla said: 'We did it as a duet, and even then he didn't concede anything. He had a microphone over the drums and I used to have to sing it bent over his kit.

Ringo also took to calling her 'Swinging Cyril'.

While still working as a secretary, Cilla began to sing with the Big Three at the Zodiac club – and was paid for it! She also sang with Kingsize Taylor & the Dominoes, the group led by Ted Taylor, Cilla's then boyfriend.

The numbers in her small repertoire were 'Fever', 'Always', 'Boys' and 'Summertime'.

On 6 July 1961, in the first issue of *Mersey Beat*, I ran a feature called 'Swinging Cilla'. It began: 'Cilla Black is a Liverpool girl who is starting on the road to fame.' It was a mistake. I'd been rushing to complete the first issue and my mind had gone blank when writing about Cilla, although I remembered her surname related to a colour and wrote 'Cilla Black'.

When the issue hit the streets, Cilla was pleased with the article and said that she liked the sound of the new name and would use it in future.

In 1963, when Cilla was being launched, her press officer concocted a story that Brian Epstein had thought of the name change. He was probably unaware that the proof lay in the issue of *Mersey Beat* published almost two years before Brian signed her.

In her autobiography, *Step Inside*, Cilla wrote: 'Not all the changes in my life met with the approval of me Dad. Although he was generally happy for me, he didn't approve of the change of name from White to Black, which began as a misprint in *Mersey Beat*.'

In an interview in the book *Secret Lives*, she said: 'The Black bit came when a local paper, called the *Mersey Beat*, had a misprint. They knew my surname was a colour and guessed wrong!'

As the Mersey scene began to thrive locally, Cilla's ambitions grew. She was still performing as an amateur, although a guy called Terry McGrath was pressing her to make him her manager.

She often dropped into the *Mersey Beat* office, requesting that I become her manager, but I was too occupied with producing the newspaper. During one of her visits, I took her to the nearby Coffee Pot, where she described the career she had in mind. Peggy Lee was her idol and she wanted to become a jazz singer. She asked me if I could form a jazz trio to back her.

This situation lasted for some time, until one evening early in 1963 at the Blue Angel club, when I noticed Brian Epstein huddled in conversation with Andrew Loog Oldham. I took Cilla over to Epstein, introduced her and asked him if he would listen to her sing. Then I arranged for the band on stage to back her singing 'Boys'.

I then left her to it. She was eventually able to tell me that Epstein had arranged a meeting at his office and she became the first female artist in his stable.

Epstein realized that he could express his creative talents in the management of Cilla. He had no real grasp of the music of the Mersey Beat scene but had displayed an interest in the theatre and he set about developing Cilla's image, even designing dresses for her to wear. Managing a female artist enabled Epstein to express part of his own personality.

'Love of the Loved' didn't prove to be the right song for her and was only a minor hit, reaching No. 35 in the charts following its release on 27 September 1963.

Initial 1963 publicity described her as 'The Gal with the Bright Red Hair and the Jet Black Voice' and she made her concert debut at the Odeon, Southport, in a show with the Beatles on 30 August, appeared with the Beatles on the all-Merseyside edition of the *Thank Your Lucky Stars* TV show and was booked for the Beatles Christmas Show at the Finsbury Park Astoria in north London from 24 December.

Not unnaturally, Brian exploited the Beatles association in the build-up of Cilla and his other artists – and also placed her with the Beatles' recording manager, George Martin.

Her career changed direction with a number Epstein picked for her, 'Anyone Who Had a Heart', which had been a big hit for Dionne Warwick in America. He heard the number while on a trip to the States and brought the record back with him, taking it to George Martin as a song for Cilla to record. George said it would be perfect for another of his artists, Shirley Bassey, and told Epstein that Cilla couldn't cope with such a song and wouldn't have a chance with it. Sticking to his guns, Epstein insisted and Cilla's version of the song topped the British charts.

Brian was delighted at the opportunity of moulding a female artist and was able to continue placing her in concerts and TV shows with his other acts. She toured with Gerry & the Pacemakers and Billy J. Kramer, appeared on *Around the Beatles* and *The Music of Lennon and McCartney* TV specials and featured in the Pacemakers' film *Ferry 'Cross the Mersey*.

Gradually, however, her image was directed away from Beat music towards the conventional world of traditional show business, with appearances at the London Palladium, the Royal Variety Show and in cabaret and pantomime.

By 1965, using his prestige and contacts, Epstein attempted to break the 22-year-old Cilla in America. She made her debut on *The Ed Sullivan Show* on 4 April and her American cabaret debut in the Persian Room at the Plaza Hotel, New York, from 26 July. However, American success was to elude her and her sole chart entry there was 'You're My World', which reached No. 26 in the *Billboard* charts in July 1964.

Success on record in Britain continued throughout the decade. She followed 'Anyone Who Had a Heart' with her second consecutive No. 1, 'You're My World', an adaptation of an Italian tune.

A Lennon and McCartney composition, 'It's for You', was her fourth release, reaching No. 7 in the charts. John and Paul visited Cilla in the studio during the recording of the track, and Paul played piano on it.

Cilla covered the Righteous Brothers' hit 'You've Lost That Lovin' Feeling' and looked like beating them to the top of the charts. There was controversy at the time because many people believed that the Righteous Brothers' single was so good it should have been given a clear run. In fact, Andrew Loog Oldham, manager of the Rolling Stones, took out an advertisement in the *New Musical Express* imploring record buyers to pick the original version rather than Cilla's. Cilla had been No. 2 in the chart and the Righteous Brothers No. 3. The following week the Righteous Brothers leap-frogged over her to the No. 1 position.

By 1966 Cilla began to feel that Brian was neglecting her. For the first time he didn't attend the opening night of one of her shows. She found she could no longer contact him by phone and had to talk to secretaries or assistants. When appointments were made he cancelled them or simply didn't turn up. She discussed the situation with her boyfriend, Bobby Willis, and they decided to seek representation elsewhere. Bobby phoned NEMS and left a message for Epstein that Cilla would soon be looking for a new manager.

Epstein had become dependent on drugs by this time, but the thought that Cilla might leave him proved so distressing that he arranged for Cilla and Bobby to meet him at his Chapel Street home for lunch.

When they were together he broke down and cried, telling her: 'There are only five people I love in the world. And that's the Beatles and you, Cilla. Please don't leave me, my Cilla, please.'

Touched by the depth of his emotion, Cilla agreed – and the next day Brian arranged for BBC TV to showcase her in her own series. This new direction was to turn Cilla into one of Britain's most popular mainstream entertainers, establishing her career for the next few decades and reaping her awards such as Best Female Entertainer of the Year for several years to come.

Epstein died in 1967, before the series he set up for Cilla was televised.

The first series of nine 50-minute shows, simply called *Cilla*, began in February 1988. Paul McCartney penned a number called 'Step Inside Love' as the show's signature tune, which became a Top 10 hit for her. This was the third song Paul had penned which Cilla had recorded and Paul made an acoustic version of the song as a demo for her.

Incidentally, George Harrison once wrote a song specially for Cilla called 'I'll Still Love You'. Arrangements were made for her to record it during a hectic summer season at Blackpool and she travelled to London on a Sunday to do so, with George producing and Ringo playing drums. Unfortunately, Cilla had toothache and a swollen mouth at the time and the session didn't work out.

The initial show was seen on Tuesday 9 February and her special guest was Ringo Starr. The two of them appeared in a comedy sketch and sang a duet, 'Do You Like Me Just a Little Bit?'. The number had been suggested by Paul's father, Jim McCartney, who used to play it when he had a jazz band. Ringo also performed 'Act Naturally' and appeared in a comedy sketch in which he was a ventriloquist and Cilla was his dummy.

As he was the first Beatle to appear solo on another artist's show, his fellow Beatles sent along a number of telegrams to the BBC studios where he was recording the show: 'Come home Jim. All is forgiven. Love. Your Buddies and Pals', 'We will be watching. Luv Herbert and Family' and 'Big Brothers are watching and wishing you well. Love from your big Brothers'.

At the beginning of 1969 Cilla and Bobby were married and during the year, to celebrate her twenty-fifth birthday, she had plastic surgery on her nose. Cilla had fractured it when she was 14, but its shape hadn't concerned her, until Bobby began urging her to have an operation to improve her profile on television.

For the next few years she continued to receive awards as Britain's Top Female Singer by publications such as *New Musical Express* and *Disc*, but by the mid-1970s she'd become firmly established as an all-round entertainer, appearing in cabaret, pantomimes and summer seasons at holiday resorts. She also became a mum, giving birth to three boys, Ben, Robert and Jack, between 1974 and 1980.

By this time she was no longer achieving any success on record and her career as a singer gave way to her new status as a television personality.

Under a lucrative contract with London Weekend Television, which made her Britain's highest-paid female TV star, she started hosting the shows *Blind Date* and *Surprise, Surprise*.

BLACK CATS, The A five-piece Mersey band comprising Jimmy Lynch (lead), Alan Stratton (bass), Benny Paige (rhythm), Peter Dobson (tenor) and Mal Thory (drums). They played mainly at social clubs and featured a lot of instrumental numbers in their repertoire. They decided on the name after nearly running over a black cat on their first gig. The members had a zany sense of humour and used to dress up as tramps or roam around in long johns.

The Black Cats appeared in the Cavern with the Beatles on Wednesday 23 August 1961.

BLACK DYKE MILLS BAND, The Famous British brass band of international repute with whom Paul McCartney recorded his composition 'Thingumybob', which he wrote as the theme tune of London Weekend Television's comedy series of the same name.

The band, which continues to perform regularly, was originally sponsored by the firm of John Foster & Sons Ltd.

On 30 April 1968, a Sunday afternoon, Paul travelled to the band's base in Bradford, Yorkshire, to record the single, which he also arranged. At the time the band was conducted by Geoffrey Brand and they also produced an instrumental version of 'Yellow Submarine' for the flipside of the single.

The Black Dyke Mills Band generally worked on a record-by-record basis and became an Apple signing for the one single, which was issued in Britain on Apple, along with singles by the Beatles, Mary Hopkin and Jackie Lomax as the very first batch of Apple releases on 6 September 1968. The record failed to register in the charts.

In America, 'Yellow Submarine' became the A-side when the disc was issued on 26 August 1968, the very first Apple single to be issued in the States, although it was also a non-charter.

The band never recorded for the Apple label again, but Paul was to feature them on a Wings album almost a decade later, in 1979, when they performed on 'Winter Rose' and 'Love Awake' for *Back to the Egg*.

BLACKJACKS, The   Pete Best's first band, formed in late 1959.

In October 1959, when John, Paul and George had a dispute with guitarist Ken Brown, who had only been a member of the Quarry Men for several weeks, Brown approached Best to form another group. As the Quarry Men had walked out on their residency at the Casbah club (in a pique over Mrs Best paying Brown when he hadn't played one night), the club were short of a resident group. Brown said to Pete: 'Why don't we form our own group. Come on! You on drums.'

Brown played rhythm, Chas Newby was on lead and Bill Barlow was on bass. Their repertoire comprised a number of rock 'n' roll classics, including 'Twenty Flight Rock', 'Whole Lotta Shakin'', 'Sweet Little Sixteen', 'Rock and Roll Music', 'Honey Don't', 'Tutti Frutti', 'Long Tall Sally' and 'Memphis Tennessee'. The quartet took over the residency at the club and Pete's mother bought him a brand-new drum kit in blue mother-of-pearl.

When the Beatles booking at the Grosvenor, Wallasey, was cancelled on 6 August 1960, the group drifted along to the Casbah and were impressed by Pete's new kit. Paul McCartney then phoned Pete and asked him to join them. As the Blackjacks were about to split because Brown was moving to London and Newby was starting college, Pete agreed.

John Lennon's original skiffle group was called the Blackjacks during the first week of their existence, when the members comprised John and Pete Shotton.

BLAIR, Isla   Scottish actress, born in India on 29 September 1944, whose solo scene with Paul McCartney on *A Hard Day's Night*, filmed on Monday 20 April 1964, ended up on the cutting-room floor.

It had originally been agreed that each of the Beatles would have a solo scene in the movie and Paul's was to take place immediately after George's sequence in the advertising agency.

Paul sets out in search of Ringo and wanders around the Notting Hill area, coming across an old church that sports a sign 'TV Rehearsal Room'. A group of figures dressed in costume emerge and pass him. He enters and notices a girl (Blair) moving about the huge room. She is dressed in theatrical costume and is quoting Shakespeare.

After some moments, the girl notices Paul and pauses in her speech.

He asks her to continue, but she tells him to go away as he's spoiled her solitary rehearsal. He remains and begins to chat with her, although she tells him he'll be thrown out when the others return. She guesses he's from Liverpool and they then discuss acting, though Paul admits he's done Shakespeare only in a school play.

She tells him she likes acting for herself and he considers such an attitude to be selfish, telling her that actors and actresses should act for an audience. He tells her that he'd approach her part in the manner of a Liverpool scrubber. He points out that this is a clearer way of explaining the character of the role she has been rehearsing.

Paul has to utter such lines as: 'I know your sort – two Cokes and a packet of cheese and onion crisps and suddenly it's love and we're stopping in an empty street doorway. Gerrout of it! Ah, you're lovely all right, you're smashin', but come round here and tell all that to me mum – you won't, will you? You're just after me body and you can't have it, so there!'

Paul remembers his mission (to find Ringo) and says his farewells. As he leaves, he hears the actress return to the rather artificial voice she'd been using when he first eavesdropped on her rehearsals. Then she pauses and begins again, using a much more naturalistic mode of speech, just as Paul had suggested.

The red-haired actress went on to establish herself on television in dramas such as *The Liars* and *An Englishman's Castle*, soaps such as *The Crezz* and series such as *The History Man*.

BLAIR, Lionel A leading British choreographer and TV personality who appeared with the Beatles on the TV show *Big Night Out* and also *Night of One Hundred Stars* at the London Palladium. He was hired to work on the choreography for *A Hard Day's Night*, although a sequence of the Beatles dancing, which he choreographed, ended up on the cutting-room floor.

BLAKE, Peter Internationally renowned British pop artist, born in Dartford, Kent, in June 1932, who was awarded the CBE in 1983.

Blake designed the famous *Sgt Pepper's Lonely Hearts Club Band* sleeve, after being commissioned by London gallery-owner Robert Fraser, who was also his agent. He was aided on the project by his then wife, American sculptor Jann Howarth, and they were paid only £200 between them.

Blake was also to use the Beatles as inspiration for some of his paintings, such as *Beatles (1963–7)* and *The Beatles (1963–8)*.

It was Paul McCartney who originally came up with the basic concept of the album and Blake was to comment: 'It'd been established that there would be another persona that they'd invented and I said, well, perhaps we could pretend that you'd just done a concert and were posing for a photograph. So what we evolved was that we'd build it in the studio. It wasn't a collage, which not many people realize: there have been a great many rip-offs of it and they've always cut up photography and stuck it down. Well, we built the whole thing life-size and made a platform for them to stand on – and the flowers were all delivered and built – and then they came in and posed and the photograph was taken.'

Blake was also to create the collage *A Souvenir for John* (*Lennon*) in 1973 and the poster for Live Aid in 1985. In 1995 he was approached to design the cover for the Beatles *Anthology*, but declined.

BONZO DOG DOO DAH BAND, The Eccentric group, originally formed as the Bonzo Dog Dada Band in 1965. They comprised Vivian Stanshall (vocals/ trumpet/devices), Rodney Slater (saxophone), Neil Innes (vocals/piano/ guitar), Roger Ruskin Spear (saxophone/props/devices) and 'Legs' Larry Smith (drums).

Their initial singles, 'My Brother Makes the Noises for the Talkies' and 'Alley Oop', were released in 1966 and their debut album, *Gorilla*, was issued the following year.

The group were featured in *Magical Mystery Tour* performing 'Death Cab for Cutie' as an accompaniment to topless strip-tease artist Jan Carson. The sequence was filmed at Raymond's Revuebar in London on Monday 18 September 1967. The Beatles inserted the word 'Censored' over her breasts to prevent the scene being cut from the television transmission.

The Beatles also hired them to perform at their special 'Magical Mystery Tour' party, held at the Royal Lancaster Hotel, London, on 21 December 1967. During their show Freddie Lennon got up to sing.

The group next entered the British Top 5 in 1968 with 'I'm the Urban Spaceman', a number produced by Paul McCartney under the pseudonym Apollo C. Vermouth. During that year they supported Cream at the Saville Theatre, Brian Epstein's West End Concert venue. They disbanded in 1970.

Songwriter Neil Innes was later involved with the Rutles and penned the songs for that Beatles lampoon. He was to become a popular guest at Beatles conventions.

George Harrison formed a friendship with 'Legs' Larry Smith, who became a regular visitor to Friar Park, and George was to write a song about him called 'Ladies and Gentlemen His Name Is Legs', which featured on the 1975 album *Extra Texture – Read All About It*.

Viv Stanshall recorded *Sir Henry at Rawlinson's End*, which was turned into a film starring Trevor Howard. He became a voice-over artist, but tragically died in March 1995 in a fire at his north London home. He was 52 years old.

BOYD, Jenny One of Pattie Boyd's two younger sisters. A former model, she joined the Beatles on their trips to Bangor and Rishikesh, India, and also worked in the Apple boutique. She later married Mick Fleetwood and moved to America, although the couple split up. Like Pattie, she has been the inspiration for songs: Donovan wrote 'Jennifer Juniper' for her. She has a Ph.D. in philosophy and in 1992 interviewed 75 musicians, including George and Ringo, for her book *Musicians in Tune*.

BOYD, Pattie Former wife of George Harrison, born Patricia Anne Boyd on 17 March 1944.

She became a model in 1962, appearing in a series of Smiths Crisps commercials, produced by Dick Lester, who hired her to appear in the Beatles debut movie, *A Hard Day's Night*, which he directed.

George fell in love with her and the two moved into his bungalow in Esher, where he proposed marriage on Christmas Day 1965.

The wedding took place at Epsom Register Office and the couple spent their honeymoon in Barbados. Pattie was to become the inspiration for a number of songs by George, including 'Something', 'For You Blue' and 'It's All Too Much'.

It was while they were living at George's Friar Park estate that Eric Clapton, George's best friend, fell in love with her. She was the inspiration behind his song 'Layla'.

After six years, her marriage to George was becoming decidedly rocky. He objected to her desire to become a model again, but she took a modelling assignment against George's wishes. She also had a brief affair with Ronnie Wood. When she left George to join Eric Clapton on his American tour, George was to comment: 'I'd rather she was with him than some dope.'

She was married to George from January 1966 to June 1977 and married Eric Clapton on 27 March 1979 in Tucson, Arizona.

That marriage also ended in divorce after seven years, when the couple broke up in 1986.

Pattie became a professional photographer for a while and settled in Fulham. In the early 1990s she invested in a modelling agency for older women called Déjà Vu, but it was a financial disappointment. She then went on to found a new charity with Barbara Bach called Sharp, which aimed to aid drug addicts and alcoholics.

BRAMBELL, Wilfred British character actor, famous for his role as Steptoe in the long-running TV series *Steptoe and Son*. He first met the Beatles when they were on the same bill at the Royal Variety Performance in 1963 and featured as Paul's eccentric grandfather in *A Hard Day's Night*. He died of cancer in January 1985.

BRAMWELL, Tony A childhood friend of George Harrison who became an office boy at NEMS in Liverpool after Brian Epstein had signed the Beatles.

George met him while he was working as a delivery boy and the two began to chat about skiffle and rock 'n' roll. George was suitably impressed when he heard that Tony had met Buddy Holly during his British tour. Tony recalls: 'I used to lend George all my Buddy Holly records so he could try to learn the various chords and riffs. We played them all so much that by the time we'd finished they were just about ready for the bin.'

From NEMS office boy he graduated to handling various assignments and soon became one of those close friends they always had around who was also capable of doing a good job of work. He travelled to America with them and wrote reports of their activities for various publications, including the *Beatles Monthly*.

Brian Epstein appointed him stage manager at the Saville Theatre and after Brian's death he joined Apple, involving himself in a number of tasks, including record production and the film company Subafilms.

He was also Apple's chief record-plugger and proved particularly adept at getting radio and TV spots for the Apple signings.

Tony was a dab hand with the camera and many of his photographs of Apple acts, such as Mary Hopkin, were syndicated throughout the world.

He remained in charge of Apple promotion until 1970 and then spent a year in Los Angeles running Apple Music.

Tony next worked for Harry Saltzmann's music-publishing company, then produced a Big Three album and became an independent promotions man, whose acts included Paul McCartney and the Moody Blues. By the end of the 1970s he was ensconced in an executive position at Polydor Records, retaining his independence.

The former NEMS office boy also became one of London's most eligible bachelors, dating an assortment of Miss Worlds and celebrities such as Christine Keeler, and for a number of years he lived with the stunning Swedish actress Julie Ege. He later married, began to represent Phil Spector in Britain and moved to the south coast.

Commenting on his own career, he was to say: 'I started in 1963 as the Beatles' roadie and toured the world with most of the Mersey Beat bands through to 1965. Then I became head of NEMS Presentations and Subafilms, Brian Epstein's production and film companies. This involved producing and directing promotional films and stage shows with the Beatles, the Who, Jimi Hendrix, the Bee Gees and Cream.'

BRAUTIGAN, Richard American author, born in 1933, whose most noted work was *Trout Fishing in America*. When the Beatles Apple Records was formed, they conceived a subsidiary label, Zapple, which was to feature experimental recordings, the first two of which were George Harrison's 'Electronic Music' and John and Yoko's 'Life with the Lions'.

Future recordings were to feature authors and poets reading from their works, with Barry Miles advising on the various projects for Zapple.

The third Zapple release was to be *Listening to Richard Brautigan* and was due to be issued on 23 May 1969, but by that time Allen Klein had taken control of the company and he cancelled the avant-garde label.

The album was issued in America the following year by Capitol Records.

Brautigan died in 1984, a suspected suicide.

BRAVO, Lizzie Brazilian Beatles fan who was asked to contribute some falsetto harmonies on the Beatles track 'Across the Universe'.

BRESNER, Buddy Miami police sergeant assigned to be the Beatles' bodyguard during their stay at Miami Beach in February 1964. They accepted an invitation to dine with his family at his home.

BRIAN POOLE & THE TREMELOES Group who auditioned for Decca on the same day as the Beatles. They were successful; the Beatles weren't. Some say it was because they came from nearby Dagenham and it was much more convenient for Decca to sign a group local to London. They made an impact, recording 'Twist & Shout', which had become popular because of the Beatles' rendition. The group comprised Brian Poole (vocals), Rick West (lead), Alan Blakely (rhythm), Alan Howard (bass) and Dave Munden (drums).

BRODAX, Al Head of the film and TV department of King Features Syndicate who approached Brian Epstein in 1964 for a licence to produce an animated series on the Beatles. The series was screened in 1965 and Brodax also secured the rights to produce a full-scale animated movie, *Yellow Submarine*.

BRODZIAK, Kenn Australian entrepreneur who organized and promoted the Beatles' June 1964 tour of 'down under'.

BRON, Eleanor Stage, screen and television actress, born in London on 14 March 1930. A Cambridge graduate, her first professional engagement was at the Establishment club, Britain's first club to specialize in satire. She was also a regular cast member of the TV series *Not So Much a Programme ... More a Way of Life*.

Eleanor made her film debut in the Beatles' second film *Help!*, when newspapers ran headlines such as 'The Beatles First Leading Lady'.

On 9 February 1965 the *Sun* newspaper announced:

> Eleanor Bron, who appears on the TV satire show *Not So Much a Programme*, did a rather satirical thing yesterday. She announced that she is to make a film with the Beatles. It was all terribly serious. Miss Bron, who has made a name for herself with pitiless send-ups of upper-class English women, will herself be an upper-class woman of a type: a mysterious Eastern princess who wants to be loved by the Beatles.

Eleanor appeared as Ahme and the film's official synopsis read: 'In the Eastern Temple of the Goddess Kaili a human sacrifice is about to be made. But the executioner, the High Priest Clang, is stopped by the beautiful Ahme, priestess of the cult, who has discovered that the victim is not wearing the sacrificial ring essential for the ritual.'

The ring ends up on the finger of Ringo Starr and the cult members attempt to capture him, but he is saved on several occasions by his fellow

Beatles and Ahme. At one point when the Beatles are being pursued by the villains across Salisbury Plain, she arrives in a tank to rescue them.

Despite a distinguished career in which she has appeared in many stage and television productions, Eleanor is still remembered for her appearance with the Beatles. She recalls an incident in the 1980s when she was shopping. She heard a man say to a woman: 'If you look around, you can see not just one but two movie stars here in this store.' The woman showed surprise and he continued: 'Yes, that woman behind you is a movie star. She was in *Help!*, the Beatles film. Her name is Fenella Fielding.'

When she was filming with the Beatles in the Bahamas, the newspapers attempted to talk her into posing in a bikini. She refused. Later she noticed a picture-story in the *Daily Mail* headed 'Bron the Beatle Tamer', which featured a photograph of Paul McCartney talking to a dark-haired girl in a bikini with her back to the camera. It wasn't her.

John Lennon struck up a friendship with Eleanor and they used to spend time together drinking in hotel bars, discussing politics and philosophy.

When the Beatles were staying in Beverly Hills prior to their Hollywood Bowl concert, she visited John and spent a few hours with him. He was later to claim that she had been one of his conquests, but Eleanor denies that they were ever lovers.

At one time, Paul mentioned that the first name in his song 'Eleanor Rigby' was probably inspired by Eleanor Bron.

BROOK BROTHERS British pop duo comprising brothers Geoffrey and Ricky Brook, from Winchester, Hampshire, who first began their musical career in a skiffle group in 1956. As a duo they made their recording debut in 1960, but it was when they joined Pye Records, with Tony Hatch as their producer, that they gained the tag 'the British Everly Brothers' and enjoyed success with hits such as 'Warpaint' and 'Ain't Gonna Wash for a Week'.

They were added to the bill of the Beatles fourth nationwide tour in November 1963. They also appeared in the film *It's Trad, Dad!*, directed by Richard Lester and starring Helen Shapiro, before they signed to Decca as the Brooks. The duo disbanded soon after.

BROOKS, Elkie Female vocalist, real name Elkie Brookbinder, who appeared on 'Another Beatles Show' at the Hammersmith Odeon, from 24 December 1964. Elkie, whose brother was Tony Mansfield, drummer with Billy J. Kramer & the Dakotas, appeared with rock bands such as Dada and Vinegar Joe before turning solo and having a string of 13 chart hits in Britain.

BROWN, Bobbie A Beatles fan from Wallasey, Bobbie organized the first Beatles fan club in April 1962, advertising it in *Mersey Beat*. In December of that year she was to report in *Mersey Beat*:

The Fan Club has now been operating since April last, and the amount of members accumulated during this time, which has risen tremendously to one thousand, has made our efforts seem well worthwhile. Our members come from all over the country, from such places as Glasgow, Lancaster, Blackpool, Essex, Doncaster, Sussex, I.O.M., Northern Ireland – and even further afield from Hamburg, Belgium and Rhodesia. My daily post is fantastic, an average of thirty letters a day!

Recently I visited the Star Club in Hamburg, with a number of fans, to see the Beatles. How pleased they were to see that they were appreciated there just as they had been by the numerous fans in this country. It is most rewarding to see after a hard struggle from the bottom that they have reached the top in their own special field of entertainment. It is the 'get up and go' quality which these boys possess that makes the Fan Club well worth running. Early next year we're going to organize a 'Fan Club Festival' in which the boys really 'meet' their fans.

Bobbie also organized two coach trips for fans: one to see the group record at the BBC's Playhouse Theatre, Manchester, and the other to watch their performance at the Plaza Ballroom, St Helens.

She became engaged to be married early in 1963 and passed the running of the club over to her friend Freda Kelly.

BROWN, Joe Lincolnshire-born singer, reared in the East End of London, who came to popularity via Jack Good TV shows such as *Oh Boy!*. Brian Epstein booked him for two consecutive gigs in 1962 in an effort to boost the Beatles image by placing them on bills with chart names. Their first gig together was at the Cambridge Hall, Southport, on 26 July 1963 and the next night Brown topped the bill at the Tower Ballroom, New Brighton, with the Beatles in support. Brown was also to have a minor hit with 'With a Little Help from My Friends' in 1967.

BROWN, Ken Liverpool guitarist who played alongside George Harrison in the Les Stewart Quartet in 1958, at a time when John Lennon's group the Quarry Men were dormant.

They were practising at a venue called Lowlands when George's girlfriend, Ruth Morrison, mentioned that a new coffee club was opening nearby and they might be seeking a resident group. Brown went along to see Mona Best and secured the band a residency, due to begin when the club opened on Saturday 29 August, 1959.

Early that Saturday Brown went to Stewart's house and sat in the lounge with Stewart and George. There seemed to be a bad atmosphere in the room and Brown asked Stewart what was up. Stewart accused him of missing practice and continued to argue after Brown explained that he'd been helping out at the Casbah in order to secure a place for them to play. Stewart accused him of receiving money for helping out, which Brown denied.

Stewart told him, 'I'm not playing there.'

Brown asked George not to back out on him too, so George followed him out of the house, with Brown suggesting they had to get a group together for that evening. George mentioned that he had two friends and would contact them.

Brown waited patiently at the Casbah for two hours, then George returned with John, Paul and Cynthia.

They decided to use the name of John's group, the Quarry Men, and began their residency that evening. Among the numbers played were 'Three Cool Cats' sung by John, and 'Long Tall Sally' sung by Paul. Brown played Hofner guitar and the group used his ten-watt amplifier.

The new club was the subject of a story in the local newspaper, the *West Derby Reporter*, which noted how Kenneth Brown, David Hughes and Douglas Jenkins had helped to decorate the club and make it shipshape, adding: 'Kenneth Brown is also a member of a guitar group which entertains the club members on Saturday nights. The other members of the group, who call themselves the Quarry Men, travel from the south end of the city to play.'

In 1965 Brown told a reporter how his days with the group came to an end, during a dispute which took place six weeks after the group had got together:

> One night, just as we were due to start a Saturday session, I felt a crippling pain in my leg. I could barely stand, but insisted on doing something, so Mrs Best asked me to take the money at the door and, for the first time, John, Paul and George played without me.
>
> Just as everyone was going home I was in the club when Paul came back down the steps. 'Hey, Ken, what's all this?' he said. 'What?' I asked him. 'Mrs Best says she's paying you, even though you didn't play with us tonight.' 'That's up to her,' I replied, as Paul bounded back up the stairs, still arguing with Mrs Best. They all came downstairs to me. 'We think your fifteen bob should be divided between us, as you didn't play tonight,' said Paul. So of course I didn't agree. 'All right, that's it then!' shouted McCartney, and they stormed off down the drive towards West Derby village, shouting that they would never play at the Casbah again.

This left the club without a resident group, so Brown approached Pete Best and suggested they form a group on their own. The result was the Blackjacks, who began playing regularly at the club until Pete was approached by the Beatles to join them for their Hamburg trip. The Blackjacks were on the verge of splitting up then, with Chas Newby soon to start college and Brown about to marry his girlfriend, Marcia, and move to London.

In December 1960, when Stuart Sutcliffe remained in Hamburg, Best suggested that Brown rejoin them as bass guitarist for some of their Liverpool gigs, even though he was then in London, but the other members vetoed the suggestion.

The last time that Brown saw the group was on 16 March 1963, when Neil Aspinall phoned him to say that they were in a jam as they'd run out of money and were due to appear in Sheffield the next night – could he lend them £20?

Brown was to relate: 'Eventually, I agreed and they all turned up at our flat. Neil came to the door, then Marcia, and I went down to the van to see the boys. I handed over the money, which they repaid six weeks later.'

BROWN, Peter A close associate of Brian Epstein who, because of their friendship, was brought on board the Beatles bandwagon and became a Beatles 'insider' until he blotted his copybook by co-authoring a kiss-and-tell book concentrating on Beatles scandals.

Brown was born in Bebington, the Wirral. He worked in Henderson's, a department store in Liverpool city centre, before moving to the larger store, Lewis's, where he became manager of the record department.

In manner and tastes he was very similar to Epstein, who, when he moved from the Great Charlotte Street branch of NEMS to manage the Whitechapel branch, appointed Brown to replace him in the first store.

A fastidious dresser who enjoyed the social life, Brown was invited to join Epstein in London when the NEMS Enterprises office relocated in 1965. As Brian's personal assistant, he proved of particular value in arranging the social events surrounding the organization, such as the special 'Sgt Pepper' party.

During the Bank Holiday weekend of August 1967, Brown and Geoffrey Ellis were at Epstein's Kingsley Hill country home, waiting for Brian to join them, when they received a phone call to say that Brian had been found dead.

While the power struggles for control of NEMS began, Peter became general manager of Beatles & Co. People were to refer to him as a 'Brian clone' and it was also suggested that he had ambitions of becoming the Beatles' manager.

The group appointed him an executive of their new Apple Corps organization and in his book *The Longest Cocktail Party* Richard DiLello describes Brown as the 'impeccable Signor Suave of the Apple diplomatic corps and personal assistant and social co-ordinator to the Beatles'.

DiLello also mentions an incident in which Peter displayed his diplomatic skills. When members of the San Francisco chapter of Hell's Angels visited Apple and attended the Apple Christmas party, a 43-pound turkey was to be served at a specific time. One of the Hell's Angels didn't like waiting and became involved in a verbal battle with John. Peter was called. He sized up the situation immediately, tapped the Hell's Angel on the shoulder and explained the delay to him. Having received a straight answer to a straight question, the Angel seemed satisfied and what could have been a nasty confrontation between him and John was averted.

It was Peter who accompanied John and Yoko to Gibraltar and acted as best man at their wedding. John mentions him by name on the single 'The Ballad of John & Yoko'.

With the onset of Allen Klein, Peter left Apple to join Robert Stigwood's organization in 1970 and moved to America, where he enjoyed considerable success.

His close association with the Beatles was destroyed when he co-wrote *The Love You Make: An Insider's Story of the Beatles*, first published in America in January 1983 by McGraw-Hill. Brown and his collaborator, Stephen Gaines, were able to obtain the cooperation of members of the Beatles' circle by stating that the book was about the 1960s in general. None of the associates would have cooperated if they had realized the true nature of the book, which portrayed the group in an unsympathetic light.

It suggested that Yoko was responsible for the Beatles' breakup and intimated that she turned John into a heroin addict. The revelations about Brian Epstein's homosexual problems caused Brian's mother, Queenie, to have a breakdown and she was hospitalized.

Brown became an independent film producer in 1975 and also worked in public relations.

BROWNE, Tara   Son of Lord Oranmore and great-grandson of the famous brewer Edward Cecil Guinness, the young Irishman was to have inherited £1 million on his twenty-fifth birthday. He frequented London clubs and was a friend of Paul and Mike McCartney, Mick Jagger, Marianne Faithfull and Brian Jones.

Tara married at eighteen and had two sons, but was separated from his wife, Nikki (Noreen), living in Eaton Row and dating Suki Poitier when a tragic accident occurred. In the early hours of the morning, with Suki as his passenger, he was driving down Redcliffe Gardens in Earls Court when a Volkswagen suddenly pulled out of a side road directly in his path and he had to swerve, crashing into a parked van. He was dead before he reached hospital. He had only recently celebrated his twenty-first birthday. Suki suffered from shock and sustained some bruising.

John Lennon noticed the story of the accident in the *Daily Mail* on 18 December 1966. He read the coroner's verdict and used it in the opening verses of 'A Day in the Life' on the *Sgt Pepper* album when he refers to 'He blew his mind out in a car.'

Marianne Faithfull claims Tara was on acid at the time, which could explain the wording of John's description.

BRYAN, Dora   Popular comedienne who recorded the first Beatles novelty record, 'All I Want for Christmas is a Beatle'. She also took part in a revue in which the Beatles were parodied as an all-girl group, the Cockroaches.

BRYCE, Leslie   Official photographer for the *Beatles Monthly* who took thousands of photographs of the group for the magazine.

BUDDY BRITTON & THE REGENTS   Band, often wrongly described as a Mersey Beat group, who recorded 'If You Gotta Make a Fool of Somebody', flipside 'Money', but on the minor Oriole label. Freddie & the Dreamers and Bern

Elliott & the Fenmen were to have hits with their versions. Buddy and his group appeared with the Beatles on a NEMS Enterprises gig at the Queen's Hall, Widnes, on Monday 18 February 1963.

BURNS, Tito British promoter, agent and manager who missed out on the opportunity of booking the Beatles on several occasions, but who almost merged his organization with that of NEMS. Burns, who managed artists such as Dusty Springfield and the Searchers, discussed a possible merger with Epstein, but they couldn't agree terms.

BYRDS, The American band who, although they'd originally formed as a folk trio called the Jet Set, became heavily influenced by the Beatles in 1964 and completely changed their style after being inspired by Beatlemania.

They comprised Gene Clark (vocals/tambourine/rhythm guitar), Jim (Roger) McGuinn (vocals/lead guitar), David Crosby (vocals/rhythm guitar), Chris Hillman (bass) and Michael Clarke (drums).

McGuinn was to comment: 'We each heard them [the Beatles], saw them in *A Hard Day's Night*, and I personally went out and got a Rickenbacker 12-string guitar like George had and David got a Gretch and our drummer got Ludwig drums and we just patterned ourselves after the Beatles individually.'

They used the pseudonym the Beefeaters for their Elektra single 'Please Let Me Love You' in 1964, but by the end of the year had changed their name to the Byrds and signed with CBS, where they had a chart hit with their first release, 'Mr Tambourine Man'. The group was then hailed as 'America's answer to the Beatles'.

When Derek Taylor travelled to England with the Byrds in 1965 he sent the Beatles copies of their debut album, also called *Mr Tambourine Man*.

The group met up with the Beatles and, at a later date, members of the Beatles attended a Byrds recording session in Los Angeles.

Dave Crosby has been credited with bringing Ravi Shankar's music to the attention of George Harrison.

Gene Clarke died on 24 May 1991, the year in which the Byrds were inducted into the Rock 'n' Roll Hall of Fame.

BYRNE, Gay Irish TV presenter who worked for Granada Television in the early 1960s, hosting a programme called *People and Places*, which focused on people and events in the north-west of England.

Byrne had originally read out a news item regarding a clip of the Beatles filmed at the Cavern and he became the first person to announce the Beatles on TV when they made their television debut and performed 'Love Me Do' for the show on 7 November 1962. The Beatles received a fee of £35. The programme was to change its name to *Scene at 6.30* and Gay later returned to Ireland, where he became the Republic's leading television personality, hosting the Dublin-based chat show *The Late, Late Show*.

On 7 November 1963 the Beatles performed in Dublin. To celebrate the thirtieth anniversary of the event, Byrne hosted a two-hour Beatles TV special in Ireland on the same day in 1993.

Byrne had also hosted their *Beat Show* radio programme, recorded at the Playhouse Theatre, Manchester, on 3 July 1963, in addition to recording an interview with the Beatles and Ken Dodd for Granada's *Scene at 6.30* on 25 November 1963.

BYRNE, Nicky Young man who made a fortune out of the Beatles due to an unfortunate decision by Brian Epstein. Byrne secured the rights to the Beatles merchandising, receiving 90 per cent of the proceeds. He formed a company called Seltaeb (Beatles spelt backwards) and went on to make millions. As a result of a dispute with NEMS, over $100 million worth of contracts were cancelled. Byrne was also to successfully sue Epstein. He bought a yacht and retired to the Bahamas.

CALDER, Tony Former associate of Tony Barrow in the Decca press office. He teamed up with Andrew Loog Oldham and worked on the publicity of 'Love Me Do'.

CALDWELL, Iris Blonde former dancer, born in Liverpool. When she was 12, her 14-year-old boyfriend was George Harrison. When she was 17, she went out with Paul McCartney and she was allegedly the inspiration for 'Love Me Do'. The sister of Rory Storm, she was to marry singer Shane Fenton in 1964. The couple had two children, but later divorced and she re-married in 1983.

CAMPBELL, William During the period of the 'Paul is dead' rumours, London's *Evening News* published a story stating that John, George and Ringo had replaced Paul with a double named William Campbell. According to the paper, Campbell had undergone plastic surgery to resemble the Beatle he was impersonating.

CANNIBAL & THE HEADHUNTERS Following their chart hit 'Land of 1,000 Dances', this American band was booked to appear on the Beatles' US tour in 1965.

CARAVELLES, The British singing duo featuring two former office girls, Lois Wilkinson and Andrea Wilson.

Their single, a reworking of Tennessee Ernie Ford's 'You Don't Have to be a Baby to Cry', was a British chart entry, reaching the No. 6 position in August 1963, and was an even bigger hit in America, where it reached No. 3 in the charts.

The girls were booked to appear with the Beatles on their very first American concert at the Coliseum, Washington DC, on 11 February 1964.

The Caravelles didn't have any further major hits and Wilkinson left to embark on a solo career under the name Lois Lane. Wilson continued using the Caravelles name for a number of years with various other female singers.

CARGILL, Patrick Actor, born in London on 3 June 1918. He featured as Superintendent Gluck in the Beatles second film, *Help!*. He also appeared in *The Magic Christian*, which starred Peter Sellers and Ringo Starr. He is more popularly known for starring in the television series *Father, Dear Father*. Following its success in Britain, he also made an Australian version of the sit-com. He died in 1996.

CARROLL, Lewis Victorian author, real name Charles Lutwidge Dodgson, who wrote *Alice's Adventures in Wonderland* and *Through the Looking-Glass*. John Lennon was influenced by his work in both his prose and his song lyrics. A prime example is 'I am the Walrus', partly inspired by 'The Walrus and the Carpenter'. Carroll is also featured in the *Sgt Pepper* tableau.

CARSON, Jan Strip-tease artist engaged by the Beatles to perform her routine in *Magical Mystery Tour*, in a sequence filmed at Raymond's Revuebar in London on Monday 18 September 1967. Jan strips off her top while the Bonzo Dog Doo Dah Band accompany her, performing 'Death Cab for Cutie'. In the editing stage the word 'Censored' was inserted to cover her bare breasts, although the BBC was one of several broadcasters to omit the scene during transmission.

CASEY, Howie A Liverpool musician who had learned to play sax while in the army. He formed Derry & the Seniors in November 1959. The line-up comprised Howie (saxophone), Derry Wilkie (vocals); Jeff Wallington (drums), Billy Hughes (rhythm/vocals); Brian Griffiths (lead) and Phil Whitehead (bass).

They appeared regularly around Merseyside at venues such as Blair Hall, Wilson Hall and the Jacaranda, and, because of the Jacaranda connection, Allan Williams booked them for the Liverpool Stadium Show with Gene Vincent on Tuesday 3 May 1960.

Williams had staged the event with London impresario Larry Parnes and the bill featured a number of Liverpool groups. Parnes was impressed and asked Williams to arrange an audition as he was seeking bands to back his various artists, such as Billy Fury, Johnny Gentle and Duffy Power.

The Silver Beetles were also present at the audition, which took place on 10 May at the Wyvern Social Club in Seel Street. When Casey was later asked what he thought of them, he said: 'Quite frankly, I wasn't too impressed and I can't remember the group singing. I believe they played a lot of instrumentals and Shadows numbers.'

Following the audition the Seniors were booked by Parnes to back one of his bands for a season at Blackpool, a deal arranged by Williams. As a result, they turned professional.

When the season was cancelled, a furious Casey arrived at the Wyvern (which Williams was transforming into his Blue Angel club) with his band, ready to give Williams a severe beating. A frightened Williams promised he would take them to London and find work for them.

They drove down south and Williams took them to the 2 I's coffee bar in Old Compton Street, Soho. Fortuitously, the German club-owner, Bruno Koschmider, was present at the 2 I's, having arrived in London to seek some bands for his Kaiserkeller club.

It was one of those million-to-one coincidences, because Williams had been in contact with Koschmider about booking groups for Hamburg, telling him that Liverpool had the best rock 'n' roll groups in the world. Koschmider had arrived in the country and, when inquiring about groups, had been directed to the 2 I's.

Williams arranged for the Seniors to go on stage and they were booked to appear at Koschmider's Kaiserkeller club for a season from 31 July 1960. Howie was to describe it as 'seven hours a night, 16 quid a week, sleeping in cupboards, being crazy'.

Koschmider asked Williams to send along another Liverpool group. Allan first approached Rory Storm & the Hurricanes, but they were booked for a season at Butlin's. He next asked Gerry & the Pacemakers, but Gerry said no. As a last resort he booked the Beatles, who had been playing in his Jacaranda cellar.

When Williams wrote to Casey, mentioning that the Beatles were due to replace them, Howie wrote back, probably remembering the Wyvern Club audition, complaining that the scene in Hamburg was a good one and that he'd be ruining it for everyone ' . . . by sending that bum group, the Beatles'.

The Beatles duly arrived, to be met at the Kaiserkeller by Howie, who told them that they were booked at a smaller club called the Indra at the shoddy end of the Grosse Freiheit.

Howie observed: 'They had very, very pointed shoes in grey crocodile. They had mauve jackets with half-belting at the back. The length of their hair caused a great stir around the area – it was thick at the back, almost coming over their collars.'

Once the Beatles appeared in Germany, Howie was able to reappraise them and was suitably impressed. At one point the Beatles' bass guitarist, Stu Sutcliffe, joined his band.

Howie commented: 'The girls used to rave over Pete Best – he was the star boy. He was a great fellow and the one I liked most. He was very quiet and didn't rave as much as the others. Pete really did fit in with the group then – but their style is more sophisticated now, as they have improved musically. He used to swap ideas with our drummer, Jeff Wallington.

'Paul had terrific talent and used to play left-handed guitar. He didn't actually play it, he had the amp turned down low.

'The manager of the Kaiserkeller decided to discontinue having a jukebox in the interval, and wanted to put a group on instead, so he split our group into two. He arranged for Stu to play with us. So the second unit of the Seniors was myself on sax, Stan Foster on piano, Stu on bass and a terrific German modern jazz drummer.

'All we could do with Stu was to play 12-bar blues – he couldn't venture out of that – and I noticed more than ever how self-critical he was about his music all the time.

'He used to sketch around the club, drawing patrons and members of the groups, such as Derry Wilkie. In fact, he left the group during the trip and remained in Germany to study at Hamburg Art college.

'The Beatles did their nut because Stu was playing with us. A woman living close to the Indra complained about the noise and the police closed the club. The Beatles then came to the Kaiserkeller and reunited with Stu.'

The Seniors finished their residency on 1 October, when they were replaced by Rory Storm & the Hurricanes. They tried to find other work, ran out of money and had to be repatriated.

When they returned to Liverpool at the end of the year, their equipment was stored at the Top Ten Club in Soho Street, a new rock 'n' roll club based on the Hamburg-style clubs, to be opened by Allan Williams. Unfortunately, it was burned down, allegedly by rival club-owners. With all their equipment destroyed, the Seniors disbanded in December 1960.

They were reborn in January 1961 as Howie Casey & the Seniors. Apart from Howie and Derry, the line-up comprised Freddie Fowell, who was later to become Freddie Starr (vocal), Frank Wibberley (drums), Brian Griffiths (guitar) and Phil Whitehead (bass). They were signed with Fontana and became the first Liverpool group to make a record.

The record company placed them with a London agent. Howie commented: 'They had no idea how to cope with us. They were used to nice boys-next-door cabaret groups – but we were the ugliest bunch of rowdy drunken gits you ever saw! Eventually they got us a residency at a club in Ilford called Twist at the Top, and we really thought we'd cracked it. We got nice new shiny bronze suits! Opening night was great, but it went downhill fast and closed!'

This line-up suffered financial problems and disbanded in December 1961. In January 1962 Howie launched the group again, with Derry, Freddie, Frank and Brian plus Frank Bowen and Lou Walters on bass guitars.

They appeared at all the major Liverpool venues, but rarely played outside the north-west, despite having three singles and an album released.

Howie decided to disband the group in June 1962. Lou returned to Rory Storm & the Hurricanes, Frank Bowen joined Lee Curtis, Derry Wilkie fronted the Pressmen, Frank Wibberley teamed up with the Lee Eddie Five, Freddie was to form Freddie Starr & the Midnighters, Brian was to join the Big Three and Howie joined the Dominoes.

After a number of years in Germany with Kingsize Taylor & the Dominoes, Howie returned to Britain and became a successful session man in London.

Paul McCartney asked him to join Wings on their 1975 world tour and 1979 tour of Britain. He also played on a number of Wings recordings, including the albums *Band on the Run* and *Back to the Egg*.

In 1995 he recorded an album in Britain with Tony Sheridan and Roy Young.

CASSER, Brian Also known as Casey Jones and Casey Valance. A Newcastle-born musician who originally led one of the top Liverpool groups, Cass & the Cassanovas, from December 1959 to December 1960.

Cass formed Cass & the Cassanovas, playing lead/vocals, and was joined by Adrian Barber on guitar and Johnny Hutchinson on drums. They were soon joined by Johnny Gustafson on bass.

When Allan Williams booked several local groups to appear at the Gene Vincent promotion at the Liverpool Stadium on Tuesday 3 May

1960, the Cassanovas topped the bill of local bands. The group were also to promote some of their own gigs and named a club the Cassanova club.

Williams asked Cass's advice about a drummer for the Beatals, as they were called at the time, and he suggested they contact Tommy Moore.

The Cassanovas were present at the Larry Parnes audition at the Wyvern Club in Seel Street on 10 May 1960. They were hired to back Duffy Power on a tour of Scotland and were away at the time when Williams needed a group to go to Hamburg, which explains why he didn't book them to appear in Germany at the time.

There has been some confusion about how Williams actually initially got in touch with Bruno Koschmider. Most reports detail his trip to Hamburg in search of his errant resident band, the Royal Caribbean Steel Band. During the trip he came across Koschmider at his Kaiserkeller club.

Cass always maintained that he made the original contact with Koschmider. Williams allowed Cass to sleep at the Jacaranda club and Cass would use the phone there after hours to contact Koschmider, through an interpreter. He said that he was arranging to book his own band in Germany. One day, in Cass's absence, Koschmider's representative phoned the Jacaranda to get hold of Cass to book groups – but it was Allan who picked up the phone, and, on finding out what it was about, he said that he'd provide the groups for Germany.

The true story is probably somewhere between the two.

Cass also suggested to John Lennon that he call his group Long John and the Silver Men.

At the end of 1960 Barber, Hutchinson and Gustafson ended their association with Cass and were to continue as the Big Three. Cass moved to London, where, for a time, he managed a club in Soho called the Blue Gardenia.

Following the Beatles' abortive trip to the Palais Ballroom, Aldershot, on Saturday 9 December 1961 for a gig which attracted only 18 customers, they drove on to London and dropped in at Cass's club, where John, Paul and Pete, minus George, played a set on stage.

In 1963 Cass wrote me a letter at *Mersey Beat* in which he said: 'Since coming to London three years ago I have been doing a great deal of film work, but films were not really my ambition. When everything started to happen in Scouseland, I really felt left out. So I decided to return to the singing scene.'

He had a number released on EMI's Columbia label, 'One Way Ticket'.

Cass also formed Casey Jones & the Engineers, a group which lasted until October 1963. Eric Clapton played guitar with the band for seven gigs. Casey was lead vocalist and other members included Tom McGuinness on bass and Ray Stock on drums.

Casey then moved to Germany and teamed up with a Bristol group as Casey Jones & the Governors. He enjoyed a successful career over there, with several hit records, including 'Don't Ha Ha' in 1965, which was No. 1 in Germany for seven weeks and sold a million copies there alone.

CATTIA German girl, surname not known, who was one of Paul McCartney's girlfriends from the early Hamburg days. When the group returned to Hamburg for a concert at the Merck Halle in June 1966, Cattia turned up backstage to visit them, along with several other friends, including Astrid and Gibson Kemp, Bert Kaempfert and Bettina, former barmaid at the Star Club.

CAVENDISH, Leslie Hair-stylist who worked for Vidal Sassoon. Jane Asher arranged for him to cut Paul's hair and he then performed the same honours for the rest of the Beatles. They set him up in his own salon. He was a passenger in the *Magical Mystery Tour*.

CHADWICK, Les Student at the Junior Art College in Gambier Terrace, Liverpool, along with myself and Cynthia Powell.

Les left the grammar school and spent two years as a National Serviceman before joining Peter Kaye, a photographic studio in Park Road, Liverpool, run by Bill Connell.

When I launched *Mersey Beat* I approached Les to become one of the main photographers for the publication. A deal was worked out with Bill Connell that in exchange for display and classified advertisements, photo credits, the promotion of prints for sale to readers and a recommendation that groups should hire the studio for publicity shots, I would commission Les to take photographs for *Mersey Beat*.

Les accompanied me all over Merseyside, taking photos of the groups. As the Beatles were the group who received the lion's share of publicity in *Mersey Beat*, he took many shots of them, accompanying me to venues ranging from the Tower Ballroom, to the Cavern and backstage at numerous theatres.

An example was the famous shot of the Beatles with Little Richard at the Tower Ballroom. All were gathered in the dressing room, where crates of light ale were supplied as refreshments, when I organized the Beatles and Little Richard in a pose together, which Les shot. Les also took pictures of Richard with the Beatles, Derry Wilkie and members of the Chants together.

My wife, Virginia, and I took Les along to so many Mersey venues that his wife, Sheila, almost became a *Mersey Beat* widow!

Rather than simply taking studio shots, which was the norm for most music publications, Les decided to take photographs of the Beatles on location around Liverpool – with resulting photos on bomb sites, outside the Liver Buildings and on ships.

In addition to the live action shots of performances, this added to the innovatory quality of the photographs published by *Mersey Beat*, which were unique to music publications at the time.

Les spent more than four years photographing the Liverpool music scene and was later to join Kodak as a manager. He currently runs their Preston branch.

CHANG, Barry Allan Williams's brother-in-law, who travelled to Hamburg with the Beatles in August 1960 and took the famous photograph of them at Arnhem Cemetery.

CHANNEL, Bruce American singer, born in Jacksonville, Texas, on 28 November 1940.

In 1962 he enjoyed his biggest hit, 'Hey Baby', which topped the American charts and reached No. 2 in Britain. The number was considerably enhanced by a haunting harmonica passage by Delbert McClinton, which was to influence John Lennon, particularly on his composition 'Love Me Do'.

Channel was booked to tour Britain and headlined a bill supported by the Beatles at the Tower Ballroom, New Brighton, on Thursday 21 June 1962.

Channel and McClinton were backed by the Barons, and, apart from the Beatles, the other groups appearing were Howie Casey & the Seniors, the Big Three, the Four Jays and the Statesmen.

The Tower show had been promoted by Brian Epstein, who had booked Channel five weeks after 'Hey Baby' entered the British charts. It was part of Epstein's plan to heighten the Beatles' profile by placing them second on the bill to chart acts. Mike McCartney, who was at the gig, took a photo of John, Paul, George and Pete Best with Channel and McClinton in the dressing room that night.

Channel next bumped into the Beatles several years later in 1968, during the recording of *The Beatles* 'White' album.

Ringo recorded 'Hey Baby' on his *Ringo's Rotogravure* album.

Channel had no further record hits in America, although he had one more entry in the British charts with 'Keep On'. He continues to record from his base in Nashville.

CHANTS, The Five-piece vocal harmony group who proved to be Liverpool's most popular black vocal act.

Their first approach to the Beatles was reported in an interview in *Mersey Beat* in 1963:

> Last year, Joe Ankrah and his brother Eddie joined a vocal group called the Shades, whose only appearances were in Stanley House, Upper Parliament Street. Due to the fact that a rock 'n' roll group in London had the same name, the group decided to call themselves the Chants.
>
> Joe went along to the Tower Ballroom during an appearance by the Beatles. He had a chat with Paul McCartney, who asked him to bring the group for an audition. The Beatles liked the group so much that they provided backing for them on a number of appearances.

In fact, when they turned up at the Cavern for an audition but didn't have a backing group, the Beatles offered to provide backing for them, but Brian Epstein objected. John Lennon overruled him and the Chants made their Cavern debut on Wednesday 21 November 1962, with the Beatles providing their backing.

The group's leader, Joe Ankrah, wanted to form an American-style vocal group and the Chants were his third attempt. The other members were Edmund Ankrah, Nat Smeda, Alan Harding and Edmund Amoo. Peter Chang was a reserve singer who supplemented the group on various occasions.

Local MP Bessie Braddock took an interest in the group as they were from her Liverpool district, the Exchange ward, and she arranged for them to be the only other Liverpool group present at the Beatles' civic reception at Liverpool Town Hall.

Despite his initial frustration at the Beatles' agreeing to back the Chants against his wishes, Epstein took over management of the group early in 1963, but only for a short time. The group found him ineffectual as a manager and he agreed to release them. They then signed with Manchester agent Ted Ross, who arranged a recording deal with Pye Records.

On the special all-Beatles edition of the TV show *Juke Box Jury*, the first record played to them was the Chants' 'I Could Write a Book', which they voted a hit – but it became a miss, despite their positive comments.

The Chants debut disc, 'Don't Care', flipside 'Come Go with Me', was released on 17 September 1963. Their second, 'I Could Write a Book', flipside 'A Thousand Stars', was released on 1 January 1964. Their third was 'She's Mine', flipside 'Then I'll be Home', in June 1964, and their final release for Pye was 'Sweet was the Wine', flipside 'One Star', on 11 September 1964.

'One Star', credited to Stanley Houseman, was written by Eddie Amoo as a tribute to Stanley House, where they'd made their first appearance.

The group never found record success, despite further releases with Fontana, Page One, Decca and RCA.

After they broke up, Joey and Edmund Ankrah joined a group called Ashanti and enjoyed a degree of success on the TV show *New Faces*. Eddie Amoo joined a Liverpool soul group, the Real Thing, who finally found UK chart success in June 1976 with 'You to Me are Everything', which also reached No. 5 on its re-release in April 1986.

CHAPMAN, Norman A Liverpool youth, who became a member of the Silver Beatles for a short time during the summer of 1960.

When Tommy Moore left the group following a gig at the Jacaranda coffee bar on 13 June that year, the Beatles were desperate for a replacement. Allan Williams and the Beatles were pondering over the problem one night when they heard the sound of distant drumbeats from across the street. Almost directly opposite the Jacaranda in Slater Street was a picture-framing establishment. Norman Chapman worked there as a picture-framer and renovator, and played drums as a hobby, practising on a hire-purchase kit in the offices of the firm in the evenings.

Williams and the Beatles went into the street, trying to find where the sound was coming from. They knocked on the doors of the National Cash Register Office and Chapman popped his head out of an upstairs window of the building. They offered him the position of drummer with the band. Chapman, an imposing six-foot-two in height, accepted the job, but only managed to appear with them on three Saturday night gigs at the Grosvenor Ballroom, Birkenhead, on 18 and 25 June and 2 July, before he was called up for National Service and was conscripted for two years in Kenya and Kuwait. In later years he was to say that he did not regret being called up.

Chapman became a teacher in the south of England and used to fascinate his students with tales of his brief spell with the Silver Beatles. He continued playing drums and was a member of a trio when he died in 1995 at the age of 58.

CHARLES, Caroline   Fashion designer who, at the age of 21, was designing clothes for the Beatles and their wives and girlfriends. By the age of 26 she was bankrupt and there was an American takeover of her company, but she then started all over again and now runs successful salons in Beauchamp Place and Bond Street, London.

CHARLES, Ray   A major musical influence on the Beatles. Born Ray Charles Robinson in Albany, Georgia, on 23 September 1930, he has been blind since the age of seven. Although 'My Bonnie' is a traditional number, Tony Sheridan and the Beatles looked to the Charles version, released in 1958, when they recorded it. He was also among the three major American stars who appeared with the Beatles during their initial seven-week season at the Star Club – the others being Little Richard and Gene Vincent. Numbers recorded by Charles which the Beatles included in their early repertoire included 'Hallelujah, I Love Her So', 'I Got a Woman', 'Don't Let the Sun Catch You Cryin'' and 'What'd I Say?'.

CHESTER, Johnny   Melbourne-born singer who was booked to appear on the Beatles Australian tour. He'd already had nine chart hits and compèred his own TV show.

CHICK GRAHAM & THE COASTERS   When Ted Knibbs agreed to sign over his act, Billy Kramer & the Coasters (who had recently been voted No. 3 in the *Mersey Beat* poll) to Brian Epstein, the Coasters refused to turn professional.

Knibbs, a pensioner who also contributed a 'Clubland' column to *Mersey Beat*, had agreed to sign the act over to Epstein for £50, although he only received £25. When the Coasters were backing Kramer, under Knibbs, they appeared on numerous bills with the Beatles. Once Epstein took over the management reins, the Coasters became increasingly unhappy and didn't enjoy being managed by him.

Drummer Tony Sanders was to recall to broadcaster Spencer Leigh many years later:

> The Beatles liked working with us because we didn't clash with them and we didn't pinch their songs. . . . Now and then Epstein sent us as guinea pigs to a place. We were playing in Colwyn Bay once and the stage was made up of snooker tables with hardboard over them. Our gear was rocking around everywhere. Epstein asked us what the place was like. We told him and it was all sorted out when the Beatles arrived the next week.

The Coasters asked Ted if he would become their manager again. He agreed and found them another lead singer – 14-year-old Graham Jennings, a St John Ambulance cadet, who had been singing for several years and had won a talent competition in Rhyl at the age of 11. He changed his name to Chick Graham. The group was to appear on a number of local gigs with the Beatles, including the Grafton Rooms on Friday 2 August 1963.

Chick Graham & the Coasters signed with Decca and their debut disc, 'I Know', flipside 'Education', was issued on 13 March 1964, followed by 'A Little You', flipside 'Dance Baby Dance' on 17 July 1964.

Chick's show business career ended by the time he was 17.

CHIFFONS, The Girl group who formed in the Bronx, New York, and comprised four teenagers: Judy Craig, Barbara Lee, Patricia Bennett and Sylvia Peterson. Their biggest hit was 'He's So Fine', penned by their manager, Ronnie Mack, and released in 1963. The number topped the American charts for four weeks and also reached No. 16 in the British charts.

A year later the girls were booked to appear with the Beatles on the group's first American concert appearance on 11 February 1964 at the Coliseum, Washington DC.

Almost a decade later in 1971, Bright Tunes, the publisher of 'He's So Fine', instituted legal proceedings against George Harrison for his first solo single, 'My Sweet Lord', which they claimed was a plagiarism of the Chiffons' hit. The case dragged on until 1976, when George settled by paying the publishing company $587,000. Ironically, by that time Bright Tunes had been acquired by Allen Klein.

CHIPMUNKS, The Novelty gimmick, the brainchild of David Seville (real name Ross Bogdasarian), who experimented with recording speeds and hit on the idea of creating a fictitious group of chipmunks. He named them Alvin, Theodore, Simon and Dave. The Chipmunks were to sell over 30 million records before Seville's death in 1972. They recorded the popular album *The Chipmunks Sing the Beatles' Hits* in 1964. Seville also created a novelty group the Bedbugs in the *F-Troop* TV series.

CIMMARONS, The A Liverpool group who appeared at the Cavern with the Beatles on Saturday 5 August 1961.

CLAPTON, Eric Premier British guitarist, born on 30 March 1945 in Ripley, Surrey.

Interestingly enough, one of the first bands he joined was Casey Jones & the Engineers, with whom he appeared for seven gigs in 1963. The group was led by Brian Casser (Casey Jones), who had fronted one of Liverpool's leading groups, Cass & the Cassanovas.

As a member of the Yardbirds, Eric appeared on the Beatles' Christmas Show at the Hammersmith Odeon. He later featured in the supergroup Cream and developed a close friendship with George Harrison, which led to several collaborations between the two, including the co-composing of 'Badge'. George also brought Eric into the recording of Jackie Lomax's 'Sour Milk Sea'.

A precedent was set when George brought Eric in to perform on the Beatles' 'While My Guitar Gently Weeps'.

John Lennon talked Eric into joining the Plastic Ono Band and he performed with them at the Toronto Rock 'n' Roll Revival Show and the Lyceum Unicef Concert, and he played on 'Cold Turkey'.

Despite the close friendship, Eric fell in love with George's wife, Pattie, and wrote a love song about her, 'Layla'. When George divorced Pattie, Eric married her – but the relationship also ended in divorce.

CLAY ELLIS & THE RAIDERS Mersey group who appeared in three Cavern shows with the Beatles in 1963 – on Wednesday 14 March, Friday 22 June and Sunday 30 September.

CLIFF BENNETT & THE REBEL ROUSERS A group that was formed in 1961, taking their name from the Duane Eddy hit. They comprised Cliff Bennett (vocals), Mick King (lead guitar), Frank Allen (bass), Sid Phillips (piano/saxophone) and Ricky Winters (drums).

The band began appearing in Hamburg and King was replaced by Dave Wendels; Winters was replaced by Mike Burt and another saxophonist, Mick Groves, joined the line-up. They were to become friendly with several Liverpool groups during their appearances at the Star Club. Frank Allen left the band to replace Tony Jackson in the Searchers and he was replaced by Bobby Thompson of Kingsize Taylor & the Dominoes. While in Germany, they were also joined by Roy Young on electric piano.

They were signed to Brian Epstein's NEMS organization in July 1964 on the recommendation of the Beatles and had their first hit with a cover of the Drifters' 'One Way Love' in November 1964. Paul McCartney was their next producer, recording 'Got To Get You Into My Life', which had just been included on the *Revolver* album. This gave them their second and final chart hit, reaching No. 6 in the British hit parade. In June 1966, they joined the Beatles on their tour of Germany and Japan.

The group later changed their name to Cliff Bennett & his Band, and then to Toe Fat. Cliff continued to seek a return to chart success, forming

Rebellion, then Shangai, but all in vain and during the mid-1970s, he took a job in advertising.

CLIFF, Edgar Paul McCartney's history teacher at Liverpool Institute. He got on well with Paul and suggested to him that he would make a good teacher and should seriously consider it as a career.

CLIFF ROBERTS & THE ROCKERS Liverpool group who were one of the handful of bands chosen to audition for Larry Parnes and Billy Fury at the Wyvern Club on 10 May 1960. The Rockers appeared after Cass & the Cassanovas, Derry & the Seniors and Gerry & the Pacemakers and immediately before the Silver Beatles.

Cliff and his group were the house band at the Grosvenor Ballroom, Liscard, during several of the Beatles' appearances there in 1961. Among the other gigs they shared with the Beatles was 'The Beatles Farewell Show' at Aintree Institute on Saturday 11 March 1961.

COCHRAN, Eddie Rock 'n' roll legend, born in Oklahoma in 1938. He was one of several influences on the Beatles, who performed four of his songs in their repertoire: 'Three Steps to Heaven', 'Twenty Flight Rock', 'I Remember' and 'C'mon Everybody'.

Cochran was due to appear in Liverpool on a bill with Gene Vincent on 3 May 1960, but was killed in a road accident on 17 April.

COCKER, Joe A singer who was born in Sheffield on 20 May 1944. He began his career in 1961 with the Cavaliers, who changed their name to Vance Arnold and the Avengers. Joe was offered a one-record deal by Decca in 1964 and recorded a lavish version of 'Georgia On My Mind' with orchestral backing. At the Decca board meeting to select new releases, Dick Rowe turned the single down and Joe had to go into the studio and record another number quickly. He reluctantly recorded the Beatles 'I'll Cry Instead'. Supporting him on the record was guitarist Big Bill Sullivan and vocal backing was from the Ivy League. The single failed to register and it was reported that Joe only received 50 pence in royalties.

His biggest hit became another Lennon and McCartney number, 'With A Little Help From My Friends'. Cocker decided to record it in 3/4 time and the single reached the top of the charts. He was also to perform it at Woodstock. A friend took the single to Apple and played it to the Beatles, who sent Joe a telegram: 'The Record's Absolutely Great. Love. John. Paul. George And Ringo.' They also took out some press advertisements in praise of the record.

Joe was invited up to Apple and initially met George, who sang 'Old Brown Shoe' and 'Something' for him. Joe later recorded 'Something'. Later that same afternoon, Paul arrived and played Joe a couple of songs on the piano. One of the numbers was 'Golden Slumbers' and Joe told Paul: 'I'd love to record that one.' Paul told him he couldn't have it, but offered him 'She Came In Through The Bathroom Window', which he did record. The number gave him a Top 30 entry in the US and he was to base himself in America from the 1970s.

Later in his career he was also to record 'You've Got To Hide Your Love Away'.

COE, Melanie Melanie was aged 17 when Paul McCartney read about her in a newspaper in February 1967 and was inspired to write 'She's Leaving Home'. Paul was to comment: 'It's a much younger girl than "Eleanor Rigby", but the same sort of loneliness. That was a *Daily Mirror* story again – the girl left home and her father said: "We gave her everything. I don't know why she left home." But he didn't give her that much, not what she wanted when she left home.'

The facts were that she'd been studying for her A-levels and had suddenly disappeared from home. A week had passed and her father told the papers: 'I cannot imagine why she should run away. She has every-thing here.' In fact, Melanie had run off with a man called David, a croupier in a gambling casino. For the song, Paul had him working in the motor trade, like his friend Terry Doran.

Ironically enough, Melanie had met the Beatles when she was 14. A member of the studio audience of the TV show *Ready, Steady, Go!*, on 4 October 1963 she had won a mime competition and received her prize from Paul. The Beatles were making their debut on the show. She's also pictured in the background of a publicity shot of the group performing that day.

Melanie now lives outside London with her two children and buys and sells jewellery.

COGAN, Alma Affectionately known as 'the girl with the giggle in her voice', Alma, who was Britain's most popular female singer of the 1950s, was born in London on 19 May 1932.

Her first Top 5 record was 'Bell Bottom Blues' in 1954. The following year she had her first and only No. 1 record, 'Dreamboat', and by the end of the decade she'd had 18 chart entries.

During the 1960s she began appearing on *Ready, Steady, Go!* along with the Beatles and they became great friends. Paul often dropped in at her flat. He played her his number 'Scrambled Eggs', which later became 'Yesterday', and he also played tambourine on the B-side of one of her singles.

Brian Epstein dated her regularly and there were rumours that they would eventually get married. She was also a close friend of songwriter Lionel Bart and there were also rumours that they'd possibly marry.

Alma was famous, talented, vivacious, had a warm personality and strong sense of humour. The Beatles, Epstein and other prominent 1960s figures were regular guests at the soirées in her home, a first-floor flat at 4 Stratton Court, near Kensington High Street, where she entertained with her mother, Fay, and sister, Sandra Caron.

Immediately prior to their June 1964 tour, the Beatles attended Alma's birthday party at her home, along with Epstein, Noël Coward, Sir Joseph Lockwood, George Martin, Chuck Berry and Carl Perkins. It was at this party that George Harrison was first introduced to Perkins.

While at art college, John Lennon used to lampoon Alma's 1958 hit 'Sugartime', pulling grotesque faces in imitation of her performance before his fellow students. Little did he know they would later become such great friends.

Just how friendly they would become is open to speculation. One of the hooks of the 1994 book *Elvis Meets the Beatles*, by Chris Hutchins and Peter Thompson, was 'How John Lennon fell in love with a cult British singer and only her untimely death threw him into the arms of Yoko Ono.' All is revealed in Chapter Ten, entitled 'Love Me Do, Alma Cogan', in which the authors contend that John was madly in love with the singer.

Chris Hutchins, a close friend and confidant of John at the time, said that he was totally smitten with Alma, who reminded him in some respects of his mother, Julia. He told Chris: 'Every time I'm with Alma, it feels right. Julia just couldn't cope with me, but Alma can read me like a book.' John nicknamed her Sarah Sequin.

Her last few records were covers of Lennon and McCartney songs. John and Paul were present at her recording of 'Eight Days a Week' on 9 October 1965. On 11 November of that year her version of 'Yesterday' was released and on 28 November her double A-side 'Eight Days a Week', flipside 'Help!' was issued – a record which nearly brought Alma back into the charts.

In March 1966 she was diagnosed as having cancer and died of the disease on 26 October of that year at Middlesex Hospital in London. She was only 34 years old.

Twenty years after her death, EMI issued a double album, *Alma Cogan: A Celebration*, which featured a gatefold sleeve in which Alma was pictured with the Beatles. The sleeve also contained a brief note penned by Paul McCartney.

COLEMAN, Bess Former journalist who worked as a press officer for the Parlophone label, publicizing the early Beatles releases. She also acted as their press representative in the States.

COLEMAN, Sid Music publisher who, in 1962, was director and general manager of Ardmore & Beechwood, EMI's publishing arm, from offices on the fourth floor of the HMV store building in Oxford Street, London.

On 8 May 1962, Brian Epstein was in London with some reel-to-reel tapes of the Beatles' Decca audition, seeking a record deal. He'd heard that tapes could be transferred on to acetate at the HMV centre and went along there to have copies made.

Epstein knew the general manager of the store, Robert Boast, and asked him if there was anyone who could listen to the tapes. Boast asked

Jim Foy, the private recording engineer of the store, for his opinion. Foy listened, was impressed and called Sid Coleman, who invited Brian to his offices upstairs.

Coleman listened to the tapes, liked what he heard and asked Epstein if the group had a recording contract. When he discovered that Brian had already been turned down by most of the record companies, he asked if he'd met with George Martin. When Brian said he hadn't, Coleman then phoned Martin's office and arranged for the two men to meet the next day. He immediately offered to publish two of the songs, 'Love of the Loved' and 'Hello Little Girl', but Brian demurred, saying he'd prefer to have a recording contract before agreeing to any publishing deal.

As a result of Coleman's introduction, Martin suggested that the Beatles' first recorded songs, 'Love Me Do' and 'P.S. I Love You', be published by Ardmore & Beechwood, which they were. However, the publishers didn't complete a contract which would have assured them of further Lennon and McCartney material. Epstein was dissatisfied with their efforts to promote the single and they weren't given the opportunity to publish any more original Beatles songs.

This was disappointing for EMI, although Sir Joseph Lockwood was to comment: 'I don't blame Sid Coleman, because he published the first two songs without a contract. He wasn't getting any support from either the record producers or the solicitors.'

There is actually some disagreement about the part Ardmore & Beechwood played in the promotion of the Beatles' debut disc. In his autobiography, *All You Need is Ears*, George Martin pointed out: 'Ardmore & Beechwood, the EMI publishers, whose Sid Coleman had first put Brian Epstein on to me, did virtually nothing about getting the record played.' On the other hand, Ted King, who worked on the BBC radio show *Twelve o'Clock Spin*, was one of the first people to play 'Love Me Do', because, he said, he was pressured to do so by Kim Bennett of Ardmore & Beechwood.

CONDON, Richard American author of such best-sellers as *The Manchurian Candidate*. The Beatles bought the rights to his Western novel *A Talent for Loving*, which they intended to film in Spain. The project was dropped and the Beatles met the author personally to explain why.

CONNOLLY, Ray Former Liverpool *Daily Post* journalist who joined London's *Evening Standard* in 1967. He was to interview the Beatles on a number of occasions and his interviews have been published in the book *Stardust Memories*. He also travelled to Toronto to stay at Ronnie Hawkins's farm during John and Yoko's visit there and is author of *John Lennon 1940–1980*. He wrote a screenplay of John's life called *Working Class Hero* and his film scripts include *That'll be the Day* and *Stardust*.

COOPER, Michael Photographer of the *Sgt Pepper* sleeve. He moved into Studio 4 of Chelsea Manor Studios in Flood Street, Chelsea, on 22 July 1966. The following year, on Thursday 30 March, the collage for the sleeve was completed in his studio and he took the famous photograph. He committed suicide in 1970 and his book *Blinds & Shutters* was published posthumously in January 1991 in a limited edition of 5,000.

CORBETT, Bill Chauffeur who was originally assigned to drive the Beatles around and was then hired to work for John Lennon in 1964.

CORDET, Louise Girl singer booked to appear with the Beatles during their tour with Roy Orbison in May and June 1963, following her only chart entry 'I'm Just a Baby'.

CORNELL, Lynn Former member of the Vernons Girls who was also a neighbour of Paul McCartney. With the Vernons she recorded 'We Love the Beatles' and when she joined another outfit, the Carefrees, they recorded 'We Love You Beatles', which entered the American charts. Lynn also appeared with the Beatles on *Shindig*, the American ABC networked pop show, and for a time was married to Andy White, drummer on 'Love Me Do' and 'P.S. I Love You'.

COTT, Jonathan American journalist who conducted the first interview with John Lennon for *Rolling Stone* magazine in November 1968. He also co-wrote the text for *Get Back*, the lavish book issued with the album *Let It Be*.

COUNTRY FOUR, The A country music band. Brian Newman, a former jazz singer, joined them on vocals/rhythm in August 1961. The other members were Tony Evans (electric banjo), Dave Stevens (ex-Vigilantes) (bass), Freddie Cain (drums) and Joe Butler (lead). The group began a Saturday-night residency at the Black Cat Club, London Road, in October 1961 and their special guests included the Tennessee Four, the Miller Brothers and Bertie Collins & the Sundowners. The previous Saturday residents at the club were the Blue Mountain Boys.

Among the gigs the Country Four shared with the Beatles was an appearance at St Paul's Presbyterian Church Youth Club on Saturday 10 March 1962.

COWAN, Norman Doctor whose patients included Brian Epstein, George Martin and Gerry Marsden. He was the man who broke down the door to Brian's room and discovered his body. Cowan was to tell the coroner that Brian had suffered from glandular fever in July 1966, was prescribed Trytizol, Librium and Carbitol and took two tablets of Carbitol every night.

COX, Kyoko Daughter of Yoko Ono and Tony Cox, who was born on 8 August 1963. After their divorce, Tony had custody of his daughter, but in 1969, after her marriage to John, Yoko wanted Kyoko back. The custody battles were so bad that father and daughter fled to America, without disclosing their whereabouts.

CRAWFORD, Marie Under her maiden name of Maguire, Marie is known to Beatles fans as the girl who helped teach Ringo Starr to read.

Marie, who was a few years older than Ringo, then known as Ritchie Starkey, lived in the same street. In June 1943 her family moved into 10 Madryn Street, in the Dingle area of Liverpool. Ritchie and his mother, Elsie, lived next door at No. 9.

Marie would come and look after Ritchie when his mother went out to work. Since Ritchie had suffered academically due to the length of time he'd spent in hospital, Marie would spend one hour, twice a week, reading to him and going over spelling lists with him. Elsie paid her 6d an hour.

When Ritchie had to spend another lengthy period in hospital, Marie brought him a present – a drumming record, 'Bedtime for Drums', by Eric Delaney.

During the 1980s, Marie became an official Beatles guide in Liverpool.

CRITTLE, John Fashion designer who came to London and was sponsored at the Royal College of Art by Lord Montague. He then set up Dandie Fashions, one of the first fashion boutiques in the King's Road, with his partner, Tara Browne. During 1966 he was designing clothes for the Beatles, the Rolling Stones, the Who, Procol Harum, Elvis Presley and Jimi Hendrix.

Through his friend Pete Shotton, he became closer to the Beatles organization and Apple bought his business. John Lennon commented: 'We bought a few things from him and the next thing I knew, we owned the place.'

His shop at 161 King's Road became 'Civil & Theatrical Apple Tailoring by John Crittle'. There was a launch party, attended by John and Yoko and George and Pattie, on 22 May 1968, but within a few weeks it became apparent that the shop would be another drain on Apple and the Beatles handed it back to Crittle on 31 July.

Crittle met Andrea Williams in a nightclub and they married at Chelsea Register Office in 1967. Their daughter, Darcey Andrea Pemberton, was born in 1969.

After the Apple Tailoring venture, Crittle opened a restaurant, GHQ, in Fulham, but he fled to Australia when the taxman chased him for £3 million in back taxes. He left his wife and daughter behind and has remained in Australia ever since, living on a cattle farm at Mullumbimby, New South Wales. His daughter, under the name Darcey Bussell, was to become the Royal Ballet's youngest-ever leading ballerina.

CUFF, Nicky Liverpool musician and comic, a four-foot-six midget whom John Lennon once described as his favourite comedian.

When he was a member of a group called the Sunnyside Skiffle Group, in the Speke district of Liverpool, he successfully auditioned for the Carroll Levis *TV Star Search* show at the Empire Theatre, Liverpool, on

9 June 1957. John's group the Quarry Men were unsuccessful entrants in the auditions. Cuff was 19 at the time.

In October 1959, John and his group once again auditioned for the Levis show at the Empire, this time calling themselves Johnny & the Moondogs. The contest was won by the Connaughts – the new name by which the Sunnyside Skiffle Group, with Cuff, were known.

CUTLER, Ivor Comedian and poet in the cast of *Magical Mystery Tour*. He portrayed Buster Bloodvessel, who falls in love with Ringo's Aunt Jessie.

CYRKLE, The American group originally formed by students of Lafayette College, Pennsylvania, under the name the Rondells. They comprised Tom Dawes (vocals/guitar/banjo/sitar), Don Danneman (piano/guitar) and Marty Fried (drums). They were joined by Fred Pickens on organ.

The group were brought to Brian Epstein's attention in 1966 by Nat Weiss, his American attorney, who had spotted the band performing in Atlantic City.

Epstein suggested that Weiss go ahead and sign them, and they became the first act of a new management company, Nemperor Artists, which Brian formed with Weiss to handle American acts.

Weiss arranged for them to perform in New York's Greenwich Village during one of Epstein's trips. Brian then suggested that they change their name to the Circle and it was John Lennon who suggested that the spelling be altered to Cyrkle (just as he suggested the 'a' be used in Beetles).

The group were signed to Columbia Records and Weiss sent Epstein several demo discs. Brian picked a number called 'Red Rubber Ball', penned by Paul Simon and Bruce Woodley of the Seekers, predicting it would sell a million copies. It did, reaching No. 2 in the American charts.

A few months later they had their second and final big hit, 'Turn Down Day', which reached No. 16 in the Billboard charts. The group were also booked to appear on the Beatles' final US tour in August, 1966.

DAKOTAS, The Manchester band who backed the singer Pete Maclaine. They began playing regularly in Liverpool and appeared at the the Cavern on the same bill as the Beatles on a number of occasions during 1962: Wednesday 25 July, Wednesday 19 September and Friday 30 November. On Friday 10 August they appeared with the Beatles and Johnny Kidd & the Pirates (whose guitarist was Mick Green) on a 'Riverboat Shuffle' along the Mersey on the *Royal Iris*. They also appeared with them at the Cavern on Wednesday 30 January 1963.

As Pete Maclaine & the Dakotas they also appeared in the Little Richard/Beatles concert at the Tower Ballroom, New Brighton, on Friday 12 October 1962.

When Billy Kramer was signed by Brian Epstein, his backing band, the Coasters, refused to turn professional. Epstein asked a number of Liverpool bands, including the Remo Four, to provide backing for Billy, but they refused.

He then approached the Dakotas. Like the Mersey groups before them, they turned his offer down. He then promised that they would also be able to record in their own right as the Dakotas and they agreed, shedding Pete Maclaine – not as traumatic as Pete Best being shed by the Beatles, but another case of a musician being tossed out into the cold.

A news item in *Mersey Beat* headed 'Manchester Furious About Dakotas Change-over' read:

> We are informed that terrific feeling has been aroused in Manchester concerning the parting of the ways between Pete Maclaine and the Dakotas. 'Billy Kramer won't fit' say many of the Dakotas' Mancunian fans. Pete Maclaine and his new group the Clan received a harsh reception at the Oasis Club, Lloyd Street. Although the fans seem up in arms about the change-over, Brian Epstein informs us that, 'All parties concerned parted amicably.'

Almost word for word what he said about the dumping of Pete Best.

The Dakotas comprised Mike Maxfield (lead guitar), Robin McDonald (rhythm), Ray Jones (bass) and Tony Mansfield (Elkie Brooks's brother) (drums).

Despite immediately being sent to the Star Club, Hamburg, to develop an act together, the Dakotas and Kramer never really got on well and didn't build a rapport.

Their first single together, the Lennon and McCartney composition 'Do You Want to Know a Secret?', topped the British charts and they followed up with a series of hits, 'Bad to Me', 'I'll Keep You Satisfied' and 'From a Window', all penned by Lennon and McCartney. Kramer then picked 'Little Children', which became their third chart-topper. Their final hit together was 'Trains and Boats and Planes', which reached No. 12.

The Dakotas did record three singles and an EP for Parlophone under their own name and their first release, an instrumental, 'The Cruel Sea', reached No. 18 in the charts in July 1963. It was their only solo hit.

Ray Jones left the band in August 1964. Robin then took over on bass and Mick Green joined as rhythm guitarist.

DALE ROBERTS & THE JAYWALKERS Liverpool group who were one of the five bands selected to audition for Larry Parnes at the Wyvern Club on 10 May 1960, along with the Silver Beatles. At that time they were known as Dale Roberts & the Rockers, but they broke up for three months during the following year, 1961, and re-formed as Dale Roberts & the Jaywalkers, without their rhythm guitarist. They now comprised group founder and leader Dave Williams (lead), Dale Roberts, a motor engineer (vocals), Phil Rogers (bass) and Bill Buck (drums).

Buck had left the Remo Four earlier that year to join his family's grocery business, but was then allowed to rejoin a group on condition they had limited engagements.

Dale Roberts & the Jaywalkers featured with the Beatles on two major shows at the Tower Ballroom, New Brighton, on Friday 1 December and Friday 15 December 1961.

They also appeared with the Beatles at the Cavern twice in 1961: on Tuesday 21 March and Wednesday 2 August. In 1962 they appeared with them on Wednesday 7 February.

DAVE CLARK FIVE, The Group from the Tottenham area of north London who were able to capitalize on the enthusiasm for Mersey groups. When the Mersey Beat scene popularized groups in general, the Dave Clark Five had their first hit with 'Do You Love Me?', a number by the Contours, which had been adapted to a Beat music style by Liverpool's Faron's Flamingos.

With the success of 'Glad All Over', the media, based in London, began to trumpet the news 'Tottenham Sound Has Crushed the Beatles', although when the group's records were promoted in America they were advertised as 'the Mersey sound with the Liverpool beat'.

The Dave Clark Five comprised Dave Clark (drums), Mike Smith (keyboards/vocals), Rick Huxley (bass), Denis Payton (tenor sax/guitar) and Len Davidson (guitar).

They became a tremendous success in America, with 22 hit records, and were the stars of a 1965 film, *Catch Us If You Can*, directed by John Boorman. They eventually disbanded in August 1970.

DAVEY, Joe A small, slightly stocky figure with a Kaiser Bill moustache and goatee. He ran Joe's Café in Duke Street, Liverpool, which became one of the regular early-morning haunts for groups seeking a meal after a gig or a drinking session at the nearby Blue Angel club.

Group members usually arrived there between two and four in the morning, when taxi drivers and ladies of the night were among the clientele. Brian Epstein and the Beatles were frequently to be found on the first floor, where Joe had established a 'Wall of Fame' in a room decorated with photographs of his musical customers.

Davey came to like the Mersey Beat scene so much that when Ray

McFall was made bankrupt, bailiffs closed the Cavern and it came up for sale, on 18 April 1966, he and an associate, Alf Geoghegan, offered £5,500 for the club and were successful in their bid.

They were able to reopen the club on 23 July 1966, in a ceremony attended by Prime Minister Harold Wilson, local MP Bessie Braddock, musicians, celebrities and members of Merseyside's two football clubs. Brian Epstein and the Beatles sent Joe and Alf a telegram wishing them a successful future. However, it proved to be a far larger economic burden than they'd imagined and they sold it to Roy Adams, another club-owner.

DAVID AND JONATHAN The songwriting team of Roger Greenaway and Roger Cook, who had appeared in the Bristol-based vocal group the Kestrels. As songwriters they'd produced the million-seller 'You've Got Your Troubles' for the Fortunes, but had flopped with their own debut disc.

It was Beatles' record producer George Martin who suggested that they record 'Michelle' as their second single. This track from the *Rubber Soul* album took them into the British Top 20 at No. 11 – where a version by the Overlanders topped the charts. They had their biggest success in America, where the single entered the Top 20, reaching No. 18.

They had their biggest British hit the following year with 'Lovers of the World Unite'. David and Jonathan next recorded a version of the Beatles' album track 'She's Leaving Home', which failed to chart.

The duo then concentrated on their songwriting and composed a number of hit songs for other artists.

DAVIES, Hunter *Sunday Times* journalist who interviewed Paul McCartney in September 1966 and suggested that he be allowed to write a book about the group. Paul referred him to Brian Epstein and Davies was given the authority in January 1967. He spent almost 18 months travelling with the Beatles and interviewing friends and relatives, although his original 150,000-word manuscript was heavily cut by the Beatles' team. The book was published in September 1968.

Davies penned Epstein's obituary for *The Times* and was commissioned to write the obituaries of all four members of the group for the publication.

DAVIS, Billie British singer, born Carol Hedges in Woking, Surrey, in 1945. She was discovered by Robert Stigwood and duetted with Mike Sarne on his hit record 'Will I What?'. In 1963 she charted in her own right with 'Tell Him'.

It was while 'Tell Him' was entering the charts that Billie was booked to appear with the Beatles on their nationwide tour on 27 February at the Gaumont, Taunton, when the headliner, Helen Shapiro, was laid low with a heavy cold. Billie also appeared with them the following night at the Rialto, York.

Helen resumed her place on the tour the following evening.

DAVIS, Pat Blonde Liverpool girl who was Cilla Black's best mate and Ringo Starr's girlfriend.

DAVIS, Meta The meter maid who claims to have inspired Paul's song 'Lovely Rita'. She worked in St John's Wood and gave Paul a ticket. She retired in 1985.

DAVIS, Rod A member of the Quarry Men from March 1957 until February 1958. He was in the same class as John Lennon at Quarry Bank School and was invited to join John's skiffle group, playing banjo. He left because of the pressures of his studies.

DAWSON, Pat A Liverpool barmaid who had a brief flirtation with John Lennon. She is nicknamed Polythene Pam because she believes John might have had her in mind when he wrote 'Polythene Pam', although, as she admits: 'It's not the kind of song you'd want dedicated to you if you listen to the lyrics.'

DEE FENTON & THE SILHOUETTES A Huyton group, formed in 1958. Lead guitarist Pete Turner worked in a shipping office, vocalist Dee Fenton was a reporter, drummer Larry King a bus conductor and bass guitarist Harry Bear a part-time miner. During 1962 they appeared twice on Cavern bills with the Beatles: on Saturday 28 July and Wednesday 22 August.

DEE YOUNG & THE PONTIACS A Liverpool band who never fulfilled their ambition of playing in the Mersey Tunnel! They comprised Sam Andrews (lead), Les Painter (rhythm), Dee Young (vocals), Mike Young (bass) and Jeff Hunter (drums). The group appeared with the Beatles on several occasions, including a gig at the Cavern on Wednesday 28 November 1962.

DEL RENAS, The A Mersey group who started out as a trio in 1958, comprising Brian Dean (drums), Brian James (piano) and a rhythm guitarist who was replaced by Derek (Del) Green in July 1960. In 1959 the group was joined by vocalist Ray Walker and turned to playing rock 'n' roll. Terry (Rex) Fisher on lead guitar also joined in July 1960, as did bass guitarist John Withing. They played at many of the local 'jive hives', including Wilson Hall, Blair Hall, Aintree Institute, Lathom Hall, Wavertree Town Hall, David Lewis Ballroom, Cassanova Club, St Luke's, Crosby and Holyoake Hall, and were inspired by Roy Orbison and the Everly Brothers.

They were renowned for their punctuality and reliability, so the audience began to get worried one night when they didn't turn up for their spot on an all-nighter. Then Ray appeared to say that the group had been involved in a car crash. The rumours then spread that they were all dead!

They played on both of Oriole's *This is Mersey Beat* albums.

The Del Renas appeared at Litherland Town Hall on 27 December 1960 on the same bill as the Beatles. This was the gig which advertised 'The Beatles – Direct from Germany' and proved to be the turning point in their local rise to fame. The Del Renas also appeared on a Cavern bill with the Beatles on Friday 11 January 1963.

DELANEY, Patrick The main doorman at the Cavern.

Patrick, more familiarly known as Paddy, a former Guardsman, had become a member of the Liverpool Parks Police, then a doorman at both the Locarno and the Grafton Ballrooms in West Derby Road.

In 1959 he was approached by Ray McFall to be a 'bouncer' at the Cavern. He said he'd do it for £1 per night. Instead of dressing in the informal gear usually worn by Cavern doormen, Paddy always turned up in a tuxedo with a cummerbund and diamond studs.

Initially, there was a strict code which barred anyone wearing jeans, and Paddy once attempted to prevent George Harrison entering the club because of his jeans.

For a time Paddy also helped with deliveries of *Mersey Beat* locally and became the paper's theatre critic.

He was an enthusiastic Al Jolson fan and once took to the stage of the Gaumont Theatre in full black face make-up to mime to Jolson songs for forthcoming presentations *The Jolson Story* and *Jolson Sings Again*.

Paddy remained at the Cavern for 15 years. He later became warden at Netherley Centre in Liverpool and wrote an unpublished manuscript about his experiences at the Cavern called *The Best of Cellars*.

DELTONES, The Liverpool band who appeared with the Beatles at Litherland Town Hall on 27 December 1960. They'd previously been booked to appear with the Silver Beetles at Lathom Hall on 21 May, but the Silver Beetles didn't turn up as they were touring with Johnny Gentle.

DEMESQUITA, Senor Bueno A commissioner of oaths. In a ceremony on the rooftop of Apple's Savile Row offices on 22 April 1969, he officially changed John's name from John Winston Lennon to John Ono Lennon.

DENNISONS, The Many people predicted major success for this highly popular Liverpool group who first formed in 1961 and began their career with a Saturday night residency at the BICC club in Melling. They comprised Eddie Parry (vocals), Ray Scragge (rhythm), Clive Hornby (drums), Steve McLaren (lead) and Alan Willis (bass).

They appeared on Cavern bills with the Beatles during 1962: on Wednesday 25 July, Saturday 13 October and Sunday 25 November. Their 1963 Cavern appearances with the Beatles took place on Sunday 20 January and Friday 12 March.

When record companies heard that they were drawing crowds in Liverpool like the Beatles used to, they rushed there and Decca managed to sign them.

The group made their recording debut in July 1963 with 'Come On Be My Girl', a number they'd written backstage at the Cavern. It reached No. 47 in the charts. They followed up with their version of Rufus Thomas's 'Walkin' the Dog' in February 1964. The B-side, 'You Don't Know What Love Is', was written specially for them by Ben E. King, with whom they were touring at the time. The record reached No. 36 in the charts and when it was played on *Juke Box Jury* one of the panellists, *Carry On* star Sid James, commented: 'If I knew who that feller was, I'd buy him a drink.'

Their third and final single was 'Nobody Like My Babe', released in November 1964. Although it sounded very commercial, it didn't enter the charts.

Vocalist Parry left in 1965 and the group disbanded two years later.

Clive Hornby became an actor and appeared in a production of *In His Own Write* at the Playhouse Theatre, Liverpool, in 1968. He found fame as Jack Sugden in the long-running British soap *Emmerdale*.

Steve contracted multiple sclerosis and died in 1993 and Eddie succumbed to a heart attack in 1995.

DENVER, Karl Folk singer, born Angus McKenzie in Glasgow on 16 December 1934. A former merchant seaman, he entered show business at the age of 23, formed the Karl Denver Trio with Kevin Neill and Gary Cottrell and enjoyed 11 British chart hits between 1961 and 1964, including the Top 10 entries 'Marcheta', 'Mexicali Rose', 'Wimoweh' and 'A Little Love, a Little Kiss'.

When the Beatles recorded for the BBC Light Programme's *Side by Side*, at the Piccadilly Studios in London on Monday 1 April 1963, they duetted with the Karl Denver Trio on the number 'Side by Side', a song originally penned by Harry Woods in the 1920s.

Denver's group were the resident band on the half-hour show in which their performances would alternate with those of their guest group. They always opened the show singing 'Side by Side' with their guest of the week.

At this particular session, the Beatles recorded two editions of the show, transmitted on 22 April and 13 May. They were to appear as Denver's guests on one further programme in the series.

The Trio also appeared with the Beatles on *Shindig*, the American ABC networked pop show, in an edition recorded at the Granville Studio, Fulham Broadway, London, in October 1964.

Denver later settled in Manchester and in 1989 had further success when he recorded 'Wimoweh' with the Happy Mondays. He teamed up with the band again in 1990 to record 'Lazyitis'.

DERLIN, Bettina Blonde barmaid at Hamburg's Star Club who became a friend of the Beatles and was at one time a girlfriend of John. She was later to work in the Herbertstrasse. She had a stroke in 1995 which left her partly paralyzed.

DESHANNON, Jackie American singer/songwriter, real name Sharon Myers, who was born in Hazel, Kentucky, on 21 August 1944.

She penned 'Dum Dum' and 'Heart in Hand' for Brenda Lee, in collaboration with Sharon Sheeley, and 'When You Walk in the Room', a number she co-wrote with Jack Nitzsche, became a hit for the Searchers.

Her own singing career took second place to her songwriting success and she penned hits for numerous artists, including Marianne Faithfull, the Byrds and Helen Shapiro.

Jackie had a Top 10 hit with 'What the World Needs Now is Love' in 1965. In 1969 she had her biggest hit with 'Put a Little Love in Your Heart', which reached No. 4 in the American charts.

Although her own version of 'When You Walk in the Room' wasn't a chart hit, it led to her being booked on the first Beatles tour of America in the autumn of 1964, for which she was paid $1,250 per week. Soon after she released an album, *Breakin' It Up on the Beatles Tour*.

DEVLIN, Johnny New Zealand rock 'n' roll singer who was booked on the Beatles' tour 'down under'. Backstage he co-wrote a song with Paul McCartney called 'Won't You Be My Baby?', which became his next single.

DEXTER Jr, David American A&R executive for Capitol Records who processed and was involved in compiling Beatles albums for the company. He died in 1991.

DIETRICH, Marlene German-born Hollywood legend. She appeared on the Royal Variety Show with the Beatles on 4 November 1963 and the group included her on their *Sgt Pepper* tableau. She died in 1992.

DICESARE, Pat Promoter who booked the Beatles at the Civic Arena, Philadelphia, on 14 September 1964. The 24-year-old entrepreneur borrowed $5,000 from his father, who mortgaged his home, to gamble on placing a deposit to book the group. His gamble paid off and the concert was a sell-out with attendances topping 12,000. Unfortunately, DiCesare didn't get to see the show – he was drafted!

DILELLO, Richard Assistant press officer at Apple. The New Yorker became known as the 'house hippie' and was to write a book of his experiences with the Beatles' company, *The Longest Cocktail Party*. He found success as a screenwriter in Hollywood, married his agent, scripted films such as *Bad Boys* and *Colours* and TV shows such as *Night Caller* and *DEA*.

DION American singer, born Dion DiMucci on 18 July 1939 in the Bronx, New York. He enjoyed his first hit, 'I Wonder Why', when he appeared as lead singer with the Delmonts in 1958 and followed with another major smash, 'A Teenager in Love', the following year. He turned solo in 1960 and had 13 chart hits in the US between 1960 and 1968, including 'Runaround Sue', 'The Wanderer' and 'Abraham, Martin and John'.

Strangely enough, Dion was the only musician, apart from Bob Dylan, to be selected to appear on the cover of the *Sgt Pepper* album, although it's not known who picked him.

DODD, Ken   Celebrated Liverpool comedian who also had a series of hit records between 1960 and 1975. The Beatles appeared in a charity show head-lined by Dodd at the Albany Theatre, Maghull, on 15 October 1961. They also indulged in 25 minutes of good-natured banter during a Granada Television *Scene at 6.30* show. Dodd had his own BBC radio programme, *The Ken Dodd Show*, and the Beatles performed 'She Loves You' on it on 3 November 1963.

DODD, Les   A dance promoter from Wallasey, 'over the water' from Liverpool, who had been promoting dances at the Grosvenor Ballroom, Liscard and the Institute, Neston since 1936 via his company, Paramount Enter-prises.

He ran '21 Plus' nights weekly in two halls, strictly for adults, with advertisements which declared 'No Jiving! No Rock 'n' Roll! No Teen-agers!'

But the impact of young music on Merseyside was so strong that Dodd reluctantly began booking local groups on Saturday night 'swing ses-sions', at the Grosvenor – and Thursday evening dances at the Institute.

When Allan Williams decided to try to get bookings for the Silver Beatles, the first gig he arranged for them was via Dodd at the Institute, sited in Hinderston Road, Neston, Wirral in Cheshire, on 2 June 1960. Dodd booked them for six Thursday night gigs at the venue. He also booked them for his Grosvenor Hall dances, beginning on Saturday 4 June 1960.

Both venues became noted for violence and a 16-year-old boy was nearly beaten to death in front of the Beatles at the Institute during one of their sessions. They were also quite nervous when they turned up at the Grosvenor without Tommy Moore – who had quit as their drummer – only to find a tough local teddy boy called Ronnie joining them on stage to play drums and telling them he was going to join the group!

The local newspaper wrote about their 16 June appearance at the Institute:

'The Big Beat' featured a double bill at Neston Institute on Thursday evening when the resident Beatles from Liverpool were supported by Keith Rowlands and the Deesiders from Heswall.

Well known locally for their performances at the Glee club and the ? Jazz Club and Le Macabre, the Deesiders are Ronnie Aston on drums, guitarists Pete Bolt and John Sanders, and the guitar-playing vocalist

Keith Rowlands, who has also been signed as a guest artiste with the Beatles on Thursday nights.

Next month the Beatles are leaving Neston to go on tour with teenage idol Dickie Pride.

From June to August 1960, all the Silver Beatles' bookings, with the exception of a single Jacaranda coffee bar appearance, were for Les Dodd at his two venues. This came to an end when the corporation cancelled Dodd's season at the Grosvenor due to the violence. The Beatles had been due to play there on 6 August, but Dodd had to cancel their appearance as the venue was now closed to rock 'n' roll.

DONEGAN, Lonnie Musician, once known as 'the king of skiffle', who was born Anthony Donegan on 29 April 1931 in Glasgow, the son of a violinist in the National Scottish Orchestra. When he completed his army service in 1949, he began playing in various jazz bands. His stage name allegedly came about in 1952, when he was appearing on the same bill as legendary blues guitarist Lonnie Johnson in London and the compere mistakenly announced him as 'Lonnie' Donegan – he decided to keep the name.

During the same year he joined Ken Colyer's Jazzmen on guitar and banjo, where he was reunited with a former army buddy, Chris Barber. During the band's show he was given his own spot, accompanied by Colyer on guitar, Barber on bass and Bill Colyer on washboard, performing the style of music generally known as 'skiffle'.

Although the skiffle boom was specific to Britain, the sound was based on an American music using home-made instruments, and the word 'skiffle' was a black American term coined in the 1920s to describe the music, which had American jazz, folk and blues influences. In 1929 country blues singer Charlie Spaniel recorded a number called 'Hometown Skiffle'.

Donegan had a massive hit with 'Rock Island Line' in 1956 and during the next six years enjoyed a total of 32 chart hits.

Among Donegan's appearances in 1956 was a concert at the Empire Theatre, Liverpool. Paul McCartney was in the audience and he became inspired. Also, during a school lunchtime he'd gone to the theatre to glimpse his idol and noticed that Donegan was writing notes to the employers of factory girls, explaining why they were late – they'd spent time in their dinner hour waiting for him. Paul was very impressed by the gesture and felt that this was the way that stars should behave.

Donegan's Liverpool appearance sparked Paul's desire for a guitar and his father, Jim, bought him one for £15.

A 14-year-old George Harrison, who'd originally met Paul on the bus on the way to the school they both attended, went round to Paul's house to look at his teach-yourself-to-play book. George recalled: 'We learned a couple of chords from it and managed to play "Don't You Rock Me Daddy-O".'

The Donegan appearance also sparked off George's desire for a guitar and he bought a second-hand one from a boy in school for £3, which his Mum had lent him.

George's brother Harry was to say: 'Lonnie Donegan was appearing at the Empire and of course George just had to go. In fact, he borrowed the money from our parents so that he could see every single show! Anyway, he found out where Lonnie was staying, which happened to be in a house in Speke, so George went round and hammered on the door until he came out and gave George his autograph. Of course, he immediately raced home to show everyone.'

In an interview with *Disc*, George Harrison was to comment: 'Lonnie and skiffle seemed made for me . . . it was easy music to play if you knew two or three chords, and you'd have a tea-chest as a bass and washboard and you were on your way.'

They were similar to the comments he made to Hunter Davies in the official biography of the Beatles, when he told him that Lonnie Donegan was the first person to make an impression on him musically: 'I'd been aware of pop singers before him, like Frankie Laine and Johnny Ray, but never really taken much interest in them. I don't think I thought I was old enough for them. But Lonnie Donegan and skiffle just seemed made for me.'

The king of skiffle was also a catalyst for the 16-year-old John Lennon. He'd listened to the music on Radio Luxembourg and thought that it wasn't difficult to play, so he asked his Aunt Mimi if she could get him a guitar. He also bought a 78rpm record of 'Rock Island Line', which he later sold to a schoolmate, Rod Davis. Rod was also inspired by Donegan and bought a banjo for £5 from an uncle and joined Lennon's new skiffle group, the Quarry Men.

Included in the Quarry Men's repertoire were several skiffle numbers popularized by Donegan, including 'Rock Island Line', 'The Cumberland Gap', 'Midnight Special', 'Railroad Bill' and 'Worried Man Blues'.

Ringo Starr also entered the music world during the skiffle era and joined the Eddie Clayton Skiffle Group in 1957.

In the late 1970s Paul suggested that Lonnie re-record some of his skiffle hits. The album *Puttin' on the Style*, produced by Adam Faith in Los Angeles, was released in January 1978. Among the musicians backing him were Ringo Starr, Elton John, Leo Sayer, Brian May of Queen and Lonnie's regular band. Ringo appeared on the tracks 'Have a Drink on Me' and 'Ham 'n' Eggs'.

Following a mild heart attack in 1986, Donegan went into semi-retirement, moving to the Costa del Sol, where he lives with his second wife, Sharon, and their three sons, Peter, David and Andrew.

DONOVAN Folk-singer, born Donovan Leitch on 10 May 1946 in Glasgow. Touted as a British Bob Dylan, he had a string of hits throughout the 1960s, ranging from 'Catch the Wind' to 'Mellow Yellow'. He was among the group who travelled to Rishikesh, India, when the Beatles were studying under the Maharishi and while he was there he wrote a song about another member of the company, Jenny Boyd, called 'Jennifer Juniper'. He also composed 'Hurdy Gurdy Man' before the four Beatles, Beach Boy Mike Love and Mia Farrow. George Harrison added a new verse to the song – although Pye Records talked Donovan out of recording the Harrison contribution.

His 'Sunshine Superman' began life as a Beatles tribute called 'For John and Paul'. Donovan was absent from the music scene during the 1980s, but returned in the 1990s to tour and record again.

DOOLEY, Arthur One of the colourful characters who was part of the Mersey scene in the late 1950s and early 1960s. A tall, powerfully built, working-class card-carrying member of the Communist Party, he became a noted sculptor and was the subject of a *This is Your Life* TV programme and a TV play by Alun Owen.

Arthur had been a friend of the Beatles during their early career and eventually created a piece of sculpture dedicated to them which, in 1974, was fitted to a wall in Matthew Street, Liverpool, directly opposite the site of the Cavern club.

Arthur worked mainly in metal and the piece is typical of his style. It depicts a Madonna holding three babies – a fourth is separated from the group and is flying away. The three babies represent John, George and Ringo and the solo figure represents Paul. The piece is surrounded by the initials MJPGR, with the M standing for Madonna. Directly above the sculpture, in a reproduction of a typical street sign, is the legend 'Beatles Street, Liverpool 2.'

Arthur died on 7 January 1994, aged 64.

DORAN, Terry One of Brian Epstein's original circle of drinking companions and gay friends. They first met in a Liverpool pub in 1959.

Once the Beatles had achieved nationwide success, Brian decided to go into business with Terry, who was a car salesman. They formed a partnership and launched a company called Brydor Auto, based in Hounslow, Middlesex. Brian reasoned that since the Beatles and other members of his organization were buying cars, it would be a sensible move to direct the business in Terry's way.

Brian immediately purchased a silver Bentley convertible and a black Mini-Cooper, and all four members of the Beatles then bought two cars each from the company.

Although Clive Epstein was in charge of the company's books, he had a difficult time balancing them because Brian kept taking cash out. If they were selling so many, Clive asked regularly, where was the money? In fact, Brian was using cash from Brydor Auto to fund his passion for gambling. Consequently, the company didn't last very long.

Terry, a charming and entertaining man, had by that time become a close friend of the individual members of the Beatles – with John and George in particular. When John tired of going out to clubs in favour of sitting at home watching television or listening to Dylan records – and George also tired of clubbing – Terry and Pete Shotton used to take Cynthia and Pattie out for nights out on the town, mainly dancing at clubs.

Terry also used to join John on his LSD trips and the two of them once began spray-painting the front of John's house with aerosol paint cans.

In the song 'She's Leaving Home', the line, 'a man from the motor trade', is a reference to Terry Doran.

When John was writing 'A Day In the Life', he was stuck for an ending to the line, 'Now they know how many holes it takes to fill' and needed something to rhyme with 'small'. It was Terry who suggested 'the Albert Hall'.

When the Beatles set up their Apple Empire, Terry was appointed head of Apple Music in September 1967. One of his first signings was a group known as Grapefruit. In November 1968, he took the group away from Apple, commenting: 'I like the Beatles as friends, but not as bosses .... there is too much driftwood at Apple.'

He then replaced Frankie Hart as George's personal assistant and worked for him for several years, at one time basing himself at the Dark Horse offices in Los Angeles. Terry then continued his duties as P.A., working from Friar Park. At one time he managed the estate for George, but George next appointed his brother Harold as manager. When George's son Dhani was born, Terry was sacked as P.A. amid rumours that George didn't want someone who was gay to be around his offspring.

Terry then returned to the motor trade.

DORN, Beno Merseyside tailor whom Brian Epstein commissioned to fashion a set of grey tweed suits for the Beatles once he'd signed them up.

DOUGLAS, Craig British singer, real name Terence Perkins, born on 12 August 1941. He had a chart hit with 'A Teenager in Love' in 1959 and reached No. 1 with 'Only Sixteen' in 1960. The following year he appeared in the film *It's Trad, Dad!*.

Between 1960 and 1963 Douglas had nine chart hits: 'Pretty Blue Eyes', 'The Heart of a Teenage Girl', 'Oh! What a Day', 'A Hundred Pounds of Clay', 'Time', 'When My Little Girl is Smiling', 'Our Favourite Melodies', 'Oh Lonesome Me' and 'Town Crier'.

On Sunday 28 October 1962, Douglas was booked to appear at the Liverpool Empire by NEMS Enterprises as part of an eight-act pop package showcase, a step in Brian Epstein's plan to place the Beatles on bills with major non-Liverpool acts.

This was also the Beatles first appearance at Liverpool's main city-centre theatre venue (although the Quarry Men had appeared there in some talent contests) and their first pop package show.

There were two houses, the first at 5.40 p.m. and the second at 8.00 p.m. In addition to their own performance, the Beatles actually backed

Craig Douglas on each of the shows that night. Little Richard was the bill-topper, followed by Douglas, who closed the first half of the show.

Other acts to appear that night were Jet Harris & the Jetblacks, Kenny Lynch, the Breakaways and Sounds Incorporated. The compère was Dave Reid.

DUNBAR, John Cambridge graduate and former husband of Marianne Faithfull, he had hitchhiked across America in 1964.

John's father, Robert, had been stationed in Russia during the war and had married a Russian, Tatiana. Their son was born in Mexico. They also had twin daughters, Jenny and Margaret.

He was 22 years old when he married the 18-year-old Marianne Faithfull in Cambridge in May 1965 and their son, Nicholas, was born in November of that year.

Together with his former school chum Peter Asher and Barry Miles, he opened an avant-garde bookshop and gallery called Indica, in Mason's Yard, London, helped by a £5,000 donation from Paul McCartney.

Dunbar took it upon himself to expand Paul's appreciation of the arts, interesting him in film-makers such as Michelangelo Antonioni and artists such as the Greek sculptor Takis. He also began making avant-garde films with Paul, using twin 16mm cameras.

It was Dunbar who invited John Lennon to Yoko Ono's first exhibition at the gallery, in November 1966, and he was the person responsible for officially introducing them. He also introduced John to Alexis Mardas.

After Marianne and John split up, Dunbar moved into Flat 11, Bentinck Mansions, Bentinck Street, Marylebone, with his parents. Paul often used to drop round and John Lennon was also an occasional guest.

Lennon also regularly sent his limousine to pick up Dunbar and take him to Kenwood, where the two of them spent the summer of 1966 on LSD trips together.

DUNNING, George Director of the Beatles' animated film *Yellow Submarine*.

DURBAND, Alan Sixth-form teacher of English at Liverpool Institute, known as 'Dusty'. Paul McCartney claimed he was the only teacher he liked and said that he told the boys about books such as *Lady Chatterley's Lover* and Chaucer's *The Miller's Tale*, pointing out that they weren't dirty books but examples of good literature.

DYKIN, John The common-law husband of Julia Lennon and father of her two daughters. He died following a car crash in 1966.

DYLAN, Bob Premier folk artist of the 1960s, born Robert Allan Zimmerman on 24 May 1941 in Duluth, Minnesota.

Saturday Evening Post journalist Al Aronowitz first roused the Beatles' interest in Dylan's music and they obtained his two albums, *Bob Dylan* and *Freewheelin' Bob Dylan*, while in Paris in January 1964.

When Dylan visited them at the Delmonico Hotel in New York later that year, he introduced them to marijuana.

John Lennon in particular was impressed by Dylan's lyrics, which inspired him when composing songs such as 'I'm a Loser' and 'You've Got to Hide Your Love Away'. John was to comment: 'I was not too keen on lyrics in those days. I didn't think they counted. Dylan used to come out with his latest acetate and say, "Listen to the words, man," and I'd say, "I don't listen to words." '

In turn, Dylan was inspired by John and took the tune of 'Norwegian Wood' and wrote his own lyrics to it, resulting in 'Fourth Time Round'.

The Beatles featured Dylan as one of the figures on the sleeve of their *Sgt Pepper* album.

EARL PRESTON & THE TTs Earl Preston, real name Georgie Spruce, was a handsome and popular lead singer with several Mersey Beat bands.

With his group Earl Preston & the TTs he appeared on a number of bills with the Beatles, including Cavern gigs on Wednesday 22 November 1961 and Sunday 3 January 1963 and a Tower Ballroom promotion on Friday 8 December 1961.

Their debut single with Fontana was 'I Know Something', in July 1963. They also backed singer Eden Kane on 'Boys Cry', which was a Top 10 hit.

Earl then led Earl Preston's Realms, who also recorded with Fontana, releasing the single 'Raindrops' in June 1964.

The Realms were among several groups managed by Jim Ireland, who owned the Mardi Gras and Downbeat clubs.

ECKHORN, Peter Hamburg club-owner. His father had left him a venue in the Reeperbahn called the Hippodrome, which he converted into the Top Ten Club in November 1960, employing Tony Sheridan & the Jets as the first resident band. He also intended featuring Derry & the Seniors, but they wanted to return to Liverpool.

He hired Horst Fascher from the Kaiserkeller and also Rosa, the toilet attendant, both friends of the Beatles, and he gave the Beatles a contract to play at the Top Ten when their Kaiserkeller term expired.

The Beatles were pleased because the pay was good and included bonuses, while the accommodation in bunk beds on the top floor of the club premises was an improvement on what they'd suffered at the Bambi Kino. However, Koschmider had a contract which forbade them to appear within 25 miles of the Kaiserkeller and when they began appearing on stage with Sheridan he saw to it that George was deported and accused Pete and Paul of attempting arson at his Bambi Kino.

Eckhorn booked the Beatles to appear at the Top Ten for a season from 17 March 1961 and renewed their stay until 2 July. He attempted to book them for a further season at his club, but Manfred Weissleder of the Star Club outbid him.

EDDIE CLAYTON SKIFFLE GROUP, The Early in 1957, Ritchie Starkey and his workmate Eddie Miles decided to start a skiffle group for a laugh. This was while they were working at H.H. Hunt & Sons.

At the time Ritchie, an apprentice engineer at the firm, hadn't really considered a career as a musician and was to recall: 'I remember my mum saying a neighbour was in a band and why didn't I have a go. I thought it was a jazz group – I was mad on jazz. When it turned out to be a silver band, playing in the park and sticking to marches and all that, I chucked it in. It lasted just one night.'

He had begun playing during the lunchbreaks in the works canteen with Eddie and three other fellow employees they enlisted. Eddie picked the stage name Eddie Clayton because he felt it sounded better than his own name.

Following their canteen appearances at Hunts, they made their actual debut as a skiffle band at the Labour Club in Peel Street. They comprised Ed Miles (guitar/vocals), Ritchie Starkey (drums), Roy Trafford (tea-chest bass), John Dougherty (washboard) and Frank Walsh (guitar).

Their nearest approach to a group uniform consisted of shirts in the same colour as their bootlace ties. Since the group were beginning to perform at local venues, Ritchie needed a proper kit and his stepfather bought him a second-hand one.

The Eddie Clayton Skiffle Group began to appear at places such as Wilson Hall in Garston and enjoyed a residency at the Boys Club meetings at the Florence Institute in Dingle.

Ritchie's mother, Elsie Starkey, was to recall in *Mersey Beat*: 'Ritchie joined the Eddie Clayton Skiffle Group with Ed Miles, the boy who lived next door, Roy Trafford and Johnny Dougherty – they all worked together in the same place. Eddie used to take his guitar to work every day. He was a smashing fellow – if ever a lad should have got somewhere he should have. I believe he's with Hank Walters & his Dusty Road Ramblers.'

The group fell apart when Eddie Miles decided to get married and Ritchie began to play in various other skiffle outfits. Obviously, Eddie continued his part-time career as a musician after his marriage.

Interestingly enough, Eric Clapton used the alias Eddie Clayton when he guested on the *Ringo* album.

ELLIOT, Bill Newcastle-born singer who was picked by John Lennon to sing lead vocals on 'God Save Us', a number he'd written specially to help the magazine *Oz* in its obscenity trial. Elliot later teamed up with another friend from Newcastle, Bob Purvis, who wrote a song called 'Lonely Man' with Mal Evans, who had also helped John produce Elliot's single. Mal brought the two lads to the attention of George Harrison and under the name Splinter they recorded a number of singles and an album for George's Dark Horse label.

ELLIS, Geoffrey Close friend of Brian Epstein who became a senior executive of NEMS Enterprises in October 1964.

ELLIS, Royston A British poet who first met the Beatles when he travelled to Liverpool in June 1960 to appear at Liverpool University for a poetry reading. Ellis, who wrote in the style of the American Beat Generation poets, became friends with members of the group, who backed him in a 'poetry-to-music' session at the Jacaranda club. He later went back to the Gambier Terrace flat rented by Rod Murray and Stuart Sutcliffe, where John Lennon also stayed, and spent a week there.

It was while he was at Gambier Terrace that Ellis introduced members of the Beatles to their first-ever drug experience. He broke open a Vick inhaler, which in those days had a strip of Benzedrine inside, and pointed out that they could chew the strip, nicknamed a 'spitball'.

Ellis told them that his ambition was to become a 'paperback writer'; his paperback books included *Jiving to Gyp, Driftin' with Cliff Richard* (co-authored with Jet Harris), *The Big Beat Scene* and a biography of the Shadows.

He met up with the group again in August 1963, when they appeared in the Channel Islands. Later he moved to Sri Lanka, where he specialized in writing travel books.

ELVIN, Carol South London female country music singer who wore a stetson hat and appeared on a short season at the Star Club, Hamburg, with the Beatles in December 1962. She later toured with Gene Vincent and appeared as an entertainer on Caribbean cruise ships.

EMERICK, Geoff Recording engineer who replaced Norman Smith as engineer on Beatles recordings in April 1966, although he first began working as a tape operator on their recordings in February 1963. Emerick became George Martin's assistant and was involved in many Beatles recordings, winning a Grammy Award for his work on *Sgt Pepper's Lonely Hearts Club Band*. He also won a Grammy for his work on Paul McCartney's *Band on the Run* album and was presented with a Lifetime Achievement Award for his services to the music industry by BASCA (British Academy of Songwriters, Composers and Authors).

Paul was best man at Geoff's wedding in January 1989.

Together with George Martin, Emerick entered the EMI vaults to work on the mass of unreleased Beatles tapes to remaster and release them as six double-CDs in the *Anthology* series.

EPHGRAVE, Joseph Fairground artist who was commissioned by Peter Blake in 1967 to paint an ornate drumskin for use in the *Sgt Pepper* tableau.

EPSTEIN, Brian Samuel The Beatles first manager, born at a private nursing home in Liverpool on 19 September 1934. His mother was Malka (known as 'Queenie'), daughter of a furniture manufacturer in Sheffield, and his father was Harry Epstein, whose family owned a furniture store in Liverpool.

At the age of ten he was expelled from Liverpool College for drawing obscene pictures and by the age of 16 had been placed in seven different schools. Brian had ambitions of becoming a dress designer, but his father forbade it and he went to work as a salesman in the family business.

At the age of 18 he was called up for National Service but was discharged after ten months on medical grounds, although it was said he had been found importuning in a public toilet while dressed in an officer's uniform. For a time he worked at Clarendon Furnishing in Hoylake, a branch of the family firm.

He then revealed to his family that he was homosexual, shocking his father and younger brother, Clive, but receiving sympathy from Queenie.

He was then allowed to study at RADA (Royal Academy of Dramatic Art), passing the audition on his twenty-second birthday.

It was alleged that he was once again found importuning in a public toilet and he left the course to return to the family business in 1957.

Scandal followed when he attempted to pick up a man in a public toilet in Liverpool and became the victim of blackmail. The family informed the police and at the trial Brian was referred to as 'Mr X'. By that time he was managing the record department at the new (North End Music Stores) (NEMS) branch in Great Charlotte Street. It was so successful that he was placed in charge of an even larger branch of the store in Whitechapel.

At the beginning of July 1961 I approached him to stock copies of a new publication, *Mersey Beat*, which contained news of the remarkable music scene in Liverpool, with the first issue featuring a biography of the Beatles written by John Lennon. Brian ordered a dozen copies, which sold out almost immediately, and he ordered increasing numbers over the next few days before ordering 144 copies of the second issue.

This was published on 20 July 1961 and the cover announced 'Beatles Sign Recording Contract!'. Below an Astrid Kirchherr photograph of the Beatles in Hamburg was the detailed story of their recording session there:

> Bert Kaempfert, who may be remembered for his golden record 'Wonderland by Night', which reached the top of the American hit parade, contracted the Beatles for Polydor, Germany's top record company. Under the contract they will make four records per year for the company.
>
> At a recording session, the Beatles provided vocals and backing for three numbers for Tony Sheridan. Tony, a first-class songwriter, penned 'Why?', a number familiar to readers through Gerry Marsden's excellent rendering. Apart from waxing 'Why?', the Beatles recorded 'My Bonnie Lies Over the Ocean', opening in waltz-time, then breaking into a rock beat. Finally, the group provided good bass and drum backing to Sheridan for 'The Saints Go Marching In', a very popular number in Germany.
>
> The Beatles recorded two further numbers for Kaempfert on their own. One side, an instrumental written by George Harrison, has not yet been named – probable titles include 'Cry for a Shadow' and 'Beatle Bop'. The other side, 'Ain't She Sweet?', featured a vocal by John Lennon. The boys weren't quite satisfied with these two numbers, so they sold the rights to Polydor. Thus, in fact, under the contract the Beatles still have four more records to make this year.
>
> Bass guitarist Stuart Sutcliffe has remained in Hamburg and will shortly be marrying a German girl. At present he is studying at Hamburg Art College and has an English tutor. The group have no plans for taking on another guitarist, but have decided to remain a quartet.

With dozens of youngsters coming into his store asking for copies of *Mersey Beat*, and with the details of the unique music scene in the city in the first two issues, Epstein became intrigued.

He invited me up to his office to discuss the local scene and was quite fascinated. He also asked if he could become the paper's record reviewer.

I agreed and in the third issue, dated 3 August 1961, his first column, 'Stop the World – and listen to everything in it. Brian Epstein of Nems,' was published.

Each time I delivered copies of *Mersey Beat*, Epstein would invite me to the office for a chat and it was obvious that he was beginning to see the potential of this huge musical movement which was literally on his doorstep.

The next issue of *Mersey Beat* featured a full-page feature by Bob Wooler extolling the merits of the Beatles, expressing his conviction that they were the No. 1 band around.

When Epstein decided to become involved in the local scene, it was the group featured in every issue of *Mersey Beat* that interested him and he phoned me to arrange for him to visit the Cavern, where he could see the Beatles perform for the first time.

Brian, accompanied by his personal assistant, Alistair Taylor, dropped into the club at 12.30 p.m. on 9 November 1961.

By then he was very familiar with the Beatles and they were aware of him. Brian had noticed the members of local groups who came into NEMS to listen to new releases in the record booths and often chatted to people like Gerry Marsden to ask them about their choice of repertoire. The Beatles also dropped into NEMS regularly and local promoter Sam Leach had arranged for Brian to sell tickets to his Tower Ballroom promotion 'Operation Big Beat'. This took place on 10 November and Brian had been selling tickets for more than two weeks prior to the gig. The posters in NEMS prominently featured the Beatles as the bill-topping band.

Brian went into the Cavern bandroom to have a brief chat with the group and dropped in to see them a month later. He left a message with George Harrison suggesting that he would like to arrange a meeting with them at NEMS.

This was arranged for 4.30 p.m. on Wednesday 3 December 1961. John Lennon asked disc jockey Bob Wooler to join them, telling Epstein that Bob was his father. Paul was 30 minutes late, which irked the punctilious record-store manager.

Another meeting was arranged for 10 December, with Alistair Taylor present, and it was agreed that Brian would become their manager. The first contract would be for a five-year period from 1 February 1962. Epstein's commission was to be 10 per cent of any income up to £1,500 per year and 15 per cent above that amount.

The formal signing took place at Pete Best's home on 24 January 1962. A second management contract for five years was drawn up on 1 October 1962. By 1963 Brian's commission had been increased to 25 per cent.

Brian might have given up control of the Beatles in the early stages of his management. According to reports, he was offering a slice of his management percentage to several different people – all of whom refused.

It was said that in 1963 he offered Joe Collins (father of Joan and Jackie) a share of the Beatles and in 1964 Epstein reputedly approached Lew Grade and told him he was ready to sell the Beatles. When John Lennon heard about it he told Epstein: 'If you do sell, we'll never play again. We'll disband.'

Mike and Bernie Winters, in the biography *Up a Pagoda Tree*, revealed that they were appearing at the London Palladium when Jack Murray called to see them in their dressing room and showed Mike a magazine picture of the group. 'They're big up North,' he said. 'Their agent has a record shop and doesn't know what to do with them. I've got them for 16 to 20 weeks, and I can have a permanent share of their contract if I want to. Do you want to come in with me?'

Mike told him: 'I'm not gambling any more, Jack. Bernie and I are going to work on our act and try to make a go of it. Thanks all the same.'

It has also been reported that Epstein offered impresario Larry Parnes a share in the Beatles, but was also rejected.

In the book *The Life and Times of Little Richard*, Richard claims that after the Beatles came off stage at the Liverpool Empire, where Richard had been topping the bill, Epstein approached him and said: 'Richard, I'll give you 50 per cent of the Beatles.' Richard commented: 'I couldn't accept 'cos I never thought they would make it.'

It was essential for Brian to secure the group a recording contract. Initially, he thought he would have a great deal of clout due to his position as a prominent north-western record dealer, but this seemed to cut no ice and he was turned down by all of the EMI pop labels (Parlophone wasn't approached regarding the Beatles at this time as George Martin was on holiday). Epstein received an official letter from EMI confirming that the company was not interested in the group. Pye and the various other labels turned him down, and he began to despair.

Through Tony Barrow, he'd put a foot in the door at Decca and followed through, stressing his position as a record dealer. Decca arranged a recording audition for the group, but they were turned down.

Brian didn't actually like pop music at the time and really had no idea of the group's intrinsic value. He'd signed the Beatles quite simply because they had been established as the No. 1 group locally, as he'd read in the pages of *Mersey Beat*.

His initial attempts to alter the Beatles' image met with some resistance from John Lennon and Pete Best, who didn't like the idea of discarding their leathers in favour of mohair suits. The leather image seemed popular: Youngsters began wearing leather jackets and coats, even Epstein took to wearing leather, yet he insisted they wear mohair suits.

This cleaning up of the image – telling them not to smoke on stage, not to swear, not to clown around – actually wasn't part of a clever plan. Brian was simply following convention in smartening up an image to make it palatable to the moguls who controlled the entertainment industry and were a generation above the kids they manipulated. Most groups on television, like the Shadows, wore smart suits, so Epstein made the Beatles conform. Although it's hypothetical, it would have been interesting to see how the Beatles fared if they'd been allowed to continue with their leather image – it would certainly have excited the youngsters they appealed to. After all, in those days rock 'n' roll meant rebellion to the kids.

Epstein attempted to make suggestions about their music – such as the type of songs to perform at their Decca recording audition – which was taking his brief too far.

As their career progressed they made sure Brian never interfered with their music again. During one recording session, he had switched on the studio intercom and said: 'I don't think that sounded quite right, John.' Lennon turned to him and said: 'You stick to your percentages, Brian. We'll look after the music.'

With the rejection by Decca there seemed nowhere else to turn, until a freak piece of luck led Brian to the Parlophone label. Even after the initial approach had been made, Epstein found that Parlophone treated him in a cavalier way and he was often driven to tears of frustration when George Martin didn't answer his calls. Eventually, he had to threaten to boycott EMI labels at his stores.

The deal he signed on behalf of the Beatles was pathetic and George Martin was to describe it as 'pretty awful'. There were no advance payments and they would receive only one penny per single – and half that on overseas sales. A 12-track album would be regarded only as six cuts. There were three one-year options with an increase of a quarter of a penny at the end of the first year and an increase of a halfpenny at the end of the second year.

Although it's true that Epstein didn't have much option at the time, the Beatles were to earn such staggering sums for EMI that he should have been able to renegotiate with the company before he eventually did, shortly before his own contract with the Beatles ran out.

John and Paul in particular were simmering with anger for years at the pathetic royalties they received – particularly when they discovered that, after the Rolling Stones had been with Decca for three years, Allen Klein had appeared and renegotiated their contract, obtaining for them an advance of almost £3 million. The Stones were then earning far more from records than the Beatles, even though they were selling much fewer.

Although Brian cultivated the image that he was an astute businessman, his deals in his brief time as a manager didn't really bear it out. Apart from the far from lucrative record deal, he signed a publishing deal for the Beatles with publisher Dick James which resulted in the group losing control of their own songs for ever. It was rumoured at the time that James's small independent music-publishing company was in financial trouble. Epstein had been rattled by being asked to wait in the reception area at one of the music-publishing companies he'd intended to negotiate with. Due to the simple fact that James managed to get the Beatles on the TV show *Thank Your Lucky Stars*, Epstein decided to sign with him.

Arguably, the initial arrangement was fair in relation to music-publishing deals at the time, but Epstein could have arranged his own publishing company and appointed James to administer it. In addition, he could have ensured that the later shares were fairer to John and Paul, whose songs were, after all, what made Northern Songs such a valuable company.

Northern Songs was formed in 1963 with James and his partner, Charles Silver, owning 50 per cent of the company. Against the wishes of John and Paul, it became a public company in 1965, with James and Silver owning 23 per cent while John and Paul had only 15 per cent each. In March, 1969 James sold his shares to ATV without offering the Beatles a chance to buy them.

If Brian's recording and publishing deals left something to be desired, his negotiations regarding their film career was also suspect. United Artists, keen to release a Beatles soundtrack album, were willing to offer the Beatles 25 per cent. At the meeting to discuss the deal, Brian pre-empted their offer by telling them: 'I wouldn't consider anything under seven and a half per cent.' Fortunately, their lawyer David Jacobs was able to finalize a deal in which they eventually received 25 per cent – but he asked only for gross, not net. Also, producer Walter Shenson's lawyer negotiated a better deal for his client.

United Artists didn't really believe that the Beatles were a long-term prospect and Shenson's lawyers suggested that the rights to the Beatles films be given to the producer after 15 years. United Artists agreed. Epstein should have taken that route on behalf of the Beatles. As a result, the films are owned by Shenson and have proved very lucrative for him.

The worst deal of all related to Beatles merchandise. Prior to the group's first trip to America, Brian asked his solicitor, Jacobs, to find someone to handle the merchandising. Jacobs met a young man called Nicky Byrne at a cocktail party and proposed he take over the merchandising for the Beatles.

Jacobs asked him what percentage he would require and Byrne said 90 per cent. Jacobs immediately agreed and informed Epstein, who also agreed. Without any advance fee or discussion, he had given away 90 per cent of the Beatles' merchandising rights to an unproved person who had no previous experience of merchandising, leaving 10 per cent to be shared by the Beatles, Brian and NEMS.

Byrne flew to New York and within a week Capitol Records had offered to buy him out for $500,000, with the money being paid into the Bahamas for him and also allowing him to retain a half interest in the company. He turned them down. The young man seemed to have more of an idea of the Beatles' value than Epstein himself.

When Epstein realized the full extent of his gaffe, he was horrified. By August 1964 Jacobs had renegotiated the deal, raising the Beatles' royalty to 46 per cent, but by that time Epstein had instructed NEMS to begin negotiating with US firms directly. Court proceedings were instigated against him.

Due to the legal problem, a large number of major firms, including Woolworth's, backed out of negotiations and it was said that approximately $100,000,000 worth of merchandising deals were lost. To make matters worse, Byrne won his case and NEMS had to settle with him for a substantial cash payment.

The fact was, Brian had never been a successful businessman. His parents initially refused to support him in NEMS Enterprises unless his brother, Clive, become a partner to look after the business side of things. At the time they had no faith in Brian's ability.

He was to take on several other ventures which lost a great deal of money. He employed the experienced agent Vic Lewis as managing director of NEMS. Lewis arranged a British tour for the Four Tops, working out that it would be profitable if it attracted the fans, but would at least break even with the deal he negotiated. Behind his back, Brian flew to Detroit and amended the contract, giving concessions such as agreeing to pay the group's tax, their air fares and adding bonuses to the deal. NEMS lost £10,000 on the tour. He also lost a greater amount when he flew in the Four Tops for a single appearance at his Saville Theatre.

Brian never understood the music young people loved. It basically didn't appeal to him. He liked classical music, jazz and middle-of-the-road. The Beatles, Gerry & the Pacemakers and Billy J. Kramer had been voted Nos. 1, 2 and 3 in the *Mersey Beat* poll when he signed them, and he also signed Cilla Black at the urging of *Mersey Beat*. Yet he was never to really understand the sort of music they'd been playing and turned the rock 'n' rollers into straight pop and middle-of-the road performers. Gerry, who'd been rocking away in Liverpool and Hamburg, was placed in the pantomime *Babes in the Wood* in 1963 and in 1965 Brian booked three of his acts into pantomimes, Cilla in *Little Red Riding Hood*, Billy J. in *Mother Goose* and Gerry in *Cinderella*.

Despite his initial success, some of the other Mersey groups he signed left him because they realized he had no idea how to manage them and had no understanding of their music – they included the Big Three and the Chants. Apart from his early Liverpool signings, he seemed to have no success with his other acts, primarily because he had no real idea about rock 'n' roll and pop music. The Rustiks, the Silkie and Michael Haslam, for example, vanished without trace. He couldn't even launch his Liverpool signing Tommy Quickly to stardom, and when he signed up the talented group Paddy, Klaus & Gibson he didn't know what to do with them and they soon disbanded.

In spite of the fact that he couldn't tell a good band from a bad one, he sat on many talent competition panels, including 'Ready, Steady, Win!' and 'Beat Time for Oxfam'.

Brian also didn't like acknowledging credit and was a great self-publicist. In the opening of his autobiography, *A Cellarful of Noise*, he created the story that he'd never heard of the Beatles until a boy came into his store and asked for their record. He made himself available for as many television and radio shows and media interviews as possible and in a relatively short time had appeared on *Juke Box Jury, Panorama, Desert Island Discs, The Eamonn Andrews Show, Late Night Line-Up, The David Frost Programme, Tonight, Celebrity Game, For Art's Sake* and *Let's Find Out*. He also compèred the American TV show *Hullabaloo*.

He was often moody and petulant with his staff, several of whom left him following disputes – Brian Somerville, Derek Taylor and Wendy Hanson among them.

In fact, there was a great deal of incredible luck during his management of the Beatles. The timing was right for a supergroup to appear, because young people were demanding their own idols for perhaps the first time. He was unable initially to get them a recording contract, and it was only by pure accident that his path led to Parlophone. Luck again intervened when leading American TV host Ed Sullivan was at London Airport to see the Beatles arrive and booked them on to his show.

Although Capitol Records in America had continued to refuse to release the Beatles' records, when they eventually did disc jockeys all over America began playing 'I Wanna Hold Your Hand' and it became a hit despite Capitol's initial lack of enthusiasm. The Beatles also arrived in America a few months after President Kennedy had been assassinated, and were able to draw America out of its mourning and put a smile on its face. Apart from Epstein's attempt at plasticizing the Beatles' image with the original mohair suits, the visual look that mattered – their 'moptop' hairstyle and collarless suits – had their origins in Hamburg. It's hard to find any specific plan or deal or management structure devised by Epstein which led to the success of the Beatles.

Towards the end of his life there were suicide attempts. He had neglected his business because of his addiction to drugs and gambling and was virtually ready to hand his show-business empire over to Robert Stigwood, who seemed to have more musical acumen than Brian with his signing of acts such as the Bee Gees and Cream.

Because he was letting his business affairs slip, Brian was neglecting his acts, and Cilla, Billy J. and Gerry wanted to find new managers. It took all his powers of persuasion to get them to remain with him. His contract with the Beatles was nearing its end and he was worried that they wouldn't renew it. Without their knowledge, he made a deal with EMI to increase their percentage, but also contracting them to pay NEMS royalties from Beatles records for years after his own contract had expired.

On Friday 25 August 1967 Brian planned to spend time at his country home with his friends Geoffrey Ellis and Peter Brown. He became restless during the evening and returned to London. His mother rang his Chapel Street home and his butler, Antonio, told her that Brian was still asleep. The following morning Antonio and his wife, Maria, attempted to contact Brian on the intercom. As there was no reply, they phoned Brian's secretary, Joanne Newfield, who arrived with Alistair Taylor. Peter Brown's own doctor, John Gallway, was contacted and he instructed that the doors to Brian's room be broken open. His body was found on the bed.

The coroner's verdict was that he had died by an accidental overdose of the drug Carbitol. His body was buried at the Jewish cemetery in Long Lane, Liverpool.

EPSTEIN, Clive Younger brother of Brian Epstein. During early life he succeeded where Brian failed, excelling at Wrekin College and becoming a sergeant in the Royal Army Education Corps.

The first major city-centre store for NEMS was opened in Great Charlotte Street, Liverpool, with both brothers managing the two-storey shop, with Brian handling the ground-floor record business and Clive looking after the electrical and domestic-goods section on the first floor.

When Brian approached his family to finance him in a company to manage the Beatles, they agreed only on condition that Clive become a partner. When NEMS Enterprises was officially launched on 26 June 1962, with share capital of £100, the brothers owned 50 per cent each of the company, with Clive appointed company secretary.

Brian's undoubted success with the Beatles led the company to increase its share capital to £10,000, with Brian's share increasing to £5,000, Clive's to £4,000 and £250 shares for each group member.

On Brian's death in August 1967, the Beatles appeared to accept Clive as Brian's successor for the two months until their NEMS contract expired. He became chairman of the new company, Nemperor Holdings, with Vic Lewis as managing director and Barbara Mattison as company secretary.

Once Clive took over, he realized that a vast proportion of their income, about £2 million, would go to the taxman unless they did something about it. He suggested they go into the retail business and open shops. The idea excited Paul McCartney, who came up with the concept of a white department store, saying: 'It would be great. We could have a department where they sell nothing but white clothes, another where they could sell white furniture – even a white grand piano – and still another where you can buy white pets.'

The department store idea never came to fruition, but Clive's original suggestion of creating a business to offset tax grew into Apple Corps.

Although there was big business pressure on him to sell NEMS to Triumph Investments, Clive felt he was morally obliged to let the Beatles have first offer and told Triumph that he would be selling NEMS to the Beatles' company, Apple.

When Allen Klein entered the picture on behalf of the Beatles, Klein suggested there had been impropriety in Brian's nine-year agreements. This infuriated Clive, who sent back a note: 'Before any meeting takes place, please be good enough to let me know precisely what you mean by the phrase "the propriety of the negotiations surrounding the nine-year agreement between EMI, the Beatles and NEMS".'

Clive, upset at Klein's style of doing business, sold NEMS to Triumph. John Eastman, whom Paul had brought in to represent him, said Klein was responsible for the lost opportunity, saying that while he'd been negotiating to buy NEMS from Clive, Klein had turned up and told the Beatles: 'Forget it, I'll get you NEMS for nothing because the Epsteins owe you money.'

Clive died of a heart attack on 2 February 1988 during a skiing holiday with his wife, Barbara. He was 51 years of age and left a son, Henry, and a daughter, Joanna. His funeral took place on 5 February at Greenbank Drive Synagogue in Liverpool.

ESCORTS, The A group who formed in 1961 and comprised Terry Sylvester (vocals/guitar); John Kinrade (lead); Mike Gregory (vocals/bass) and John Foster (drums). Foster, also known as Johnny Sticks, was Ringo Starr's cousin and it was Ringo who arranged for them to have a residency at the Blue Angel club in 1962.

Johnny was replaced by Pete Clarke the following year and they entered a talent competition at the Philharmonic Hall. The judges included George Harrison and Ringo Starr. Eighty groups entered and the Escorts won. The prize included a television appearance on *ABC at Large* and a recording contract with Decca.

Unfortunately, it then transpired that Decca said the prize was only for a recording test and they didn't take an option on the group, who had hoped to record 'Fortune Teller' as their debut disc.

They made their recording debut in April 1964 with 'Dizzy Miss Lizzy', but it failed to register – although it went to No. 1 in Texas! The group considered that Jack Baverstock, their recording manager at Fontana, didn't have any feeling for their type of music and were unhappy with the recordings they made with him.

Their next release, 'The One to Cry', reached No. 49 in the British charts. Their third single was a version of the Drifters' 'I Don't Want to go on Without You', but soon after it was released the Moody Blues covered it and the Brum group's version charted.

When Terry Sylvester left to join the Swinging Bluejeans, he was replaced by the ubiquitous Paddy Chambers. The group split and Mike Gregory joined Sylvester in the Swinging Bluejeans, where he remained until 1972, although Terry had left earlier to become a member of the Hollies, replacing Graham Nash.

Their last single release was 'Head to Toe', flipside 'Night Time', which featured Paul McCartney on tambourine. At that time the line-up comprised Kinrade, Gregory, Chambers and Paul Comerford on drums.

The disc failed to register and the band broke up several weeks later.

The Escorts appeared with the Beatles on several bills, including one at the Cavern on Saturday 3 August 1963, the Beatles' final appearance at the venue.

EUBANKS, Bob Head of Hollywood radio station KRLA who booked the Beatles for the Hollywood Bowl in August 1964.

EVANS, Mal The Beatles' second road manager. He was a telecommunications engineer who worked part-time as a bouncer at the Cavern when Brian Epstein offered him the job as equipment manager to the Beatles, helping Neil Aspinall in his duties as road manager.

The 26-year-old, six-foot-two engineer lived in Mossley Hill with his wife, Lil, and their baby son, and he took the job despite his wife's misgivings.

He remained close to the Beatles throughout their career, reporting his experiences in *Beatles Monthly* and appearing in *Help!*, *Magical Mystery Tour* and *Let It Be*. He also had a cameo role in Ringo's film *Blindman*.

He was present at the Beatles recording sessions and was often asked to participate. He played Hammond organ on 'You Won't See Me', sang in the chorus of 'Yellow Submarine', played bass harmonium on 'Being for the Benefit of Mr Kite', played one of the pianos on 'A Day in the Life', played tambourine on 'Dear Prudence', played trumpet on 'Helter Skelter', 'played' the anvil on 'Maxwell's Silver Hammer' and sang backing vocals on 'You Know My Name (Look Up the Number)'.

When the Beatles ceased touring he was appointed one of their personal assistants and in 1968 became an executive at Apple, where he discovered the Iveys, who were to become Badfinger.

Allen Klein appeared on the scene and the majority of the Apple staff were sacked. Mal then went to America. By that time he had two children, but he became estranged from his wife. He was living in Los Angeles in 1975 when he completed his autobiography, *Living the Beatles Legend*, aided by John Hoernle, but it remains unpublished.

In January 1976 Mal was living with a woman and her four-year-old daughter. She rang the police when he got into a depressed state. They arrived to find him waving an air pistol and the two policeman fired six shots, killing him instantly.

EVANS, Malcolm One of the shareholders of the merchandising company Seltaeb. Not to be confused with the Beatles' road manager of the same name.

EVANS, Shirley Buxom actress who appeared as one of the passengers in *Magical Mystery Tour*. Shirley played accordion on the trip, but a number specially written for her by John and Paul, 'Shirley's Wild Accordion', wasn't released.

◀ **BERYL MARSDEN** on stage at the Cavern reopening in 1984. Colin Manley is on guitar.

▼ **THE UNDERTAKERS,** a Liverpool band who appeared frequently with the Beatles and whose lead singer, Jackie Lomax, became one of the first Apple signings.

▲ **CHUCK BERRY,** a seminal influence who acknowledged Liverpool's contribution to the revival of rock 'n' roll by writing 'Liverpool Drive'.

▶ **GERRY MARSDEN,** leader of the Pacemakers, on stage at the Cavern in 1963.

◀ **NEIL ASPINALL,** (left) the man most deserving of the tag 'the fifth Beatle', with the author.

▲ **CLIVE EPSTEIN,** Brian's partner and younger brother, outside a 'mock' NEMS store in 1984.

◄ **MIKE BERRY** with Tommy Bruce. Mike appeared on several bills with the Beatles.

▼ **BRIAN EPSTEIN** chats with Billy J. Kramer backstage at the Empire Theatre, Liverpool.

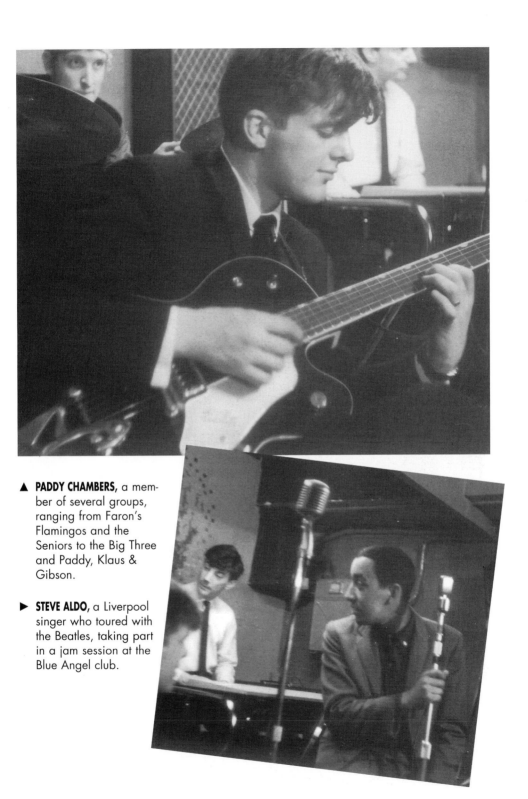

▲ **PADDY CHAMBERS,** a member of several groups, ranging from Faron's Flamingos and the Seniors to the Big Three and Paddy, Klaus & Gibson.

▶ **STEVE ALDO,** a Liverpool singer who toured with the Beatles, taking part in a jam session at the Blue Angel club.

▶ **EDDIE PARRY,** lead singer with the Dennisons. He died in 1995.

▼ **JOE ANKRAH,** leader of the Chants. The Beatles once backed them at the Cavern.

◄ **TOMMY QUICKLY** on stage at the Cavern in 1963.

▼ **SONNY WEBB** and **JOE BUTLER** of Sonny Webb & the Cascades, later to become the popular C&W band the Hillsiders.

▲ **MARK PETERS**, a leading Liverpool singer but one of the many talented local musicians who never made it nationally.

◄ **EARL PRESTON** on stage at the Mardi Gras in 1963. He continues to perform in Liverpool clubs.

◄ **RORY STORM & THE HURRI-CANES,** the legendary outfit consisting of Johnny 'Guitar' Byrne, Ringo Starr, Lou Walters and Ty Brien.

▼ **HOWIE CASEY & THE SENIORS.** A 1963 line-up which included Paddy Chambers, Gibson Kemp, Bobby Thompson and Steve Hardie.

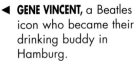

◄ **GENE VINCENT,** a Beatles icon who became their drinking buddy in Hamburg.

► **BILLY J, KRAMER** with Virginia Harry at the reopening of the Cavern in 1984.

▼ **RAY McFALL,** owner of the Cavern, who ran 'the best of cellars' during its heyday.

▲ **MIKE McCARTNEY** (right) and the author discussing the Beatles on American television.

▶ **ALISTAIR TAYLOR,** Apple's 'Mr Fixit'.

▲ **MITCH MURRAY,** composer
of 'How Do You Do It?'.

▲ **TONY BARROW**, the Beatles' press officer, with **BRIAN O'HARA** of the Fourmost.

▶ **ARTHUR BALLARD,** tutor to John Lennon and Stuart Sutcliffe at Liverpool College of Art.

◀ **RICHARD LESTER**, the director of the Beatles' first two films: *A Hard Day's Night* – 'the *Citizen Kane* of jukebox movies' – and *Help!*.

▲ **JANE ASHER,** Paul McCartney's former fiancée. Their romance lasted for five years and inspired several hit songs.

EVERETT, Kenny Zany British disc jockey and television personality, born Maurice James Christopher Cole in Liverpool. After working in an office and in a bakery, he joined the pirate ship Radio London and was the official pirate radio reporter invited to accompany the Beatles on their final US tour in August 1966.

On Saturday 20 May 1967 the BBC show *Where It's At* transmitted a pre-recorded feature by Everett on 'Sgt Pepper's Lonely Hearts Club Band', including interviews with John, Paul and Ringo. Another pre-recorded interview by Everett, in which he talked to Paul McCartney and discussed 'All You Need is Love', was transmitted on *Where It's At* on Saturday 1 July 1967.

On the edition of *Where It's At* on Saturday 25 November 1967, an 18-minute interview with John Lennon by Everett and Chris Denning was broadcast.

The Beatles' fifth and final Christmas fan club records were edited by Kenny Everett, who used his real name, Maurice Cole, on the 1969 edition.

On Saturday 27 January 1968, Everett visited John at his home in Weybridge to record an interview for *The Kenny Everett Show*, which was broadcast on Radio 1 on 4 February.

Everett also visited the group while they were recording at Abbey Road on Thursday 6 June 1968 and recorded an interview which was broadcast on *The Kenny Everett Show* on Sunday 9 June.

On Thursday 14 August 1969, Everett again dropped by the Abbey Road studios while the Beatles were mixing some tracks and recorded an interview with John Lennon which was broadcast in two parts on his *Everett is Here* radio series on Saturday 20 and Saturday 27 September.

It wasn't merely the fact that Kenny shared the same Liverpool roots as the Beatles that led to his becoming such a personal friend of the group; he also had a wacky sense of humour that appealed to them, particularly to Lennon. Kenny was also anarchic in his approach to his radio and television shows, another aspect of his talent which they liked.

His autobiography, *The Custard Stops at Hatfield*, published in October 1982, featured many anecdotes about his relationship with the Beatles.

Kenny died from an AIDS-related illness on 4 April 1995. He was 51 years old.

EXCITERS, The New York quartet who appeared with the Beatles on their first American tour. Led by Herb Rooney and his wife, Brenda Reid, the group had reached No. 4 in the US charts with their single 'Tell Him' in 1962.

FAITHFULL, Marianne Singer, born in Hampstead, London, on 29 December 1946, the daughter of Baroness Erisso Sacher-Masoch and Major Glynn Faithfull. The family initially lived in Ormskirk, on the outskirts of Liverpool, while Marianne's father worked on his doctorate at Liverpool University. They then settled in Oxfordshire.

She was six years old when her parents separated, attended St Joseph's Convent School in Reading and was still at the school when her first record, 'As Tears Go By', was released.

Marianne married John Dunbar and they had a son, Nicholas. Paul McCartney became friendly with John and used to spend many evenings with him and Marianne at their Bentinck Street flat. The couple became estranged because Marianne went to live with Mick Jagger of the Rolling Stones. When interviewed by Andrew Tyler for the *New Musical Express* in 1974, she was to say, rather cynically: 'My first move was to get a Rolling Stone as a boyfriend. I slept with three and decided the lead singer was the best bet.'

Marianne appeared on the Granada Television documentary *The Music of Lennon and McCartney*, recorded on Monday and Tuesday 1–2 November 1965. Paul began singing 'Yesterday' for 22 seconds and Marianne completed the song. In fact, Marianne was Paul's personal choice to record the number and during an evening at a party he played her an acetate of his version, and also attended her recording session at Decca Studios on 11 October 1965.

Arguably, her record company didn't push her version as enthusiastically as a Matt Munro cover, which reached No. 8 in the charts, while Marianne's single barely reached No. 36.

As a 1960s icon and Mick Jagger's girlfriend, she was present at various Beatles functions, beginning with the 'Yellow Submarine' recording on Wednesday 1 June 1966, when she joined several others in producing background noises to the track. She was also present at Abbey Road, along with various other celebrities, including Mick Jagger, Keith Richards, Donovan and Mike Nesmith, during the recording of 'A Day in the Life', on Friday 10 February, an event which was filmed by Tony Bramwell.

On Sunday 25 June 1967 she was also one of the several Beatles buddies sitting cross-legged on the floor of the studio during the broadcast of 'All You Need is Love' for the *Our World* international television spectacular.

She also travelled with the Beatles and their entourage to Bangor for a seminar with the Maharishi Mahesh Yogi.

Marianne later became dependent on drugs, her relationship with Jagger floundered and she ended up a registered heroin addict, living in a squat.

She conquered her addiction and received critical acclaim for albums such as *Broken English*, released in 1979. Other albums have included *Strange Weather* (1987), *Rich Kid's Blues* (1988) and *Blazing Away* (1990). Her autobiography, *Faithfull*, was published in 1994.

FALLON, John Canadian-born booking agent, based in London, who booked the Beatles several times during 1963. He was also a session musician and played on Ringo Starr's 'Don't Pass Me By'.

FARON'S FLAMINGOS A group who, at one stage in their career, had the potential to become major stars.

Nicky Crouch (guitar/vocals), Trevor Morais (drums), Billy Jones (guitar/vocals) and Eric London (bass) comprised the group the Ravens, who formed in 1959.

Singer Faron, real name William Russley, originally led Faron & the Tempest Tornadoes in 1960 and the group appeared on a number of bills with the Beatles, including Aintree Institute on Saturday 7 January, Hambleton Hall on Wednesday 25 January and the 'Rock Around the Clock' all-night session at the Liverpool Jazz Society on 11 March, all in 1961. In the meantime, the Ravens had changed their name to Robin & the Ravens, with the addition of singer Mike McPhillips (Robin). Faron then replaced him as lead singer with the group in September 1961 and the group changed its name to Faron & the Crossfires, which became known as Faron & the Burnettes and then, at the suggestion of local compère Bob Wooler, Faron & the Flamingos.

Bob also dubbed Faron 'the panda-footed prince of prance', because of his dynamism as a performer.

When they decided to turn professional, in January 1962, Eric London left to form Group One and was replaced by Mushy Cooper, a former member of the Undertakers. When they appeared on their first tour of US bases in France that year, they were accompanied by singer Pam Connelly. For their second tour they were accompanied by Barbara Harrison and Paddy Chambers also joined the band.

Their most exciting line-up in 1963 had Faron on vocals and bass guitar, with Chambers, Crouch and Morais. They were a formidable quartet and became one of the most popular of the Liverpool bands.

During their shows a highlight was their arrangement of the Contours 'Do You Love Me?' Like several local bands, they included what became known as the 'Mersey-Motown Sound', an adaptation of Motown music performed in the Liverpool group style. The Contours, for instance, were purely a vocal group. The Flamingos changed the number into an exciting piece of rock 'n' roll.

When they recorded it, their record company, Oriole, considered it to be a stunning record debut and a possible chart-topper. Unfortunately, being a small label without the necessary funds to promote in a big way, they relied on Don Agnes of Leeds Music to plug the group on the radio. Agnes would do this only if another track, 'See If She Cares', which Leeds published, was issued as the A-side. This decision robbed Faron's Flamingos of fame.

Brian Poole & the Tremeloes heard Faron's Flamingos perform the number on stage and rushed out their version of the song, which reached No. 1 and established them as a major group. It also became the first hit for the Dave Clark Five. With two versions in the Top 10 both almost identical to Faron's arrangement, there is no doubt that the decision to issue it as a B-side killed the group's chances.

Disillusioned and frustrated, they disbanded at the end of the year. Trevor was to join the Peddlers, Nicky joined the Mojos and Faron and Chambers became members of the Big Three.

While they were together, Faron's Flamingos appeared on several bills with the Beatles, including a show at the Cavern on Friday 12 March 1963.

FARRELL, Bernadette A blonde hairdresser's apprentice from Liverpool who was George Harrison's girlfriend at the time of their special Cavern 'Fan Club Night'. Bernadette was officially member No. 596. Later she was Paul McCartney's girlfriend for a brief period.

One of the Beatles' earliest local fans, she was featured in 'The Face of Beauty' column in *Mersey Beat*.

Bernadette became one of Liverpool's first official Beatles guides and was to marry Mike Burns, a local musician and compere. Together with Mike, she made great sacrifices to open 'The Beatles Story' museum in the basement of the Britannia Pavilion at the Albert Dock, Liverpool, in April 1990.

FARROW, Mia American screen actress, born in 1945, who first came to prominence in the TV series *Peyton Place*. She was married to Frank Sinatra between 1966 and 1968.

According to Mia, when she lived with Sinatra in their Bel Air home, they would listen to music and their favourites were the Beatles.

She was interested in Eastern philosophy, which she described as 'a mathematical formula for mind expansion. They've always said the kingdom of heaven is within – the trick is how you get there.'

Both Mia and her sister Prudence were close friends of the Beatles, whom they had met in London prior to the filming of *Rosemary's Baby*. They weren't overawed by the Beatles, which was something John, Paul, George and Ringo appreciated. One of Mia's friends was to comment: 'Sure the Beatles were the biggest thing around, but after all, Mia had been Mrs Frank Sinatra, which put her almost on the same footing.'

It was due to the Beatles that Prudence tried out Transcendental Meditation and she in turn interested Mia in the teachings of the Maharishi. When they heard that the guru was to speak to a group of Harvard law students, Mia and Prudence flew to Boston to hear him in January 1968. They then decided to spend three months at his ashram in Rishikesh, India, to study with him personally.

There was huge press interest in her spiritual odyssey and on arriving in India she said: 'Life is important, love is important. Giving is important. Here are people who are like children, brought up with no false standards.'

The sisters had been at Rishikesh for a month when they heard that the Beatles were to arrive. Mia was disturbed because she knew that they would be accompanied by reporters and photographers, she said: 'I got into a panic. I had nightmares of armies of press invading. The press was already here in droves, in the trees, everywhere. It was bad enough when I was here by myself.' She decided to leave the ashram and embarked on a three-week trip across India.

Many Beatles scribes have inaccurately written that John and George decided to part company with the Maharishi because he had made sexual advances to Mia. This is untrue. It was a member of the Beatles' entourage, Alexis Mardas, who reported to them that there had been sexual impropriety between the Maharishi and a young girl meditator from California, and this was what led them to confront their guru and leave the ashram.

FARROW, Prudence   Actress Maureen O'Sullivan and film director John Farrow had seven children: Michael, Patrick, Mia, John, Prudence, Stephanie and Tisa.

During the 1960s Prudence was in London with her older sister, Mia. The two became close friends of the Beatles, who they met in London shortly before Mia starred in *Rosemary's Baby*.

The Beatles introduced Prudence to the teachings of the Maharishi Mahesh Yogi and she in turn interested her sister in the guru. Both sisters flew to Boston in January 1968 to hear the Maharishi and Mia was so taken by what he said that she decided to go with Prudence to Rishikesh in India for three months to stay at the Maharishi's ashram to study with him.

The sensitive Prudence took an almost obsessive interest in Transcendental Meditation, to the extent that her periods of meditation became excessive. She would go into her quarters, in the same building as the Beatles, and enter deep meditation for so long that her sister, her friends and even the Maharishi began to worry.

She involved herself in deep meditation against the Maharishi's advice and retired to her room for three weeks. Her skin turned white, friends were concerned about her sanity and the Maharishi hired a full-time nurse to look after her.

John remarked that she'd gone barmy and was trying to reach God quicker than anyone else, but he was, like the others, concerned about her.

The Maharishi placed her in an after-lecture discussion group with John and George and she eventually adjusted.

She'd been unaware that John had used the situation to compose a song called 'Dear Prudence', and it was George who mentioned it to her at the end of the course.

On his demo of the number, John is heard commenting, 'No one was to know that sooner or later she was to go completely berserk, under the care of Maharishi Mahesh Yogi. All the people around were very worried about the girl because she was going insane. So, we sang to her.'

She first heard the song when *The Beatles* double album was re-leased.

Prudence and her husband live in Florida, where she teaches medi-tation.

FASCHER, Horst Former featherweight boxer, born in Hamburg on 5 February 1936, who was a bouncer on the door of the Kaiserkeller club when the Beatles made their first appearance there in 1960. He then moved to the Top Ten Club at the invitation of Peter Eckhorn, before being head-hunted by the Star Club, where he later began managing the venue on behalf of Manfred Weissleder.

Horst had a fearsome reputation because he had served a prison term for manslaughter following a street fight in which he'd accidentally killed a sailor.

He became a good friend of the Beatles, although observers say there was an initial tension. It was alleged that, when George Harrison made a remark about him being a Nazi, Horst punched him. When John Lennon made a similar remark, he took him into the gents' toilet and urinated over him. Horst particularly objected to such comments as his family had hidden a Jewish family from the Nazis during the Second World War.

When Adrian Barber recorded the Beatles during their December 1962 appearances at the Star Club, Horst could be heard singing on two of the tracks, 'Be-Bop-a-Lula' and 'Hallelujah, I Love Her So', although he is credited as Herr Obber – German for 'waiter', – as the sleeve-note writers were unsure of who was on the tracks. This recording took place at a Star Club party when various people were invited on stage to do a turn.

Horst was to marry Ali, the daughter of Faron, leader of Faron's Flamingos, and the couple had a child, Rory. The marriage didn't last and, sadly, the baby died in an accident in Hamburg caused by a faulty cot.

Horst and his next partner had a baby girl who suffered from a rare heart problem. Paul McCartney generously came to his aid by hiring a team of specialists to fly over from New York and operate at Great Ormond Street Hospital, London. Paul also arranged for Horst and his partner to fly to London and stay while the operation took place. Un-fortunately, the baby couldn't be saved and Horst was plunged into depression, having seen both his children die within a year of each other.

Since the 1960s, Horst has reopened a venue called the Star Club on several occasions in different parts of Hamburg and did so once again in 1994. When he opened a Star Club in the Grossnerumark district on 15 December 1978, headlined by Tony Sheridan, both Ringo Starr and George Harrison were present for the first night.

FAWCETT, Anthony Art critic who was to become a personal assistant to John and Yoko. He then penned a book of his experiences with them called *One Day at a Time.*

FELIX, Julie American folk-singer based in Britain during the 1960s. She appeared regularly on television on *The David Frost Show*. Paul arranged for a mutual friend to phone her on his behalf and fix up a date. They went out together for a time, but the affair was relatively unpublicized.

FELL, Ray Liverpool comedian who co-compèred the Beatles' second 'Christmas Show' at the Hammersmith Odeon in west London.

FENTON, Shane Singer who led a group called the Fentones. Born Bernard Jewry, he was later to change his name to Alvin Stardust and enjoyed success on record in the 1970s. He appeared with the Beatles at the Albert Hall on 18 April 1963 and also at the Empire Theatre, Liverpool. Following his Empire appearance, Epstein chatted with him backstage and offered him 'Do You Want to Know a Secret?' if he would let Brian become his manager. Fenton turned him down as he already had a manager. Fenton married Iris Caldwell, Rory Storm's sister, and had 13 chart hits between 1973 and 1985. After his divorce from Iris, he married actress Liza Goddard, but that marriage also ended in divorce.

FIELD, Alan British comedian who was booked to compère the Beatles' tour of Australia. He caused controversy as his material was considered to be of 'too adult a nature' for the young audiences.

FINLEY, Charles O. President of the Kansas City Athletics baseball team who discovered that the Beatles were not scheduled to appear in Kansas City during their first American tour. He approached Brian Epstein and offered $50,000 for them to appear at the Municipal Stadium. He was turned down and his offer of $100,000 was also refused. When he upped the offer to $150,000, a world record fee for an artist, Epstein decided to accept for the prestige such an offer would bring. The reverse side of each ticket had a photo of Finley in a Beatles wig and the slogan 'Yeah! Yeah! Yeah! Today's Beatles Fans are Tomorrow's Baseball Fans'. The concert took place on Thursday 17 September 1964 and although he lost money on the deal he gained a massive amount of publicity.

FLINTSTONES, The Mersey band who were originally known as the Pegasus Four. Their gimmick was to wear furry waistcoats. For a time they had a female vocalist and were also known as Ogi & the Flintstones.

The group appeared with the Beatles at the Cavern on Friday 12 March 1963.

FONDA, Peter Actor brother of Jane and star of the movie *Easy Rider*. At a party attended by the Beatles in Hollywood he kept saying to John, 'I know what it's like to be dead,' which inspired John to write 'She Said, She Said'.

FONTAINE, Dick The first television director to film the Beatles. The event occurred on 22 August 1962 during a Cavern lunchtime session. They performed two numbers, but the film wasn't considered suitable for the programme *Know the North*, due to technical difficulties in the club. Film of one the numbers, 'Some Other Guy', survived.

FOOL, The Design group who became involved with Apple Corps for a time.

Josie Leeger, Marijke Koger and Simon Postuma ran a boutique in Amsterdam called the Trend before moving to London in 1966. They were joined by Barry Finch and Simon Hayes.

The Fool were commissioned by Brian Epstein to undertake design work for the Saville Theatre and then began to design clothes for the Beatles and their wives. In addition, they painted George's fireplace, his Mini and his guitar and John's Rolls-Royce, piano and caravan.

At one time they prepared a design for the *Sgt Pepper* album, but it was discarded after Robert Fraser was appointed consultant.

The Fool convinced the Beatles that they should have a boutique selling fashions they designed and the Apple Boutique in Baker Street was opened on 7 December 1967, sporting a huge psychedelic design on its exterior walls. This raised such a cry of outrage from nearby traders that it had to be painted over with whitewash.

The venture lost an incredible amount of money and was abandoned. The group then moved to America and made their debut album, *The Fool*, for Mercury.

Barry and Josie married, settled in Holland and had six children. They continued to design fashions until Josie's death in July 1991. Simon and Marijke recorded some singles under the name Seemon and Marijke, but split up in 1975.

FORD, Clinton Popular jazz singer from the north-west of England who appeared regularly on Merseyside. His first chart hit was 'Old Shep' in 1959, followed by 'Too Many Beautiful Girls' in 1961, 'Fanlight Fanny' in 1962 and 'Run to the Door' in 1967. He appeared at the Cavern with the Beatles on 9 September 1962.

FORD, Emile Singer, born Emile Sweetman in Nassau on 16 October 1937. Ford arrived in London at the age of 17 and formed his group the Checkmates in 1959. He topped the charts that year with 'What Do You Want to Make Those Eyes at Me For?' and followed up with 'Slow Boat to China'. After several other hits, his final chart entry was 'I Wonder Who's Kissing Her Now' in 1962.

He met the Beatles on 24 November 1961. Ford dropped in at the Tower Ballroom, New Brighton, and took the stage to sing with Rory Storm & the Hurricanes, whose drummer at the time was Ringo Starr.

Mersey Beat arranged for him to be photographed by Dick Matthews backstage with the Beatles and published the picture on their front cover.

On 6 April 1962 Sam Leach booked Emile Ford and the Checkmates to top the bill of a Tower Ballroom, New Brighton, 'A Night to Remember' concert with the Beatles (advertised as 'The Beetles' on posters for the event). Also on the bill were Gerry & the Pacemakers, Howie Casey & the Seniors, Rory Storm & the Hurricanes, the Big Three and the Original Kingtwisters.

From 1962 Ford began producing records by other artists, moved to Sweden for ten years, then returned to Britain to set up a company, EFOS (Emile Ford Objective Sound Monitoring System). In 1993 he won the Black Music Industry Association's Award for Businessman of the Year.

FORSHAW, Dave Teenage Merseyside promoter who was impressed with the Beatles' performance at Litherland Town Hall on 22 December 1960 and rushed backstage to book them for three appearances at St John's Hall, Bootle, beginning on 6 January 1961. Dave was later to manage a stable of lesser-known local bands.

FOURMOST, The Formed in 1959 as the Four Jays. They comprised Joey Bower (vocals/rhythm), Billy Hatton (vocals/bass), Brian (Owie) O'Hara (lead) and Brian Redman (drums). The group had a rock/jazz/comedy act, but each member was pursuing a career and initially decided to remain semi-pro. Joey turned down an offer to join Jan Ralfini's Band at the Locarno, Billy turned down the opportunity of backing his former schoolmate Billy Fury, Owie refused the offer of joining a television group and Brian a position with the Nat Allen Band.

As the Four Jays, their Cavern appearances with the Beatles in 1961 took place on Wednesday 26 July, Wednesday 18 October, Wednesday 15 November and Wednesday 13 December. Appearances in 1962 were on Wednesday 24 January, Thursday 5 April, Saturday 9 June, Sunday 15 July and Wednesday 10 October. They also appeared as special guests on a 'Beatles Fan Club Night' on Thursday 5 April 1962 and on a bill with the Beatles at the Tower Ballroom on Thursday 21 June 1962.

The group then changed their name to the Four Mosts after discovering that a southern group called the Four Jays was managed by London impresario Lou Praeger. Under their new name they appeared with the Beatles in 1962 on Sunday 21 October, Sunday 25 November, Sunday 9 December, Wednesday 12 December and Sunday 16 December. Their 1963 Cavern appearances with the Beatles as the Fourmost (their name slightly altered once again) were on Wednesday 23 January, Sunday 3 February and Friday 12 April.

By the time Epstein signed them on 30 June 1963, their line-up had changed to Mike Millward, Billy Hatton, Brian O'Hara and Dave Lovelady.

According to Dave, they were the second group that Brian approached and asked to turn professional. They turned him down, preferring to remain semi-pro. He made them a management offer three times and it was only after Gerry & the Pacemakers and Billy J. Kramer had their initial chart hits that they decided to sign up with NEMS.

The quartet appeared in many other Merseyside gigs with the Beatles. As the Four Jays they were billed on the 'Operation Big Beat 3' at the Tower Ballroom on Friday 29 June 1962 and the Little Richard/Beatles Tower concert on Friday October 12 1962.

Following his usual practice, Epstein placed them with George Martin, but they found they had no original material strong enough for them to record. Owie asked John Lennon if he had a number he could give him and John told him he had one which he'd written while sitting on the toilet. When they appeared with the Beatles at the Queen's Theatre, Blackpool, on 4 August 1963 John told them that the number they could have was called 'Hello Little Girl', which he'd penned in his teens and had included in the group's repertoire since 1958. The Beatles had also recorded it at their Decca and Parlophone recording auditions.

John was to say: 'This was one of the first songs I ever finished. I was then about 18 and we gave it to the Fourmost. I think it was the first song of my own that I ever attempted to do with the group.'

He also commented that it was loosely based on a couple of old standards which his mother used to sing to him when he was a small child and was an attempt to capture the mood of those songs written in the 1930s.

Billy Hatton told *Mersey Beat*:

We arranged to go to John Lennon's house, and they gave us a copy of the words. We hadn't heard the number before, and George and John gave us a rough idea of it by taping the tune. We received the tape at 4 o'clock on Monday morning.

As we had to record on the following Wednesday, we had two days in which to make an arrangement good enough to put on disc. As a matter of fact, when we were recording, we were just learning the song as we went along and were tremendously encouraged by A&R man George Martin.

'Hello Little Girl' reached No. 9 in the British charts. Their next release was unusual in that it was a Lennon and McCartney number which the Beatles hadn't used on an album and was written specifically for the Fourmost. A romantic number called 'I'm in Love', it reached No. 17 in the British charts.

They appeared in 'The Beatles Christmas Show' at the Finsbury Park Astoria in north London in December 1962, during which they performed 'Hello Little Girl'.

The group were arguably the very first Beat group to perform impressions. Dave Lovelady was to comment: 'We did them long before the Barron Knights and the Rockin' Berries.'

The Finsbury Park audience were given an opportunity to see this side of the Fourmost as Brian O' Hara sang 'White Christmas', during which he did impressions of Elvis Presley, Gracie Fields, Adam Faith, Dean Martin – and the Beatles. They issued an EP called 'The Fourmost

Sound' and appeared in the film *Ferry 'Cross the Mersey*, with their NEMS stablemates Gerry & the Pacemakers and Cilla Black.

Their biggest hit, 'A Little Loving', which reached No. 6 in the charts, wasn't by Lennon and McCartney. The Fourmost had gone to see Dick James to ask him if he had a number to record and he played them several tracks which didn't excite them. Then James remembered a song which had come in that morning's post. He played them the demo of 'A Little Loving', written by Juliet Mills's husband, Russell Alquist, and, although Owie hated it, the others liked the number enough to vote it in as their next single.

They had three remaining hits in their career, 'How Can I Tell Her?', 'Baby I Need Your Lovin'' and 'Girls Girls Girls', but they were never to have a hit in America.

From 13 May 1964 they were booked to appear for a four-month season at the London Palladium on a bill with Frankie Vaughan, Cilla Black and Tommy Cooper. It was so popular that the run was extended until December.

Sadly, just before the Palladium season began, Mike Millward became seriously ill with leukaemia and needed radium treatment. He had to enter Clatterbridge Hospital in the Wirral, where he died. A special show, 'A Night for Mike', was presented at Liverpool's Grafton Ballroom on Tuesday 5 April 1966.

Mike's place was filled by a number of different Liverpool musicians over a period of time, including George Peckham, Ian Edwards and Frank Bowen. Eventually, Joey Bowers, an original founder member of the band, returned to the fold.

Paul McCartney discovered a song called 'Rosetta', which he felt would be suitable for the group, and offered to produce it for them, which he did.

Dave Lovelady commented: 'Paul liked the way we could mimic instruments with our voices, our "mouth music", if you like. Brian O'Hara was a trumpet and we were the trombones. We used it on "Rosetta" and the Beatles did the same thing on "Lady Madonna". There were proper instruments on our record as well. I was playing piano at the session, but Brian O'Hara told me to play it badly. I soon found out why. Paul said, "Look, I'll do the piano bit," and so he ended up playing on our record.'

The number was released by CBS on 21 February 1969, but failed to reach the charts.

Although the band continued appearing in cabaret during the 1970s, members drifted away until the only original Fourmost left was Brian O'Hara. When he eventually left, the band continued – but without a single member of the original Fourmost.

On the other hand, three of the members – Joey Bower, Billy Hatton and Dave Lovelady – teamed up with Joey's wife to form a quartet called Clouds, which performed on a semi-pro basis in Liverpool clubs until 1993.

FRANKLAND, Rosemarie A former Miss World who appeared as a long-legged showgirl in *A Hard Day's Night*. She adds a touch of glamour to the film when she bumps into the lads in some backstage scenes.

FREDDIE & THE DREAMERS Manchester group who developed a comedy act. Originally formed as a semi-professional outfit in 1959 by leader Freddie Garrity, they turned professional in 1963.

As with other Manchester bands such as the Hollies and Herman's Hermits, they played regularly in nearby Liverpool and the group appeared with the Beatles at the Cavern on Wednesday 12 September 1962.

Apart from vocalist Garrity, the group comprised Roy Crewsdon (guitar), Derek Quinn (guitar), Peter Birrell (bass) and Bernie Dwyer (drums).

They had a string of hits, beginning with 'You Were Made for Me', and were booked to appear with the Beatles on 'Another Christmas Show' at the Hammersmith Odeon in West London December 1964.

The group also became popular in America, where Freddie's awkward-looking dance routines gave birth to 'Do the Freddie', and appeared in two movies, *Just for You* and *Cuckoo Patrol*.

At the close of the decade, the original band split up, but Garrity has re-formed it on numerous occasions, mainly for appearances on the cabaret circuit.

FREEMAN, Robert Photographer who took numerous pics of the Beatles between 1963 and 1965. He suggested a black-and-white cover for their *With the Beatles* album (*Meet the Beatles* in America), which EMI initially resisted. Freeman also designed John's two books and provided covers for the albums *A Hard Day's Night, Beatles for Sale, Help!* and *Rubber Soul,* in addition to the EP cover for 'Long Tall Sally'.

His Beatles photographs have been collected in several published works, including *Beatles Ltd, Yesterday: Photographs of the Beatles* and *The Beatles*.

FREYMAN, Dr Robert Said to be the inspiration for the song 'Dr Robert', featured on the *Revolver* album. The number was penned by John, with help from Paul on the middle section of the number.

Freymann was a 60-year-old German doctor whose surgery was on East 78th Street in New York. He had been the doctor present at the death of legendary jazzman Charlie Parker and many New York musicians used his services. John was one of a number of celebrities who obtained amphetamines from him. Prescribing amphetamines was not illegal, although Freymann was to lose his licence for six months in 1968 and was eventually struck off by the New York Medical Society for malpractice. He died in 1987.

Other sources have cited Dr Charles Roberts, who reputedly had a practice on 49th Street, also in New York, although writer Steve Turner says that Charles Roberts didn't exist, but was an alias used by biographer Jean Stein in her book on Warhol protégée Edie Sedgwick, which hid the identity of another doctor who freely prescribed amphetamines.

Commenting on the song, Paul McCartney said: 'Well, he's like a joke. There's some fellow in New York, and in the States we'd hear people say, "You can get everything off him; any pills you want." It was a big racket, but a joke too, about this fellow who cured everyone of everything with all these pills and tranquillizers, injections for this and that; he just kept New York high. That's what "Dr Robert" is all about, just a pill doctor who sees you all right.'

FROST, David Television personality who came to prominence as a member of the *That Was the Week That Was* team. He interviewed individual members of the Beatles on several occasions on his radio and television shows.

FURY, Billy Liverpool singer, born Ronald Wycherley on 17 April 1940. His parents were Albert and Jean and he also had a brother, Albert, three years younger than himself, who became a pop singer, calling himself Jason Eddie.

Prior to the Beatles, he was Liverpool's most successful pop artist.

In a small Liverpool studio in 1958 Ronnie cut several songs and sent a demo tape and picture to Larry Parnes. He then went to a Parnes Extravaganza Show at the Essoldo, Birkenhead, for a successful audition. Parnes was to rename him Billy Fury.

He became Decca's biggest-selling artist of the time, with 26 hits between 1961 and 1966. During this period he spent 268 weeks in the charts. His hits included 'Halfway to Paradise', 'Jealousy', 'I'll Never Find Another You', 'Last Night was Made for Love', 'Once Upon a Dream', 'Like I've Never Been Gone' and 'In Summer'.

Fury was reared in the same area of Liverpool as Ringo Starr, the Dingle, where he attended St Silas's junior school and Dingle Vale Secondary School, along with Ringo and Fury's best friend, Billy Hatton, who was later to become a member of the Fourmost.

On 10 May 1960, Billy and his manager, Larry Parnes, attended an audition at the Wyvern Club in Seel Street, Liverpool. Parnes had been impressed by the Liverpool bands appearing in a Gene Vincent concert and had asked one of his assistants, Mark Foster, to contact Allan Williams to arrange an audition. He wrote: 'Duffy Power will be touring Scotland from June 2nd to 11th inclusive and Johnny Gentle will be touring Scotland from June 16th to 25th. For these two periods, as agreed, we are willing to pay your groups £120, plus the fares from Liverpool.'

The letter also added: 'We will make arrangements for Mr Parnes to come and audition your groups to select the most suitable. He will also bring Billy Fury as Billy will want one of these four groups for his own personal use. Incidentally, the idea of Billy wanting a group from his own home town will provide several interesting press stories and publicity tie-ins.'

There were actually five Mersey groups at the audition: Gerry & the Pacemakers, Cass & the Cassanovas, Cliff Roberts & the Rockers, Derry & the Seniors and the Silver Beatles.

During the afternoon, Stuart Sutcliffe drew Fury's portrait and John Lennon asked for and received his autograph. Although Fury didn't get his backing group, the Silver Beatles were chosen to tour Scotland with Johnny Gentle.

Fury made his film debut in 1962 in Michael Winner's *Play It Cool* and also starred in *I've Gotta Horse* in 1965.

The singer had been plagued by ill-health since he was a child, when rheumatic fever had left him with a weak heart. Several tour appearances had to be cancelled due to his recurring heart problems and he was hospitalized on a number of occasions, which caused him to cease live performances in 1967 and spend most of his time on a farm, breeding horses.

He appeared with Ringo Starr in a cameo role as Storm Tempest in *That'll Be the Day* in 1973, performing 'Long Live Rock', a number written specially for him by Pete Townshend. As the character led a group performing in a holiday camp, it must have reminded Ringo of his days with Rory Storm at Butlin's. During the filming there was a jam session with Ringo on lead guitar, David Essex on bass, Graham Bond on drums, Harry Nilsson on tambourine and Billy Fury on vocals.

Billy's heart finally gave out on 28 January 1983, at a time when he was in the process of recording a new album and had just had a single enter the charts.

GARLAND, Judy   The legendary Hollywood star moved to Britain in the 1960s. A biography of the notorious Kray Brothers, called *Doing the Business*, related how Reg Kray took Judy Garland to the Establishment, a club in London's Soho which specialized in satire: 'They met a group of youngsters starting to make a big name for themselves in the music business. They thought it was just fabulous to meet Judy Garland and Judy was just as pleased to meet John, Paul, George and Ringo – otherwise known as the Beatles.'

Judy was, in fact, to meet the group on a number of occasions. She became a close friend of composer Lionel Bart and recorded several songs from his musical *Maggie May*, which was set in Liverpool. She accompanied Bart to the world première of the show in Manchester, where Lionel introduced her to Brian Epstein. She also attended the show's party, held in Liverpool's Blue Angel club later that evening.

Judy was the hit of 'The Night of One Hundred Stars' at the London Palladium on 23 July 1964, when she sang her most famous song, 'Over the Rainbow'. The Beatles were also on the bill that evening; they had introduced 'Over the Rainbow' into their own repertoire in 1960.

Paul McCartney spent most of the evening talking to Judy at a party held in Epstein's Knightsbridge flat on 12 August 1964. It was said that he had offered to write a song specially for her.

Brian Somerville, the Beatles' press agent, had also had Judy as a client and she was represented by the Beatles' solicitor, David Jacobs.

In October 1964, Lionel Bart and Brian Epstein announced that they would be promoting a Garland concert, but they never did.

The singer died in London in 1969.

GARNER, Frank   The Beatles' first road manager. He worked for them for a couple of months in 1961, but, as he also worked as a bouncer at the Casbah club, he couldn't continue and Neil Aspinall was brought in.

GAUL, Tom   The McCartneys' Liverpool neighbour. Gaul moved into 18 Forthlin Road two years before Jim McCartney and his two sons moved in at No. 20. He enjoyed a friendly relationship with Paul and when fans used to gather outside the front door of No. 20 he'd let Paul clamber over the backyard fence and rush out the front of his house and into a waiting car. According to Gaul, Paul told him that the essence of some of the lyrics of 'Yesterday' concerned the death of Paul's mother.

GENTLE, Johnny   Liverpool singer, real name John Askew. As an amateur, he sang under the name Ricky Damone, then wrote off to Larry Parnes in London, enclosing a photograph of himself. He visited Parnes, who arranged for him to audition for Philips Records, and his first release was the self-penned 'Wendy'.

Parnes suggested that Askew change his stage name from Ricky Damone to Tim McGee, but Askew told him that he preferred to use his real first name, Johnny, and Parnes added the Gentle because he considered the singer had a placid personality.

Along with other Parnes artists Duffy Power and Vince Eager, Gentle was booked to appear in several dancehalls in Scotland by promoter Duncan McKinnon.

On 10 May 1960 Larry Parnes auditioned several local bands in Liverpool, including Cass & the Cassanovas, Derry & the Seniors, Cliff Roberts & the Rockers and the Silver Beetles, primarily to find backing bands for the Gentle and Power Scottish tours and also a possible band for Billy Fury.

The Silver Beetles were chosen to back Gentle at a fee of £120, plus their fares from Liverpool. The group comprised John Lennon, Paul McCartney, George Harrison, Stuart Sutcliffe and Tommy Moore.

The 20-year-old Gentle, a former apprentice carpenter and merchant seaman, has been quoted as saying: 'When I first saw them I wondered what on earth Parnes had sent me.' But he was later to deny this, claiming that he immediately liked their youth and enthusiasm.

The tour began on 20 May 1960 at the Town Hall, Alloa, Clackman-nanshire, and the other gigs were on 21 May at the Northern Meeting Ballroom, Church Street, Inverness; on 23 May at the Dalrymple Hall, Fraserburgh, Aberdeenshire; on 25 May at St Thomas's Hall, Keith, Banffshire; on 26 May at the Town Hall, Forres, Morayshire; on 27 May at the Regal Ballroom, Leopold Street, Nairn, Nairnshire, and on 28 May at the Rescue Hall, Peterhead, Aberdeenshire.

The group name was never actually used in the promotion of the tour, as the billing read 'Johnny Gentle and his group'. However, three members of the band decided to use stage names. Paul used the name Paul Ramon, George adopted the name Carl Harrison and Stuart called himself Stuart de Staël. It has been suggested that John called himself Johnny Silver, but he denied this.

Johnny first met the group half an hour before they were due to go on stage together and they had time for only 20 minutes of rehearsals before their performance. Duncan McKinnon wasn't impressed with the show but Johnny explained that they needed rehearsal time together, and after practising the next day the stage show improved.

McKinnon had also complained about their stage gear, so Johnny gave George a black shirt to wear, as Paul and John were wearing black shirts and it was the nearest they got to a uniform appearance on stage.

Johnny had a room to himself and the Silver Beetles shared two rooms. Sometimes they were put in different hotels. Johnny recalled that the best hotel they stayed in together was in Inverness, overlooking the river. It was while they were at the hotel that he played a song he'd written called 'I've Just Fallen for Someone' to George and John. Gentle was having difficulty with the middle eight and John came up with something he'd written which fitted in. Johnny decided to use Lennon's middle eight in his song and he actually recorded the number for Parlophone the following year under the name Darren Young. The record sold about 3,000 copies.

Gentle was to say that, despite their rawness as a group, he was impressed with them and urged his manager to sign them up. However, Parnes specialized in representing solo singers and wasn't interested in the problems associated with managing bands.

Parnes commented: 'Johnny used to phone me virtually every night and say, "Come up to Scotland and see these boys. I've given them a spot in my act and they're doing better than I am." He was very honest. I always said that if I'd found the time to go up to Scotland he might have been the fifth Beatle. Who knows?'

Following the tour, Johnny appeared with them once more. He visited Merseyside and on 2 July dropped into the Jacaranda club with his father. He was told that the group were appearing that night at the Grosvenor Ballroom, Liscard, and went over to the gig and joined them on stage.

Gentle asked Parnes to book them again as his backing band, but they were appearing in Hamburg and Cass & the Cassanovas were hired instead.

In 1965, after he'd been performing as Darren Young, he was asked to join the Viscounts, replacing Gordon Mills, who'd left to manage Tom Jones. When the Viscounts broke up, he went to Jersey to work in hotels as a singer.

He was never to find success as an entertainer and eventually settled in Kent, where he currently has a joinery and carpentry business.

GERRY & THE PACEMAKERS   Gerry Marsden was born in Liverpool's Dingle area on 24 September 1942, the second son of Mary and Frederick Marsden.

He lived in Menzies Street, close to where Ringo Starr was brought up, and left school at 15, initially working as a coalman, then for a short spell in the Kardomah tea factory, before becoming a railway delivery boy.

After his father bought him an acoustic guitar, he decided to form a skiffle group, with his elder brother Fred on drums, Tommy Ryan and Dixie Dean on washboard, Jimmy Tobin on tea-chest bass and Marty Summers on guitar. Brian O'Hara was also to join as a guitarist. Known simply as Gerry Marsden's Skiffle Group, they made their debut at the Peel Street Labour Party Club in 1958.

Their next line-up comprised Gerry, Freddie, Jimmy Tobin on bass, Dixie Dean on washboard and Arthur MacMahon on piano.

Gerry then bought his first electric guitar, a Futurama, at Frank Hessy's for £40.

Now 16, Gerry named his group Gerry & the Mars Bars and his father, who was managing the group at the time, wrote to the confectionery company Mars for permission to use the name. They refused, so Gerry, after watching an athletics programme on TV in which the commentator mentioned a 'pacemaker', decided to call the group the Pacemakers. By this time Les Chadwick had joined as bass guitarist. The group were to have a repertoire which comprised 250 numbers, including songs such as

'What'd I say?', 'Skinny Minnie', 'I'll be There', 'Hallelujah, I Love Her So', 'You'll Never Walk Alone', 'Save the Last Dance for Me', 'Will You Still Love Me Tomorrow?' and 'Jambalaya'.

They began to build a strong following on Merseyside and were one of the groups Allan Williams initially asked to go to the Kaiserkeller club in 1960. Still a railroad worker, Gerry didn't want to give up his job at the time and turned him down.

That they were a bigger Liverpool name than the Beatles at the time is proved by the fact that Williams booked them on the Liverpool Stadium bill with Gene Vincent on Tuesday 3 May 1960. They also auditioned with the Silver Beatles for Larry Parnes at the Wyvern Club.

When Gerry was approached in 1961 to appear at Peter Eckhorn's Top Ten Club, he agreed and the group turned professional. The trip was a success and the Pacemakers returned to Hamburg on 29 July 1961, enjoying a three-month season at the Top Ten, also taking local singer Faron with them as a second vocalist.

Merseyside disc jockey Bob Wooler featured a list of his personal Top 10 local bands in *Mersey Beat*, with the Beatles in the No. 1 position and Gerry & the Pacemakers at No. 2. When the official *Mersey Beat* poll was published in January, 1962, the Beatles and Gerry were voted into the first and second positions respectively by the readers.

Having already signed up the No.1 group in the poll, Brian Epstein decided to sign up Liverpool's No. 2 band, and he took over the management of Gerry & the Pacemakers in May 1962.

He immediately arranged for the Beatles' recording manager George Martin to see them perform in Liverpool, and had them learn 'How Do You Do it', a number penned by Mitch Murray which the Beatles had originally been given to record as their second release.

Murray had written it with Adam Faith in mind and was initially unhappy when Dick James recommended it to George Martin for the Beatles. The Beatles didn't like the number and deliberately recorded a lacklustre version. As James was still convinced it would be a hit, he suggested it for Gerry and Ron Richards, Martin's assistant, recorded the Pacemakers version – which topped the charts.

Steve Day remembers being present at NEMS in Liverpool with Gerry when John and Paul arrived to meet Epstein and Gerry said to them: 'How does it feel to be Brian Epstein's No. 2 group?'

Gerry's second single, another Mitch Murray composition, 'I Like It', also topped the British charts. Murray offered them a third number, 'You Can't Fool Me', but Gerry decided to record 'You'll Never Walk Alone' instead, giving him a hat trick of No. 1s, the first artist in British recording history to achieve such a feat (it placed Gerry & the Pacemakers in *The Guinness Book of Records*). No one has bettered this feat, although it was equalled by another Liverpool band, Frankie Goes to Hollywood, exactly 20 years later, with, ironically, Gerry's 'Ferry 'Cross the Mersey' featured on the flipside of one of the No. 1 hits, 'Relax'.

Hits in 1964 were 'I'm the One', 'Don't Let the Sun Catch You Crying',

'It's Gonna be All Right' and 'Ferry 'Cross the Mersey'. His two final hits were in 1965, 'I'll be There' and 'Walk Hand in Hand'.

Brian tried to steer Gerry & the Pacemakers down the same path as the Beatles – smart stage suits by Dougie Millins, photos by Dezo Hoffman, a Gerry & the Pacemakers Christmas Show, a film, *'Ferry 'Cross the Mersey'*, a magazine and an American tour, with an *Ed Sullivan Show* appearance in May 1964.

But Gerry & the Pacemakers weren't the Beatles. Gerry had already tackled Epstein on the fact that he was taking on too many artists and, since he wouldn't delegate, this had a bad effect on the artists. As the world's No. 1 sensation, the Beatles needed a great deal of attention and as a result the other acts suffered.

Gerry eventually became an all-round entertainer, appearing in pantomimes and children's television shows. His 'You'll Never Walk Alone' was adopted by Liverpool FC supporters and became a football anthem throughout Britain. Following the Bradford City Football Club disaster in May 1985 in which 55 people were killed when a fire destroyed a stand, Gerry recorded the number again as a charity disc to raise funds for the relatives of the victims. Under the name the Crowd, he enrolled 50 artists to join him on the record. They included Paul McCartney, Zak Starkey, Jim Fagin, Rolf Harris and Kenny Lynch. The number reached No. 1 in the charts in June 1985. This provided Gerry with another unbeaten record – the first time an artist had topped the charts with two different versions of the same number.

After some time appearing on the cabaret circuit he re-formed Gerry & the Pacemakers with different personnel and continues to tour. He issued his own tribute to the Beatles in 1985, the album *The Lennon/McCartney Songbook*, with his own interpretations of Beatles classics. Paul McCartney provided the sleeve notes and wrote: 'In Liverpool his group was probably the biggest competition to the Beatles and I remember all too well sweating the outcome of our local newspaper popularity poll, hoping that we could scrape together the necessary points to beat their band. That's how close it was.'

Gerry's autobiography, *I'll Never Walk Alone*, written in collaboration with Ray Coleman, was published in 1993. It formed the basis of *Ferry 'Cross the Mersey: The Liverpool Musical*, which opened at the Liverpool Playhouse in February, 1996.

Gerry & the Pacemakers appeared on dozens of bills with the Beatles. Tower Ballroom gigs with the two bands performing included Friday 10 November, Friday 24 November and Friday 8 December 1961; Friday 6 April 1962; and Friday 14 June 1963. They appeared with the Beatles at the Grosvenor Ballroom on Monday 6 June 1960 and at the Liverpool Jazz Society on Wednesday 15 March 1961. The two bands were also among the many local groups appearing on the 'Rock Around the Clock' all-nighter at the Liverpool Jazz Society on Saturday 11 March 1961. They appeared with them at Litherland Town Hall on Thursday 21 September 1961 and the following month, on 19 October, they teamed up at the same venue as the Beatmakers. Another of their many Liverpool gigs together took place at the Riverpark Ballroom on Thursday 30 May 1962.

When Brian Epstein asked me for permission to use my copyright name for a series of '*Mersey Beat* showcases', the Beatles and Gerry appeared on several of them together, beginning on 7 March 1963.

Their Cavern appearances with the Beatles in 1961 were on Tuesday 25 July, Wednesday 27 September, Saturday 21 October, Wednesday 25 October, Wednesday 1 November, Tuesday 14 November, Wednesday 22 November, Friday 1 December, Wednesday 13 December, Saturday 23 December and Wednesday 27 December. The 1962 dates were Wednesday 24 January, Saturday 3 February, Wednesday 7 February, Friday 9 February, Saturday 24 February, Wednesday 28 February, Tuesday 6 March, Wednesday 14 March, Thursday 22 March, Wednesday 28 March, Wednesday 1 August, Wednesday 22 August, Sunday 16 September, Wednesday 5 December and Sunday 16 December. Their only Cavern appearance with the Beatles in 1963 was on Friday 11 January. The group also toured with the Beatles and Roy Orbison in May and June 1963.

GIBBS, Russ Disc jockey and programme controller with the Detroit radio station WKNR who, on 12 October 1969, reported that Paul McCartney had been dead since 1966, when he was killed in a road accident, and had been replaced by a lookalike. He'd received information by telephone from a listener who told him that the Beatles had been hinting to the world what had happened via clues on their album covers and in the lyrics of their songs. Gibbs began to be inundated with thousands of calls and the 'Paul is Dead' rumours swept America like an epidemic. Gibbs pointed out that one of the clues had been on the *Magical Mystery Tour* US album sleeve. The stars which composed the word 'Beatles' became a telephone number when studied upside-down, he said. He presumed that the number, 537 1438, was in London and called up. The phone was answered by a journalist who didn't know what Gibbs was talking about. When Gibbs tried the number the following week, it had been discontinued.

GIBSON, Wayne Minor British singer who was in Hamburg in 1961 at the same time as the Beatles. Paul offered him original Beatles material to record, but Gibson turned him down. He was later to record some cover versions of their songs.

GOLDMANN, Peter Swedish director who was engaged to work on the promotional videos for 'Strawberry Fields Forever' and 'Penny Lane' in February 1967. He was to comment: 'I found that Ringo was very well informed on camera and photographic techniques, and Paul was a most entertaining conversationalist. But the group had all informed me that I was the director and so I must direct.'

GOOD, Jack A London-born impresario who originally devised one of Britain's first TV rock shows, *The 6.5 Special*. His other shows included *Oh Boy!*, *Boy Meets Girl* and *Wham!* before he moved to America in 1962. He returned to England specially to produce the 1964 show *Around the Beatles* and a British edition of his American show *Shindig*, in which the Beatles starred.

GRADE, Sir Lew Along with his brothers Leslie Grade and Bernard Delfont, Sir Lew ran a show-business empire in Britain in the 1960s. As the head of ATV, he took control of Northern Songs, which owned the copyright of most of the Beatles songs. Paul appeared for him in the TV special *James Paul McCartney* and John appeared on the TV tribute *Salute to Sir Lew Grade*.

GRANT, Erkey Comedian booked to appear on the Beatles tour with Roy Orbison in May 1963.

GRANT, Julie Pretty dark-haired British singer, managed by Eric Easton, co-manager of the Rolling Stones. Her hits between 1962 and 1964 were 'Up on the Roof', 'Count on Me' and 'Come to Me'. She appeared in a gig with the Beatles in 1962.

GRAVES, Elsie Ringo's mother, born Elsie Gleave. While working in a bakery, she met fellow worker Richard Starkey and they were married in 1936. The couple moved to a tiny terraced house at 10 Admiral Grove, where their only son, Richard, was born in 1940. Elsie was 28 at the time. Three years later her husband had left the marital home and she moved into premises at 9 Madryn Street, where the rent was cheaper.

She became a barmaid and was to meet Harry Graves, whom she married on 17 April 1953.

When her son became famous as Ringo Starr, he arranged for his mother and stepfather to retire and move into a bungalow in Gateacre Park in 1966.

GRAVES, Harry A Romford-born painter and decorator who moved to Liverpool to work for Liverpool Corporation. He was introduced to Elsie Starkey by mutual friends, the Maguires, and married her on 17 April 1953, with the approval of her son, Ritchie, who called him his new 'step-ladder'.

The 13-year-old Ritchie liked Harry, who, as stepfather, took an interest in the boy. He persuaded the engineering firm Henry Hunt & Sons to engage Ritchie as a trainee joiner.

During a visit to Romford, he bought his stepson a drum kit for slightly under £10 and lugged it to Liverpool by train.

When Ritchie, now known as Ringo Starr, wanted to continue playing with groups in Liverpool, Elsie and Harry attempted to persuade him to remain at Hunts, without success.

Once Ringo had become wealthy, he bought Elsie and Harry a bungalow in the Gateacre Park area of Liverpool.

Harry died on 27 August 1994 at the age of 87 and was buried at Huyton Cemetery, Liverpool, on 1 September. Ringo was at the funeral.

GRETTY, Jim A local entertainer on Liverpool's clubland circuit since the 1930s who also worked as a demonstrator at Frank Hessy's music store. He suggested to Hessy that a good way of selling guitars would be for him to give free lessons to anyone who bought a guitar, so Hessy rented another shop and each Monday Jim would spend an hour and a half teaching a group of 30 to 40 youngsters.

It was Jim who sold a guitar to Mimi Smith when she dropped in one day in 1957 with her nephew, John Lennon.

The rotund chief salesman built a 'Wall of Fame' at the store's Stanley Street branch, with photographs of scores of local bands stretching along the showroom wall.

Jim was also well known locally as a country music singer-guitarist. He performed regularly on the clubland circuit and acted as a variety agent, occasionally booking artists for various clubland events.

He organized a number of charity events and booked the Beatles to appear on a variety bill at the Albany Theatre, Maghull, on 15 October 1961.

Sadly, he died in 1992.

GRIFFITHS, Eric A neighbour of John Lennon who was invited to become the original lead guitarist with the Quarry Men. He was eventually forced out of the group after Paul McCartney joined. Eric was a member of the skiffle group from March 1957 until mid-1958.

GROUP ONE A Mersey band who appeared with the Beatles at Cavern gigs and also on the television programme *The Mersey Sound*. Ex-members of several different bands got together to form Group One and they made their debut at the Cavern on 1 May 1962. They were Eric London, ex-Faron & the Flamingos (bass), Dave Williams, ex-Jaywalkers (lead), Keith Stokes (vocals) and Harry Prytherch, ex-Remo Four (drums).

Their Cavern gigs with the Beatles in 1962 were on Friday 15 June; Wednesday 14 July, Wednesday 12 September, Saturday 13 October and Wednesday 17 October. During 1963 they appeared with the Beatles at the Cavern on Friday 12 March.

GRUENBERG, Erich Leader of the orchestra of 41 male musicians on the 'Day in the Life' track on the *Sgt Pepper* album. Gruenberg, who had attended the Guildhall School of Music at the same time as George Martin, was one of

Europe's foremost violinists and was previously leader of the London Symphony Orchestra and the Royal Philharmonic.

Recording manager George Martin realized that when they recorded the track Gruenberg had a giant monkey's paw on his bow hand and was wearing coloured-paper spectacles, novelties which the Beatles had been handing out to the musicians.

The Beatles sent Gruenberg a copy of the album, which he still has in his possession.

He also led the musicians on 'She's Leaving Home' and was leader of eight violinists who performed on 'Within You, Without You'.

GUNTHER, Carl   American photographer who travelled with the Beatles on their American tour in 1964. His pictures appeared in several prominent magazines and in the book *Beatles '64: A Hard Day's Night in America*, published in 1989.

He died in 1991.

GUSTAFSON, Johnny   His first group was Cass & the Cassanovas, founded by Brian Casser in December 1959. With Cass on rhythm/vocals, Johnny on bass, Johnny Hutchinson on drums/vocals and Adrian Barber on lead, they became one of Liverpool's top bands.

Despite this, Johnny says that they became disenchanted with Cass: 'So we hatched this plot to disband and re-form without him. Later he went to London and became Casey Jones.'

The group toured as a backing band to some of Larry Parnes's artists, such as Johnny Gentle and Duffy Power, before becoming the Big Three in January 1961.

While at the Star Club, Hamburg, in July 1962, Adrian left the band and was replaced by Brian Griffiths, primarily because they were considering an offer from Brian Epstein. From August to November 1962 they were managed by Epstein, who attempted to steer them in a purely pop direction, which didn't suit their music or their temperaments.

Gus and Griff felt that there were some financial improprieties taking place and left to form the Seniors, with drummer Ian Broad, in November 1963. Four months later, Johnny received an offer to join the Merseybeats. Since Brian and Ian were financially compensated for the transfer, he agreed, although he was to comment; 'I didn't like the watery style of the Merseybeats at all – but money flashed before my eyes!'

Ian went on to join Heinz, and Griff became a member of the Griff Parry Five.

Johnny was with the band from February until December 1964, but was fired after inquiring into the group's finances.

From January until September 1965 he teamed up with Griff again in the Johnny Gus Set; along with Ron Parry on drums and Vinnie Parker on keyboards.

Johnny then joined various other bands, including the Quotations, Quatermass, Hard Stuff and Bullet, and during the 1970s became a popular session musician, also touring with bands such as Roxy Music, in addition to writing a hit for Status Quo in 1982, 'Dear John'.

He did team up again with Griff and Elton John's drummer Nigel Olsson in 1973 to record an album, *Resurrection*, for Polydor as the Big Three.

HAGUE, Jonathan Classmate of John Lennon at Liverpool College of Art. John and Paul sponsored an exhibition of his work at the Royal Institute Gallery in London in 1968 and John bought him a house in Leamington Spa.

HAIGH, Kenneth Established British actor who appeared as an advertising executive in *A Hard Day's Night*. It was rumoured that he wanted his name kept from the credits and initially didn't mention his appearance in the film when seeking other roles. He also starred as the male lead in the Alun Owen/Lionel Bart musical *Maggie May*, which was set in Liverpool.

HALSALL, Peter John 'Ollie' Actor/musician who portrayed the fifth Beatle, Leppo, in the Rutles lampoon 'All You Need is Cash'. Ollie worked with Mike McCartney in the 1970s and died of a heart attack in Madrid on 29 May 1992.

HAMILTON, David Disc jockey who introduced the Beatles on *ABC at Large* in 1963. He also compèred a Beatles show at Urmston on 5 August of that year and in the 1980s was to introduce a 'Beatles Break' into his show for Capital Radio.

HAMILTON, Richard Prominent artist brought in by Robert Fraser to design the Beatles follow-up to *Sgt Pepper*. He suggested that *The Beatles* double-album should have a plain white sleeve, individually numbered to give the effect of a limited edition and containing a collage of photographs. The album then became known as 'the white album'.

HAMP, Johnny A British television producer. Hamp was producer of the Granada Television early-evening show *People and Places*, which screened the Beatles television debut on 17 October 1962 with a clip of them performing at the Cavern. Their next appearance took place on 2 November, which was their first broadcast from an actual television studio. The group's third appearance on *People and Places* occurred on 17 December of that year.

Hamp continued to book them after the show had been renamed *Scene At 6.30* and they appeared on 19 August 1963. He was later to comment: 'I first saw the Beatles in a club in Hamburg. They were very scruffy characters but they had a beat in their music which I liked.'

Henry Henriod has a slightly different recollection. He worked for Don Arden at the time and remembers that Brian Epstein asked him if Don could get the Beatles on an Everly Brothers tour in exchange for a share in the group. Arden decided to ask Johnny Hamp's opinion. Johnny, who was booking acts into the Granada cinema chain at the time, was in Hamburg and saw the Beatles. He told Arden: 'If I booked that bunch of scruffy bastards, Sid Bernstein would sack me.'

When he was appointed Head of Light Entertainment at Granada,

Johnny decided to pay tribute to the songwriting talents of John and Paul. After discussions with the group, he decided to make *The Music Of Lennon & McCartney*, a major music spectacular. Produced by Johnny and directed by Phil Casson, the 50-minute programme was filmed over a two-day period in one of the station's largest studios (Studio 6) on specially constructed sets. The completed show was fully networked at 9.40 p.m. on Friday 17 December 1965.

In 1982, Johnny intended to produce a Granada television show to tie in with the twentieth anniversary of the 'Love Me Do' release. However, he found such a wealth of interesting material in the archives that the programme wasn't finished until 1983. Called *The Early Beatles*, it was first broadcast at 5.40 p.m. on Sunday 1 January 1984.

Johnny commented that it would probably become the most video-pirated programme of the holiday season. He added: 'Putting together this archive material was more a labour of love than work. We decided we didn't need any commentary – the film speaks for itself.'

He later left Granada Television to become an independent producer.

HANK WALTERS & THE DUSTY ROAD RAMBLERS A Liverpool country music group comprising Hank Walters (vocal/accordion), Bob Kelly (twin-arm steel guitar), Tex Mason (rhythm/vocals), Jimmy Thomas (banjo) and Spud Ward (bass).

Jim Gretty booked them to appear on a special star matinée on Sunday 15 October 1961 at the Albany Cinema, Northway, Maghull. The Beatles were also on the bill, along with Ken Dodd and a number of variety acts.

Walters's group was one of the traditional country bands, unlike some of the other Mersey country groups who were attempting to give the music a fresh image.

Backstage, John Lennon was amused by Walters's stetson and, in his typical manner, said: 'I don't go much on your music, lad, but give us your hat.'

A furious Walters told him that he didn't think much of the Beatles music and they'd never become successful unless they started playing country music.

HANSON, Wendy Cousin of financier Lord Hanson, she was born in Huddersfield and when she was 18 moved to America, where she became secretary to conductor Leopold Stokowski and temporary secretary to President Kennedy.

She acted as temporary secretary to Brian Epstein on his first visit to America and he later hired her as his personal assistant, replacing Derek Taylor.

Wendy eventually resigned, due to Brian's moods, whims and tantrums, and took up a post with film producer David Puttnam. However, Brian enlisted her help when he sought permission to use their images from the numerous people featured on the *Sgt Pepper* sleeve.

She died on 27 January 1991, at the age of 56, after falling down the stairs at her home in Cortona, Italy.

HANTON, Colin The original drummer with the Quarry Men.

Colin, who lived in King's Drive, was two years older than the other members of the skiffle group and worked in a local factory as an apprentice upholsterer. Despite his age, he was quite small and used to carry his birth certificate around with him to prove his age. His friend Eric Griffiths immediately thought of him when the Quarry Men needed a drummer.

Colin had recently acquired a £38 Broadway drum kit from Hessy's and was invited to join the group. His father was manager of a Co-operative shop and the Quarry Men were often able to practise at his house on Saturday afternoons.

The relationship came to an end early in 1959 during an argument when the members of the group had had too much to drink, particularly Hanton, who liked Black Velvet, a mixture of Guinness and mild bitter.

George Harrison's father had booked the group for a Saturday night dance at the Picton Road Busmen's Social Club and had told them he'd arranged for the manager of a local cinema to see them perform, with a view to booking them to appear in the intervals between films. Because they'd been drinking, their performance that night was quite bad, which obviously caused the loss of the cinema bookings.

Hanton was upset and had a furious argument with the others during their bus journey home from Wavertree. He was so angry that he got off the bus with the drums before he'd even reached his own stop – and didn't see the other members of the group for many years.

In the early 1990s he got together with some former members to record a selection of their original repertoire under the name the Quarry Men and also began to appear at conventions. When the Beatles *Anthology I* was issued in November 1995, he was originally offered £500 from Apple for a one-time royalty payment for his drumming on 'In Spite of All the Danger', and finally settled for £1,500.

HARRIS, Ginny Paul's auntie, who lived in Dinas Lane, Huyton. In 1958, John, Paul and George used to rehearse in her front room. Her home was also the setting for Paul's twenty-first birthday bash.

HARRIS, Rolf Born in Perth, Australia, on 30 March 1930, the son of Welsh parents, Harris became an artist, cartoonist, sculptor, pianist and composer. Following his first British chart hit, 'Tie Me Kangaroo Down Sport', in 1960, he moved to Britain, where he had four further chart entries during the 1960s: 'Sun Arise', 'Johnny Day', 'Bluer Than Blue' and 'Two Little Boys', which topped the charts.

He was asked by the BBC to conduct an interview with the Beatles and broke the ice by saying: 'Ringo, what do you think of spaghetti?' He then appeared in 'Swinging Sound '63' with the Beatles at the Royal Albert Hall on Thursday 18 April 1963. He was also a guest of theirs when they recorded the first of their series of radio shows *From Us to You* at the Paris Studios in London on Wednesday 18 December. Rolf acted as host and was joined by the Beatles in a humorous version of 'Tie Me Kangaroo Down Sport'.

Rolf was then booked to appear on the Beatles 1963 Christmas Show at the Astoria, Finsbury Park, where he had a 15-minute spot immediately before the Beatles took the stage. He used his artistic talents to produce a cartoon souvenir of the show, which was posted to all members of the Beatles Fan Club.

In 1966 he had his own BBC TV series, *It's Rolf,* and received the MBE in 1968 and the OBE in 1977. He became almost a cult figure when he recorded Led Zeppelin's 'Stairway to Heaven', and hosted TV's top-rated *Animal Hospital* in 1995.

HARRISON, Dhani   Only child of George and Olivia Harrison. George named him Dhani because of '*dha*' and '*ni*', notes of the Indian music scale, although it is also the Sanskrit word for 'wealthy'.

Dhani was born on 1 August 1978 at Princess Christian Nursing Home in Windsor, some four weeks before his parents were married. He was reared at George and Olivia's huge 33-acre Gothic mansion, Friar Park, and has lived a somewhat cosseted life, being chauffeured around in a gold Mercedes or various of George's Porsches.

Initially educated in the Montessori method at the Dolphin School, near Twyford, he was then enrolled at the fee-paying Shiplake College. From an early age he has been schooled in a spiritual way of life and meditates regularly. George and Olivia commented: 'We can instil the right values in our son. It is his nightmare that he should grow up spoiled.'

George invited him on stage to play guitar at the Albert Hall during an appearance to promote the Maharishi's political party in 1992, although Dhani says he does not want to become a musician. He also denies press reports that his ambition is to become a botanist. Following his final term at Shiplake in 1995, he decided to study design technology.

HARRISON, Harold Hargreaves   Born in Liverpool on 28 May 1909, the son of Henry Harrison and Jane Thomson. His father was killed in the First World War and his mother had to raise several children by herself. Harold left school at 14 to become a delivery boy and at the age of 17 went to sea. He joined the White Star line, serving on cruise ships, eventually becoming a First Class Steward.

In 1929, during one of his trips home, he met his future wife, Louise, while she was working in a Liverpool greengrocer's, asked for her address and began writing regularly to her. They were married on 20 May 1930.

Long sea voyages were not conducive to married life and he left the sea in 1936, spending 15 months on the dole before finding a job as a bus conductor. By the beginning of the Second World War he had been promoted to driver.

Harold and Louise lived in Liverpool's Wavertree area, where their four children, Louise, Harry, Peter and George, were born.

Harold's social life revolved around the Liverpool Corporation Centre for Conductors and Drivers at Finch Lane. He became a leading union official and also the Saturday evening master of Ceremonies at the Speke Depot Social Club, of which he was Chairman. He and Louise also ran a ballroom-dancing class at the club for over ten years.

On 1 January 1959 Harold booked his son's group, the Quarry Men, to appear at a special social club Christmas party at the Wilson Hall, Garston.

When the Beatles became internationally famous, Harold and Louise were particularly close to fans, inviting them into their home and answering fan mail by the sackload.

In 1965 George asked Harold how much he earned as a bus driver. Harold told him his pay was still £10 a week, so George offered to pay him £50 a week if he'd retire early. He then bought his mum and dad a bungalow in three acres of land in the village of Appleton, near Warrington in Cheshire.

Harold continued to visit George at Friar Park and occasionally travelled with him on tours – for example, the Dark Horse tour.

After a lifetime of heavy smoking, he died of emphysema in May 1978.

HARRISON Jr, Harold   Eldest son of Harold and Louise Harrison, born in 1934. While he was away on National Service, his fiancée Irene used to take his younger brother, George, to concerts. When Harold and Irene were married, George arranged for the Quarry Men to play at their reception. When George sacked Terry Doran as estate manager to Friar Park, he gave the job to Harold.

HARRISON, Louise   George Harrison's mother. As Louise French she was working in a greengrocer's in 1929 when she was spotted by Harold Harrison, who asked for her address, telling her he was going to sea and would like to send her a bottle of perfume – which he did. The couple were married on 20 May 1930 and settled in Arnold Grove in the Wavertree area. They had a daughter and three sons (Louise was 33 years old when George was born) and moved to a council house in Speke in 1949.

Louise and Harold conducted ballroom-dancing lessons for ten years at the bus conductor's club. Louise encouraged her youngest son, George, in his interest in music and bought him a guitar for £3. When he joined the Quarry Men she allowed them to rehearse in the front room of the Harrison household.

A proud George was able to buy his parents a house in the village of

Appleton, near Warrington, in 1965. By that time Louise was well loved by Beatles fans around the world. She attempted to reply personally to fans' letters, collecting the mail sent to George at the fan club HQ in Hackin's Hey and dealing with it herself. She even attended one fan's wedding.

She was taken ill in July 1969 and a brain tumour was eventually diagnosed. She died on 7 July 1970, with George at her bedside. Fans were to organize the Louise F. Harrison Memorial Cancer Fund.

HARRISON, Louise Older sister of George Harrison, born in 1931. She moved to America in July 1954 after marrying Gordon Caldwell.

Her brother made his first trip to the States in 1963, staying with Louise and her family in St Louis, Illinois.

When the Beatles arrived in America in February, 1963 and George was taken ill, Louise moved into the adjacent room at the Plaza Hotel to look after him.

In 1965 she appeared on a number of American radio shows and released an album of her interviews the same year, called *All About the Beatles*.

Louise appears regularly at Beatles conventions around the world.

HARRISON, Olivia Born Olivia Trinidad Arias in Mexico in 1948, she was educated in America and graduated at Hawthorne High School, California. She remained in Los Angeles and went to work in the merchandising office at A&M Records. She was then moved to Dark Horse Records as a secretary – George's Dark Horse was a small subsidiary label of A&M.

Olivia was 27 in 1974, when George first met her in the company offices. They talked together on the phone on numerous occasions and when George was returning to the States to work he asked a friend to check her out.

Their relationship deepened and they became virtually inseparable. When George fell ill following a number of problems relating to his marriage breakdown and a slump in his recording career, she recommended that he visit Dr Zion Yua, a noted Chinese acupuncturist, who cured him.

George and Olivia then spent the winter in Britain, preferring a traditional cold Christmas to the heat of Los Angeles. George also took her to visit Liverpool.

The pair lived together in Los Angeles, initially at George's $700,000 Beverly Hills mansion, which had a guest house, tennis court, swimming pool and all the trimmings. They found that it was too big for their needs and sold it for a smaller home with a greater sense of privacy.

When they stayed with Ringo and Nancy Andrews for a time in Hollywood Hills, an observer commented: 'There was a serene and calming presence that George and Olivia gave off. George had fresh flowers placed in the home and there was incense burning, pictures of holy men, the smell of curried rice dishes – long-grain rice – wafting in from the kitchen. They're both health-food eaters.

'You know something is going on when they're around but it isn't something George shoves down your throat. They are both very thoughtful, and he has a great sense of humour. She is a lovely woman, far from the Hollywood-model type, far too spiritual. The harmony between them is clear and apparent to anyone around them.'

It became obvious that Olivia was not particularly impressed by the lavish lifestyle in Los Angeles and the two of them moved to the tranquillity of the English countryside, to George's mansion, Friar Park, in Henley-on-Thames.

The couple were unable to marry until George's divorce from Pattie was finalized. This took place on 9 June 1977 and they then planned their wedding for May 1978, but postponed it due to the death of George's father. Their son, Dhani, was born on 1 August 1978 and the couple were eventually married by special licence at Henley Register Office some four weeks later, on 2 September.

HARRISON, Peter Second son of Harold and Louise Harrison. He was the first member of the family to own a guitar and his younger brother George played the washboard. Briefly they were in a group together, the Rebels. Eventually, George was to engage his brother to oversee the gardens and gardening staff at Friar Park.

HARRY, Virginia Yorkshire-born, auburn-haired girl who first met me at a Beatles gig at the Jacaranda club in 1960. She was 16 at the time. Virginia gave up her job to devote herself to the creation of the *Mersey Beat* newspaper, becoming its only original full-time member of staff. The Beatles would often drop in and help her in the office.

With her encouragement and help to the various bands and her regular 'Mersey Roundabout' column, she did much to promote the rise of the Beatles and the other groups on Merseyside.

HASLAM, Michael Vocalist from Bolton, Lancashire. When journalist Godfrey Winn was dining with Brian Epstein and Cilla Black in London one evening, he mentioned that he'd discovered a promising singer. Epstein, accompanied by Winn and Derek Taylor, went to see Haslam perform one Sunday night in May 1964 at the White Hart pub in Bolton.

The 24-year-old Haslam was a semi-pro entertainer who performed only locally and worked in a leather tannery by day. His two-hour show impressed Epstein, who taped the performance and drove Haslam home that evening. In an excited state he told Haslam he wanted to manage him and would immediately put him on the Beatles' next tour.

The following day Haslam received a telegram: 'The tapes are great. Consider yourself under personal management. Brian Epstein.'

Brian then made his rather predictable management moves, having Haslam's mohair suits made by the Beatles' tailor, Dougie Millings, the singer's hair styled by Brian's hairdresser and placing him with the Beatles' recording manager George Martin on the Parlophone label.

Haslam joined the Beatles autumn tour of Britain, from 9 October until 10 November 1964, and was also included on 'Another Beatles Christmas Show' at the Hammersmith Odeon from 24 December 1964, during which he performed two numbers, Presley's 'Tonight is so Right for Love' and 'Scarlet Ribbons'.

His debut single, 'Gotta Get a Hold of Myself', despite the George Martin production and the musical direction of Johnnie Spence, failed to register after its release on 25 September 1964.

His second release, 'There Goes the Forgotten Man', proved an unfortunately prophetic title for the singer, as it was also a failure, and his last release.

Brian Epstein didn't bother to renew his contract.

Interestingly, Haslam's sister Annie was also a singer and during the 1970s she achieved a degree of fame as lead singer with Renaissance.

HAWKE, Jim Former British soldier who, with his German wife, Lilo, and daughter, Monica, ran the British Sailors' Society in Hamburg. When the Beatles first arrived in Germany, they'd visit the 'Mission' regularly to relax and eat. Hawke, aware of the fact that they had little money, allowed them to have meals at a fraction of the normal price. John and Paul also used to compose songs on the 'Mission' piano.

HAWORTH, Jann An American sculptress who was married to British artist Peter Blake. Gallery-owner Robert Fraser, who acted as their representative, commissioned both of them to devise an album sleeve for *Sgt Pepper's Lonely Hearts Club Band* and paid them £200.

Haworth had exhibited at the 'Young Contemporaries' show at the ICA in 1963 and one of her exhibits from that show, a doll of Shirley Temple, was placed on the sleeve wearing a 'Welcome Rolling Stones' shirt.

Paul McCartney invited Jann and her husband to his home to hear tracks from the album as an inspiration. Once, when Jann was travelling in a car with Paul in Hammersmith, she pointed out a municipal flower clock and suggested that, rather than lettering, a grouping of flowers spelling 'Beatles' should be used.

In photographer Michael Cooper's studio, Jann helped to build the background to the tableau and, together with her husband, pasted the life-size photographic blow-ups to hardboard. She also tinted all of the original black and white photographs.

Together with Blake, she also designed the special colour card contained inside the sleeve which featured a set of army stripes, badges and a moustache which could be used as cut-outs. In addition, the card contained a painting of Sergeant Pepper and a Beatles photograph.

Haworth and Blake separated in 1979.

HENROID, Henry   Another of the unsung heroes of the Beatles story. Henry, a former boxer from London, became heavily involved in the music scene in the late 1950s and was road manager and later manager to Gene Vincent. He helped to discover groups such as the Animals and Herman's Hermits.

He acted for a time as Manfred Weissleder's right-hand man at the Star Club in Hamburg, travelling regularly to Liverpool to book bands. At one time Manfred gave the Beatles the sack and Paul came to Henry to ask for his help. Henry went to see Manfred, who told him that he was only putting the frighteners on them and hadn't really intended to sack them.

Henry has a host of gemlike anecdotes about the Beatles and their early career, particularly during their Hamburg days, from 1960 to 1962.

HENRY, Clarence 'Frogman'   American singer born in New Orleans on 19 March 1937. His hits included 'Ain't Got No Home', 'But I Do' and 'You Always Hurt the One You Love'. He appeared with the Beatles at the Civic Arena, Philadelphia, on 14 September 1964.

HESSY, Frank   Frank Hesselberg opened his musical instruments store, Frank Hessy, in Whitechapel, Liverpool, in 1934 and it became the city's most famous music store. In the mid-1950s, with the burgeoning music scene, local youngsters flooded the shop, wanting musical instruments on hire purchase.

Mimi Smith bought her nephew John Lennon his first guitar at Hessy's for £15 – and later threatened to throw it into the dustbin, after telling him: 'The guitar's all right as a hobby, but you'll never make a living out of it.' Years later he had the phrase engraved on a silver plaque which he sent to her.

Stuart Sutcliffe also purchased his first bass guitar, a Hohner President, from Hessy's. Although the story goes that he bought it with the £65 he received for selling a painting to John Moores, he actually took out a hire-purchase agreement and did not buy it outright, as is popularly supposed.

Hessy funded a music magazine, *Frank Comments*, mainly written and illustrated by myself when I was a local art student, and which was a forerunner of *Mersey Beat*.

His chief salesman was Jim Gretty, a local entertainer who encouraged the groups and occasionally booked them on his own promotions.

Although there were other musical instruments stores in Liverpool city centre such as Crane's, Rushworth & Dreaper's and Cramer & Lea, Hessy's had a particular affinity with the local groups.

The shop was featured in the film *Ferry 'Cross the Mersey*, and had its own 'Wall of Fame', a panoramic display of photographs of dozens of local groups.

Frank Hesselberg retired to Tel Aviv, where he died in 1983 at the age of 74. His store continued to supply instruments to local groups, but eventually closed down after 61 years in July 1995, when the premises were bought by a fashion chain.

HOFER, Walter   Brian Epstein's American attorney. He died in November 1985.

HOLDER, Owen   Screenwriter who penned a script for the Beatles' proposed third film, called *Shades of a Personality*, which was originally to have been shot in Spain by Michelangelo Antonioni, but the project was dropped.

HOLLIES, The   Northern group, once referred to as 'Manchester's Beatles', who appeared on the same bill as the Beatles at the Cavern on Sunday 3 February 1963.

Allan Clarke and Graham Nash had been singing together for a number of years as a vocal duo using various names, including the Guytones, the Two Teens and Rikky & Dane. It has been suggested that they possibly appeared on a Carroll Levis talent-show bill with the Quarry Men when they were known as Rikky & Dane.

The Hollies themselves were formed in 1962, with Eric Haydock on bass, Don Rathbone on drums and Tony Hicks on guitar. They signed to the Beatles record label, Parlophone, and had hits with their first two singles, 'Just Like Me' and 'Searchin''. Rathbone became their road manager and was replaced on drums by Bobby Elliott.

When their cover of George Harrison's 'If I Needed Someone' entered the charts in December 1965, Harrison made some uncomplimentary remarks about it; 'They've spoilt it. The Hollies are all right musically, but the way they do their records they sound like session men who've just got together in a studio without ever seeing each other before.'

This caused a great deal of controversy and Graham Nash replied: 'Not only do those comments disappoint and hurt us, but we are sick of everything the Beatles say or do being taken as law. The thing that hurt us most was George Harrison's knock at us as musicians. And I would like to ask this: "If we have made such a disgusting mess of his brainchild song, will he give all the royalties from our record to charity?" '

The Hollies were one of the most successful groups to emerge from the Beat boom and had a total of 31 hit singles and several hit albums, including 'Stay', 'Just One Look', 'Yes I Will', 'I'm Alive', 'I Can't Let Go' and 'He Ain't Heavy, He's My Brother'.

HOLLY, Buddy   American rock legend, born Charles Hardin Holley in Lubbock, Texas, on 7 September 1936.

He was a major influence on the Quarry Men, whose repertoire included a number of Holly's hits, including 'Words of Love', 'Crying, Waiting, Hoping', 'Think It Over' and 'It's so Easy'. In fact, the very first song John Lennon learned to play was Holly's 'That'll be the Day'.

When the group decided to change their name, it was Stuart Sutcliffe who pointing out that Holly's backing group were called the Crickets, and suggested that they follow their lead and name themselves after an insect – Beetles. John Lennon was to add the 'a'.

Beatles scribes, and even George Harrison, have theorized that they might had got their name from the film *The Wild One*, in which Lee Marvin featured as leader of a motorcycle gang called the Beetles. This couldn't have been the case, as the film was banned in Britain until the mid-1960s and no member of the group had seen it at the time of their name change.

Tragically, Buddy Holly died in an air crash in February 1959, along with the other rock legends the Big Bopper and Ritchie Valens.

Paul McCartney was to acquire the Buddy Holly music catalogue of 38 Holly compositions and from 1976 has presented an annual 'Buddy Holly Week' in Britain.

HOLLY, Ida Erstwhile girlfriend of John Lennon. John used to date her, even when he was going out with Cynthia. She became a compère at local venues, then moved to London, where she changed her name to Stevie Holly.

HOPKIN, Mary Blonde Welsh singer, born in Pontardawe on 3 May 1950.

It was Twiggy who spotted her on *Opportunity Knocks*, the TV talent show, and called Paul McCartney, who signed her to Apple, personally producing her debut single, which he chose himself – a vintage number called 'Those were the Days'. The single topped the British charts and was a hit internationally, selling over 5 million copies.

Paul also produced her second single, 'Goodbye', which reached No. 2 in the charts. He next produced her debut album, *Postcard*, and even designed the album sleeve. Finally, he produced her version of 'Que Sera Sera'.

Mary became disenchanted with Apple, primarily because of the managers they chose to look after her, and she appointed her sister Carol to the position, with her next recordings being produced by Mickie Most and Tony Visconti.

She left Apple in 1972 and was to have no further hits, although she married Visconti and the couple had a daughter, Jessica. They were later divorced and Visconti went on to marry May Pang, John Lennon's former live-in lover.

Cynthia Lennon was to record 'Those were the Days' in 1995.

HOPKINS, Nicky Nicky Hopkins was one of Britain's leading session musicians in the late 1960s and 1970s.

The Beatles brought him in to play piano on 'Ob-La-Di, Ob-La-Da', recorded at Studio Three in Abbey Road Studios on Thursday 11 July 1968.

Hopkins went on to back the Rolling Stones on tour and appeared on many best-selling albums by various artists, including the Stones, the Who, the Small Faces and the Kinks. In fact, the Kinks' number 'Session

Man' was written in his honour. He was also to perform on solo albums by John Lennon, George Harrison and Ringo Starr, while George Harrison was to play on four tracks of Hopkins' 1973 album *The Tin Man was a Drummer*.

Nicky first entered the musical field as a member of Screaming Lord Sutch's Savages in the early 1960s. During the decade he also toured with the Jeff Beck Group and was keyboard player for Jefferson Airplane at Woodstock in 1969.

In 1994 he moved to Nashville, where he died on Tuesday 6 September in hospital after suffering from abdominal and heart trouble. He was 50 years old.

HORN, Tom American flautist who was at Rishikesh in India at the same time as the Beatles. He claims that a New York schoolteacher, more interested in the Beatles than meditation, told them a phoney story about the Maharishi making a pass at her, which led John and George to confront him with the accusation.

HOT CHOCOLATE Tony Wilson and Errol Brown approached Apple, requesting permission to alter the lyrics to 'Give Peace a Chance', which they wanted to record. John Lennon suggested that they record it for Apple and press girl Mavis Smith suggested the name the Hot Chocolate Band. It was their only Apple release, in October 1969, but the group went on to have a string of major hits over the next two decades. As the Hot Chocolate Band they appeared on a bill with the Plastic Ono Supergroup at the Lyceum, London, on Monday 15 December 1969.

HOWARTH, Don Producer specializing in documentaries for BBC TV. In 1963 he produced the successful 30-minute film *The Mersey Sound*, which featured the Beatles and several other Mersey Beat bands.

HOWES, Arthur British promoter of pop package shows who booked the Beatles on a series of nationwide tours between 1964 and 1966.

Brian Epstein contacted Howes and pressed him into giving the Beatles an audition by including them on the bill of a concert at the Embassy, Peterborough, headlined by Frank Ifield.

The group didn't go down well with the audience that night, but Howes decided to take a chance and placed them on the bill of a Helen Shapiro tour. By time the tour began, in February 1963, the Beatles had begun to make a stir, and by their Howes second tour, headlined by Tommy Roe and Chris Montez, they'd made an impact with 'Please Please Me'.

Apart from a tour with Roy Orbison and some mini-tours, the rest of the British tours by the Beatles were promoted by Howes.

He died in London at the age of 63 on 12 February 1987.

HUGHES, Geoffrey Former member of Mersey Beat group the Travellers who became an actor after his appearance in the stage musical *Maggie May*. It was Geoff who dubbed the voice of Paul McCartney for the *Yellow Submarine* film. His biggest role was as Eddie Yates, the good-hearted lodger in *Coronation Street*. He also starred in the popular sit-com *Keeping Up Appearances*.

HUNTLEY, Ted Former EMI recording engineer who was cutting discs for customers at the HMV store in London when Brian Epstein wanted some acetates made of the Beatles' Decca recording audition. When he found that the group didn't have a publishing contract, he phoned Sid Coleman and sent Epstein up to meet him – which eventually led to the group's Parlophone contract.

HUTCHINS, Chris British journalist and former reporter for the *New Musical Express*. At the time of the Beatles' rise to prominence in Britain, *NME* was the most influential music publication in the country.

Hutchins first met the Beatles in Hamburg in November 1962, when he visited the Star Club to interview Little Richard.

Once the Beatles had made their impact in Britain, Hutchins, whom they called Chrisp Hutchy or Chrispy Hutch, covered their activities on a regular basis, travelling to America with them in February, 1964 and staying at the Plaza in New York.

Following their appearance at the Albert Hall on 18 April 1963, Shane Fenton drove Paul, John, George and Jane Asher to Chris Hutchins's Chelsea flat, and that's where Paul's romance with Jane began.

His biggest contribution to the Beatles story took place when he arranged their famous meeting with Elvis Presley during their American tour of 1965.

Chris was later to become a gossip columnist for several British tabloids, including the *Sunday Mirror*, the *Daily Express* and *Today*.

His reminiscences of his days with the Beatles are to be found in *Elvis Meets the Beatles*, a book he wrote in collaboration with Peter Thompson in 1994.

HUTCHINSON, Johnny Reputed to be the leading drummer of the Mersey Beat scene. 'Hutch', a former upholsterer, had never played drums prior to making his debut with Cass & the Cassanovas at the Corinthian Club at the age of 18 in December 1959.

He also played with a Modern Jazz group at the Princess Road Club and turned down a two-year contract with Johnny Kidd & the Pirates to remain with the Cassanovas.

After edging leader Brian Casser out of the group, the Cassanovas became the Big Three, one of Liverpool's best bands. Together with the Silver Beetles, they auditioned for Larry Parnes at the Wyvern Club when the London impresario was seeking Liverpool groups to back his singers. Like the Beatles, the Big Three were to tour Scotland backing Johnny Gentle.

At the Parnes audition, the Silver Beetles' drummer, Tommy Moore, turned up late, so Hutch sat in with them during the first part of their performance.

The Big Three appeared on many bills with the Beatles and Johnny Hutch was also to sit in with them on other occasions immediately after Pete Best's sacking and prior to Ringo's joining them.

Brian Epstein actually wanted Hutch to be Best's replacement with the group. Hutch was to tell Radio Merseyside broadcaster Spencer Leigh: 'Brian asked me to join the Beatles and I said, "I wouldn't join the Beatles for a gold clock. There's only one group as far as I'm concerned and that's the Big Three. The Beatles can't make a better sound than that, and Pete Best is a very good friend of mine. I couldn't do the dirty on him."'

Cilla Black was to confirm this, telling writer Ray Coleman: 'He [Hutch] was the first choice. Johnny Hutch was renowned as *the* drummer with *the* band in Liverpool. But he must have thought that because the Beatles were going to be big he didn't want to be part of them as he had the Big Three.'

While the discussions about a new drummer definitely included Johnny Hutchinson, the Beatles themselves wouldn't accept Epstein's choice. Hutch was too domineering and belligerent to fit in. Paul didn't like him and he would in all likelihood have begun bullying John Lennon. Epstein also realized that he'd be a difficult person to handle.

In fact, Epstein experienced problems when he took over management of the Big Three and he eventually had to let them go, as his style of management and their style of music were incompatible.

Hutch parted company with Gus and Griff over a dispute about the handling of the group's money. Hutch retained the name and hired two members of Faron's Flamingos, Faron and Paddy Chambers, to join him. However, he now controlled the group and only paid them a wage. Chambers left after four months to join Kingsize Taylor & the Dominoes and was replaced by Paul Pilnick, but the group finally called it a day in October 1964.

After disbanding the Big Three, Hutch took a job in the building trade, but never played again. He was to tell Spencer Leigh: 'I've still got my drums, I'll never let them go, but the only way I'd do it now is to go back with a couple of musicians who are as good as Griff and Gus. I'd practise for six or eight months and then I'd go out and knock everybody flat.'

IAN & THE ZODIACS Popular band from Crosby who appeared on various gigs around Liverpool with the Beatles.

Ian Edwards, rhythm guitarist with the Deltones, left the group to join the Zodiacs in 1960, and they became Ian & the Zodiacs.

They were among the host of groups who recorded for the Oriole *This is Mersey Beat* albums, produced by John Schroeder, from which two singles were issued, 'Beechwood – 45789' and 'Let's Turkey Trot'.

From their base in Crosby, they began to appear all over the Merseyside area and became regulars at the Cavern club, where they appeared on many bills with the Beatles.

The gigs they shared with the Beatles in 1961 took place on Wednesday 6 September, Wednesday 20 September, Wednesday 18 October, Wednesday 8 November and Wednesday 29 November. The 1962 appearances were on Wednesday 17 January, Wednesday 25 June, Sunday 7 October and Wednesday 21 November.

Billed simply as the Zodiacs, they also appeared with the Beatles on Tuesday 20 March 1962.

Edwards recalls that on many occasions, while they spent their time in the Grapes pub in Matthew Street, the Beatles remained in the Cavern bandroom, practising.

There had been two changes in line-up by 1965, when the personnel was Ian Edwards (lead vocals/rhythm), Pete Wallace, a founder member of the Zodiacs (lead), Jeff Bamford, formerly with the Memphis Three (drums) and Charlie Flynn, ex-member of Kingsize Taylor & the Dominoes (bass).

By this time they'd made four trips to Germany, where they'd had one LP and two singles released which entered the Top Ten. *Ian & the Zodiacs* was the album title and the singles were 'covers': 'Spartacus' (previously recorded by Sounds Inc.) and 'Message to Martha' (a British hit for Adam Faith).

Their German A&R man, Siegfried Loch, then working for Philips Records, arranged for the US release of a track from their album, 'The Crying Game', which sold over a quarter of a million copies and reached No. 1 in Texas. They had a British single released on 12 March 1965, 'Just the Little Things That I Like', flipside 'This Won't Happen to Me', and later had an album released on the Wings label, *Gear Again*. Under the name the Koppykats, they recorded an album of Beatles hits which was their best-selling release, although they received no royalties, having accepted a session fee.

IFIELD, Frank Coventry-born, Australian-raised singer who had 15 chart hits between 1960 and 1966. Promoter Arthur Howes booked the Beatles on a bill with Ifield at the Embassy Cinema, Peterborough, in December 1962. Vee-Jay Records in America released *Jolly What! The Beatles and Frank Ifield on Stage* in February 1964.

JACKLEY, Nat A British music-hall comedian whose gimmick was an ability to twist his neck as if it were rubber. He appeared in *Magical Mystery Tour* and John Lennon personally directed him in one scene.

JACKSON, Simone London singer who was only 16 when the Beatles provided backing for her during their Cavern appearance on Wednesday 12 September 1962.

JACOBS, David A British television personality who was the host of *Juke Box Jury* throughout the 1960s. He travelled to Liverpool with the Beatles for their civic reception at the northern première of *A Hard Day's Night* and presented an all-Beatles *Juke Box Jury* from the stage of the Empire Theatre. Brian Epstein, Jane Asher and individual members of the Beatles also appeared on various editions of his show.

JACOBS, David Show-business lawyer who represented Brian Epstein. Ringo and Maureen were to spend their honeymoon at his home in Hove. Jacobs placed the rights to the Beatles merchandise in the hands of a youth he met at a party, Nicky Byrne, a move which was alleged to have eventually lost them $100,000,000 in American orders. He was found hanging in his garden in December 1968 and the inquest recorded a verdict of suicide.

JAMES, Carroll Disc jockey at WNDC-AM, a Washington DC radio station, who was credited as the first person to play a Beatles record on American radio: it was 'I Wanna Hold Your Hand', on 17 December 1963. He also introduced them at their Washington Coliseum appearance on 11 February 1964 and conducted an interview with them which was issued 20 years later as *The Carroll James Interview with the Beatles – February 11, 1964*.

JAMES, Dick Former singer turned music publisher. Born Richard Leon Vapnick in 1920, he became a professional singer at the age of 17 and is best remembered for his chart hit 'Robin Hood', the theme tune for the television series starring Richard Greene.

George Martin was his record producer and their association was to have an influence on the Beatles' future career.

When Brian Epstein became disenchanted with Ardmore & Beechwood's handling of the promotion for 'Love Me Do', it was George Martin who suggested he try James.

James had the publishing rights to 'How Do You Do It?' and when Martin originally suggested that he give it to the Beatles, a group from Liverpool, James said: 'Liverpool? A group from Liverpool – you gotta be kidding?'

It was rumoured that James was having financial problems with his publishing company, which was relatively unsuccessful, and that the appearance of Brian Epstein and the possibility of his injecting capital into his business saved James's bacon.

James was able to obtain the Beatles' publishing rights after securing the group a spot on the TV programme *Thank Your Lucky Stars*. From the moment Epstein signed with James, the Beatles lost control of their own songs and were never able to recover it.

James suggested that a separate company be formed, called Northern Songs, which would be administered by Dick James Music, with himself having the majority shares. He persuaded Epstein to make Northern Songs public in 1965. John and Paul were against the move, but had no choice. After the flotation, James and his accountant Charles Silver had the largest shareholding, 37 per cent, between them and were managing director and chairman respectively of the company.

The Beatles gradually began to resent James and felt that he patronized them. Together with Silver and without the Beatles' knowledge, James sold his shares to Sir Lew Grade and ATV in 1969.

In succeeding years, James continued to thrive as a publisher, representing stars such as Elton John, although Elton John was eventually to sue him in a lengthy court case which ended in James's favour.

He died at the age of 65 on 1 February 1986.

JAMES, Ian A classmate of Paul McCartney during his Liverpool Institute days. The two friends virtually taught each other to play guitar – passing on tips, jamming together. They also used to wander round the visiting funfairs, trying to pick up girls. The two began to look and dress alike, sharing the same hairstyle (like Tony Curtis's, nicknamed the DA, which was popular at the time) and both wore white sports jackets and drainpipe trousers. Paul said they wore the jackets because of the song 'A White Sports Coat' and described his jacket as having 'speckles in it and a flap on the pockets'. It was Ian who taught Paul the chords he played to John at their first meeting.

JANICE THE STRIPPER A buxom brunette, surname unknown, whom Allan Williams booked from a Manchester agency for a number of appearances in Liverpool during late June and early July 1960, despite the fact that striptease was banned in the city at the time by order of the local Watch Committee.

Williams was in partnership at the time with Lord Woodbine, running an illicit strip-club they called New Cabaret Artistes at 174a Upper Parliament Street, in the Toxteth area, Liverpool's equivalent of Harlem.

Janice told Williams that she wouldn't perform to records and insisted that a live band should back her. He approached John Lennon and asked if the Silver Beatles would do the honours, but they refused. He then promised them ten shillings (50p) each per night, which met with their approval. For this they were required to perform two 20-minute spots each evening.

Janice handed the lads printed sheet music of Beethoven and Khachaturian, but they explained they couldn't read it and suggested they play some old standards, including 'Begin the Beguine' and 'It's a Long Way to Tipperary'.

Paul McCartney was to recall the experience in a letter to me: 'John, George, Stu and I used to play at a Strip Club in Upper Parliament Street, backing Janice the Stripper. At the time we wore little lilac jackets ... or purple jackets, or something. Well, we played behind Janice and naturally we looked at her, everybody looked at her, just sort of normal. At the end of the act she would turn round and ... well, we were all young lads, we'd never seen anything like it before, and we all blushed ... four blushing red-faced lads.

'Janice brought sheets of music for us to play all her arrangements. She gave us a bit of Beethoven and the Spanish Fire Dance. So in the end we said, "We can't read music, sorry, but instead of the Spanish Fire Dance we can play 'The Harry Lime Cha Cha', which we've arranged ourselves and instead of Beethoven you can have 'Moonglow' or 'September Song', take your pick ... and instead of the 'Sabre Dance' we'll give you 'Ramrod'. so that's what she got. She seemed quite satisfied anyway."'

JETS, The Group who became the first British band to perform at the Kaiserkeller club in Hamburg. Bruno Koschmider, who came to Britain seeking bands for his club, had been recommended to try two cities – Liverpool and London. Luckily for the Jets, he arrived in London first and, after some inquiries, made his way to the 2 I's, a coffee bar in Soho where various musicians used to meet.

Iain Hines, a Scottish musician, and Del Ward, a drummer, were sitting at a table when Koschmider, through an interpreter, asked them if they knew of any bands he could book for a season in Hamburg. The quick-witted Hines made up a group name, the Jets, and was booked for six months at the club. The group he put together comprised himself, Tony Sheridan, Ricky Richards, Colin Milander and Del Ward.

Hines had to return to Britain on a personal matter after his first night at the club, but the Jets continued for the next few months, led by Tony Sheridan.

Following their Kaiserkeller season, they next appeared at the Top Ten Club, with a slightly altered line-up and the return of Hines. They were joined on stage one night by members of the Beatles, who were still under contract to Koschmider, an action which infuriated Koschmider and led to his planning their deportation.

The Beatles were due to take over the Jets' season at the Top Ten, but when they were deported Peter Eckhorn asked the group to stay. As some of the members had already left, the new line-up comprised Hines on piano, Milander on bass, Sheridan on guitar/vocals and Ward on drums. The group remained at the Top Ten for a further two months, until Gerry & the Pacemakers took over, and then they disbanded.

JOHN FRED & HIS PLAYBOY BAND   American eight-piece outfit led by John Fred on lead vocals/harmonica. Fred, real name John Fred Gourrier, was born in Baton Rouge, Louisiana. The other members of the band were Charlie Spinosa and Ronnie Goodson (trumpets), Andrew Bernard (baritone sax), Jimmy O'Rourke (guitar), Howard Cowart (bass), Joe Micelli (drums) and Tommy Dee (organ).

Their first chart entry, 'Agnes English', was followed by their biggest hit, the million-seller 'Judy in Disguise (with Glasses)'. The number was penned by Fred and Bernard and was an obvious play on 'Lucy in the Sky with Diamonds'.

Fred was playing this particular track from the *Sgt Pepper* album while shaving and thought the lyrics were 'Lucy in disguise with diamonds'.

He remembered the number while he was on a beach in Florida and noticed lots of girls were wearing sunglasses, so he came up with the basic song 'Beverly in Disguise (with Glasses)', which later had a name change to Judy.

Ironically, the single knocked the Beatles' 'Hello Goodbye' from the top of the American charts on its release in November 1967. The single also reached No. 3 in the British charts.

JOHNNY & THE HURRICANES   American instrumental outfit, formed in 1957 by tenor sax player Johnny Paris. The group, who had hits such as 'Red River Rock', 'Reveille Rock' and 'Rocking Goose', topped the bill, above the Beatles, at the Star Club, Hamburg, in December 1962.

JOHNNY & THE MOONDOGS   Name the Quarry Men adopted in October 1959 when they entered the Carroll Levis talent competition at the Empire Theatre, Liverpool. Soon afterwards they came up with the name Silver Beetles.

JOHNNY KIDD & THE PIRATES   Johnny Kidd was one of the leading British rock 'n' roll stars at the beginning of the 1960s.

Born Frederick Heath in Willesden, north-west London, on 23 December 1939, he formed his first group, Freddie Heath & the Nutters, during the skiffle boom. An EMI recording contract brought him his first hit with his debut record, 'Please Don't Touch', which reached No. 25 in the charts in 1959.

By that time he'd changed his name to Johnny Kidd and dubbed his backing band the Pirates. The group comprised Brian Gregg on bass, Art Caddy on lead and Clem Cattini on drums. This line-up left him in 1961 to become the Tornadoes.

With a touch of showbiz, Johnny capitalized on the Pirates name, presenting a show which featured a pirate theme. He wore swashbuckling leather gear and a black eye-patch over his left eye. It was rumoured that he had originally worn the patch one night on stage after a guitar string broke into his eye. Joe Brown used to comment that Jack Good made Johnny wear the patch to stop him winking at the Vernons Girls! It became a trademark and he always carried six of them, due to the fact that fans kept pinching them.

When his original backing group left, he took on Cuddly Dudley's former backing band and later formed the trio which was to have some influence on the heavy metal bands of the future – Mick Green on guitar, Johnny Spencer on bass and Frank Farley on drums.

'Please Don't Touch' was followed by 'You Got What It Takes', which also reached No. 25. His next release, the classic 'Shakin' All Over', reached the No. 1 spot. This was followed by 'Restless', also in 1960, which reached No. 22.

There were several other hits, which included 'A Shot of Rhythm & Blues' and 'I'll Never Get Over You'.

Johnny Kidd & the Pirates appeared for a week at the Cavern from Monday 14 May 1962 and later topped the bill, above the Beatles, on Friday 10 August 1962 during the 'Riverboat Shuffle' on the *Royal Iris*.

In the midst of a hectic schedule of one-nighters, Johnny was killed in a car crash at Radcliffe, Lancashire, on 7 October 1966. He was 26 years old.

JOHNNY RINGO & THE COLTS   Mersey group who formed in the latter part of 1962. They comprised Johnny Ringo (vocals/rhythm), Les Hold (lead), John Smith (bass) and Derek Kay (drums). They appeared with the Beatles in their final Cavern show on Saturday 3 August 1963.

JOHNNY TEMPLAR'S HI-CATS   Lead guitarist Vic Grace left the Cyclones early in 1962 to found the Hi-Cats with Johnny Sanchez on rhythm, Tony Tarson on bass and Chick Broderick on drums. Johnny Templar replaced Danny Havoc as vocalist and Barbara Harrison was also a vocalist with the band until she left for France with Faron's Flamingos.

The group appeared on several local bills with the Beatles during 1962, including 'Operation Big Beat 3' at the Tower Ballroom on Friday 29 June and the Cavern on Wednesday 21 November.

JOHNS, Glyn   British recording engineer who was invited by Paul McCartney in December 1968 to work as a balance engineer on the Beatles' project 'Get Back'.

Johns and George Martin worked for some time on the tapes, but these were then handed over to Phil Spector and were eventually to be issued as the *Let It Be* album.

A frustrated Johns commented: 'I cannot bring myself to listen to the Phil Spector version of the album – I heard a few bars of it once, and was totally disgusted, and think it's an absolute load of garbage.'

JONES, Brian   Founder member of the Rolling Stones, born in Cheltenham on 28 February 1942.

Brian was particularly impressed by the Beatles' music and at one time sought to persuade the Stones to attempt Beatle-style harmonies. He was also influenced by ethnic music and tried to introduce some innovative ideas into the group. However, his position as one of the main figures in the band was seriously weakened when Andrew Loog Oldham encouraged Mick Jagger and Keith Richard to compose original songs for the band. The Rolling Stones were soon to revolve around the two, and Brian became increasingly disenchanted and turned to drink and drugs, until he left the band in 1969, saying: 'The music of Mick Jagger and Keith Richard has, to my mind, progressed on a tangent as far as my own tastes are concerned.'

Brian believed that there was a possibility that he could join the Beatles and he actually played saxophone on their track 'You Know My Name (Look Up the Number)', which was recorded in May 1967.

At the age of 27, on 3 July 1969, Brian was found drowned in the swimming pool of his home.

JONES, Davy Black American artist who was backed by the Beatles on three separate occasions in Liverpool.

Jones made his Liverpool debut on Tuesday 3 May 1960 at the Liverpool Stadium, on a bill headed by Gene Vincent. Allan Williams had promoted the concert, which also featured Liverpool bands Cass & the Cassanovas, Rory Storm & the Hurricanes and Gerry & the Pacemakers. Williams hadn't booked the Beatles as they were still relatively unknown locally, although he was to engage them for a series of gigs at his tiny Jacaranda club later that same month.

On Friday 24 November 1961, the Beatles appeared on Sam Leach's second 'Operation Big Beat' concert at the Tower Ballroom. Two black singers turned up unannounced at the venue that evening – one was Emile Ford, who took to the stage and performed with Rory Storm & the Hurricanes, the other was Jones, who went on stage during the Beatles performance and sang two numbers with them.

His first official booking with them was a Cavern lunchtime session on Friday 8 December 1961. Ray McFall booked the singer and, as Jones didn't have a backing band, arranged for the Beatles to do the honours.

During the evening he was booked by Sam Leach to headline at the Tower Ballroom. 'The Davy Jones Show' also featured the Beatles, Rory Storm & the Hurricanes, Dale Roberts & the Jaywalkers, Kingsize Taylor & the Dominoes, Derry & the Seniors and Steve Day & the Drifters. Once again, the Beatles provided backing for Jones, who had been advertised as '*Saturday Spectacular* television star and Reprise recording artist'.

He was photographed on both occasions for *Mersey Beat*.

Jones was later to renew his acquaintance with Liverpool bands when he began appearances at the Star Club in Hamburg.

JONES, Pauline A former Essex University student who married John Lennon's father, Freddie.

She worked for a time at John's Weybridge home and the couple married, even though she was only 19 and Freddie was 56. In 1990, as Pauline Lennon, she penned the book *Daddy, Come Home*, based on Freddie's unpublished manuscript.

JONES, Peter As editor of *Record Mirror*, he became the first journalist from a national music paper to interview the Beatles, in August 1962. He also penned the first published book about the group, *The True Story of the Beatles*, under the pseudonym Billy Shepherd. He became European representative for *Billboard* magazine and retired in 1995.

JONES, Philip Producer of the popular television show *Thank Your Lucky Stars*. He booked the Beatles to make their debut on the programme after Dick James played him 'Please Please Me' over the phone. It was their first national television appearance and Jones was to book them on a number of subsequent occasions.

JUNKIN, John British actor/comedian/scriptwriter who tried to pass himself off as a Liverpudlian when auditioning for *A Hard Day's Night*. The Beatles saw the joke and he appeared as one of their road managers, Shake.

KAEMPFERT, Bert Prominent German bandleader, songwriter and recording manger, born 16 October 1923 in Hamburg, Germany. It was while he was working as an A&R man for Polydor Records, the pop division of Deutsche Grammophon, that he was approached by publisher Alfred Schacht with the suggestion that he visit the Top Ten Club to watch artist Tony Sheridan perform.

The 37-year old Kaempfert decided to record Sheridan and, on his recommendation, engaged the Beatles to back him. The sessions took place over a three-day period from 22 May 1961 at the Haburg Friedrich Ebert Halle, a local school. The children were not at school because of holidays and Kaempfert arranged for mobile recording equipment to be installed on the stage of the school auditorium.

When they began recording 'My Bonnie' there were some Coke bottles on the stage and George Harrison knocked one over. Kaempfert told him: 'All Coke bottles off the stage.'

The other numbers recorded were 'The Saints', 'Why?', 'Nobody's Child', 'Ain't She Sweet?', 'Cry for a Shadow' and 'If You Love Me Baby'.

When Polydor released two of the songs in Germany they were credited to Tony Sheridan & the Beat Brothers. Kaempfert had decided that the name 'Beatles' was not suitable for use on the record as, according to rumour, he felt that it sounded too much like the north German slang word 'Peedles', denoting the male sex organ.

When they'd finished backing Sheridan, the Beatles asked Kaempfert if they could record some other numbers. He asked them what original material they had, but they didn't come up with anything original – although they'd recorded the George Harrison instrumental 'Cry for a Shadow'. Kaempfert then suggested that they begin writing their own material if they wanted to make a name for themselves.

The Beatles were paid a flat fee of 300 marks for the session and did not receive any royalties. They later said that they had opted for the flat fee because they weren't satisfied with the session – although it also seems likely that at the time they preferred the cash.

Prior to the recording sessions they signed a recording contract with Bert Kaempfert Produktions. The one-year contract was renewable for periods of one year, with an agreement to record four songs per year.

On 20 February 1962, Brian Epstein was to write to Kaempfert, asking him to release the group from this commitment. He replied: 'I do not want to spoil the chance of the group to get a recording contract elsewhere, but I do think that we should have the chance to make recordings with the group for the Polydor label whilst they are in Hamburg.'

But they never recorded for him again. The last time he saw them was at the Ernst Merck Halle in Hamburg on 26 June 1966. When he visited them backstage, they began singing 'Strangers in the Night'.

Kaempfert was to earn his major fame as a composer and bandleader. His orchestra was voted No. 1 Band of the Future in the 1961 *Cashbox* poll and he was to pen a series of major hit songs, including 'Wonderland by

Night', 'Strangers in the Night', 'Bye Bye Blues', 'A Swinging Safari', 'Spanish Eyes' and 'Danke Schön'.

Sadly, Bert died of a heart attack while on holiday in Spain on 22 June 1980.

KARL TERRY & THE CRUISERS   A Mersey group who appeared on numerous gigs with the Beatles and were, in fact, advertised above them for a Cavern lunchtime session on Friday 1 September 1961. They also appeared in a Cavern evening session with the Beatles on Wednesday 20 September 1961.

Leader Karl began his career in a skiffle group called the Gamblers. His Bob Wooler-inspired nicknames included 'The Sheik of Shake' and 'Lover Boy'.

He also appeared with the Beatles and Gerry & the Pacemakers at Litherland Town Hall on 19 October 1961, and when he saw the Beatles and the Pacemakers merge into a band they called the Beatmakers, he also got up on stage to join them.

The early line-up of the group comprised Karl Terry (vocals), Dave Hamilton (lead), Don McGough (bass) and Roy Dyke (drums). They were an immensely popular band, coming fifteenth in the first *Mersey Beat* poll. They wore purple and lilac jackets with white jeans. Karl went on to join various other Mersey outfits, including the Delemeres and the Tempest Tornadoes and is still performing on Merseyside today.

KASS, Ron   Former Liberty Records executive hired to head Apple Records. Kass, who was married to film actress Joan Collins at the time, was based in Savile Row, London, but also opened an Apple office in California.

He left the company in August 1968, when Allen Klein became involved in the Beatles affairs, and he became head of Warner Bros. Records in London. He died of cancer at the age of 51 in 1986.

KAUFMAN, Murray   New York disc jockey, known as Murray the K. He received a copy of 'She Loves You' in October 1963. He recalled that he played it on a record contest he ran and it came third, so he continued playing it for a few weeks. Nothing seemed to happen, so he dropped it and went off to Miami for his Christmas vacation. Suddenly, while listening to the radio there, it seemed as if every other record being played was by the Beatles. Then he received a phone call from his programme director at 1O1O WINS, telling him to return to the station as the Beatles were coming. 'Get yourself an exterminator,' Kaufman told him, but his director was firm and Kaufman had to cut short his holiday and attend their airport press conference.

He contacted the Beatles by phone at the Plaza Hotel, where they were staying, and conducted a radio interview with them. They were apparently aware of him from the sleeve notes he'd made on various record albums, and he told them: 'You're what's happenin', baby.'

Murray was to become the omnipresent disc jockey during that first trip and even had the audacity to call himself 'the Fifth Beatle', a liberty which infuriated Brian Epstein so much that he threatened legal action.

Soon he was literally running their social life, taking them to New York nightclubs to meet starlets such as Tuesday Weld and Stella Stevens, visiting the Playboy Club – all the time recording interviews.

When the group booked into the Deauville Hotel in Miami, to record another *Ed Sullivan Show*, Murray flew to Florida and shared a room with George Harrison. He continued taking them to nightclubs, such as the Peppermint Lounge in Miami, where they watched a show by country singer Hank Ballard.

Over the years, Murray kept in touch, visiting them in London, where he attended their appearance at the NME Award Winner's Concert at Wembley Stadium and interviewed them during the filming of *A Hard Day's Night*.

He also travelled to the Queen Elizabeth Hotel, Montreal, some years later when John and Yoko had a bed-in, and was one of the celebrities present (including Petula Clark and Timothy Leary) who provided the background clapping on the 'Give Peace a Chance' recording.

His interviews from New York, Miami, London and Washington were contained on an EP, 'The Beatles and Murray the K As It Happened'. The interviews he conducted in 1965 are to be found on bootleg albums such as *Soldier of Love* and *Murray the K Fan Club*.

His autobiography, *Murray the K Tells It Like It Is, Baby*, was published in America in 1966 with an introduction penned by George Harrison. He also appeared as himself in the film *I Want to Hold Your Hand* in 1978.

Kaufman participated in a major Beatles festival held at Knotts Berry Farm in 1980. Tragically, he died of cancer on 2 February 1982.

KAYE, Peter When Bill Connell launched his photo studio in Park Lane, Liverpool, he decided on the name Peter Kaye. This became a generic name for all the photos taken by the studio, whether by Bill himself or by Les Chadwick. When I launched *Mersey Beat* I wanted Les to take photos for me and commissioned the Peter Kaye studio to take photos of the groups – and in particular the Beatles. The range of early Beatles photos by Peter Kaye is quite extensive. Sadly, Bill Connell died in 1987, the year his book *Beatles in Liverpool* was published.

KELLY, Arthur One of George Harrison's childhood friends. The two were members of the Rebels and when the Quarry Men re-formed in August 1959 Arthur was offered the job as bass player, but turned it down. He became an actor and appeared as Bert in the Willie Russell play *John, Paul, George, Ringo ... and Bert*.

KELLY, Brian One of the handful of Liverpool promoters who helped to build up the network of local venues which provided Mersey groups with the opportunity to develop their music in front of live audiences on a regular basis.

Kelly promoted 'Beekay' dances, the first of which took place at the Savoy Hall, Bath Street, Waterloo on 11 May 1959. He then built up a number of other regular promotions at Lathom Hall, Seaforth, Alexandra Hall, Crosby, Aintree Institute, Litherland Town Hall and a venue in Skelmersdale.

Like several other promoters, Kelly would have bands appearing at 'auditions'. In other words, if he hadn't seen a band perform before, he would let them play at his venue for no fee as an 'audition'.

He first booked the Silver Beats for an audition at Lathom Hall on 14 May 1960 on a bill which included Kingsize Taylor & the Dominoes, Cliff Roberts & the Rockers and the Deltones.

They passed the audition! Kelly next booked them to appear the following week, on 21 May. However, they never turned up, because they had set off on their brief Scottish tour with Johnny Gentle.

One of their most important early bookings took place at Litherland Town Hall on 27 December 1960. It was their debut appearance at the venue. Kelly hadn't booked the Beatles since their failure to turn up at his Lathom Hall promotion, but Bob Wooler talked him into booking them at a fee of £6.

As it was a late booking, their names didn't appear in the local newspaper advertisements, which had already been placed, announcing the groups: Kingsize Taylor & the Dominoes, the Searchers, the Del Renas and the Deltones. Entrance to the show was 3s (15p) and Kelly managed to place their name on a number of posters: 'Direct from Hamburg, the Beatles!'

Their line-up that night was John, Paul, George, Pete and Chas Newby. They had just returned from Hamburg, where they had literally transformed their music and appearance, and gave a dynamic performance. Fans in the audience, due to the posters, actually believed they were a German group, because they weren't that well known locally at the time.

Present at that particular gig were Pete Best's brother Rory and the Bests' lodger, accountancy student Neil Aspinall, who saw the Beatles perform for the first time.

Over two decades later, John Kennedy of Kingsize Taylor & the Dominoes, who opened the show, told Radio Merseyside reporter Spencer Leigh: 'We used to open and close the show there. We'd do our spot and then go to the White House for a few pints. We never got to the pub that night. We'd just reached the door when they started off, and that was it. We stayed there all night and watched them. They were brilliant. There was something raw and animal about them.'

Discussing his involvement in the Beatles career in an article published in *Mersey Beat*, Brian revealed:

I was organizing a dance at Litherland Town Hall to be held on Boxing Day, 1960, but I was short of a group. On Christmas Day I received a phone call from Bob Wooler who said, 'I've found a group for you at the Jacaranda and they're free. They want eight pounds. will they do?'

'Not at that price they won't,' I said. 'A group won't increase my attendance enough to warrant that'. .... we finally agreed to pay them six pounds.

On their first appearance I was completely knocked out by them. They had a pounding, pulsating beat which I knew would be big box office. When they finished playing, I posted some bouncers on the door of their dressing room to prevent other promoters who were in the hall entering. I went inside and booked them solidly for months ahead.

I had a huge poster made with 'The Beatles' written in large fluorescent lettering. The poster caused a certain amount of curiosity and I remember the first reaction to their name. 'Beatles – you've spelt it wrong, mister.' 'Beatles – where've you dragged them from?' 'Beatles – who are they?'

The group went from strength to strength at Litherland and built up a fantastic following. Even then, the songwriting talents of Lennon and McCartney were evident. On stage they'd say, 'Here's a song we've just written – if you don't like it you needn't clap.'

The group went away to Germany. When they returned we did reasonable business with them, but they had lost Stuart and seemed downhearted and had temporarily lost their lustre.

They were the first really noisy group to appear on Merseyside – and amplifiers were insufficient to cope with their sound. I worked on the amplification for them – and received a great deal of business for Alpha Sound. Groups on Merseyside seemed to play wilder and louder and more of them approached me to help with their amplification.

Brian booked them for Lathom Hall during a two-month period in 1961 – on 20, 21, 20 and 30 January and 4, 6, 10, 11 and 25 February. Their final performance on 25 February took place on George Harrison's eighteenth birthday.

Their Litherland Town Hall appearances during 1961 took place on 5 and 26 January; 2, 14, 16, 21 and 28 February; 2 March; 24 and 31 July; 7 August; 7, 14, 21 and 28 September; 19 and 31 October; and 9 November.

Kelly also booked the Beatles for a total of 31 appearances at Aintree Institute. They made their debut there on 7 January, 1961, and also appeared on 13, 14, 18, 21, 27, 28 January; 8, 10, 15, 18, 22 February; 1, 4, 8, 11 March; 21, 28 July; 4, 12, 18, 19, 26 August; 2, 9, 16, 23, 28 October; and 11 November.

They made a single appearance in 1962, their last at the venue, on 27 January 1962.

Their fee for the gig was now £15 – and Kelly paid them in coins. A furious Brian Epstein was to recall the incident in his autobiography and said they were paid ' ... in sixpences and florins and even halfpennies and I kicked up an awful fuss, not because £15 isn't £15 in any currency, but because I thought it was disrespectful to the Beatles.' As a result, Epstein ensured that they never appeared at the venue again.

Brian Kelly died in 1993.

KELLY, Freda Irish-born Freda arrived in Liverpool with her family at the age of 13. On leaving school she began to work at Princes food firm and became a Cavern regular. At the club she met Bobbie Brown, who was then running the Beatles Fan Club, and began to help her with the club work. She was able to get a job as a shorthand typist at NEMS Enterprises and when Bobbie became engaged in 1963 Freda took over the running of the club.

When NEMS Enterprises relocated to London, Freda's father wouldn't allow her to move south, so she continued to run the club with the help of part-time workers.

The club's headquarters was established in London and Freda handled the northern area, becoming joint national secretary in 1966.

She was married to a local musician, Brian Norris, former member of the Realms and the Cryin' Shames, on 4 April 1968 and soon left her fan-club activities to concentrate on raising her first child.

KELLY, George Employed as a butler by Paul in 1966, he was to sell a story to the tabloid press revealing 'wild parties' at Paul's house.

KELLY, John The photographer whose colour portraits of the Beatles were part of *The Beatles* 'white' album package. He'd also had his photographs used in the *Magical Mystery Tour* booklet, which was issued with the record package. In 1969 he was hired as the official photographer at the wedding of Paul and Linda.

KEMP, Gibson A Liverpool drummer who, in 1962, at the age of 16, left the Memphis Three to replace Ringo Starr in Rory Storm & the Hurricanes, inheriting Ringo's pink stage suit.

Gibson was to leave the Hurricanes and join Kingsize Taylor in Germany, where he married Astrid Kirchherr, Stuart Sutcliffe's former fiancée.

He was later to team up with Klaus Voormann and Paddy Chambers to form Paddy, Klaus & Gibson, at one time managed by Brian Epstein on the recommendation of the Beatles.

His contacts in Germany stood him in good stead and he became an executive with Polydor in Germany, Australia and England, although his marriage to Astrid didn't last.

KEN DALLAS & THE SILHOUETTES Liverpool group who appeared numerous times with the Beatles. Their Cavern gigs on Beatles bills during 1962 included Wednesday 21 February, Saturday 24 February, Wednesday 18 July, Sunday 22 July, Tuesday 7 August and Wednesday 10 October. They also appeared with the Beatles at the club on Wednesday, 23 January 1963.

KENNEDY, Adrienne Afro-American playwright, born in 1931, who had the idea of writing a play based on John Lennon's two books. Victor Spinetti helped her to complete *The Lennon Play: In His Own Write*, which was presented at the Old Vic in June 1968.

KESTRELS, The British vocal group from the West Country, comprising Tony Burrows and Roger Greenaway. They were one of the acts to be booked on the Helen Shapiro tour from 2 February to 3 March 1963, which was also the Beatles' first major tour. They were later booked to appear on the Beatles fourth tour, which lasted from 1 November to 13 December 1963.

The duo's recording manager was Tony Hatch, but they never enjoyed success on record, despite recording the Lennon and McCartney song 'There's a Place' for release as a single and a version of 'Please Please Me' for their first album.

When the Kestrels disbanded in 1965, Greenaway formed a partnership with Roger Cook in the vocal duo David and Jonathan. Greenaway became David and Cook became Jonathan. The two then recorded a version of 'Michelle', which became their first chart hit, reaching No. 11 in the British Top 20. They swiftly followed with a Top 10 entry, 'Lovers of the World Unite', but found greater success as a songwriting team, penning hits for a range of artists including the Hollies, Andy Williams, the Seekers and Cilla Black.

Burrows became a member of the Ivy League in 1966 and the Flowerpot Men in 1967, before becoming a session singer. In 1969 he became lead singer with Edison Lighthouse.

KING CURTIS American saxophonist who appeared on the Beatles' US tour in 1965. John Lennon hired Curtis to play on his 'Imagine' sessions in 1971. He was stabbed to death in Harlem shortly afterwards.

KING, Tony A promotions man who worked for Apple, plugging the company's record releases.

KINGSIZE TAYLOR & THE DOMINOES The Dominoes claim to have been the first rock group on Merseyside (disputed by the Seniors and Cass & the Cassanovas) and also the first Liverpool group to have broadcast on Radio Luxembourg.

Ted 'Kingsize' Taylor had been with a skiffle group called the James Boys from 1956. The Crosby-based band had named themselves after watching a film about Jesse James. He then switched to the Dominoes in August 1957. Another original member of the band was Keith 'Sam' Hardie on keyboards. Sam left the Dominoes for two years to work as a policeman, but later returned.

The drummer was Dave Lovelady, who was with the Zodiacs prior to joining the Dominoes.

Bass guitarist Bobby Thompson was originally rhythm player with the James Boys, but switched to bass when his rhythm guitar was destroyed in a car crash.

The band appeared regularly at a number of local venues, especially the jive Hive (St Luke's Hall, Crosby). By 1960 they had changed their name to Kingsize Taylor & the Dominoes and made their Cavern debut on 25 January 1961. Cilla Black, who was Ted's girlfriend at the time, got up to sing with the band and there was talk of her becoming a permanent member.

The group were voted No. 6 in the first *Mersey Beat* poll.

They made numerous appearances on bills with the Beatles and their Cavern gigs with them included three spots in 1961, on Wednesday 23 August; Tuesday 21 November and Wednesday 27 December.

Their 1962 Cavern appearances with the Beatles took place on Wednesday 3 January, Wednesday 31 January, Wednesday 20 June, Sunday 2 September and Wednesday 26 September.

They also appeared at the Cavern with the Beatles on Friday 11 January 1963 and were billed simply as the Dominoes when they appeared with the Beatles on Sunday 3 February 1963.

Kingsize was one of the best vocalists to emerge from the Mersey scene and the group had an extremely strong repertoire, comprising some of the more obscure but nevertheless brilliant American rock numbers. This was achieved by Taylor writing to the States for release lists from labels such as Chess, Imperial, Aladdin and Cameo-Parkway and having the records mailed to him.

When they appeared at the Star Club in 1962 they proved so popular that they were offered a residency.

Lovelady had taken time off from his architectural studies to appear for the short season, but couldn't remain for a residency, so Taylor had to find a new drummer.

He wrote to Ringo Starr at Butlin's, Skegness, offering him £20 a week to take over Lovelady's place in the band and Ringo agreed. A few days later Ringo wrote again saying he'd received an offer to join the Beatles, which he'd decided to accept. It was claimed at the time that the only reason he opted for the Beatles' seat was because they offered him £5 more per week than Taylor.

Brian Redmond joined and the group remained in Germany. While at the Star Club they appeared with several American rock stars, including Jerry Lee Lewis, Little Richard, Johnny & the Hurricanes and Joey Dee & the Starliters. Like the Beatles, they also provided backing for singer Davy Jones.

Redmond was replaced by Gibson Kemp, who'd taken over from Ringo Starr in Rory Storm & the Hurricanes.

Adrian Barber, stage manager at the Star Club, recorded them performing on stage – he recorded most of the groups at the time as he was developing a system for Manfred Weissleder to record artists on stage for a series of Star Club records.

Taylor asked Adrian if he could have a tape of the band and Adrian also gave him one on which he'd recorded the Beatles.

The Dominoes were to spend a great deal of their time abroad over the next few years, particularly in Hamburg, Berlin and Kiel, a decision which Taylor felt caused them to miss capitalizing on the Mersey Beat boom. They did return to Britain in 1964 for a Chuck Berry tour and made an appearance on *Ready, Steady, Go!* performing their Decca single 'Stupidity', but their residencies in Germany certainly prevented them building any national image in Britain.

The group had a No. 1 hit in Germany with 'Stupidity'.

They were to make a large number of records because Ted signed the group to Polydor, Fontana, Philips and Decca at the same time, recording under different names, ranging from the Shakers to Boot Lacey & the Toecaps.

During the years in Germany there were various changes in personnel, new members including saxophonist Howie Casey, singer Steve Aldo and Paddy Chambers, a former member of Faron's Flamingos.

In 1965 Taylor was appearing in Hamburg and Frankfurt with his group, renamed Kingsize Taylor & his Band, but was having problems with gangsters in certain clubs and the group weren't being paid. They had to be repatriated back to Britain later that year and the band broke up.

Taylor became a butcher and gave up his musical career entirely. Several years later he was to dig out Adrian Barber's recordings of the Beatles and sold them.

Ted Taylor had a distinctive voice and his bands were among the best ever to emerge from Liverpool; they were certainly superior to a great many of the bands who found success on record during the 1960s.

KINNEAR, Roy British actor who appeared as the incompetent Algernon, the assistant to a mad scientist in *Help!*. Kinnear also appeared with John Lennon as Private Clapper in Dick Lester's *How I Won the War*. He died in a freak accident on 20 September 1988, during the making of *The Return of the Musketeers*.

KIRCHHERR, Astrid Blonde-haired German photographer, born in Hamburg in 1938 and raised in a three-storey house at 42 Eimsbutteler Strasse in the suburb of Altona with her widowed mother, Nielsa. Her late father had been an executive for the West German branch of the Ford Motor Company.

She'd initially considered a career as a fashion-designer and had enrolled at the Meister Schule. However, she showed a talent for photography and the Schule's main photographic tutor, Reinhardt Wolf, talked her into switching courses, promising her that he would employ her as his assistant when she graduated.

In 1958 Astrid began going steady with a fellow student, Klaus Voormann, a 17-year-old doctor's son from Berlin. The two became part of a group of 'Exis', young followers of Existentialism, who generally wore black clothes and listened to modern jazz music.

One evening in October 1960, Astrid and Klaus had a row and Klaus took a long walk around the city. He found himself in the Grosse Freiheit in the St Pauli red-light district, where he was attracted by the sounds emanating from a club called the Kaiserkeller.

The music was performed by Rory Storm & the Hurricanes, but Klaus was even more enchanted by the group which followed: the Beatles.

He tried to convey to Astrid his excitement about the group and asked her to accompany him to the club. Eventually he persuaded her to come with him, also accompanied by another friend, Jurgen Vollmer. They too became captivated by the Beatles and began to visit the club regularly with a group of other friends, who included Peter Penner, Peter Mark-mann and Detlev Birgfeld.

The day after Astrid first became acquainted with the Beatles at the club, she arranged to take photographs of them and they all met at the Hamburg funfair, Der Dom.

After completing the shots Astrid took them all to lunch in a Chinese restaurant, then on to her home to introduce the Beatles to her mother and have tea at her home. Then she drove them back into town for their first set at the Kaiserkeller.

Despite John and Paul being the obvious leaders of the band, it was Stuart Sutcliffe to whom Astrid, Klaus and the other Exis were mainly attracted. In fact, Astrid was later to reveal: 'I fell in love with Stuart that very first night.'

Two weeks after they'd met, Astrid bought Stuart a chocolate heart and, while Klaus was in Berlin visiting his parents, Astrid and Stuart declared their love for each other.

Embarrassing as it might have been for Klaus, he accepted the situation and was replaced not only as Astrid's boyfriend but also in the Kirchherr home, as Frau Kirchherr, concerned about the deplorable state of the Beatles' accommodation in the Bambi Kino, invited Stuart to become their lodger in place of Klaus.

During this first trip Astrid took other shots of the Beatles, escorting them to various locations, including the docks and the railway yards. Her Beatles photographs at this time included some atmospheric portraits in which one half of the face was in shadow, a style which showed the influence of American photographer Richard Avedon. These pre-dated the famous Robert Freeman portraits for the *Around the Beatles* album cover, which were very similar in style.

One of the shots taken at the first location setting in the fairground was used as the front cover of issue No. 2 of *Mersey Beat*, giving the Beatles their first-ever cover. The photograph dominated the front page, alerting Liverpool to the fact that the Beatles had made a record in Germany, and it also intrigued Brian Epstein.

Almost two months after Astrid and Stuart first met they became engaged, exchanging rings in the German fashion.

While still at the Kaiserkeller, the Beatles had taken to visiting a rival club, the Top Ten on the Reeperbahn, much to the frustration of Bruno Koschmider. When he discovered that they intended moving on to the

Top Ten after their Kaiserkeller season ended, he pointed out the clause in their contract that stated they'd need his permission for such a move.

In his determination to sabotage their Top Ten plans, Koschmider allegedly arranged for George Harrison to be deported because he was under-age. Astrid and Stuart were the only ones to see him off back to Liverpool, from the Hauptbahnhof station on 21 November 1960.

Astrid was to recall: 'Stu and I drove George to the train station. He looked so lost and pathetic standing there on the platform holding his battered guitar case and his little duffle bag of laundry. Tears were welling up in his eyes, and just at the last moment he threw his arms around me and gave me a big hug.'

Koschmider next had the police arrest Paul and Pete on the pretext that they'd attempted to set fire to his cinema; they were also deported. John was the next to go, returning to Liverpool in early December. Stuart had contracted tonsillitis and Astrid paid for him to fly back home.

Astrid's influence was soon to affect the group as a whole. Her interest in fashion design and style in general had led her to alter Stuart's general appearance. She initially changed his hair style into the *pilzen kopf* ('mushroom head') which was sported by the male 'Exis' and was popular in Germany and France at the time. She shaped his hair across his forehead and created the style which became the basis for the famous Beatle 'moptop'.

Initially, the other members of the group ridiculed Stuart's new style. Then George agreed to try it and Astrid shaped his hair. Paul was next and finally John agreed to allow her to do his hair. Pete Best, however, decided to retain his own style, one of the moves which may have begun to isolate him from the others.

Astrid next fashioned a leather jerkin and trousers for Stuart, which resulted in the other members of the group buying some leather outfits from a store in Hamburg. When Astrid made Stuart a black corduroy jacket without lapels, in the style then being popularized by Pierre Cardin in Paris, the other members initially ridiculed him, but the collarless style was later to feature in the Beatles' image.

Astrid was invited over to Liverpool to meet Stuart's mother, sisters and friends. During this period it became obvious that Stuart's interest in being a Beatle was waning and his desire to pursue a career in art was gaining pace.

He returned to Hamburg on 15 March 1961 and the Beatles were to commence a season at the Top Ten Club. It was during this trip that the group recorded for Bert Kaempfert, although Stuart suggested that he did not take part in the recording – and Paul was to play bass.

Paul had been continually frustrated by Stuart's position as bass guitarist. He felt he should take over, and began to needle Stuart. The resentment finally spilled over one night on stage at the Top Ten, when Paul made some disparaging remarks about Astrid. Stuart lept on him and a furious fight took place. Soon after, Stuart decided to call it a day and left the group.

The Beatles had been impressed with Astrid from the start. She was two years older than Stuart, had her own car, her own private section of the house in Altona and was very sophisticated compared to the girls they were used to.

During the April trip, John's and Paul's girlfriends, Cynthia Powell and Dot Rhone, came over to join them. Cynthia stayed at Astrid's house, where Astrid changed her hairstyle, showed her how to put on make-up and lent her some of her clothes.

Cynthia was particularly impressed with Astrid's room, which was painted black, with silver tin-foil accessories. The bed also had a black velvet bedspread with black satin sheets and concealed spotlights lit the room.

After the Beatles returned to Liverpool, Stuart resumed his art studies in Hamburg under the tutelage of Eduardo Paolozzi. Tragically, during the latter part of 1961, Stuart began experiencing intolerable headaches and blackouts, which various doctors and medical institutions were unable to diagnose. There have been several theories regarding the cause – ranging from Millie Sutcliffe's conviction that it was a fall down the stairs at Astrid's house to Allan Williams's theory of a Liverpool punch-up.

Stuart and Astrid visited Liverpool in February 1962, but he looked exceedingly ill. On his return to Hamburg, his condition began to deteriorate. On Tuesday 10 April, he collapsed in his attic room. Frau Kirchherr called for a doctor and they carried him downstairs. A cerebral haemorrhage was suspected and an ambulance was called to take him to the neurological clinic at Heidbert Hospital.

Neila rang her daughter and when Astrid arrived home, Stuart went into a coma. Astrid sent a telegram to Mrs Sutcliffe, informing her Stuart was seriously ill, then accompanied him in the ambulance, where Stuart died at 4.45 p.m., before reaching the hospital.

On 12 April the Beatles arrived in Hamburg to begin their Star Club residency. Astrid met John, Paul and Pete at the airport and told them the tragic news. Brian Epstein arrived the next day with George and Millie Sutcliffe.

To shake Astrid out of her state of depression, John encouraged her to visit them regularly at the Star Club and she began taking photographs of various other Liverpool bands, such as the Undertakers and the Searchers.

Astrid was to say: 'It was John who saved me. He convinced me that I shouldn't behave like a widow. "Make up your mind," he said. "You either live or die, you can't be in the middle." '

She was later to marry Gibson Kemp, the young drummer who had replaced Ringo Starr in Rory Storm & the Hurricanes, who was eight years her junior.

In 1964 Astrid decided to give up photography and became a barmaid. When the Beatles appeared in Hamburg for a concert at the Ernst Merck Hall on 26 June 1966, Astrid and Gibson visited them and Astrid was able to give John a present of the letters he'd written to Stuart years previously.

In 1968 she was commissioned to take a photograph of George for his *Wonderwall* album sleeve.

Astrid and Gibson were to divorce after seven years and she later married a Bavarian businessman called Fink. This marriage was also unsuccessful. During the 30 years since she first met the Beatles, she endured various periods of hard times when she was penniless, homeless and suicidal.

She took on numerous jobs, ranging from working as a cleaner to becoming a dancer in a lesbian bar. When her second marriage collapsed a friend hired her to run his luxury hotel on the German-Danish border, but this also fell through in 1991. She returned to Hamburg with no money and nowhere to live until a friend provided her with a flat.

At last, good fortune came along when her friend Ulf Kruger became her manager, gaining acknowledgement for her photographic archive, which had been ripped off over the years by publishers who never paid her or credited her for the early Beatles pictures of hers which they published.

The biggest change came with the 1994 release of *Backbeat*, a feature film based on her romance with Stuart; she was reputedly paid £100,000 for her story.

Astrid was 55 years old when the film was released and American actress Sheryl Lee, who played Laura Palmer in *Twin Peaks*, portrayed her.

KLAATU Group who issued an album, *Klaatu*, in 1973 which many people believed was the Beatles under an assumed name. As a result the album sold 300,000 copies in a very short time.

KLEIN, Allen American manager and music publisher, born in Newark, New Jersey, on 13 December 1931.

When he entered the music business, after studying accountancy, he formed some music-publishing companies and became manager of the Shirelles, Sam Cooke and Bobby Vinton.

Klein's great strength was in discovering overlooked fees and royalties and obtaining monies for the artists from recording companies. This much-publicized activity led to his being given the nickname the 'Robin Hood of Pop'.

He was a tough negotiator and together with his wife, Betty, set up his ABKCO Industries (short for Allen and Betty Klein).

When the British invasion of America occurred he was able to take over the management of several UK bands, including the Rolling Stones, the Dave Clark Five, Donovan, Herman's Hermits and the Animals.

Ironically, it was Paul McCartney who first suggested that Klein should act on behalf of the Beatles.

When Klein read the issue of *Disc* in which John Lennon had revealed to editor Ray Coleman, 'If Apple goes on losing money, all of us will be broke in six months,' he saw his opportunity. He contacted Lennon and met up with him and Yoko Ono at the Dorchester Hotel in London on 28 January 1969.

Lennon was impressed and sent a message to Sir Joseph Lockwood of EMI, which read: 'Dear Sir Joe – from now on Allen Klein handles all my stuff.'

Klein also met up with George and Ringo and they agreed to arrange a meeting for him with all four Beatles. Paul walked out of the meeting.

By that time Paul had decided he wanted John Eastman to represent him and a compromise was agreed for a while – that Eastman and Klein should both work as the Beatles advisers.

There was a great deal of conflict, during which the Beatles lost their opportunity of buying NEMS Enterprises, and also Northern Songs.

Klein was one of the factors in the break-up of the group, although he had boosted their income by renegotiating their contracts with EMI and Capitol and by sacking almost all of the staff at Apple.

However, Paul was disenchanted and on 31 December 1970 he instigated a High Court action to place the group's affairs in the hands of the receiver, a move he was advised to take as the only way of ridding himself of Klein.

Although the Beatles' finances weren't as bad as they'd been pictured (they had £6,549,668 in the bank), it was revealed that their affairs were in a mess, that they didn't have enough money to pay their taxes and that there were hardly any accountants left at Apple to tackle their accounts.

Paul was successful in his action, although it took six years for Apple to be finally rid of Klein, who agreed to a pay-off of $4 million. The other three had eventually come to the same conclusion about Klein as Paul.

In May 1979 Klein was jailed for two months for tax evasion – this related to income he'd taken from illegal sales of George Harrison's charity album *The Concert for Bangladesh*.

In 1995 Klein was still living in New York, although he was suffering from ill-health.

KOSCHMIDER, Bruno Hamburg club-owner, a former circus clown, fire eater and acrobat. He was the first club-owner to book British rock bands into the city.

The actual steps leading to his booking mainly Liverpool groups has not been clearly defined. Allan Williams claimed that he went to Hamburg in search of his Royal Caribbean Steel Band and happened on to the Kaiserkeller club by accident, where he discovered that Koschmider was looking for acts to present at the club.

It seems unlikely that someone running a tiny coffee bar in Liverpool would travel all the way to another country in search of an act he had booked for a few pounds. While not dismissing the story, it is interesting to note that other versions exist. Casey Valence says that he stayed overnight in the Jacaranda and was contacting Koschmider in Hamburg in an effort to get him to book Cass & the Cassanovas. He relates that a Koschmider representative phoned the club, asking for him when he wasn't there, and Williams took the call, and as a result said that he would book the groups.

What has been established is that Koschmider arrived in London, seeking bands, and was directed to the 2 I's club in Soho. While there he booked the Jets, who were literally formed on the spot by Iain Hines. By sheer coincidence, Williams was also at the club, with Derry & the Seniors, and Koschmider booked them as the second act for his club.

Williams attempted to secure the booking rights for all British bands with Koschmider and sent over the Beatles, followed by Rory Storm & the Hurricanes.

Koschmider originally put the Beatles into his smaller club, the Indra, but it was closed by the police and they opened at the Kaiserkeller on 4 October 1962, second on the bill to Rory Storm & the Hurricanes.

Koschmider's idea of bringing British rock 'n' roll groups to Hamburg was immediately taken up by Peter Eckhorn of the Top Ten Club, who booked the Jets. The Beatles began to play at the club and accepted Eckhorn's offer of a season.

When Koschmider heard about it, he allegedly arranged for George Harrison to be deported, because he was under-age, and accused Paul McCartney and Pete Best of trying to set fire to his Bambi Kino, which resulted in their deportation as well.

Unable to compete with the Top Ten and the Star Club, he changed the name of the Kaiserkeller to the Colibri and reverted to booking strip acts.

KRAMER, Billy J Born William Howard Ashton on 19 August 1943 in the Bootle area of Liverpool, Billy began his musical career with Billy Forde & the Phantoms, who were to change their name to Billy Kramer & the Coasters.

The group were managed by pensioner Ted Knibbs and, in 1962, they appeared on Cavern bills with the Beatles on Sunday 9 September and Wednesday 3 October. They also appeared with the Beatles at Queens Hall, Widnes on Monday 17 September 1962 and Tower Ballroom on Friday 23 November 1962.

The group were voted No. 3 in the *Mersey Beat* poll, but Billy had, by that time, decided to take up a full-time position with British Rail. However, Knibbs interested Brian Epstein in his artist and Epstein was to sign him up.

The Coasters refused to turn professional, so Brian had to find another backing group for Billy. When the Remo 4 turned him down, Epstein made an offer to the Manchester band, the Dakotas, who were backing Pete Maclaine at the time. They initially refused, but finally agreed when Epstein arranged for them to make records in their own right.

Considering that Billy only teamed up with the Dakotas in 1963, their American press release, issued in 1964, read:

> Billy and the Dakotas chose their name when they were called to audition in England four years ago. They were told to return dressed as Indians. Unable to afford the $100 apiece for buckskins, the group skipped the audition but kept the name.

It was John Lennon who came up with the idea of the initial 'J' – which stood for Julian, his son.

Billy topped the charts with his first release, the Lennon and McCartney number, 'Do You Want to Know a Secret?'. His other Lennon and McCartney hits included 'Bad To Me', 'I'll Keep You Satisfied' and 'From a Window'.

It was Kramer himself who found the number 'Little Children' and had to talk Brian Epstein into letting him record it. The song became his biggest hit. Epstein seemed to have lost interest in Billy's career by this time, so the singer approached Paul McCartney to ask him if he could provide him with a song. Paul offered him 'Yesterday', but Billy didn't consider it suitable.

Billy embarked on a solo career in 1967 and has been performing ever since.

KUBAS, The Mersey group who formed in April 1963. Their original drummer, John Morris, who became their co-manager, said: 'Our first break came from Rory Storm, who suggested we audition for the Star Club, Hamburg. Bill Harry finally clinched the deal and we were off for a three-week stay. We came home Christmas Eve 1963 and soon after based ourselves in London under the Roy Tempest Organization.'

The group next appeared in Spain, for a time were managed by Brian Epstein and were in the film *Ferry 'Cross the Mersey*, although their sequence ended up on the cutting-room floor.

There were several variations in personnel, but their basic line-up was Keith Ellis (bass), Stu Leithwood (rhythm), Tony O'Reilly (drums) and Roy Morris (lead).

They signed a contract with Columbia and their first release was 'Magic Potion' in January 1965. By the time of their second release, 'Take Me for a Little While' in November 1965, which was issued by Pye, they'd altered the spelling of their name to the Koobas. The following month they appeared on the Beatles' final tour of Britain from 3 to 12 December.

Late in 1965, Tony Stratton-Smith became enthusiastic about the group and signed them up. Unfortunately, despite major promotion, they never made the big time. Following the release of their album *The Koobas* in 1968 and an appearance as support band on a Jimi Hendrix Experience tour of Switzerland the same year, they disbanded.

LADDERS, The When Paul left the Beatles there was a degree of acrimony and John, George and Ringo considered continuing as a band with Klaus Voormann replacing Paul on bass. They decided not to use the name the Beatles and were going to call themselves the Ladders. Klaus met John, George and Ringo at the Apple offices on 19 March 1971 and the *Daily Mirror* ran a story about the potential new band the next day. However, Apple printed a denial a few days later.

LEACH, Sam Innovative Liverpool promoter who initially began local promotions at Mossway Hall in 1958, in partnership with Dick Matthews.

He first booked the Beatles for his Cassanova club on 11 February 1961, where they were featured with the Big Three, Rory Storm & the Hurricanes and Mark Peters & the Cyclones, and for his Iron Door all-night session on 11 March.

His biggest promotions took place at the Tower Ballroom, New Brighton, beginning with 'Operation Big Beat' on 10 November, followed by 'Operation Big Beat 2' on 24 November and another Tower promotion on 15 December.

Sam's most interesting Beatles booking took place on 9 December, when he featured them on their first foray down south, at the Palais Ballroom, Queen's Road, Aldershot.

He'd decided to arouse interest in Mersey groups in the south by holding gigs there and inviting prominent promoters along. He mistakenly chose Aldershot, which is 37 miles from London and a place where no agent would venture to see an unknown band.

He booked the venue for five consecutive Saturdays and had leaflets printed announcing a 'Battle of the Bands'. This was to be a 'Liverpool vs. London' gig, with the Beatles representing Liverpool and Ivor Jay & the Jaywalkers representing the south.

The party set off at five on Saturday morning with Sam, Dick Matthews and the Beatles travelling in a van with their equipment, driven by one of Sam's bouncers, Terry McCann.

The drive took nine hours. Sam had told the group that he'd promoted them in a big way and bought a copy of the *Aldershot News*, expecting to see a large advertisement for the gig. It wasn't in, and when he went to the newspaper office they explained that they hadn't placed the advertisement because they required cash up front from first-time advertisers – and hadn't been able to contact him to explain the rule.

Only four people turned up at the hall and Sam went to coffee bars and pubs pleading with youngsters to attend. Eventually 18 people gathered in the ballroom. A neighbour complained about the noise and three police cars and four police vans arrived at the Palais, instructing them to leave town and never return!

Sam continued booking the Beatles locally in 1962 and his last promotions with them took place in September of that year, beginning with a Leach Entertainments presentation of 'The Beatles Show' at the Rialto, with the Big Three, Rory Storm & the Hurricanes and the Mersey

Beats and the 'Operation Big Beat V' at the Tower on 14 September.

Brian Epstein was now the Beatles' manager and, according to Sam, prevented them appearing for him again. Sam says they played for him a last time at the Rialto gig because: 'there was some money owing from the night before, £19. I paid everyone else except them, I said. "I'll pay you tomorrow for the two bookings," as we hadn't done very well ... but Epstein got upset and that was the last time they played for me.'

Despite what Sam said, the Beatles hadn't played for him for some time prior to the Rialto gig – and it wasn't their last appearance for Sam, as he featured them at the Tower Ballroom a week later.

During 1961 and 1962 Epstein had been relying on the knowledge and expertise of members of the local scene to help him in his plans. As Sam had successfully established the Tower Ballroom as the biggest venue on Merseyside, Brian suggested they become partners in further Tower promotions. At a meeting at the Kardomah coffee bar, Sam suggested that they split 50–50, but Brian insisted that his brother Clive be part of the deal and they should split three ways. Leach refused.

Sam had booked Little Richard for the Tower, but says that Brian offered more money to the American star and the next Tower promotion headlined Richard and the Beatles on 12 October in a NEMS Enterprises promotion.

Sam Leach intended seeking management of the Beatles, until Epstein appeared on the scene. He'd wanted to sign them to a record label he hoped to start called Troubadour Records and intended recording them performing 'Twist & Shout' and 'Stand by Me'.

He was able to capitalize on his association with them when he published *The Beatles on Broadway* in 1964, which sold a million copies and brought him enough money to establish himself in his own business.

LEARY, Timothy Prominent figure of America's drug culture of the 1960s. His book *Psychedelic Experience* influenced John Lennon when he wrote 'Tomorrow Never Knows'. Leary was to say: 'The Beatles are prototypes of a new race of laughing freemen: revolutionary agents sent by God, endowed with a mysterious power to create a new human species.' He died in 1996.

LEE, Debbie Female vocalist who appeared on the Chris Montez, Tommy Roe, Beatles tour in March 1963.

LEE CURTIS & THE ALL STARS Lee Curtis was the stage name of Peter Flannery, younger brother of Joe Flannery, who became his manager.

Joe was determined to emulate Brian Epstein and spent a lot of money and energy promoting his brother's group, initially known as Lee Curtis & the Detours when they were launched in March 1961. Apart from lead singer Lee, a handsome Elvis clone, there was Ritchie Quillam on rhythm, John D. Puditter on drums, Chez on bass and Billy Churchill on guitar. As a gimmick they were given a set of unfortunate stage names: Consyd Waytis, Xystus Cornelius, Derry Lucas and Lord Joseph Beatty.

The band appeared with the Beatles on 'Operation Big Beat 3' at the Tower Ballroom, New Brighton, on Friday 29 June 1962 and then major personnel changes were made and the name altered to Lee Curtis & the All Stars.

Lee recruited a new backing band. Wayne Bicketon on bass had been with the Bobby Bell Rockers and had just spent six months playing in London with another Liverpool outfit, Steve & the Syndicate. Drummer Bernie Rogers, former member of the Travellers, was to leave the band after a short time to join Denny Seyton & the Sabres, who'd secured a record contract. Tony Waddington on rhythm had been a member of the Comets and Frank Bowen on lead was a legendary Liverpool guitarist who died at an early age. Frank's first group was the Teenbeats, followed by Cliff Roberts & the Rockers, the Strangers, the Lonely Ones, the Cyclones and Howie Casey & the Seniors. After the All Stars he joined the Pathfinders and the Trends.

Bickerton and Waddington were to remain a team for over two decades and found great success in London as songwriters and record producers.

When Pete Best was ejected from the Beatles, Joe talked him into joining Lee's group to fill the gap left by Rogers, and the band was then renamed Lee Curtis & the All Stars. Among several bills they appeared on with the Beatles was the 'Riverboat Shuffle' on the Mersey on 28 September 1962, Little Richard and the Beatles concert at the Tower Ballroom on Friday 12 October 1962, the 'Showdance' at the Queen's Hall, Widnes, on Monday 22 October 1962 and the Cavern on Tuesday 19 February 1963, the latter being the last time Best ever saw the Beatles.

As a result of Pete Best's joining them so soon after he left the Beatles, the group were voted No. 2 in the second *Mersey Beat* poll, although this reflected the popularity of Best rather than the standing of the group.

There was another major change in July 1963, when Lee left to pursue a solo career and Pete Best took over as leader of the All Stars. Lee performed at the Star Club and was to remain in Hamburg for several years, recording a number of singles and albums in Germany.

Lee had three singles issued by Decca, 'Little Girl', 'Let's Stomp' and 'What About Me?', although his relationship with Decca proved frustrating and he blamed them for hindering his career. 'Let's Stomp', with Pete Best on drums, was a Bobby Comstock number which was popular with the group's fans. However, Decca forced him to keep repeating the words on the single – a total of 36 times – which he felt ruined the recording and stripped it of any commercial impact.

He then wanted to record 'Twist & Shout', but Decca refused, and later had Brian Poole & the Tremeloes release the number and they topped the charts with it. The group asked if they could record 'Money'. Decca refused and later released the number by another of their southern acts, Bern Elliot & the Fenmen. Curtis then asked Decca if they could record

'Shout'. Decca refused and later released a single of 'Shout' with Lulu with the Luvvers. He next requested that they record 'It's Only Make Believe', but Decca once again refused but later released a version by Billy Fury which charted.

This, like the examples with other Liverpool bands such as the Undertakers and Faron's Flamingos, is undeniable evidence of how London recording companies undermined the careers of Liverpool bands while putting their energies and promotion behind bands from the south in order to regain ground lost when northern groups such as the Beatles began to dominate the charts.

LENNON, Alfred John Lennon's father, born in Liverpool on 14 December 1912, who has perhaps been maligned in Beatles books much more than is warranted.

One of six children, he was bundled off to the Bluecoat School orphanage, along with his sister Edith, when his father died of a liver disease in 1921.

At the age of 15 he took a job as a clerk, before becoming a merchant seaman at the age of 16. He first met the 14-year-old Julia Stanley in Sefton Park in 1927, chatted her up and began to date her regularly over a period of ten years. They were finally married at Mount Pleasant Register Office on 3 December 1938. No member of her family was present at the wedding and in the evening Julia returned to her home and Freddie to his digs. He went off on a three-month trip to the West Indies the following day.

Fred was also at sea when his son John was born in October 1940. While in New York, he was told to report to a ship leaving for Britain, but, as this would have meant a demotion, he took the captain's advice, got drunk and missed the ship, which resulted in his internment on Ellis Island. He was then placed on a ship going to North Africa. He was given a bottle of vodka by one of the cooks and then accused of stealing it, which led to a three-month jail sentence.

In the meantime in Liverpool, his wife was dating other men and gave birth to a baby girl in 1945 following her affair with a Welsh soldier. The baby was put up for adoption. Julia then went to live with another man and left John to live with his Aunt Mimi.

In 1946, when Fred docked in Southampton, he contacted Mimi and asked if he could take John to Blackpool. He then decided that he and John could forge a new life for themselves in New Zealand and was making plans when Julia arrived, demanding the return of John. As John wanted to go with his mother, Fred agreed.

As soon as Julia returned to Liverpool, she placed John back in the hands of her sister and went off to live with John Dykins, by whom she had two daughters. Fred did not see his son again for 20 years.

By 1964 Fred had ceased his seafaring life and worked as a porter in a London hotel. The *Daily Express* traced him and wanted to set up a meeting between him and his son.

During the years John was raised by Mimi, his aunt had poisoned his mind about his father and when Fred was interviewed by Hunter Davies for the authorized Beatles biography, Fred's version of events was vetoed and Mimi's version was put to the fore.

John and his father became reacquainted and John gave him an allowance. Freddie made an autobiographical record, 'That's My Life (My Love and My Home)', and married a 19-year-old girl, Pauline Stone. With John's help, they eloped to Scotland. The couple had two sons.

There was another period in which John turned against his father, but, shortly before Fred died of cancer, John spoke to him several times by phone and they were reconciled.

He'd been writing his autobiography at the time of his death and the book was completed by his wife and published in 1990 as *Daddy, Come Home*.

LENNON, Charles Brother of Alfred and uncle to John. While John lived at Weybridge, the press discovered the whereabouts of his father, but John refused to become reconciled. Charlie wrote to him to explain that his brother was not the black sheep people had made out. John then established a relationship with Alfred and also invited Charlie to his home. During one of his Weybridge visits, John said: 'Uncle Charlie, whenever you're confronted by the press you have two left feet and a stub of an arm.'

Charlie was later to move to Liverpool. He is a regular guest at local conventions and chats with fans of John who visit the John Lennon club in Mathew Street.

LENNON, Cynthia John Lennon's first wife, born Cynthia Powell in Blackpool on 10 September 1939, the week war broke out. Her mother, Lillian, and father, Charles, had been relocated to Blackpool because most pregnant women were moved away from the Liverpool area for fear of the inevitable bombing raids. Cynthia's two older brothers, Charles and Tony, had been sent to Wales.

The family eventually returned to their home in Waverley Road, Hoylake.

At the age of 12 Cynthia won a scholarship to the Junior School of Art in Gambier Terrace, Liverpool, where she was to meet her lifelong friend Phyllis MacKenzie.

Her father died of cancer when Cynthia was 17 and it looked as if her hopes of continuing her education at the Liverpool College of Art were doomed. However, her mother insisted that the insurance money be used for her education and Cynthia entered the college in September 1957.

The first two years at college were spent on the Intermediate Course, in which the basics of art were taught in lessons ranging from life drawing to architecture. Students also had to pick a subject which they would specialize in following the Intermediate exams and Cynthia and Phyllis chose lettering.

John and his friend Jonathan Hague were also in the same class and John would often tease her about her 'posh' accent and the fact that she came from 'over the water' in the Wirral. Despite the barbs, she found she was becoming fascinated by him and one day, in the lecture hall, when she saw fellow student Helen Anderson stroke his hair, she felt a pang of jealousy. From then on she was love-sick, changing her clothes, her hair style, leaving off her glasses, dieting, all in an attempt to capture his attention.

The romance took off following a college end-of-term party. When John began chatting her up, she blurted out: 'I'm awfully sorry, I'm engaged to this fellow in Hoylake.'

'I didn't ask you to marry me did I?' he said, but later invited Cynthia and Phyl to join him at Ye Cracke, the local pub. She wasn't used to drink and went back with John to the Gambier Terrace flat, where they made love for the first time.

Now that they were going out together, Cynthia began to alter her appearance further in her efforts to please him. She knew he was besotted by Brigitte Bardot so she allowed her blonde hair to grow long, began to wear tight black sweaters, very short, tight skirts, high-heeled shoes and black stockings and suspenders.

As the Beatles began to gain a following in the local Liverpool venues, Cynthia had to stay in the background so as not to upset the female fans. He'd taken her to meet his Aunt Mimi, who seemed to approve of her, but, when she took John to meet her mother, Lilian made no attempt to hide her disapproval and told her daughter she could have done better. The tension between John and Lilian continued over the years, even when she came to stay with them at their Weybridge home.

Cynthia became friendly with Paul McCartney's girlfriend, Dot Rhone, and the two girls were invited to join the group in Hamburg when the Beatles appeared at the Top Ten Club, from 27 March to 2 July 1961. On her return home, Cynthia found that her mother had received an offer to move to Canada with her nephew and his wife, who were emigrating and wanted her to act as nanny to their children. Cyn then lodged for a time with Mimi Smith, but it didn't work out and she moved into a small flat and coaxed Dot into taking an adjoining room.

Cynthia failed her exams and then discovered she was pregnant. When the doctor told her the news she was shocked. Her mother was in Canada, John was away, she couldn't go back to college and had no job or money.

When John turned up a couple of weeks later she told him, apprehensively, but was relieved when he said: 'We'll have to get married.'

His Aunt Mimi was furious, accusing him of ruining his life and told him she wouldn't attend the wedding. Brian Epstein insisted that any marriage must be kept secret from the press, as he felt it would damage the Beatles' career. He arranged a special licence for them and the ceremony took place at Mount Pleasant Register Office at 64 Mount

Pleasant on 23 August 1963. This was the same register office where John's parents had been married.

Also present were Brian Epstein, Paul McCartney, George Harrison and Cynthia's brother Tony and his wife, Margery. Ringo Starr, the new member of the Beatles, hadn't been invited. Paul signed the certificate as witness to the civil ceremony, which had been so disrupted by nearby construction work that Cynthia could hardly hear the words of the ceremony. They then went to Reece's Restaurant, where Brian Epstein was to host their wedding breakfast. However, the restaurant was packed with lunchtime office workers milling about and as Brian hadn't booked a table they had to wait for 20 minutes before they could sit down to their set menu of soup, chicken and trifle.

Brian also gave them the key to his private flat in Falkner Street and told them they could live there for as long as they wished. However, as John was on the road most of the time, Mimi was concerned about the pregnant girl being on her own and, after she had a near miscarriage in her third month, insisted that she move in with her.

Julian was born at Sefton General Hospital on Monday 8 April 1963 and the birth, like the marriage, was also kept secret from the media.

Six months later Cynthia's mother returned from Canada and moved into a flat in Trinity Road, Hoylake, where Cynthia and Julian were to join her. At one point John was able to take a break from touring and the two had a belated honeymoon in Paris.

On her return to Hoylake the inevitable happened and the press, discovering that the famous Beatle had a wife and son, besieged the Trinity Road flat and the story was given extensive coverage. John decided they should move to London and all find a flat together, living as a family. Photographer Bob Freeman suggested they move into a vacant flat at Emperor's Gate in Kensington. However, it was on the sixth floor and there was no lift, which proved problematic for Cynthia, having to climb six flights of stairs with a child. On the advice of the Beatles' accountants Bryce Hanmer, John paid £40,000 for Kenwood, a house in Weybridge, 20 miles from London, in July 1964, spending a further £30,000 on renovations.

Cynthia soon settled down to becoming a housewife, although she experienced some exciting times travelling to America with the Beatles and socializing with the other Beatles' wives and girlfriends.

She claims that things started to go wrong when John began taking drugs and in her autobiography, *A Twist of Lennon*, she wrote: 'As far as I was concerned the rot began to set in the moment cannabis and LSD seeped its unhealthy way into our lives.'

Because John and other members of the Beatles' inner circle also partook of various substances, she began to feel estranged from John and decided she'd have to make some attempt to save her marriage. She succumbed to John's constant suggestion that she take LSD – he had said he'd help her through her first experience of a trip. She found it horrific. During the experience, John kept saying that he loved her and would never leave her, but when she looked at him she hallucinated and saw an animal-type person with razor-sharp teeth laughing at her.

She was relieved when the Beatles took an interest in Transcendental Meditation and felt that the teaching of the Maharishi Mahesh Yogi would wean John off drugs. They all travelled to India to study at the Maharishi's ashram in Rishikesh and Cynthia believed that meditation had a positive effect on John.

By this time Yoko Ono had entered the picture. Cynthia first met her at a meditation session. She then noticed letters Yoko had been sending to John, requesting his help in promoting her book *Grapefruit*.

When the Beatles were due to go into the studio for some extended recording sessions, John suggested that she take up the offer of a two-week holiday in Greece in the company of Jenny Boyd, Alexis Mardas, Donovan and Gypsy Dave. She returned home to find John and Yoko together wearing matching purple dressing gowns. Instead of reacting with anger and throwing Yoko out, she broke down in tears and left, staying at the house Jenny shared with Alexis. In the evening she sat up drinking wine with Alexis and woke up the next morning to find herself in bed with him.

Years later John's Aunt Mimi was to scold her for not trying to save the marriage, telling her: 'How could you have allowed it to happen, Cynthia? You should have fought. You should have battled.'

Cynthia returned to Kenwood, found Yoko had left and accepted John's explanation that he'd become bored with Yoko. There was a brief reconciliation, but John left for New York a few days later, refusing to take Cynthia along with him. Not wishing to remain at Kenwood alone, she took Julian with her on an Italian holiday, accompanied by her mother and her Uncle Bill and Auntie Daisy.

While there she saw reports in the English newspapers of John and Yoko attending the *In His Own Write* play together, with John declaring his love for Yoko. Her despair deepened when Alexis Mardas turned up and informed her that John was seeking a divorce, with Alexis willing to testify that Cynthia had committed adultery with him. She returned to London to find a petition citing her adultery with Mardas, but this was dropped when it was agreed that it would be far better for all concerned if John admitted his adultery with Yoko. This done, Cynthia was granted a decree nisi on 8 November 1969.

Several months later, on 31 July 1970, Cynthia remarried at Kensington Register Office. The man in question was Roberto Bassanini, the son of the owners of the hotel where she'd stayed in Italy.

It was a short-lived marriage and she was later to marry businessman John Twist. Initially, the newly married couple moved to Ireland, then settled in Ruthin, North Wales, where they opened a restaurant.

Cynthia's autobiography, *A Twist of Lennon*, was published in 1978, Her marriage to Twist was also to end in divorce a short time later.

Following John's death, Cynthia dropped the Twist from her surname and replaced it with Lennon.

Once Julian had left home to carve a career for himself in show business and with the rather small settlement she'd received from John (small in relation to his earnings) almost gone, she had to make a living for herself and achieved a modest degree of success as a designer.

At one point she became a partner in a West End restaurant, Lennons, but it didn't succeed and she later settled on the Isle of Man and was to sell most of her personal memorabilia relating to John at auction in 1991.

Cynthia lived in a chalet-style house on the Isle of Man with longtime boyfriend and business partner, Jim Christie, her spokesman. Her life story was serialized in *Hello!* magazine, starting in April 1994. During the 1990s she began appearing regularly at Beatles conventions around the world and in January 1995 made her recording debut with 'Those were the Days'. In 1996 Cynthia and Jim relocated to Dorset.

LENNON, Jack John's paternal grandfather. Born in Ireland, he moved to Liverpool before setting off for America, where he joined a minstrel show. He later returned to Liverpool and raised a family before his death in 1921.

LENNON, Sean Second son of John Lennon and the only child of John and Yoko Ono. The couple had tried for a child for some years and Yoko had suffered three miscarriages.

When Sean was born, an excited John said, 'I feel higher than the Empire State Building,' although it was a good thing he didn't carry through his original plan to name the boy George Washington United States of America Citizen Lennon.

Just as John had been raised without the presence of a father, he'd done the same with his first son, Julian, rarely seeing him during his formative years. With Sean he decided to devote himself to the child and retired for a period of five years, during which he spent all his time looking after the boy.

His very close relationship with Sean came to a cruel end when he was gunned down in 1980.

Sean enjoys a much more lavish lifestyle than his stepbrother Julian and is heir to John's £250 million fortune. He lives in a £2 million luxury apartment adjoining his mother's in the Dakota Building in New York.

In 1995 he ran his own pop group, the Pits, in which he sang and played lead guitar.

LENNON, Sydney Freddie Lennon's older brother, who was witness to Fred and Julia's marriage on 3 December 1938. At the time he lived in a suburb of Liverpool called Maghull.

LENNON, John Charles Julian First son of John Lennon, born at Sefton General Hospital, Liverpool, on Monday 8 April 1963.

When Cynthia became pregnant, John proposed marriage and an

unpublicized ceremony was arranged by special licence. John was to make many hurtful comments about the birth in the years to come.

Julian was born at 7.45 a.m. and there were complications, because the umbilical cord was wrapped around his neck. John saw his son for the first time a week after his birth. Brian Epstein wanted the marriage to be kept secret, so Cynthia and Julian went to live with her mother in Hoylake.

In November of that year Julian was christened at Trinity Road Parish Church. John didn't attend that ceremony either.

The baby's first name was chosen in honour of John, the second in memory of Cynthia's father and the third in memory of John's mother. Over a period of time he became known simply as Julian.

Eventually, news of the marriage broke in the national press and Cynthia and Julian moved to London to be with John. They settled in a flat in Emperor's Gate, Kensington, for a time. John then bought a large house in Weybridge and Julian began to attend the local prep school.

At the age of four he brought home a picture he'd painted of one of his school chums. John asked him what his painting was about and Julian told him, 'It's Lucy in the sky with diamonds.' John was then inspired to write a song of that title for the *Sgt Pepper* album.

The arrival of Yoko Ono heralded the end of the marriage and after the divorce John saw little of his son. He did take him out on a number of occasions, but they were few and far between.

Cynthia married Roberto Bassanini in 1970, but was divorced in 1973. She married John Twist in 1976 and Twist, Cynthia and Julian moved to Ruthin, North Wales, where Julian attended the local school.

In 1980, when he was first given the news of his father's violent death, Julian lay on the floor in a state of shock for hours.

Cynthia and Twist were divorced and Julian left home to settle in London, where he began to hit the headlines frequently, as a result of his affairs with several models.

His interest in music grew and he formed a group called the Lennon Drops. Then, for a short time, he joined Quasar. He turned solo and his debut album, *Valotte*, provided him with a major hit, but subsequent releases saw a steady decline in his success.

For a time he began to drink Jack Daniels to excess and also took drugs, but he eventually freed himself from the addictions.

Julian currently owns three homes: one in London, one in Los Angeles and one in Monte Carlo. Although his father's fortune exceeded $200 million, Julian was only given £70,000 as a lump sum when he reached 25 and the bulk of John's estate is said to have gone to Sean.

LENNON, Julia Born Julia Stanley on 12 March 1914, she was one of the five daughters of George and Annie Stanley.

On 3 December 1938 she married Alfred Lennon and their son John was born in October 1940. While her husband was at sea she had another child by a Welsh soldier, 'Taffy' Williams, but had to give the baby up for adoption. She continued dating other men and eventually went to live with John Dykins, with whom she had two daughters.

In the meantime, she left John to be raised by her sister Mimi, although he began to see more of Julia as he was growing up. Julia used to sing to him and play a banjo and John was to comment: 'My mother could play any stringed instrument there was.'

She was killed on 15 July 1958 after visiting Mimi. Nigel Whalley, John's friend, witnessed the accident in which a car driven by an off-duty policeman knocked her down. She died instantly.

John was to be haunted by memories of her for the rest of his life – feelings which he is said to have exorcized during his course of 'Primal Scream' therapy.

He was also inspired to write some songs about her, including 'Mother', 'My Mummy's Dead' and 'Julia'.

LENNY THE LION Puppet featured by ventriloquist Terry Hall, whose catchphrase was 'Don't embawass me!' He was featured on the children's television show *Pops and Lenny*, and the Beatles made their second national BBC TV appearance on it on Thursday 16 May 1963. They performed 'From Me to You' and 'Please Please Me' and joined the finale with Patsy Ann Noble, the Raindrops, the Ben Hayes Octet and Terry and Lenny to sing 'After You've Gone'. The puppet was later featured on a show aiding children with reading difficulties, 'Reading with Lenny the Lion', until Terry decided to retire following the death of his wife in 1980 and settled in Coventry.

LES STEWART QUARTET, The During 1959, when the Quarry Men had all but disbanded, George Harrison joined the Les Stewart Quartet, who had a residency at Lowlands club in West Derby. When Ken Brown, who was also in the group, fixed up a residency at the new Casbah club, Les Stewart refused to let the group appear, accusing Brown of missing rehearsals to help out in decorating the new club. George and Brown left the band to team up with John and Paul to re-form the Quarry Men and take up the Casbah residency.

LESTER, Richard American film director, born in Philadelphia on 19 January 1932. He was a psychology student at the University of Pennsylvania who began writing music and formed a vocal group. He worked in a television studio as floor manager, then took some time off in the mid-1950s to travel to England, just as the commercial ITV channel was being launched. He began directing comedy and music shows in Britain, including a television show featuring Peter Sellers, *A Show Called Fred*. He made his film directing debut with *The Running, Jumping and Standing Still Film* in 1959, starring Sellers and Spike Milligan.

In 1962 he directed *It's Trad, Dad!*, which featured several British and American pop artists, including Helen Shapiro, introducing some of his fast cutting and hand-held camera innovations. The following year he directed *Mouse on the Moon* for Walter Shenson. When Shenson was asked to produce the Beatles' debut film, he hired Lester to direct it.

Discussing the movie, he said: 'The shooting of the concert sequence was astonishing. We used six film and three TV cameras to shoot the final 17 minutes of film in a single day.' He also commented: 'I made it for a tiny salary. No share in the profits.'

Lester had also made a number of TV commercials, including a series for Smith's Crisps, which featured Pattie Boyd, whom he cast to appear in *A Hard Day's Night*.

In 1965 he directed the Beatles in *Help!* and his other films included *The Knack* (1965), which won the Best Film Award at Cannes, *A Funny Thing Happened on the Way to the Forum* (1966), *How I Won the War* (1967), which featured John Lennon, *The Bed Sitting Room* (1969), *The Three Musketeers* (1973), a project he'd originally wanted to use as a vehicle for the Beatles third film, featuring Brigitte Bardot as Lady De Winter, *Robin and Marian* (1976) and *Superman* (1977).

Twenty-five years after directing *A Hard Day's Night*, he approached Paul McCartney and requested the opportunity of directing a film about his 1989–90 world tour. Paul agreed and the result was *Get Back: The Movie*, released in 1991.

In 1984 *Beatles, Musketeers and Supermen: The Films of Richard Lester*, by Neil Sinyard, was published. Ten years later, in 1994, another book, *The Man Who Framed the Beatles: A Biography of Richard Lester*, by Richard Yule, was published, with an introduction by Paul McCartney.

LEWIS, Jerry Lee American rock 'n' roll singer/pianist born in Ferriday, Louisiana, on 29 September 1935.

His career suffered after it was revealed that he had married his 13-year-old cousin Myra Gale Brown.

On 17 May 1962 he appeared at the Tower Ballroom, New Brighton, on a bill with ten Mersey Beat bands, including the Big Three, the Undertakers, the Strangers, Vince Earl & the Zeros, Billy Kramer & the Coasters, Steve Day & the Drifters and Kingsize Taylor & the Dominoes. He was also to appear at the Star Club in Hamburg.

Lewis, whose hits included 'Whole Lotta Shakin' Goin' On', 'High School Confidential', 'Breathless' and 'Great Balls of Fire', wanted the Beatles to appear on his British tour, but they were committed to a Roy Orbison tour at the time.

The Beatles were to request Jerry Lee Lewis as a guest on their *Around the Beatles* TV special, but he couldn't appear because of prior commitments.

His colourful life provided the meat for a screen biography, *Great Balls of Fire*, in 1988, in which Dennis Quaid portrayed the controversial singer.

LEWIS, Vic Former jazz musician turned showbiz agent. Brian Epstein bought out his Vic Lewis Organization in 1965 and appointed him to the board of NEMS Enterprises. After Epstein's death, Lewis became managing director of the company. In October 1969 he issued an orchestral album of covers of Beatles songs, *Beatles My Way*, on the NEMS label.

LIANE Blonde German barmaid who was dated by Paul McCartney during the Beatles' season at the Kaiserkeller. Iain Hines of the Jets recalled: 'I personally struck up quite a friendship with Paul McCartney. He was at the time going out with a barmaid called Liane, whilst I was going out with her friend Gerda. Every morning at two Paul would arrive from the Kaiserkeller, which was closed at that hour, and would listen to our last session. The four of us would go in Gerda's VW to Liane's flat, where we would cook hamburgers and listen to Everly Brothers records.'

LIBERACE American superstar entertainer and pianist, born Wladziu Valentino Liberace in Milwaukee on 16 May 1919.

His closer association with the Beatles appeared at the Convention Centre in Las Vegas on 20 August 1964, Liberace was appearing at the Riviera. He turned up for the matinée performance of the Beatles concert and went backstage after the show.

Despite Brian Epstein's instructions that no celebrities be invited backstage to meet the Beatles, Derek Taylor decided that he would leave such decisions to the Beatles themselves.

Liberace had arrived to say, 'I want to meet these young artists who are doing such amazing things,' and the personal meeting was arranged.

In his autobiography, Derek Taylor recalls the event: 'Pat Boone was nice but Liberace was nicer; strangely quiet and polite, we thought, and interestingly clad in a little pale-blue Eton jacket and matching trousers. Plump and smiling, he seemed pleasantly in contrast to the rest of Vegas that we saw, which was mean and dangerous.'

Liberace died of an AIDS-related disease on 4 February 1987.

LINDSAY-HOGG, Michael Lindsay-Hogg was director of the celebrated weekly TV show, *Ready, Steady, Go!*, on which the Beatles appeared several times.

His closer association with the Beatles began when he was engaged to direct some of their promotional films, beginning with *Paperback Writer* and *Rain*, filmed at Abbey Road studios and on location at Chiswick House on Thursday and Friday, 19 and 20 May 1966. Lindsay-Hogg was also to direct Wings' *London Town* promo in 1978. He also directed the unreleased *The Rolling Stones Rock 'n' Roll Circus* in 1968, which featured John and Yoko.

Lindsay-Hogg was hired to direct their final film, the documentary *Let It Be* in 1970, from which two clips were taken and used as promo films – *Hey Jude* and *Revolution*. A review by Michael Goodwin in *Rolling Stone* magazine savagely criticized his direction of the film, saying that with a good director the audience can sit back and relax, knowing that everything is under control, but: 'Here, you are constantly busy doing work that Lindsay-Hogg should have done, but didn't; cutting the bad stuff, rearranging the good stuff, placing the camera properly – really basic directorial responsibilities.'

Lindsay-Hogg was given an opportunity to speak in his own defence in a *Rolling Stone* interview in which he commented: 'It's lucky there is a movie. There was a big push all the time to get them going. Even though half of them always were behind it, the trouble was it was never the same half.

'It was a terribly painful, frustrating experience. It's not that I don't like them – I do. It's just that when we were trying to make the film, every day there was a different one to hate.'

Lindsay-Hogg was later to direct the acclaimed television series *Brideshead Revisited*.

LITTLE RICHARD Legendary rock 'n' roller, born Richard Penniman in Macon, Georgia, on 25 December 1935. He had nine singles in the American charts between 1956 and 1958, but his hit-parade success seemed to dry up at the same time as the other legendary rockers of the 1950s.

Paul McCartney was the Richard fan in the Quarry Men and performed several of his numbers in the act: 'Long Tall Sally', 'Lucille', 'Ooh! My Soul', 'Tutti Frutti', 'Good Golly, Miss Molly' and 'Kansas City/Hey Hey Hey'.

The Beatles first made his acquaintance when they appeared on the same bill for a short season at the Star Club in Hamburg in April and May 1962.

Liverpool promoter Sam Leach intended bringing Richard to Liverpool, placing him on a bill with the Beatles at the Tower Ballroom. He'd been in negotiation with Brian Epstein about a possible business partnership on Tower Ballroom promotions, but it fell through and NEMS Enterprises presented the Little Richard/Beatles bill at the Tower on 12 October 1962.

Backstage in the ballroom, I commissioned photographer Les Chadwick to cover the event on behalf of *Mersey Beat* and the famous photograph of Richard and the Beatles was taken.

NEMS then booked Richard to top the bill locally at the Empire Theatre on 28 October, also featuring the Beatles.

In the 1984 biography *The Life and Times of Little Richard* by Charles Wood, Richard claimed that, after the Beatles left the stage at the Empire, Brian Epstein came up to him and said: 'Richard, I'll give you 50 per cent of the Beatles.'

Although there is plenty of evidence that Epstein approached several people offering a percentage of the Beatles, there is also a deal of extravagant and inaccurate comment in the book by Richard himself regarding his influence on the group.

LIVINGSTONE, Alan President of Capitol Records in the 1960s who persistently refused to issue the Beatles records and made the famous remark: 'We don't think the Beatles will do anything in this market.' He eventually had to bow to the inevitable.

LOCKWOOD, Sir Joseph The chairman of EMI Records from 1954 to 1974.

During the 20 years of his stewardship of EMI, he turned the label into one of the biggest recording companies in the world, astutely buying the American record label Capitol when it was still a relatively small outfit.

He advised and aided the Beatles in personal and financial matters during their years with his company, although there were times when he wouldn't allow them a completely free hand – he vetoed John Lennon's choice of Gandhi for the *Sgt Pepper* album and refused to handle the *Two Virgins* album because of the full frontal nudity on the cover.

The man the Beatles called 'Sir Joe' died at the age of 86 on 6 March 1991.

LOMAX, Jackie Merseyside musician, former lead singer with the Undertakers.

After failing to achieve success on record in Britain, members of the band moved to America, but there they split up. Jackie and drummer Bugs Pemberton teamed up with two American musicians to form the Lomax Alliance.

Brian Epstein signed them up, showcased them at his Saville Theatre and arranged for them to record an album, which remains unreleased.

The group disbanded and after Epstein's death Jackie was signed to Apple as a solo artist. 'Sour Milk Sea', his debut single, penned by George Harrison, was among the first four Apple releases on 26 August 1968. Appearing on the record with him were George Harrison, Paul McCartney, Ringo Starr, Eric Clapton and Nicky Hopkins.

His debut album was called *Is This What You Want?*, which was followed by another single, 'New Day'.

Paul McCartney next produced Jackie singing 'Thumbin' a Ride', issued as a flipside to 'New Day' in America and 'How the Web was Woven' in Britain.

Jackie's final Apple single was a re-release of 'Sour Milk Sea' in June 1971.

Once Allen Klein entered the picture, Jackie left Apple and went to Warner, where he recorded two albums. He then signed with Capitol and appeared with a group called Badger.

Jackie moved to Los Angeles, where he still lives. In 1995 he was making regular appearances at the Café Voltaire in Ventura and the Coconut Teaser on Sunset Strip and also performed at Libby Park in Ojai.

LONG JOHN BALDRY British blues singer who appeared on the radio show *Pop Go the Beatles* on Thursday 1 August 1963 and on the television special *Around the Beatles*.

LONG JOHN & THE SILVER MEN A name suggested to John, Paul and George by Casey Jones, leader of Cass & the Cassanovas after they decided to dispense with the Quarry Men and Johnny & the Moondogs. Cass told them that they should have the name of the group leader up front, as was the fashion in those days. They didn't like the suggestion and called themselves the Silver Beetles, adapting it to Silver Beatles.

LOPEZ, Trini   Singer from Texas whose biggest hit was 'If I Had a Hammer'. He shared the bill with the Beatles for a season at the Olympia, Paris, from 16 January to 4 February 1963.

LOWE, John Charles   John Lowe, nicknamed 'Duff', shared the same class as Paul McCartney at Liverpool Institute. In January 1958, he joined the Quarry Men as pianist, appearing at a number of gigs with them, but leaving the band in January 1959.

During the summer of 1958, he recorded 'That'll Be The Day', flipside 'In Spite Of All The Danger' with them at a small studio in Liverpool. Lowe maintained the only existing copy of the acetate and 23 years after it was recorded (in July 1981), he sold the disc to Paul McCartney.

He then moved to Ashton, near Bristol, where he works in the investment business. In the 1990s, he teamed up with Mike Wilsh, former member of the Four Pennies, to form the Pennies – a number of their gigs took place in the new Cavern in Liverpool during the annual Mersey Beatle conventions.

LYFORD, Jimmy   One of the two male members of the Apple Scruffs, that devoted group of Beatles fans who haunted the steps of the Apple offices. Jimmy died of an AIDS-related disease in San Francisco in October 1988.

McBAIN, Charlie One of the earliest of the Liverpool rock 'n' roll promoters. He originally booked groups such as the Quarry Men at his promotions at Wilson Hall in Garston, where he also ran talent contests for skiffle groups. McBain promoted at venues such as the New Clubmoor Hall as well and booked the Beatles there on 18 October 1959. His other promotions took place at Garston Swimming Baths, Holyoake Hall and Wavertree Town Hall. He was one of the pioneers of the local scene, but died in the early 1960s.

McBEAN, Angus Noted British photographer who took the photos used on the Beatles debut album, *Please Please Me*. He re-created the same pose several years later for the cover of the 1970 release *The Beatles 1962–1966*. He died in June 1990.

MACBETH, David Former soccer player who became a singer and had one minor hit, 'Mr Blue', in 1959. He enoyed a brief career in the spotlight, appearing on the Cabaret circuit for a number of years, and made several appearances in Liverpool during 1962.

In May 1963 he was booked to appear as one of the support acts on the Beatles/Roy Orbison tour, during which he was backed by the Terry Young Combo and performed 'Oh! Lonesome Me', 'A Very Good Year for Girls', 'My Golden Chance' and 'Mr Blue'.

McCAFFREY, Laurie Liverpool Beatles fan who became receptionist at both the Liverpool and the London branches of NEMS Enterprises. She then accepted the Beatles' offer of joining Apple and, when the Savile Row building was closed, she went to work for Capital Radio.

McCARTNEY, Angela The second wife of Jim McCartney. The Liverpool-born widow agreed to marry the widower after they'd met only three times. Jim was 62 and Angie 34 when they married on 24 November 1964. Jim also legally adopted her five-year old daughter, Ruth.

Following Jim's death in 1970, the relationship between Paul and Angie deteriorated. She set up a rock group agency in Liverpool and Paul felt she was trading on the McCartney name. She then reverted to her first husband's name, Williams, in 1981 after a series of articles in the *Sun* newspaper, ghosted by Tony Barrow, which were highly critical of Paul.

Together with Ruth, she went to live abroad, first in Australia, then in Munich, followed by Los Angeles and finally Nashville, where, by the 1990s, she'd taken up a job as a £12,000 a year secretary, having reverted back to the McCartney name and launched a company, McCartney Music.

In 1995 she once again appeared in the tabloid press, pleading for money from Paul. Paul refused to have anything to do with her, quoting the fact that she'd sold his birth certificate: 'She then sold my original birth certificate without saying anything to me or letting me know that she was putting it up for sale at auction – so some bugger has got my birth certificate now and I don't know who it is.'

McCARTNEY, Florence Known as 'Florrie', she was Paul's paternal grandmother, who married Joseph McCartney in 1896. She gave birth to seven children and died in 1944.

McCARTNEY, Heather Born in Colorado on 31 December 1963, the daughter of Linda and Melvin See.

Linda split from her husband and moved with Heather to New York. When she began her romance with Paul McCartney, Linda noticed how Paul enjoyed looking after Heather and took a photograph of them together. When they were married in 1969, Paul formally adopted Heather as his daughter.

The young girl travelled with them during the touring days of Wings, but when she reached her early teens Paul began to worry about the people she was mixing with in London and decided to move the family into the country. They settled in Sussex.

Heather has had a variety of jobs since, ranging from darkroom technician to barmaid, and generally keeps a low profile.

McCARTNEY, James Paul's father, born 7 July 1902 in the Everton district of Liverpool, one of the nine children of Joseph and Florence McCartney.

Despite bursting his right eardrum in an accident at the age of ten, he taught himself to play the piano. At the age of 14 he went to work for the Cotton Exchange. In his spare time he formed a band called the Masked Melody Makers and wrote an original composition called 'Eloise'.

During the Second World War he met Mary Patricia Mohin. They married in April 1941 and their first son, James Paul, was born on 18 June 1942, to be followed by Peter Michael on 7 January 1944.

At the time of Mary's death from breast cancer in 1956, Jim was earning £8 a week at the Cotton Exchange and was left with the task of raising the two boys alone.

When the Beatles achieved success, Paul asked his father to retire in 1964, bought him a house and assured him of a regular income. Paul also put words to his father's composition 'Eloise', when he recorded the number 'Walking in the Park with Eloise'.

In November 1964 he remarried. His new wife was a widow, Angela Williams, who had a daughter, Ruth.

Jim died on 18 March 1976.

McCARTNEY, Linda Born Linda Louise Eastman on 24 September 1941 to Lee and Louise Eastman. Her mother was the daughter of a Cleveland family, the Linders, owner of a department store chain, and her father, the son of Russian immigrants, was a former Harvard Law School graduate turned attorney who specialized in copyright law in the show-business field. Ironically, his family name was Epstein, but he changed it.

Linda was raised in an affluent atmosphere in the family home in Scarsdale, Westchester County, in upstate New York. The Eastmans also owned a luxurious apartment in Park Avenue and a house in East Hampton. She had an older brother, John, and two younger sisters, Laura and Louise.

One of her father's clients was songwriter Jack Lawrence and Lee undertook some legal work on his behalf in exchange for his writing a song about his daughter. Lawrence wrote the song about the six-year-old girl called 'Linda' in 1947 and it was featured in the film *The Story of GI Joe*. It was initially a hit for Buddy Clark in 1947 and was also recorded by Perry Como and Charlie Spivak and His Orchestra. The most famous version is that by Jan & Dean. The number was also recorded in Britain by Jimmy Young and Dick James.

From an early age she became accustomed to the company of celebrities, thanks to the number of famous people who dined at the Eastman homes. They included William (Hopalong Cassidy) Boyd, the abstract artist Robert Rauschenberg, songwriter Hoagy Carmichael and jazzman Tommy Dorsey.

She graduated from Scarsdale High School, but admits: 'I wasn't a very good student.' The High School Yearbook entry described her as 'a strawberry blonde with a yen for men' and Linda was to comment: 'All I cared about were animals, rock music and photography, it was a great disappointment to my family.' She then enrolled at the exclusive Sarah Lawrence School in Bronxville, followed by Princeton University, where she was studying history and art. Then her world was shattered by the death of her mother in a plane crash. Linda was 18 at the time. Her father was to remarry soon after.

She next moved to the University of Colorado to study art and history and there she met and married fellow student John (also referred to as Bob and Melvyn) See. The marriage seemed to be Linda's reaction to her mother's death and she commented: 'My mother died in a plane crash and I got married. It was a mistake.'

She realized the marriage wouldn't work and was to say: 'When he graduated he wanted to go to Africa. I said, "Look, if I don't get on with you here, I'm not going to Africa with you. I won't get on with you there." '

By that time they'd moved to Tucson, Arizona, where Linda gave birth to their daughter, Heather, on 31 December 1963.

See, a geophysicist, had gone to Africa, hoping she would follow him, but she wrote him a letter informing him of her intention to get a divorce. The marriage had lasted for only a year.

By that time Linda had begun to study art history at the University of Arizona. She also attended a course in photography which was given by Hazel Archer at the Tucson Art Centre and commented: 'Arizona opened my eyes to the wonder of light and colour.' Linda bought herself a Pentax camera and she began taking a serious interest in photography.

In 1966 she moved back to New York, where she took a job as receptionist at *Town and Country* magazine. When an invitation arrived at the office to attend a press launch on a yacht on the Hudson for the Rolling Stones, she intercepted it and caught a cab to the quay. She recalled: 'I must have caught the band's eye because a woman came down the gangway and said I was the only photographer they would allow on board. I got well into it, using black and white. Then back on the quay all the journalists came up and gave me their cards because they needed the pictures. I got them back from the lab and, lo!, they were wonderful. After that I started to get a lot of work with bands like the Jimi Hendrix Experience, Lovin' Spoonful, the Doors, Jefferson Airplane, the Grateful Dead and the Beatles.'

Danny Fields, editor of *Datebook*, commented: 'And the pictures she got that day – there were the other pictures, the official pictures of the Stones taken by some professional news photographer, and then there were Linda's pictures. The Stones were doing things, striking poses, being arrogant and beautiful and fantastic and sexy. They did it, they danced for her camera, and she always had this quality. She took the best portraits of beautiful people of anyone.'

As a result of the Stones shoot, she was able to turn to photography full-time and also had an unpaid, but prestigious appointment as house photographer at the famous Fillmore East rock venue, in addition to receiving photo assignments from groups such as the Beach Boys.

She also met the Beatles for the first time officially at the Shea Stadium in 1966 and was to comment: 'It was John who interested me at the start. He was my Beatle hero. But when I met him the fascination faded fast and I found it was Paul I liked.'

Seeking work in England, Linda sent a portfolio of her photos to Peter Brown at Apple. He was particularly struck by a photo of Brian Jones which he liked. He said: 'I sent the portfolio back and told her, "You'll find one picture missing." '

In 1967 writer J. Marks, who needed photos of big-name groups for a projected book *Rock and Other Four-Letter Words*, invited Linda to London. During her trip she was taken on 15 May to the Bag o' Nails club at 9 Kingly Street by Chas. Chandler, to see Georgie Fame & the Blue Flames perform.

Paul was at the club with Peter Brown and recalled: 'I saw this blonde across the room and I fancied her. So when she passed my table I said something stupid like, "Hello, how are you? Let me take you away from all this." '

Linda commented: 'It was like a cartoon. It sounds silly, but our eyes met and something just clicked.'

They were introduced, began chatting together and Paul took her to another club, the Speakeasy, but they got separated as Paul began to talk to members of the Who.

As Brian Epstein had been undergoing treatment for his drug dependency, Brown arranged the invitations for a select group of journalists and broadcasters to attend a special preview of *Sgt Pepper's Lonely Hearts Club Band* at Brian's house at 24 Chapel Street on 19 May. Remembering he owed Linda a favour for the Brian Jones photograph, he invited her along. During the party Paul sat in a chair by the fireplace and Linda took rolls of film of him sitting there.

She returned to America, but was to meet Paul exactly a year later when he and John flew to the States to appear on *The Tonight Show* on 15 May to publicize Apple. At an early press conference she slipped him a note with her phone number on it and he called her and asked her to meet him at lawyer Nat Weiss's apartment. They spent the next few days together and Paul even baby-sat for Heather while Linda photographed groups at the Fillmore East in the evenings. Paul, always the family man at heart, was enchanted with Heather and after he'd returned to London Linda sent him a poster-sized blow-up of Paul with his arms around her four-year-old daughter.

He was back in America in June, travelling to Los Angeles with Ron Kass to attend a convention of Capitol Records' executives. Linda paid for a flight to LA and they spent a few days together. She returned to New York with Paul, Kass and party and once he'd returned to London she phoned him and wrote letters to him regularly.

When Paul's five-year-romance with Jane Asher ended because of his dalliance with Francie Schwartz, he contacted Linda.

He says: 'I persuaded Linda to come to London for a visit.' After some weeks they both began to miss Heather and Paul said: 'I rang Heather in New York and said, "Heather, will you marry me?" She was five. "No, don't be silly," she said, "I'm too young." "Well I can't wait," I said. So we went to New York and brought her back to London to live with us.'

In February 1969, doctors confirmed that Linda was pregnant and the couple decided to get married, going to Marylebone Register Office on 11 March to book their wedding for 9.45 a.m. the next day.

At the time Paul was busy recording Jackie Lomax and forgot to buy a wedding ring, so he had to persuade a local jeweller to reopen his shop. He bought a plain gold ring for £12.

The next morning the wedding had to be held up when Mike McCartney, the best man, arrived an hour late because his train from Liverpool had been delayed.

Fortunately, no other weddings were booked that morning and the ceremony went ahead with Heather as bridesmaid and Peter Brown and Mal Evans as witnesses.

None of the other members of the Beatles attended the ceremony as Paul had already begun litigation to dissolve the group.

The ceremony was conducted by registrar Mr E. R. Sanders. Afterwards, the marriage was blessed at the Anglican Church in St John's Wood by the Reverend Noel Perry-Gore.

By this time, Linda's father and brother represented Paul. John Eastman was a graduate of Stanford and NYU Law School and joined his father's firm in New York. When Paul asked Lee for advice on how to sort out the financial mess at Apple Corps, Eastman recommended John.

John flew to London and met the Beatles. John, George and Ringo were considering hiring Allen Klein, but decided they could also hire Eastman, if only to placate Paul, and he was hired as general counsel.

The first thing he suggested was that the Beatles buy NEMS. He started negotiations, but they fell through and the company was sold to Triumph Investments. Eastman blamed Klein and Klein blamed Eastman. The Beatles would have been satisfied retaining both men to look after their interests, but it was obvious that the two couldn't work together, so Eastman was in the McCartney camp and Klein with Lennon, Harrison and Starr.

Paul's ties with Eastman became stronger when he married Linda and John became his brother-in-law. Paul refused to sign with Klein and retained Eastman as his representative. It was Eastman who advised him that he had no choice but to file writs against John, George, Ringo and Apple in order to dissolve the Beatles partnership.

After the wedding Paul formally adopted Heather and also composed the song 'The Lovely Linda'.

An interesting incident had taken place the previous year, before Paul had finally parted with Jane Asher. He'd visited a clairvoyant in Brighton who had told him that he would marry a blonde and have four children.

The couple had three more children: Mary, Stella and James Louis.

After the Beatles' partnership had been dissolved, Paul formed Wings, insisted that Linda be a part of the band and taught her to play keyboards. She also recorded in her own right, using the alias Susie & the Red Stripes for her single, 'Seaside Woman'.

Linda's personal achievements were to be considerable. She established herself as a leading photographer, with several books of her work and exhibitions in various countries around the world. Together with Paul she appeared in a cameo role in the popular TV series *Bread*, set in Liverpool. It was scripted by Linda's friend, Carla Lane. She also wrote a best-selling book based on her vegetarian recipes and has a range of vegetarian foods stocked in major supermarkets on both sides of the Atlantic.

On 30 July 1991, her father died of a stroke in New York. He was 81 years old. It was Lee who advised Paul on investing in music-publishing copyrights, with the result that Paul's MPL publishing company, with over 1,000 major copyrights, including many standards, together with a range of popular musicals, is the largest independent music publisher in the world.

McCARTNEY, James Louis Only son of Paul and Linda McCartney, named after the respective fathers of Paul and Linda. James was born at the Avenue Clinic in St John's Wood, London, on 12 September 1977.

Rather publicity-shy, little has been heard of him apart from a few of the accidents he has been involved in. In September 1989 he had a brush with death while surfing in high seas and apparently vanished for 40 minutes. Then on 3 May 1995 he was driving a Land Rover which overturned, trapping him beneath. He was airlifted to hospital, but the only injury he'd sustained was a broken ankle.

James is interested in becoming a drummer.

McCARTNEY, Mary Mother of Paul and Michael McCartney, born Mary Patricia Mohin, at 2 Third Avenue, Fazakerley, Liverpool, on 29 September 1909.

When Mary was four years old her mother, Mary Theresa Mohin, died while giving birth to a baby girl, who also died. When her father, Owen, remarried, Mary couldn't accept her new stepmother, Rose, and went to live with a maternal aunt.

At the age of 14 she entered nursing and worked at Alder Hey Hospital. She then moved to Walton Road Hospital in Rice Lane, Liverpool, and after ten years became a full nursing sister.

Mary first met Jim McCartney at the McCartney family home at 11 Scargreen Avenue, West Derby. Still a nurse at Walton Hospital, she was staying temporarily with Jim's newly wed sister Jin and her husband, Harry. She was 31 years old and Jim was eight years her senior when the two were married at St Swithin's Roman Catholic Chapel in Gill Moss, Liverpool.

Although Mary had been raised as a strict Roman Catholic, she married Jim, a Protestant, after promising that her children would be baptized Roman Catholics. Both her sons were baptized – and also circumcised.

Paul was born on 15 April 1941 in a private ward at Walton Hospital, because Mary had once been the sister in charge of the maternity ward.

When she was able to resume work she became a health visitor and then returned to the practice of midwifery, taking domiciliary posts in which a council house was provided for her and her family. Each of the various houses they moved to proved better than the last and they finally settled at 20 Forthlin Road in 1955.

Her second son, Michael, was born in 1944 and soon afterwards she developed mastitis, an inflammation of the breasts. It was in 1955 that she began suffering pains in her breast which were so agonizing that she had to lie down. When a concerned Jim sought to find out what was wrong, she put it down to the menopause. As the pain increased she began to take Bisodol, an over-the-counter medicine. Her son Michael once found her crying in her bedroom while she was clutching a crucifix. When he asked her what was wrong, she answered: 'Nothing, love.'

She eventually consulted a specialist who told her she had breast cancer. She was immediately sent to the Northern Hospital for an operation, but it was too late. The operation revealed that the cancer had spread.

Just before she died she told a friend: 'I would love to have seen the boys growing up.' She died on 31 October 1956, soon after being given the last rites by a Catholic priest. She had a pair of rosary beads tied to her wrists.

The 14-year-old Paul, when told that his mother had died, said 'What are we going to do without her money?' That night he and Mike cried themselves to sleep.

It was just after his mother's death that Paul took up the guitar, which became an obsession with him. He was later to say: 'You lose a mother – and you find a guitar.'

Mary was laid to rest on 3 November 1956 at Yew Tree Cemetry, Finch Lane, Liverpool.

Mary was devoted to her sons and had wanted Paul to become a teacher. She was ambitious for both boys, wanting them to get on in the world, and gave Paul elocution lessons to rid him of his Scouse accent.

Friends who knew the family said that Paul would never have become a member of a group if Mary had lived.

He was finally able to pay tribute to her in the song 'Let It Be' and was to say: 'I had a dream one night about my mother. She died when I was 14 so I hadn't really heard from her in quite a while, and it was very good. It gave me some strength "in my darkest hour, Mother Mary comes to me".'

McCARTNEY, Mary Paul and Linda's first child, born at 1.30 a.m. on Thursday 29 August 1969 at the Avenue Clinic, St John's Wood, although an earlier announcement had said she was due in December. She weighed 6lb 8oz and arrived slightly less than six months after the couple had married. Two months later Paul and Linda took their new baby up to Scotland with them. It was during this period that the 'Paul is Dead' rumours first sprang up in America. In November they took Mary to America to show her to Linda's family.

For her twenty-fifth birthday, Paul and Linda organized a party for 1,000 people, allegedly costing £90,000. The glamorous brunette seemed the most confident of the McCartney offspring and began appearing in public in 1994 at opening nights. For the première of *Sirens* she wore a micro-mini and thigh-length leather boots. When the photographers gathered, she said: 'Why are they taking my picture? I'm nobody.'

Mary works in the offices of a music publisher and in 1995 her name was linked romantically with that of Paul Weller of the Jam/Style Council fame.

McCARTNEY, Mike Peter Michael McCartney, Paul's younger brother, was born at Walton Hospital, Liverpool, on 7 January 1944.

A highly talented singer, composer, photographer and artist in his own right, he teamed up with Roger McGough and John Gorman in 1962 to form the Scaffold, a satirical trio who became very successful during the 1960s and recorded several major hits.

During this time, in an effort to succeed on his own talent, he was known as Mike McGear.

In 1968 he married Angela Fishwick and Paul was his best man. The couple had three daughters, but the marriage ended in divorce in 1979. Mike married Rowena Home in 1982 and the couple had three sons.

Mike's first collaboration with his brother took place in 1968, when Paul produced the album *McGough & McGear*. Paul also produced the single 'Liverpool Lou' and the album *McGear*.

When Scaffold finally disbanded, Mike authored a number of children's books and in 1981 published *Thank U Very Much: Mike McCartney's Family Album*, the story of the McCartney family in words and pictures. Others of his photo books were *Mike Mac's White & Black's* in 1986 and *Remember* in 1992.

Mike's first photographs were published in *Mersey Beat* in 1961 under the pseudonym Francis Michael. He has continued to take photos over the years and during the 1990s was able to establish himself as a photographer of note, being commissioned to take several visual portfolios of Liverpool.

McCARTNEY, Ruth Paul's stepsister. Her mother, Angie, married Paul's father, Jim, when she was five. The little girl was legally adopted by Jim and her name changed to McCartney by deed poll. She lived in Rembrandt, the McCartney home in Hoylake, and has fond memories of growing up there.

She recalls that when she was nine years old and learning to play the piano she tried to perform a traditional hymn, 'Golden Slumbers'. She asked Paul to help her with it and as a result he penned his own 'Golden Slumbers', which appeared on the *Abbey Road* album.

Ruth spent a total of 12 years as a member of the McCartney family. Following Jim's death in 1976, she and her mother became estranged from the rest of the family, with Angie declaring that Paul had made a vow to his father on his deathbed that he'd look after them for him.

Ruth attempted to make her name in show business and led a dance trio called Talent. In 1981 she moved to King's Lynn with her mother and worked as a shopgirl. She then returned to show business and appeared in successful tours of Russia and Eastern Europe, where she was dubbed the Moscow Madonna.

She lived in various countries with her mother and they settled in Nashville in an apartment shared by Angie, Ruth and her boyfriend, Martin Nethercutt.

Ruth is currently writing her autobiography.

McCARTNEY, Stella Nina Paul and Linda's second child, born at King's College Hospital in London on 13 September 1971. Stella was delivered by Caesarean section. Paul, who was banned from the operating theatre, was to comment: 'I sat next door in my green apron praying like mad. The name Wings just came into my mind.' He then decided to call his new band Wings.

On 12 June 1995, at the age of 23, Stella graduated as a fashion designer from St Martin's School of Art in central London. When the final-year students demonstrated their designs at Islington's Business Design Centre, Paul and Linda were in the audience and Paul commented: 'I am the proudest dad in the world. Stella has come such a long way since she started out.' The highly paid supermodels Kate Moss, Naomi Campbell and Yasmin Le Bon modelled her clothes at the show for no fee. Stella was immediately offered a job with leading designer Ralph Lauren.

McCLINTON, Delbert American musician, born in Lubbock, Texas, who specialized in the harmonica. While with a band in Fort Worth, he was hired to work on the Bruce Channel recording session for 'Hey Baby' and provided the haunting solo which helped to make it a hit.

When Channel toured Britain he brought McClinton with him and the two appeared with the Beatles at the Tower Ballroom, New Brighton, on Thursday 21 June 1962.

During the evening John Lennon chatted with McClinton, who showed him how to play the harmonica passage. When the Beatles came to record 'Love Me Do', Lennon used the style McClinton had taught him.

McClinton was one of the country music artists who contributed to the 1995 Liberty Records release *Come Together: America Salutes the Beatles,* a tribute to the group by the stars of country music. McClinton contributed the track 'Come Together'. During the press call for the release, he was interviewed by Matt Hurwitz. His recollections of the Beatles indicate how perceptions and memories can differ, whether through point of view or passage of time.

He said: 'The Beatles were the opening act on about four of the shows we did . . . We were in New Brighton the first night we played with them, at a place called the Castle. It was an old castle, if I remember right, because when you looked out of the dressing-room window it was a sheer drop to the ocean.'

In fact, the Beatles appeared at only the one gig with Channel and McClinton – at the Tower Ballroom, New Brighton. It wasn't a castle and didn't look down on the ocean: just the River Mersey!

Channel and McClinton were backed by the Barons and the rest of the bill comprised the Beatles, the Big Three, the Four Jays and the Statesmen.

McDONALD, Phil Balance engineer at the Abbey Road studios who worked on various Beatles recordings, including *Revolver* and *Abbey Road*. He was later to be involved in the recordings of solo works by John Lennon, George Harrison and Paul McCartney.

McFALL, Ray Liverpool accountant who became owner of the famous Cavern club. Ray was born in the Garston area of Liverpool on 14 November 1926. It was while he was handling the accounts for the Sytner family, who ran the Cavern and the Temple Jazz Club, that he had the opportunity of buying the club, which he did on 1 October 1959 for £2,750.

Although the Cavern had been strictly a jazz club, forbidding rock 'n' roll to be played on the premises, Ray noticed that there was a huge interest in rock 'n' roll in the city, with thousands of youngsters attending the promotions at local 'jive hives'. As a result he began to book groups. This proved so successful that he introduced the innovation of lunchtime sessions. These went so well that he also began all-night sessions and Saturday-afternoon under-16s promotions.

He hired Bob Wooler as Cavern compère and Bob suggested the Beatles for regular lunchtime sessions, as they didn't have full-time jobs. The Beatles made their debut on a 'Swinging Bluejeans Guest Night' and were also given their own evening residency. They were to make a total of 274 appearances at the club, ending on 3 August 1963.

Ray travelled with the Beatles to New York in February 1964 and is the man with the fur hat (bought in Hamburg) alighting from the plane with them in many photographs.

He began a rapid expansion of the club, but eventually had to declare himself bankrupt and moved to London, where he re-established himself as an accountant before retiring in 1993.

McGIVERN, Maggie When Paul's long romance with Jane Asher came to an end in 1968, Paul often frequented the Revolution Club in Bruton Place, London. He took a shine to one of the waitresses there, Maggie McGivern, and the two of them went off on holiday to Sardinia together. News of the couple's vacation appeared in the Sunday newspaper the *People*.

McGOUGH, Roger One of Britain's leading contemporary poets. Roger was born in Liverpool and educated at St Mary's College and the University of Hull. Back in Liverpool, he was part of the poetry movement which evolved on Merseyside at the same time as the music scene.

Roger began his poetry readings regularly at Streates coffee bar in Mount Pleasant. He teamed up with Mike McGear (McCartney) and John Gorman in the Scaffold, one of Liverpool's offbeat groups, and enjoyed a series of chart records.

Roger also married Thelma Pickles, former girlfriend of John Lennon and Paul McCartney, and composed a book of poems about her, *Summer with Monika*.

He provided input for the *Yellow Submarine* film, when he was brought in to add a touch of Liverpool humour. He was paid £500 for his efforts, but received no acknowledgement – although he said he would have preferred a credit to the money.

Together with fellow Liverpool poets Adrian Henri and Brian Patten he compiled a collection of poems, *The Mersey Sound*, published in the late 1960s. The work was tremendously popular and has sold over a quarter of a million copies in many editions.

Roger and Thelma were divorced and Roger has settled in London, where, in addition to his popular stage readings, he is in demand for numerous television shows, particularly those appealing to younger audiences.

Penguin Books have published approximately two dozen volumes of his work, which displays his prowess as a first-class humorist and wordsmith.

McGOUGH, Thelma Former student at Liverpool College of Art. At the age of 16 she became John Lennon's girlfriend for a six-month period. Later Paul McCartney began dating her. She married Roger McGough of the Scaffold, the group of which Paul's brother, Mike, was a member, though the marriage ended in divorce. She became a TV producer and worked on Cilla Black's *Blind Date* for London Weekend Television.

McKENZIE, Tom Compère who believed he was the inspiration behind 'Father McKenzie' in 'Eleanor Rigby'.

Tom, who first began compèring in 1936, was born in Toxteth, Liverpool, and went to the same school as Ringo's stepfather. He compèred the Beatles in shows for promoter Lewis Buckley on several occasions from early 1962 and was compère and master of ceremonies at the Memorial Hall, Northwich, for five years after it opened in 1961. The Beatles appeared at the venue on six occasions.

Tom recalled that the Beatles were booked on 6 July 1963 to crown the Northwich Carnival Queen and then played at a dance at the Memorial Hall. He said it was extremely hot and the Beatles were picked up from Ringo's aunt's home at Leftwich in a Parks' steelworks van. The procession took so long to get round its route that the four were shut up inside the van, being driven round and round the town from half-past one to four in the afternoon. The crowning was a hurried affair because of fan fervour in the crowd and Paul put the crown on upside-down! Hundreds queued outside the Memorial Hall while the Beatles played inside, in spite of the torrential rain which followed the sunshine.

At one of the gigs George had been left behind in the dressing-room toilets and had to be smuggled out to the others, at Tom's suggestion, wearing a coach-driver's hat and coat.

Tom fervently believed that he inspired Father McKenzie and commented: 'I think that when they wrote that song they had never forgotten me. They used to say that I treated them like a father and they were very amused when I told them of my days in the anti-aircraft artillery at Coventry, when I darned my socks at night to keep awake.'

Sadly, he died at the onset of the 1990s.

McKERN, Leo Actor, born in Australia in 1920, who featured in *Help!* as Chang, the leader of a religious cult. He'd previously worked with director Richard Lester on *The Running, Jumping and Standing Still Film* and with producer Walter Shenson in *The Mouse That Roared*. He is best known now for his portrayal of Rumpole, in the TV series *Rumpole of the Bailey*.

McKINNON, Duncan Scots promoter who booked the Larry Parnes package featuring Johnny Gentle and the Silver Beatles in May 1960. The tour was to cover Alloa, Inverness, Fraserburgh, Keith, Forres, Nairn and Peterhead, but McKinnon wasn't impressed by the Beatles and immediately phoned Parnes to complain. McKinnon, a chicken farmer from Dumfries, wanted to send them home on the next train. He told Gentle he could find four buskers who played better. However, Gentle promised to make them smarten up their appearance and talked McKinnon into letting them continue.

MACMILLAN, Iain Photographer who took the classic shot of the Beatles walking across the zebra crossing on Abbey Road on 8 August 1969. He was given only a short time to work in and took six shots, one of which was used on the cover of the *Abbey Road* album.

MAHARISHI MAHESH YOGI Eastern guru, born Mahesh Prasad Verma in 1918. For a brief time he became the Beatles spiritual teacher.

They first attended one of his lectures at the Hilton Hotel in London's Park Lane on 24 August 1967 and were invited to join his course in Transcendental Meditation at University College, Bangor. It was while they were in Wales that they were informed of Brian Epstein's death.

They also decided to spend three months at the Maharishi's ashram in Rishikesh, India. Paul and Ringo were less interested in the guru's teachings than John and George and left early, although both John and Paul wrote a considerable number of songs during their stay and meditation seemed to have a positive effect on John.

However, their relationship was soured when they were told that the Maharishi was acting improperly with one of the female students. John and George confronted him and left the ashram.

John was furious at what he considered a betrayal by the Maharishi and wrote a song called 'Maharishi'. Due to legal reasons he had to rewrite it, and called it 'Sexy Sadie'.

The association with the Beatles established the Maharishi's name on an international level and his Spiritual Regeneration Movement thrived – and continues to do so today.

MAHON, George Graphic designer, born in Dublin, who became art director of the back sleeve of the *Sgt Pepper* album. He then worked on other design projects for Apple, including the apple logo and design used on the actual record releases.

MALTZ, Stephen Staff accountant of Apple, who also became a member of the board of directors of the company. He contacted the members of the group to inform them that Apple finances were in a mess and warned them of major problems ahead. Because of what he considered mismanagement and profligacy, he resigned.

MANDERS, Alf The driver who was hired to drive the coach for the Beatles' *Magical Mystery Tour*.

MANSFIELD, Jayne Buxom blonde Hollywood star who featured in one of the Beatles' favourite films, *The Girl Can't Help It*. She dropped by to see them in Bel Air in August 1964 and also arranged a rendezvous with them at the Whiskey A Go Go on Sunset Strip to attract publicity for herself.

MANSON, Charles Born on 12 November 1934, he became leader of a cult which he named 'the Family', which he formed on his release from prison.

From the time of the release of *Sgt Pepper's Lonely Hearts Club Band* in 1967, Charles Manson believed that the Beatles were attempting to convey messages directly to him. He was convinced that there were biblical predictions which applied to the Beatles, particularly in the Book of Revelations. He told one of his girlfriends that in verse 15: 'The four angels were loosened.' To him, the four angels were the Beatles. He pointed out that verse 3 said: 'And there came out of the smoke locusts upon the earth: and unto them was given power as the scorpions of the earth have power.' As locusts and beetles are the same word in Hebrew, he believed this confirmed the prediction. Another verse stated: 'Their faces were as the faces of men. And they had hair as the hair of women.' References to 'breastplates of fire' and 'out of their mouths issued fire and smoke and brimstone', Manson interpreted as pointing to the electric guitars and voices.

As he gathered his notorious 'Family' and moved to Death Valley, he began to believe he was a new Messiah, and, when he returned to his group shortly after Christmas 1968 with *The Beatles* 'white' album, he believed it had been written with him in mind.

In January the group moved from Death Valley to a house in Gresham Street in the San Fernando Valley. Manson was feverishly studying the album, interpreting the 'messages'. 'Blackbird', for instance, meant that the black people intended to destroy the white race, specifically the radical group the Black Panthers. He believed that 'Piggies' was a derogatory name the blacks had devised for their white enemies, whom they would give 'a damn good whacking'. In 'Happiness is a Warm Gun' he believed the black race were being told how to exact their vengeance on the whites – 'bang, bang, shoot, shoot'.

Unaware that 'Helter Skelter' was the name of a British fairground ride, he believed it was the code word for an uprising in which the blacks were to destroy the whites. He regarded 'Sexy Sadie' as referring to one of his female acolytes whom he'd renamed Sadie Mae Glutz. 'Rocky Raccoon', was to him a reference to black people: 'coons'. 'Revolution No. 1' and 'Revolution No. 9' also referred to the coming holocaust – Revelations predicts a coming Armageddon.

Manson's acolytes set out on his orders and committed a series of horrific murders at three separate places, the first involving five killings, including that of Sharon Tate, the pregnant wife of film producer Roman

Polanski. The second killings were of a married couple, the LaBiancas.

The words smeared in blood at the murder scenes were from the Beatles' songs and the message 'death to pigs' was daubed on a wall near the dead Leno LaBianca, who had a fork piercing his stomach. In fact the LaBiancas had been stabbed with knives and forks, which are mentioned in the last line of George Harrison's 'Piggies'.

Other words smeared in blood at the crime scenes came from 'Helter Skelter' and 'Revolution No. 9'.

Los Angeles District Attorney Vincent Bugliosi, who prosecuted, had a book of the trial published in 1971 called *Helter Skelter*.

Manson, together with three of his female followers who had committed the murders, were sentenced to death, although this was commuted to life imprisonment.

On the subject of Manson believing that the Beatles were sending special messages to him via the double album, John Lennon commented: 'Well, he's barmy. He's like any other Beatles fan who reads mysticism into it. I don't know what "Helter Skelter" had to do with knifing somebody.'

MARDAS, John Alexis The man the Beatles appointed to be head of Apple Electronics, who was dubbed 'Magic Alex' by John Lennon. The Beatles were impressed by some electronic gadgetry he made for them and were intrigued by the various inventions he said he could devise, including an invisible curtain of ultrasonic vibrations and a paint which glowed when connected to an electrical current.

Apple created an Apple Electronics division specially for Alex, but apart from a few gadgets he never came up with any of the inventions he promised – including the 78-track recording studio he'd said he would construct in the Apple basement.

He mixed with the group socially and travelled to Rishikesh with them, and is said to have caused the rift between John and George and the Maharishi by reporting that the guru had been making sexual advances to some of the female meditators.

When Allen Klein was brought in to save Apple Corps from near bankruptcy, Alex left the company.

MARK PETERS & THE CYCLONES/SILHOUETTES A group who featured in both *Mersey Beat* polls and appeared on various bills with the Beatles. They were also popular in Hamburg. Their 1961 gigs with the Beatles at the Cavern took place on Wednesday 27 September and Wednesday 20 December.

Mark's real name was Peter Fleming and he'd been entertaining from the age of seven. In the skiffle era he formed a band called Dean Fleming & the Flamingos and appeared for a week at the Pavilion, Lodge Lane, in 1956 in a revue, 'The Backyard Kids'. He was 13 and sang 'Kisses Sweeter Than Wine'. Freddie Starr and Steve Aldo were in the same show. He then joined a vocal group, the Teen Tones, prior to becoming a member of the Hi-Spots. He became a disc jockey at the Locarno Ballroom in 1959 and in May 1961 he formed the Cyclones, with his brother Steve 'Tiger' Fleming on piano. They later merged with another group, Ken Dallas & the Silhouettes, and called themselves Mark Peters & the Silhouettes.

It was Dave May of the Silhouettes who originally gave bass guitar lessons to Stuart Sutcliffe. He was a student at Liverpool College of Art along with Stu and John Lennon at the time and when Stu bought his Hofner bass Dave would go across to the flat in Gambier Terrace, where he showed Stu how to play 'C'mon Everybody'.

Mark recorded for both Oriole and Piccadilly and his records included 'Fragile', 'Cindy's Gonna Cry' and 'Don't Cry For Me'.

MARMALADE Scottish band who formed in 1961 under the name Dean Ford & the Gaylords. They changed their name to Marmalade when they moved to London and had their first chart entry with 'Lovin' Things' in May 1968.

They comprised Dean Ford (vocals), Graham Knight (vocals/bass), Pat Fairley (rhythm), Junior Campbell (vocals) and Alan Whitehead (drums).

Their only No. 1 record was their cover version of 'Ob-La-Di, Ob-La-Da', their third release, which topped the charts in December 1968. They faithfully re-created the Paul McCartney composition with its reggae beat.

This number was the third and final cover of a Beatles number to top the British charts and was taken from *The Beatles* 'white' album.

Another group, the Bedrocks, covered the number, but they reached only No. 17 in the charts with their version of the song. 'Ob-La-Di, Ob-La-Da' actually suited this particular band quite well, as they were a London-based West Indian outfit.

Marmalade had two further hits, were later to change labels and sign with Dick Rowe of Decca, had some line-up changes and were continuing to perform in cabaret over 25 years later.

MARRION, Albert Liverpool photographer who took 30 shots of the Beatles during two sessions on behalf of Brian Epstein. One of the photos, featuring them in black leather, was used as the famous cover of issue No. 13 of *Mersey Beat*, when the Beatles topped their first poll.

MARSDEN, Beryl At the age of 15, young Beryl Hogg began to sing with local groups such as the Undertakers and Faron's Flamingos. She adopted the stage name Marsden, although she was no relation to Gerry Marsden of Gerry & the Pacemakers.

A pint-sized rock 'n' roller, she was looked on as Liverpool's own answer to Brenda Lee and many considered her the best female vocalist of the Mersey Beat scene.

She was managed by various people, including Spencer Lloyd Mason and Joe Flannery. Under the aegis of Flannery, she appeared for a time with his brother's group, Lee Curtis & the All Stars. At the age of 17 she appeared at the Star Club, Hamburg, although she had to obtain a special licence to be able to perform there.

At one time I asked John Lennon if he could provide a Lennon and McCartney number for her to record and John was keen to let her have 'Love of the Loved'. Brian Epstein vetoed this and gave the song to Cilla Black instead.

Unfortunately, when manager Flannery booked her for shows such as *Thank Your Lucky Stars*, he garbed her in inappropriate party frocks when she should have been presented in her own tomboyish fashion, belting out rock 'n' roll numbers – Lulu later proved there was room for such a singer. On the other hand, Beryl flustered Flannery with her tendency not to turn up to gigs if she found something else to interest her. Flannery cited one example where he'd booked her to appear with a big band backing and she failed to turn up because she went to see the Rolling Stones instead.

Her first single 'I Know', originally recorded in America by Barbara George, was released by Decca in August 1963 when she was 16 and was in the Marsden style local audiences were used to. This wasn't true of her second release, 'When the Lovelight Starts Shining Through His Eyes', issued in January 1964.

Beryl was booked to appear with the Beatles on their last concert tour of Britain, from 3 to 12 December 1964. Of interest is the fact that this tour also featured two other Liverpool artists, the Koobas and Steve Aldo.

Married at the age of 18, she gave birth to a son, Tony. Two years later her daughter, Kim, was born, then a few years later her second son, Neil. After his birth her marriage fell apart and she left for London to find work.

Her new manager was Tony Stratton-Smith, who almost succeeded in establishing her name nationally. She had two more singles released, this time on the Columbia label: 'Who You Gonna Hurt?' in October 1965 and 'Music Talk' in December 1965.

Stratton-Smith paid a 'fixer' to hype the single 'Who You Gonna Hurt?', but it only scraped into the *NME* Top 30 for a single week, although it entitled her to an appearance in the 'Newcomers to the Chart' spot in the paper, where Beryl commented: 'I don't actually like the record. I've never cared much for it and I didn't think it had a chance of getting into your Top 30.'

'Stratters', as he came to be known, was experiencing Beryl's lack of discipline, just as Flannery had. He commented: 'Beryl was a marvellous girl flawed by a kind of Liverpudlian bloody-mindedness. There is a Liverpool thing and if you're not part of it, it's very difficult to cope with. I had to hire a Liverpool minder for her and he was the only guy who could actually get some sense out of her. Often, if a gig didn't suit her, she would actually lock herself in her flat so that nobody could get in and she couldn't get out. Many a time, this minder had to go through a window to get her.'

He was also to comment: 'Once she was due to go to Germany for an important television show. She knew exactly what it involved. But when she got to the airport she refused to fly. I knew she'd flown before. God knows what was going through her mind. It caused a terrible commotion: police were involved, British Airways said they'd virtually ban her from coming near the airport. After a few months of that I had to have an emergency operation brought on by nervous exhaustion, overwork and anxiety.'

In March 1966 she teamed up with Rod Stewart, Peter Green, Peter Bardens, Dave Ambrose and Mick Fleetwood in Shotgun Express and the band were only to make one single, 'I Could Feel the Whole World Turn Around'. She later returned to Liverpool to join Paddy Chambers in a soul group called Sinbad, before settling in London again.

She discovered Buddhism and was to become district manager for the Nichiren Shoshu Japanese Buddhism movement, during which time she became a close friend of another female singer, Sandie Shaw.

A leading British songwriter is currently preparing a stage musical based on her life.

There are several tracks recorded by Beryl and Paddy Chambers which have never been released. They include 'Here We Go Again', 'Take Me in Your Arms Again' and 'You and Me'.

MARSH, Tony Compère who appeared on both the Chris Montez/Tommy Roe and Roy Orbison tours with the Beatles. A practical joker, he was banned from the tour circuit when a member of the audience complained after an incident on a Rolling Stones tour when he dropped his pants.

MARTIN, George The Beatles' recording manager, often dubbed 'the fifth Beatle'. He was born in London in 1926. George joined the Fleet Air Arm when he was 17 and at the age of 21 was to enter the Guildhall School of Music for a three-year-course, during which time he was tutored on oboe by Jane Asher's mother, Margaret.

It was during his course at the Guildhall that he married his girlfriend Sheena, a former Wren. The couple were to have two children, Bundy and Gregory.

After working for a spell in the BBC Music Library, he was offered a job in 1950 working as an assistant to Oscar Preuss, head of the Parlophone label, which was part of EMI Records. EMI had several pop labels, such as Columbia and HMV, but Parlophone specialized in classical, jazz, comedy and middle-of-the-road music.

Among the artists recorded by Martin for Parlophone were Peter Ustinov, Bernard Cribbins, Sophia Loren, Johnny Dankworth, Cleo Laine, the Temperance Seven, Stan Getz, the Goons, Sir Malcolm Sargent, Sir Adrian Boult, Jimmy Shand, Shirley Bassey, Flanders & Swann and the cast of *Beyond the Fringe*.

The classically trained A&R man was more at home with artists of this nature. In 1957 he was taken to the 2 I's coffee bar in Soho to see Tommy Steele, but decided to turn him down. Decca Records signed him the next day and Steele became Britain's first major rock 'n' roll star.

It was purely by chance that he became involved with the Beatles. Despite all the flak Decca were to receive in hindsight because they didn't sign up the group, they were the only company to at least give the band a recording audition. The three pop labels of EMI, in addition to Pye, Philips and the other major record companies, had turned the Beatles down flat without even allowing them the opportunity of a recording audition.

Sid Coleman called Martin's office, but George was out. He chatted to Judy Lockhart-Smith, George's secretary, and arranged for Brian Epstein to meet Martin. Even then, the situation was not straightforward. Epstein, continually frustrated by his failure to obtain a recording contract for the group, began to apply what pressure he could.

Alistair Taylor, Brian's assistant at that time, confirms that Parlophone began to play around with Epstein to the extent that he became frustrated and threatened to withdraw his business if EMI didn't give the Beatles a recording contract.

Taylor was to tell writer Ray Coleman: 'EMI took them on sufferance because Brian was one of their top customers. I saw Brian in tears, literally, because Martin promised to phone back, and day after day went by and George Martin was never available, always "in a meeting". I saw Brian thumping the desk and in tears because George Martin hadn't phoned back.'

According to Taylor, when Epstein finally got hold of Martin he told him that NEMS as a shop would jettison EMI's HMV, Parlophone and Columbia labels.

Martin admits that EMI had nothing to lose financially by taking on an unknown group such as the Beatles. He said: 'To say I was taking a gamble would be stretching it, because the deal I offered them was pretty awful.'

He then arranged an audition for Wednesday 6 June 1962. It was Ron Richards, Martin's assistant, who actually took on the role of recording manager at the session. He was the one who usually dealt with the pop-style records and produced the discs for acts such as Paul Raven (Gary Glitter), Shane Fenton & the Fentones, Jerry Lordan and Judd Proctor.

After he'd recorded four numbers with them, Richards was intrigued by their original material and, having listened to 'Love Me Do', sent for George Martin, who was in the canteen. Martin then took over the rest of the session.

It was while listening to the playback that Martin told them: 'You must listen to it, and if there's anything you don't like, tell me, and we'll try and do something about it.' George Harrison replied: 'Well, for a start, I don't like your tie.'

Over the succeeding weeks, Martin had to decide whether to sign the group and initially began thinking in terms of altering the structure to that of the more conventional line-up of the time – a lead singer with a backing group in the style of bands such as Cliff Richard & the Shadows. He was attempting to figure out who should be the frontman – John or Paul, a case of Paul McCartney & the Beatles or John Lennon & the Beatles. Finally, he decided to leave them as they were, and at the time seemed to have no quibble about Pete Best – although in hindsight, in his books, he has slightly altered the opinions he held at the time.

Having decided to sign the Beatles, Martin presented them with a contract which paid a paltry royalty. Although their records were to make immense fortunes for EMI in subsequent years, the Beatles didn't receive a better slice until Allen Klein intervened.

When the Beatles returned to the EMI studios on Tuesday 4 September, they'd ousted Pete Best and replaced him with Ringo Starr. Ron Richards began rehearsing them in the afternoon and decided on two songs for the evening recording session: 'How Do You Do It?' and 'Love Me Do'. George Martin produced the session and insisted they record the Mitch Murray song, which Richards had obtained from Dick James. The Beatles were reluctant to do so and produced a lacklustre version.

Engineer Norman Smith was to comment: 'I've a feeling that Paul wasn't too happy with Ringo's drumming, and felt that it could be better. He didn't make a good job of it.'

This seemed to be confirmed by Richards, who was sole producer of the Tuesday 11 September session, during which they recorded 'Love Me Do', 'P.S. I Love You' and 'Please Please Me'.

Richards hadn't been satisfied with Ringo Starr's drumming on 'Love Me Do' during the 4 September session and had booked a session man, Andy White, to play instead. This wasn't such an unusual move. As Richards was to remark: 'I used him [White] a lot at the time – he was very good.'

Martin was also unhappy with Ringo's drumming. He had commented that he was dissatisfied with the Beatles' drum sound when he'd originally heard them, but this was mainly because Martin and other A&R men were used to a different style of drumming in the recording studios, where they used show drummers rather than ones from rock 'n' roll bands. It wasn't unusual for A&R men to employ a session drummer and this shouldn't have reflected on the ability of either Best or Starr.

Richards was used to working with White and preferred him at the session and a worried Ringo thought, 'They're doing a Pete Best on me,' when he noticed White in the drum seat. When the first number, 'P.S. I Love You', was recorded, an unhappy Ringo sat next to Richards in the control box until the producer asked him to play maracas on the track. When they came to record 'Love Me Do', Richards asked Ringo to play tambourine. Fortunately for Ringo, Richards allowed him to play drums on one of the cuts for 'Love Me Do', and versions by both White and Ringo were released.

If the version with Ringo had not been released, they would never have got away with the suggestion that it was Pete Best who was 'not a good enough drummer'.

When 'Love Me Do' was issued, both Martin and Epstein were disappointed at Ardmore & Beechwood's promotion of the record and Epstein decided to sign with another publishing company. It was Martin who steered him into the arms of Dick James and a contract which was to lose Lennon and McCartney the rights of their songs for ever.

For their second single, Martin wanted them to release the Mitch Murray composition 'How Do You Do It?'. He told them it would turn them into a household name and was upset when they said they didn't like the number and would rather record one of their own songs. Martin ticked them off and told them: 'When you can write material as good as this, then I'll record it. But right now we're going to record this.'

When they performed their new interpretation of 'Please Please Me', following advice he had given them about improving the song, he acknowledged that their own composition was better than 'How Do You Do It?' and 'Please Please Me' provided them with their first chart-topper.

Epstein then presented Martin with a string of acts: Gerry & the Pacemakers, Billy J. Kramer, Cilla Black and the Fourmost, almost guaranteeing him amazing success as an A&R man. The year 1963 brought him unprecedented acclaim, making him the first A&R man ever to achieve the top three places in the record charts, with 'I Like It' by Gerry & the Pacemakers at No. 1, 'Do You Want to Know a Secret?' by Billy J. Kramer at No. 2 and 'From Me to You' by the Beatles at No. 3, with Martin's Mersey productions being placed at No. 1 for 37 weeks of the year.

This was largely due to the popularity of the artists and the songs themselves, not to any specific input that George contributed. Almost any A&R man would have had the same success given the artists and the material.

Yet he was not entirely supportive of all the new acts he was presented with. Billy J. Kramer still resents to this day the disparaging remarks made about him by Martin in his autobiography *All You Need is Ears*, and when Brian Epstein brought him the song 'Anyone Who Had a Heart' for Cilla Black to record Martin wanted Shirley Bassey to perform it as he didn't think Cilla was capable, even though it was to give her a No. 1 hit.

His knowledge of the Mersey acts, if his autobiography is anything to go by, is quite rusty. To take one example, he states that Brian brought him a singer 'named Priscilla White. All her friends called her Cilla, and Brian, for some reason best known to himself, didn't like the idea of Cilla White, so he'd gone to the other end of the spectrum and called her Cilla Black.' She had first been dubbed Cilla Black in the 6 July 1961 issue of *Mersey Beat* and had used the name ever since – over a year before Brian ever met her and over two years before she met Martin.

Having achieved such unprecedented success for EMI, George was taken aback when the company didn't even give him a Christmas bonus. When he asked why, he was told that his salary of £3,000 per annum was quite adequate and he was therefore not entitled to a bonus. Discovering that his productions had made a profit of £2,200,000 for EMI during 1963, he suggested that he should receive some form of commission or bonus. Being refused either, he left the company. The Beatles, who had been signed to the company with such disgracefully low royalty arrangements by Martin, couldn't do the same.

So, 14 years after joining EMI, Martin left to form Associated Independent Recordings (AIR), taking a number of EMI's leading A&R men with him, including Ron Richards, John Burgess and Peter Sullivan. In addition, a large number of the acts agreed to continue having their records produced by the new company. They included the Beatles, Gerry & the Pacemakers, the Fourmost, Billy J. Kramer, Cilla Black, P. J. Proby, the Hollies, Peter and Gordon, Adam Faith and Manfred Mann.

This resulted in a staggering loss of revenue for a company which didn't have the foresight or generosity to pay a modest bonus to the person who had completely transformed their fortunes.

Although the artists still had their product released by EMI, the independent producers now received a percentage commission on the recordings.

The success he'd achieved through the luck of having such a stable of acts placed in his hands established his reputation as the most successful A&R man in the world and the offers poured in for him to orchestrate music for movies. He even began recording in his own right with the George Martin Orchestra.

He released singles based on Lennon and McCartney numbers and an album, *A Hard Day's Night: Off the Beatle Track*. He composed a number of instrumental versions of their numbers for the soundtrack album of *A Hard Day's Night*. Other ventures included his album *George Martin Scores Instrumental Versions of the Hits*. Virtually all of his individual projects over those years were with Beatles or Beatles-related material.

Although he was to admit himself that any A&R man could have achieved the same success with the Beatles during the first few years of their recording career, his real participation and input came in what were regarded as 'the studio years', when they ceased touring, and particularly in the production of *Sgt Pepper's Lonely Hearts Club Band*.

This process evolved gradually. In the first stage of their recording career, which Martin called the first era of recording, John and Paul would play their numbers on acoustic guitars and George would make his suggestions. This was called a 'head arrangement', and it was to change at the next stage of their career, which occurred with 'Yesterday'. This number was the first Beatles track to use orchestration and was the first record on which George scored music for them, in addition to being the first time that instruments other than those used by the Beatles were included. With 'Yesterday', George began to exert a greater influence on their music and as their records grew more sophisticated his input became more important.

By this time George had divorced Sheena and he married his secretary, Judy, in August 1967. Brian hosted a dinner party for the couple in his

Charles Street house, with the Beatles and their wives and girlfriends. George and Judy were to have two children, Lucy and Giles.

The close relationship in the studio foundered when the studio takes for the 'Get Back' project were handed to Phil Spector for him to fashion into *Let It Be*. Ominously, this was the Beatles thirteenth album.

George became the subject of a BBC TV documentary, *A Little Help from My Friends*, in December 1969.

Although he was to run a successful studio at AIR, Martin could never escape his association with the Beatles, and in the succeeding years people would be hard pushed to name his other record successes or any major artists he created.

In November 1976 Robert Stigwood approached him to compose the musical score for the movie *Sgt Pepper's Lonely Hearts Club Band*. The film proved a box-office disaster.

Capitol Records contacted him in 1977 to listen to tapes from their vaults of recordings of the Beatles Hollywood Bowl concerts in 1964 and 1965, which Martin had supervised. With the aid of Geoff Emerick, he worked on the tapes at AIR Studios, enhancing them for commercial release by transferring the three-track recording to multi-track tape and remixing and filtering until they had cleaned up the sound. The album *The Beatles at the Hollywood Bowl* was issued in May 1977.

All You Need is Ears, written with Jeremy Hornsby, was published in 1979. In 1993 he became involved in the production of a documentary on the making of *Sgt Pepper* for London Weekend Television's *South Bank Show* and his book *Summer of Love: The Making of 'Sgt Pepper'*, was published the same year.

Martin then became involved in his biggest Beatles venture since the 1960s: the three sets of double-CDS which were to comprise the *Anthology* releases, with 150 tracks which Martin selected from the Abbey Road vaults. With the help of Geoff Emerick and the latest state of the art technology, he enhanced the numbers for the series, with *Anthology I* being issued in November 1995.

The Beatles also recorded a new single 'Free as a Bird', flipside 'Real Love', released at the same time as the double-CD. This release saw Paul, George and Ringo perform together using demo tapes John had recorded in New York in the 1970s. However, the Beatles selected Jeff Lynne rather than Martin to produce their new recordings.

When *New York Times* music critic Allan Kozinn asked Paul McCartney why they chose Lynne rather than Martin, Paul commented: 'George is a very noble guy, and he's old now, and he will tell you that his hearing's not as good as it used to be. So when it came to who to work with, George Harrison brought up the fact that George Martin's hearing wasn't as good as it was. So George Martin was OK on all the old stuff. But perhaps for new stuff it required someone who's hearing was 100 per cent.'

In January 1996, at the age of 70, George decided to retire after producing a tribute album featuring Beatles songs performed by a variety of famous artists.

MATTHEW, Brian Veteran British broadcaster who hosted the Beatles ten times on his *Saturday Club* show, four times on *Easy Beat* and twice on *Top Gear*, all BBC radio shows.

Brian also covered the American tour and interviewed the group on a number of occasions.

A theatre lover, he once went into business with Brian Epstein to launch a new theatre, the Pilgrim, in Farnborough. Unfortunately, the project collapsed when planning permission was refused.

Although Brian has officially retired from the BBC, in 1995 he continued working with a Saturday show on BBC Radio 2, *The Sound of the Sixties*.

His voice appeared on the Beatles *Live at the BBC* album and in 1995 he was featured as a guest at his first Beatles convention.

MAYLES, Albert and David American documentary film-makers. They filmed the Beatles in 1964 for a documentary, *The Beatles in New York*, commissioned by Granada Television. David died in 1987.

MEEHAN, Tony Former member of the Shadows who turned A&R man and joined Decca Records. When the Beatles were turned down by Decca, Dick Rowe suggested to Brian Epstein that he should pay Tony £100 to produce a session with the group. It was Tony who discovered a Scots band called the Pathfinders and they recorded for Apple under the name Trash.

MENDEZ, Carlos Portuguese bandleader. When Paul was on holiday in Portugal, he wrote a song called 'Penina', which was the name of the hotel at which he was staying. Mendez heard Paul singing the number and liked it so much that Paul allowed him to have the song to record. His version was released in Portugal on 18 July 1969. The following year a Dutch band, Jotte Herre, also recorded it. At the time, Paul had forgotten to inform Northern Songs about the number and the fact that he'd let someone record it without telling them.

MERSEYBEATS, The Originally called the Mavericks when they formed in 1960, the group changed their name to the Pacifics. At the beginning of 1962 they approached me at *Mersey Beat*, as copyright holder of the name, for permission to call themselves the Mersey Beats. I agreed and they adopted the name in February.

Their personnel at the time comprised Billy Kinsley (bass), Tony Crane (lead/vocals), Dave Elias (rhythm), Frank Sloane (drums) and Billy Butler (vocals). Butler left after three months to join the Tuxedos and later became a disc jockey. He is now a leading DJ on Radio City. Elias and Sloane left in the summer of 1962 to form the Nocturnes.

The group had a Monday night residency at St John's Hall in Bootle and on one occasion were able to pick the Beatles as their guests.

The Mersey Beats appeared on several Cavern bills with the Beatles in 1962: Tuesday 19 June, Wednesday 1 August, Sunday 18 November and Wednesday 12 December. During 1963 their appearances included Sunday 20 January, Sunday 3 February and Saturday 3 August, the Beatles' final Cavern appearance.

Other bills they shared with the Beatles included the Rock and Twist Spectacular at the Rialto Ballroom on Thursday 11 October 1962, the Little Richard Show at the Tower Ballroom on Friday 12 October 1962, the 'Showdance' promotion at the Queen's Hall, Widnes, on Monday 22 October 1962 and La Scala, Runcorn, on Tuesday 11 December 1962.

When Pete Best was sacked from the Beatles, Brian Epstein suggested that he join the Mersey Beats, telling him: 'I have an idea that might work. I'm thinking of signing the Mersey Beats and I'd like you to join them.' Pete turned him down.

At the beginning of 1963 they became the third group to be signed by Brian Epstein, in the wake of the Beatles and Gerry & the Pacemakers. But their association was short-lived: they had a dispute with him and left after only a few months.

They signed a recording deal with Fontana in June 1963 and reached No. 24 in the charts with their debut single, 'It's Love That Really Counts'. Their second release, 'I Think of You', reached No. 5. The group at this time comprised Kinsley, Crane, Aaron Williams (rhythm) and John Banks (drums).

They developed a Spanish-inspired act, wearing shirts with frilled cuffs and collars and Spanish-styled suits, and featured maracas and tambourines. They also became the first group to appear on colour TV when they played Stockport Town Hall, where closed-circuit colour TV was being demonstrated.

Between 1963 and 1966 the Merseybeats had seven chart entries, the others being 'Don't Turn Around', 'Wishin' and Hopin'', 'Last Night', 'I Love You, Yes I Do' and 'I Stand Accused'.

Billy Kinsley formed his own band, the Kinsleys, in April 1964 with Denny Alexandre (rhythm/vocals), Dave Austin (drum/vocals), Dave Percival (lead/vocals) and himself (bass/vocals). He said: 'It was untrue to say that I left the Mersey Beats because I couldn't stand the pace. This was just an excuse I had to make. In actual fact I left because of personal disagreements with the other members.'

Bob Garner from Warrington group the Barkers deputized until Johnny Gustafson replaced Kinsley in the group's line-up. By this time they'd contracted the name into a single word: Merseybeats.

When 'Gus' began to make inquiries about the band's finances he was fired and Kinsley rejoined in December 1964. That line-up remained the same until January 1966. Williams left the music business and Banks teamed up with Gus in a duo called Johnny and John. Crane and Kinsley became the Merseys and had a single chart hit in April 1966 with 'Sorrow', which reached No. 4. George Harrison said that their version of the song was one of his favourite records and took a line from the number, relating to a girl with 'long blonde hair and eyes of blue', and included it on 'It's All Too Much', a track on *Yellow Submarine*, in tribute to his wife, Pattie. David Bowie was to record 'Sorrow' in 1973.

At one time John Lennon intended to produce a single of the Merseybeats performing 'I'll Be Back', but it never materialized.

Crane later reformed the Merseybeats and still runs the group today. Kinsley formed Liverpool Express and enjoyed some success with four chart entries: 'You are My Love', 'Hold Tight', 'Every Man Must Have a Dream' and 'Dreamin''. He later teamed up with Pete Best on a number of musical projects and rejoined Crane in the Merseybeats.

The Merseybeats' recordings of 'Soldier of Love' and 'Cry Me a River' have never been released and there is an unreleased version of the Merseys performing 'Sorrow', backed by Jack Bruce, Clem Cattini, John Paul Jones and Jimmy Page.

MERSEYSIPPI JAZZ BAND, The Liverpool's premier jazz band in the late 1950s. The Quarry Men supported them on Saturday-evening dances at Liverpool College of Art and at the Cavern on 25 January 1958.

MIKE COTTON SOUND, The Band who appeared with the Beatles on 'Another Beatles Show' at the Hammersmith, Odeon, west London, in December 1964. A former jazz band who had altered their direction to keep pace with the burgeoning Beat scene, they comprised Mike Cotton (trumpet), Johnny Crocker (trombone), Stu Morrison (banjo), Dave Rowberry (keyboards), Derek Tearle (bass guitar) and Jim Garforth (drums). Rowberry was later to join the Animals.

MIKE SAMMES SINGERS, The Established group of British middle-of-the-road singers who were hired to provide backing for the Beatles on Wednesday 27 September 1967 on the track 'I am the Walrus'. There were eight female vocalists, Peggy Allen, Wendy Horan, Pat Whitmore, Jill Utting, June Day, Sylvia King, Irene King and G. Mallen, and eight males, Fred Lucas, Mike Redway, John O'Neill, F. Dachtler, Allan Grant, D. Griffiths, J. Smith and J. Fraser. Eight of the Mike Sammes Singers provided vocals for another Beatles recording on Monday 22 July 1968, Ringo's 'Don't Pass Me By'. They were Ingrid Thomas, Pat Whitmore, Val Stockwell, Irene King, Ross Gilmour, Mike Redway, Ken Barrie and Fred Lucas.

MILES, Barry One of the owners of the Indica Gallery, which advised the Beatles on the various contemporary arts. He was commissioned to advise on the Beatles Zapple label and later became a biographer, working on books about Allen Ginsberg, William S. Burroughs and Paul McCartney.

MILLINGS, Dougie Show-business tailor who, with his son Gordon, produced over 500 garments for the Beatles and made the suits for their Madame Tussaud's waxworks. He also appeared in *A Hard Day's Night*.

MODERN JAZZ QUARTET Famous jazz outfit comprising John Lewis (piano), Milt Jackson (vibes), Percy Heath (bass) and Connie Kay (drums) who signed to Apple Records in 1968. They recorded two albums for the company.

MOHAMMED, Jeff Manchester student who entered Liverpool College of Art and became a firm friend of John Lennon. The two lost contact and in his *Playboy* interview John mentioned that he had heard Jeff had died.

MOJOS, The Drummer John Kinrade and bassist Keith Karlson formed a group called the Nomads with lead guitarist Roy Woods, but he didn't fit in and was replaced by Adrian Wilkinson in September 1962. Stu Slater, a student at Liverpool University, joined them as vocalist/pianist, changing his name to Stu James.

As the Nomads they appeared with the Beatles at the Cavern on Sunday 3 February 1963 and recorded on the *This is Mersey Beat* album. However, they discovered a London group had registered the name and changed to the Mojos. They entered 'The Lancashire and Cheshire Beat Group Contest' at the Philharmonic and, although the group didn't win, were awarded a songwriters' contract with Carlin Music.

It was ironic that Carlin leased their tapes to Decca, because the Escorts, the group who won the competition, failed to be given the promised Decca recording contract.

They were joined by Terry O'Toole on piano and Stu became lead vocalist.

Now managed by Spencer Lloyd Mason, they saw their first record, 'Forever', released in October 1963. Adrian left to join the Mastersounds and was replaced by Nicky Crouch, a former member of Faron's Flamingos. They appeared for a five-week season at the Star Club and while in Germany they recorded 'Everything's Alright', which became a Top 10 hit. The group also toured Britain with the Rolling Stones and the Dave Clark Five.

Soon after the release of 'Seven Daffodils', Keith Karlson and Terry O'Toole left because the group couldn't agree on musical policy. Lewis Collins on bass and Aynsley Dunbar on drums became the new members of the quartet in December 1964. The name was changed to Stu James & the Mojos.

This line-up continued until September 1966. Lewis Collins was to join other bands before becoming an actor and Dunbar joined John Mayall's Bluesbreakers.

MOLYNEUX, Bob A Merseyside teenager in 1957 when, on 6 July, he recorded the Quarry Men performing at the Woolton Garden Fête in Liverpool. Molyneux had recently bought a Grundig TK8 portable tape recorder for 82 guineas and had taken it along to the fête.

The Quarry Men first appeared on stage at approximately 4.15 p.m.

and comprised Eric Griffiths on guitar, Colin Hanton on drums, Rod Davis on banjo, Pete Shotton on washboard, Len Garry on tea-chest bass and a 16-year-old John Lennon on guitar and lead vocals. The skiffle group took a half-hour break and then continued performing at 5.45 p.m.

The group were actually on a supporting bill with the George Edwards Dance Band, who played mainly waltzes and foxtrots, and Molyneux approached both acts asking permission to record them.

Later he was to record over the tapes, but fortunately he had transferred one of the tapes on to another, Emitape reel. This contained a couple of numbers from the George Edwards Dance Band and two Quarry Men numbers. One was 'Putting on the Style', a Lonnie Donegan hit then at No. 1 in the charts, the other was 'Baby, Let's Play House', the flipside of Elvis Presley's 'Rip It Up'.

Bob forgot about the tapes until he bumped into Ringo Starr at the Blue Angel club in the early 1960s and told him that John could have the tape if he wanted it. No one got in touch so he forgot about the tape for 35 years.

In 1994 Molyneux, now a retired policeman, put it up for auction at Sotheby's, where on 15 September it was bought by EMI Records for £78,500.

MONKEES, The   The Monkees were a pop group created specially for television by two American producers, Bob Rafelson and Bert Schneider. They formed the Raybeat Company to produce a pilot sit-com for Screen Gems, based on *A Hard Day's Night*.

Acknowledging the work of director Richard Lester on the Beatles' debut film, Schneider commented: 'The Beatles made it all happen, that's the reality. Richard Lester is where the credit begins for the Monkees and for Bob and me.'

They initially considered using an existing group, the Lovin' Spoonful, but decided to use actors and organized a casting call by advertising in the newspaper *Daily Variety*: 'MADNESS!! Auditions – folk and rock 'n' roll musicians/singers. Running parts for four insane kids, ages 17 to 21, with the courage to work.'

Some 437 hopefuls were interviewed, including Steve Stills, Paul Williams, Danny Hutton (who became leader of Three Dog Night) and Charles Manson, who was to become involved in the Sharon Tate murder.

David Thomas Jones (vocals/guitar), more familiarly known as Davy Jones, had already been selected. Born in Manchester on 30 December 1946, he'd appeared as the Artful Dodger in *Oliver!* on Broadway, the stage version of *Pickwick* and in the TV series *Ben Casey*.

In fact, it was as a member of the *Oliver!* cast that he appeared on the same *Ed Sullivan Show* as the Beatles making their American debut, in February 1964.

Robert Michael Nesmith (vocals/guitar) was born in Dallas, Texas, on

30 December 1942 and later moved to Los Angeles, where he appeared in several bands.

Peter Halsten Thorkelson (vocals/keyboards/bass guitar), more familiarly known as Peter Tork, was born in Washington DC on 13 February 1942 and George Michael Dolenz (vocals/drums), known as Mickey, was born in Los Angeles on 8 March 1945. Under the name Mickey Braddock he'd appeared as Corky in the series *Circus Boy*, had made appearances on shows such as *Peyton Place* and had formed several bands.

The first name considered for the group was the Turtles, then the Inevitables and finally the Monkees.

NBC launched the series on 5 September 1966, the same day they launched another new series, *Star Trek*. A month before the debut of the show, a Monkees single, 'Last Train to Clarksville', was released and it was to top the charts.

Although the group had been formed specially for the series, it was decided to include music in all the shows and the producers hired Don Kirshner to produce the material. He gathered songs from a variety of songwriters, including Neil Diamond, Leiber and Stoller, Neil Sedaka, Carole King, Gerry Goffin and Barry Mann, and produced backing music to which the Monkees had only to add their voices.

Interestingly, on the programme's theme song the group sang 'no no no', a counterpoint to the Beatles' 'yeah yeah yeah'.

By 1967 the Monkees were at odds with Kirschner and wanted to produce their own material and perform the music themselves, which they were then allowed to do.

There were 58 episodes of the TV series, which lasted until 25 March 1968. The main audience for the group was a very young one and their appeal was described as 'Monkeemania'.

Brian Epstein's NEMS Enterprises was the company which first presented the group in Britain, booking them into the Empire Pool, Wembley, from 30 June to 3 July 1967. NEMS also held a party in their honour at the Speakeasy club in London, which was attended by the Beatles, Lulu, the Bee Gees and numerous other celebrities.

In 1968 the group starred in a feature film, *Head*, written by Bob Rafelson and Jack Nicholson, which also featured Annette Funicello, Victor Mature, Carol Doda, Teri Garr, Sonny Liston and Frank Zappa, with choreography by Toni Basil. Soon after Tork left the group, they recorded a TV special, $33\frac{1}{3}$ *Revolutions per Monkee*, on 14 April 1969. This was conceived and produced by Jack Good and also featured the Brian Auger Trinity, Julie Driscoll, Fats Domino and Jerry Lee Lewis.

In addition to the TV series, the Monkees had nine albums and 14 singles released between August 1966 and May 1970. In their song 'Randy Scouse Git', they refer to the Beatles as 'the four kings of EMI'.

MONTEZ, Chris American singer, born Christopher Montanez on 17 January 1943 in Los Angeles. 'Let's Dance' in 1962 was his first and only million-seller.

Although it was his only British hit at the time, the singer was booked by promoter Arthur Howes to co-headline a tour with another American artist, Tommy Roe. When told that the second act on the bill was the Beatles, Montez commented: 'Who are these guys the Beatles? I try to keep up to date with the British scene, but I don't know their work.'

Despite the fact that the Beatles were now more famous in Britain than either of the two Americans, no British artist had previously topped the bill above an American act.

It was the Beatles' second package tour, which got under way five days after their first and commenced on Saturday 9 March 1963 at the Granada, East Ham.

'Let's Dance' was Montez's only claim to fame, but he did well by the number, taking it into the charts on three occasions: in 1962, 1972 and 1979.

MOODY BLUES, The Birmingham group who formed in 1964. They originally comprised Denny Laine (vocals/harmonica/guitar), Mike Pinder (piano/keyboards), Ray Thomas (flute/vocals/harmonica), Graeme Edge (drums) and Clint Warwick (bass).

Laine had actually appeared on a bill with the Beatles with his previous group, Denny & the Diplomats. This took place at the Plaza, Old Hill, on Friday 5 July 1963.

Brian Epstein took an interest in the band when he interviewed them in Britain for the American NBC show *Hullabaloo* and signed them to a management and agency deal. They entered the charts with their single 'Go Now', and were booked to appear on the Beatles' 1965 British tour.

Epstein seemed to lose interest in the band. As Ray Coleman reported in his biography of Epstein:

> The gifted group from Birmingham, which then featured Denny Laine, should have been steered to the top by Epstein with all his influence and expertise. But Brian failed to show the patience or strategy necessary to realize their potential. Although he knew they could scale the peaks, he seemed unable or unwilling to devote the time necessary to reposition them for the golden future that surely awaited them.

Brian passed over their management to his assistant Alistair Taylor, but NEMS didn't do much for the band and in October 1966 NEMS Enterprises announced that the Moodies had disbanded.

Actually, Laine and Warwick left but the group continued with the replacements, Justin Hayward and John Lodge. The Moody Blues then embarked on the most successful phase of their career, with singles such as 'Nights in White Satin' and album hits such as *Days of Future Past, In Search of the Lost Chord* and *On the Threshold of a Dream.*

In 1971 Denny Laine was to team up with Paul McCartney in Wings and co-penned the No. 1 smash-hit 'Mull of Kintyre' with him.

MOORE, Tommy Acted as drummer for the Silver Beatles in 1960. The group had been performing without a drummer as the Quarry Men, but began changing their name and felt they needed someone in the drum seat. After Brian Casser had said the name the Beatals was no good, they changed it to the Silver Beetles (also Silver Beatles) and, on Casser's recommendation, they invited Tommy Moore to join them.

At the time, Tommy was a fork-lift truck operator at the Window Lane branch of the Garston Bottle Works. He was 26 years old, in contrast to Lennon, who was 19. Apparently, during the short time he was with them there was continual tension between him and John, who was reputed to have needled him mercilessly. Initially, he rehearsed with them at Gambier Terrace.

When they were due to audition for Larry Parnes at the Wyvern Club, playing four numbers in a ten-minute set, Moore was late and didn't turn up until halfway through their set. They began playing with Johnny Hutchinson of the Big Three taking Moore's place – and photographs of the audition show Hutch in the drum seat – so the image of Moore as a member of the group was lost to posterity.

As a result of the audition, the group were booked for a short tour of Scotland, backing Johnny Gentle, although they weren't selected as Billy Fury's backing group. Parnes said that this was because of Moore, whom he felt was far older than the other members, and also because he didn't dress in the same manner. Parnes didn't like the fact that Moore had turned up late, either.

Despite the pressure from his girlfriend, Moore took time off from his job to join them on their tour of Scotland, which took place between 20 and 28 May. When their regular driver, Gerry Scott, needed to rest, Gentle took over as driver, but crashed the car into the back of a Ford Popular at the crossroads outside of Banff. Moore was injured and his front teeth were knocked out. He was lying in his hospital bed, dazed with sedatives, when John Lennon, accompanied by the manager of the Dalrymple Hall arrived to drag him out of bed insisting that he play the gig that night. At the end of the tour, Moore found he had only profited by £2.

Tommy decided to leave the group following their appearance at the Institute, Neston on 9 June and he didn't turn up at the Jacaranda on 11 June to set off with them for their Grosvenor Hall booking. Allan Williams and the Beatles went to Moore's house in Fern Grove, Toxteth to get him, but received a torrent of abuse from his girlfriend, who leaned out of an upstairs window and shouted: 'You can go and piss off! He's not playing with you any more; he's got a job at Garston Bottle Works on the night shift.'

They all rushed to the works and found him driving his fork-lift, but he refused to go on the gig with them. So they arrived at the Grosvenor with Tommy's kit, but no drummer. When John mentioned this over the mike, a teddy boy called Ronnie got up on stage and joined them, thumping away at the drums and damaging Moore's kit.

Tommy actually made one further appearance with the band – at the Jacaranda on 13 June. He was to die of a stroke in 1981, soon after joining a local jazz band.

MOROCKANS, The A group from the Wirral, led by lead guitarist Pete Weston, who appeared at the Cavern with the Beatles on Wednesday 11 July 1962.

MORRISON, Ruth One of George Harrison's early girlfriends. It was a suggestion by Ruth which indirectly led to George, John and Paul teaming up again after a time apart.

When she was in the company of George and Ken Brown, she told them of the plans Mona Best had of turning her basement into a club called the Casbah, suggesting they contact her. George and Ken were members of the Les Stewart Quartet and, after Ken had made arrangements for them to begin a residency at the club, Les Stewart refused to play and George asked John and Paul to join Ken and himself. It was during the Casbah residency that George, aged 16, refused to take Ruth to the cinema, an incident that led to their breaking up.

Ruth moved to Birmingham to become a nurse.

MOYNIHAN, Vyvienne A prominent British figure in the arts and media whose career began immediately after the Second World War, when she joined the Q Theatre as assistant stage manager. She was soon to progress to stage director and company manager before moving to the West End.

She joined Associated Rediffusion, the original London television weekend contractor in the mid-1950s, initially as casting director, then as manager of drama and eventually as manager of light entertainment. It was in this capacity that she was initially contacted by Brian Epstein in the autumn of 1962.

Moynihan, then 38 years old, listened to what Epstein had to say about the Beatles and suggested that she have someone see the group before she considered booking them. Epstein insisted that he come down to London to discuss the matter with her personally, which he did, and as a result Moynihan booked the Beatles for Rediffusion's *Tuesday Rendezvous*.

Epstein also dealt with Vyvienne when he began negotiations for the *Around the Beatles* television special, and she was also involved in the production of a Cilla Black TV show.

Brian then offered her a position in his own organization, in charge of all work associated with theatres. He set her up in her own office London's Cork Street, where, as director of productions, she was involved in presentations featuring the Beatles and other artists and was also involved with the Saville Theatre.

Following Epstein's death, she moved to the Soviet Union for two years to produce documentaries, then returned to London, where she joined the Central Office of Information. She moved to the advertising agency McCann Erickson, then formed her own consultancy business in 1984, which she ran successfully until retiring due to illness in 1993.

She died at the age of 74 on 19 August 1994.

MURPHY, Paul Liverpool singer, real name Paul Rogers. He made his stage debut at the age of 13 in a school pantomime version of *Cinderella*, then became a member of various skiffle groups before appearing with the Rhythm Quintet. At the beginning of 1959 he was vocalist/guitarist with Rory Storm's group the Raving Texans. He became a solo singer, using the stage name Paul Murphy, which had been given to him by Jim Gretty.

While appearing at Liverpool's the Latin Quarter he was spotted by comedians Mike and Bernie Winters, who recommended him to Walter Ridley of HMV. He appeared briefly with Johnny Kidd & the Pirates and sang with a big band, then made various solo appearances at the Zodiac Club in Duke Street.

HMV released his version of 'Four and Twenty Thousand Kisses' in 1961, a song which had been a hit at the San Remo Festival.

Paul moved to Germany and in 1963 became A&R man for Polydor in Hamburg. He signed up Tony Sheridan and commented: 'I want to show everyone in England "the Teacher". I also intend to send him to Liverpool and launch him from there.'

Paul also recorded a humorous disc about the Mersey Beat scene with Alex Harvey and produced an album with Kingsize Taylor & the Dominoes. He moved to various companies in Germany before returning to England in the 1970s to run Buk Records and achieve his ambition of launching Sheridan in Liverpool with a concert at the Philharmonic Hall.

When he was heading Buk Records he heard of the Adrian Barber tape of the Beatles at the Star Club which was in the hands of Kingsize Taylor and Allan Williams. He persuaded them to let him put the tapes through his company, Lingsong, and released them as a double album. He later sold the distribution rights to Double H Licensing Corporation in America.

MURRAY, Mitch Under his real name of Lionel Michael Stander, he worked for the family business, selling handbags in Golders Green, north-west London. He bought a four-string ukelele primarily as an excuse to chat up girls on the beach while on holiday. Using old sheet music, he'd play a couple of songs.

'I wrote my own words to them,' he said. 'I found it very easy to write songs. I got a tape recorder and began to make demos of my ideas and started doing the round of music publishers. My family gave me three months' leave to make it.

'I had the B-side of Mark Wynters's "Go Away Little Girl", and Terry Scott recorded "My Brother". Then I got a telephone call from Dick James, who said that he thought one of my songs, "How Do You Do It?", would be suitable for a group called the Beatles. I said, "What's a group?" The Beatles made "Love Me Do" at the time and I said, "It's awful." '

The Beatles didn't release 'How Do You Do It?' and it was recorded by Gerry & the Pacemakers. Mitch Murray, as he was now called, said: 'It became No. 1 in most countries, a Top 5 in the States and was covered by the Supremes on their LP. "I Like It", another number by Gerry, went to No. 1 and "I'm Telling You Now", by Freddie & the Dreamers went to No. 1 in the States and No. 2 in Britain, and Freddie also reached No. 2 with "You Were Made for Me". I also wrote "By the Way" for the Big Three.'

Murray originally had the demo disc of 'How Do You Do It?' recorded at Regent Sound Studios, Denmark Street, in the summer of 1962, with vocals by Barry Mason and backing by the Dave Clark Five. Initially, he'd conceived it as a number for Adam Faith.

George Martin sent the Beatles an acetate disc of the number for them to record on Tuesday 4 September 1962 and had originally decided that it should be their debut single. The Beatles also recorded 'Love Me Do' at the same session, apparently putting more effort into their own number than into Murray's and Martin eventually decided to issue the Lennon and McCartney original.

After his initial flush of success penning hits for Beat groups, Murray later teamed up with Peter Callendar and formed Bus Stop Records. They also managed and wrote hits for Paper Lace. After finishing with Paper Lace, Murray went to live in Holland, producing records for Dutch artists and recording English groups such as Peter Noone in Germany. Bus Stop Records was sold and Callendar retired to Farnham, Bucks, while Mitch moved to the Isle of Man, where he began producing jingles for advertising agencies and making documentary albums.

MURRAY, Rod A youth from the West Derby area of Liverpool, who enrolled at Liverpool College of Art in 1958. He befriended Stuart Sutcliffe and eventually invited Stuart to share a flat he rented at 8 Gambier Terrace. John Lennon also began staying at the flat on a regular basis.

John, Stu, Rod and I used to get together regularly and at one time I suggested we called ourselves 'the dissenters', in an effort to use our talents to make Liverpool famous.

When John needed a bass guitarist for his group, he offered the job to both Rod and Stu, without telling either one about the other. Rod began to make a bass guitar, but Stuart sold a painting and was able to buy a guitar on hire-purchase, and thus became a Beatle instead of Rod.

After the Beatles left for Germany, Rod found he couldn't afford the rent on the flat by himself and moved out. Among the items he took with him were copies of some early John Lennon manuscripts. I tracked him down a couple of years later and obtained one of the exercise books back on John's behalf, and in 1984 Rod was to sell another at a Sotheby's auction for more than £16,000.

He later became a lecturer at a prominent London art college.

NEWBY, Chas A guitarist who had originally played with the Blackjacks, the group formed by Pete Best and Ken Brown, which had a residency at the Casbah club.

When the Beatles returned to Liverpool from their first season in Hamburg in December 1960, Stuart Sutcliffe remained in Germany. The group needed a bass player to sit in with them for some of their local gigs and Pete Best suggested Brown, who was currently living in London. John and Paul didn't like the idea as they had originally sacked him from the Quarry Men and reasoned that there would still be some bad blood between them. Paul McCartney felt that this might be his opportunity to become the group's bass guitarist, but Pete then suggested Chas Newby, who was currently on holiday from college, where he was a chemistry student.

When approached, Newby agreed to join the Beatles for a short time, borrowed a leather jacket and bass guitar, and made his debut with the band at the Casbah club on 17 December 1960.

Newby was only to make four appearances as a Beatle, the other dates being the Grosvenor Ballroom on 24 December, Litherland Town Hall on 27 December and finally, a return to the Casbah club on 31 December. John Lennon then approached him with the offer of joining them on their next Hamburg season, but Newby turned him down, preferring to continue his college studies.

Years later, he was to meet up again with Pete Best, who was researching his book *Beatle!*. Chas was then working in industrial management in Birmingham and had fond memories of his brief time with the Beatles, observing how exciting it had been. Recalling those few gigs, he told Pete: 'I remember them vividly. It used to make my feet ache with all the stamping we had to put into the act, but I loved every minute.'

He also said that he had no regrets about turning down the offer to join the Beatles as a permanent member.

NEWFIELD, Joanne Personal secretary to Brian Epstein after he'd relocated to London. In 1966 she became his personal assistant and it was she who raised the alarm when Brian was found dead in September 1967. She then became PA to Peter Brown. The following year she married Colin Peterson, drummer with the Bee Gees, and later resettled in Australia.

NEWLEY, Anthony Major British actor/singing star whom Brian Epstein chose to open the Whitechapel branch of NEMS in 1959. George Harrison also met Newley during a visit to his sister Louise in St Louis and commented: 'America was really great. I met Tony Newley over there. He'd never heard of any of our numbers so I played him some of our recordings. When I left he said he wanted to record "I Saw Her Standing There".' Newley was as good as his word and the single was released in October 1963, making him the second artist to cover a Beatles number in America.

NICOL, Jimmy A British drummer who had started his career as a drum repairer for Boosey & Hawkes. He'd begun playing drums with the Spotniks prior to forming his own group, the Shubdubs. When Ringo Starr was diagnosed as having tonsillitis on the morning of Wednesday 3 June 1964, on the eve of the first leg of the Beatles' world tour, Brian Epstein felt that they should go ahead with the tour using a substitute drummer, despite protests by George Harrison, who said: 'If Ringo's not going then neither am I, you can find two replacements.'

It was George Martin who suggested Nicol, as the drummer had recently played on sessions for Martin with Georgie Fame & the Blue Fames and Tommy Quickly. Nicol had also performed on a Beatles soundalike album, *Beatlemania*, on the Top Six label and knew most of the Beatles' numbers.

Martin rang Nicol and arranged for him to audition and rehearse with the Beatles at Abbey Road at three that afternoon. At the rehearsal the four of them performed six numbers and Paul commented: 'This fellow is fine, but we just can't afford to be without Ringo at a real recording session, because the kids would always know that a record was one without him.'

Jimmy was then called into Brian Epstein's office and offered the job and given details of his remuneration in front of John, Paul and George.

He rehearsed with them again the following day prior to their appearance at Copenhagen. Making his stage debut with them at the Tivoli Gardens that evening, he wore Ringo's stage suit, although the trousers were too short for him, and the band performed ten numbers, cutting down from the 11 originally planned by leaving out Ringo's spot with 'I Wanna be Your Man'.

Nicol then appeared with them in Holland, Hong Kong and on the first four shows in Australia, before Ringo rejoined them in Melbourne on 14 June, when a press conference with all five of them took place. During his time with the group, Jimmy was invited to all their personal appearances and press conferences.

On his return to Britain he recorded with the Shubdubs, but his single 'Husky', flipside 'Don't Come Back' failed to register. He met the Beatles one more time when the Shubdubs were asked to substitute for the Dave Clark Five on 12 July 1964 at the Hippodrome, Brighton, on a bill with the Beatles and the Fourmost. He met them backstage and they had a brief, polite chat.

Nicol later moved to South America and returned to Britain in the 1980s, then moved on to Australia.

NILSSON, Harry An American singer, born Harry Edward Nilsson III in Brooklyn, New York, on 15 June 1941, whose debut album, *Pandemonium Shadow Show*, was released in 1967. One of the tracks, 'You Can't Do That', featured a medley of Beatles numbers and brought him to the attention of Derek Taylor, who then sent the album to Brian Epstein.

His recording of 'Everybody's Talking' was chosen as the theme song for the film *Midnight Cowboy* and earned Harry his first Grammy award.

He also recorded a number penned by Pete Ham and Tom Evans of the Apple band Badfinger, 'Without You', which became his biggest hit. It was featured on his most successful album, *Nilsson Schmilsson* and the single release earned him another Grammy.

His *Son of Schmilsson* album featured George Harrison and Ringo Starr as guest musicians. John Lennon also acted as recording manager for his *Pussy Cats* album.

Nilsson made two films with Ringo Starr, *Harry & Ringo's Night Out* and *Son of Dracula*, and he released a *Son of Dracula* soundtrack album.

After John Lennon's assassination, Nilsson toured America on a campaign for tighter handgun control.

In 1993 he suffered a heart attack from which he never fully recovered and died in Los Angeles on 15 January 1994 at the age of 52. Ringo played on his posthumously released 1995 album, *The Harry Nilsson Anthology*.

NORRIS, Steven A classmate of Paul McCartney at Liverpool Institute who also used to travel to school with him on the No. 80 bus. He was later to become the Conservative MP for Oxford East.

NURK TWINS, The Name used by Paul and Mike McCartney in their pre-teen years when they performed for relatives in the family home. In April 1960 Paul and John used the name the Nurk Twins when they performed at a pub owned by Paul's cousin Mike Robbins and his wife in Berkshire.

NUTTER, David Photographer commissioned by Apple to take shots of John and Yoko on a regular basis, including pictures of the couple getting married in Gibraltar.

NUTTER, Tommy Savile Row tailor who was hired regularly by the Beatles and their entourage. Three of his suits are featured on the *Abbey Road* cover. He died at the age of 49 in August 1992 of an AIDS-related disease.

O'DELL, Chris American girl who joined Apple as a receptionist. She then became Peter Asher's secretary and also took charge of bookings for the Apple studio. George Harrison penned a song about her, 'Miss O'Dell'.

O'DELL, Dennis Associate producer of the Beatles debut film, *A Hard Day's Night*. The Irish-born O'Dell also worked on *The Family Way*, for which Paul wrote the score, and *The Magic Christian*, which featured Ringo. When Apple Films was formed in February 1968, the Beatles appointed him one of the company's directors and he was involved in the making of *Magical Mystery Tour*, *Let It Be* and *The Concert for Bangladesh*. He's also mentioned by name in the song 'You Know My Name (Look Up the Number)'.

O'DONNELL, Lucy Indirectly responsible for inspirating 'Lucy in the Sky with Diamonds'. She was attending Heath House infant's school in Wey-bridge in 1967 in the same class as Julian Lennon. Julian drew a picture of her and showed it to his father and, when John asked him what it represented, Julian said it was 'Lucy in the sky with diamonds'.

OLDHAM, Andrew Loog The illegitimate war child of a wealthy English woman and a Dutch-American bomber pilot who was killed before his birth, Andrew Loog Oldham adopted both his parents' names. In 1962 at the age of 17, he was working as a runner for Mary Quant. By the end of the year he was acting as a press agent for Mark Wynter and had formed a partnership in a PR firm with Tony Calder.

Calder, who had formerly worked in the Decca press office with Tony Barrow, was approached by Barrow and asked if he could set up inter-views and issue the press releases for 'Love Me Do' for the Beatles. Oldham and Calder obliged and they were also asked to handle the release of the 'Please Please Me' press information. Brian Epstein offered Oldham the post of Beatles press officer, but he turned it down.

In April 1963, on a tip from journalist Peter Jones of *Record Mirror*, he went to see a new band called the Rollin' Stones. He then contacted agent Eric Easton, who agreed to co-manage the group and provide the finan-cial back-up to launch them. Oldham added a 'g' to Rollin'.

In the 1970s, in an interview in the *New Musical Express*, he recalled attending an early Beatles concert: 'I sat there with a lump in my throat. In one night you knew they were going to be very big. It was just an instinctive thing. From that night on, it registered subconsciously that when they made it, another section of the public was going to want the opposite.'

As a result he created an aggressive 'bad boy' image for the Rolling Stones – something which peeved John Lennon, who always claimed that the Stones had stolen the Beatles' original image.

Oldham also came up with the line: 'Would you let your daughter marry a Rolling Stone?'

In London early in the afternoon of 10 September 1963, when John

Lennon and Paul McCartney were returning from a Variety Club lunch-eon at the Savoy Hotel to their flat in Green Street, they spotted Oldham and invited him into their cab. He then talked them into attending a Stones rehearsal at Studio 51 in Great Newport Street, where the two Beatles finished a number, 'I Wanna Be Your Man', which gave the Stones a No. 2 hit and launched them into the major league.

Oldham formed a company, Forward Look, with Lionel Bart to pro-duce records by new talent and their first release was 'As Tears Go By' by Marianne Faithfull. In 1967 Oldham was supplanted as the Stones manager by Allen Klein.

He's been a resident of Bogotá, Colombia, since 1982, from where he manages top Argentinian band Ratones Paranoiacos (the Paranoid Mice) and in 1995 teamed up with Tony Calder and journalist Colin Irwin to write the book *Abba – The Name of the Game*.

OLIVER, Jack He originally joined Apple as assistant to Terry Doran of Apple Music. To everyone's surprise, he was swiftly promoted to head of Apple Records after Allen Klein took over the operation and sacked Ron Kass.

OLYMPICS, The A Liverpool group who appeared with the Beatles at the Cavern on Sunday 3 February 1963.

O'MAHONY, Sean Enterprising publisher of the *Beatles Monthly*.

Sean was working for a magazine called *Pop Weekly* when he contacted Brian Epstein to see if he would advertise 'Love Me Do' in the magazine. He then set up his own magazine, *Beat Monthly*, and got in touch with Brian once more to see if he could feature a Beatles interview.

Sean later arranged to meet Brian at the Westbury Hotel in London, where he suggested producing a magazine devoted solely to the Bea-tles.

Beatles Monthly was highly successful and at its peak sold 350,000 copies an issue. After 77 issues, Sean decided to cease publication, but was to relaunch in May 1975 and the magazine is still running today.

Similar magazines which he attempted to launch at the time, includ-ing a Gerry & the Pacemakers and a Rolling Stones monthly, didn't fare so well. However, he did launch a highly successful monthly called *Record Collector*, which is one of Britain's most respected music publica-tions.

ONO, Yoko A figure who was to loom large at the tail end of the Beatles' career.

Born at 8.30 p.m. on 18 February 1933 in Tokyo, her name means 'Ocean Child'. Yoko's parents were Eisuke and Isako Ono and her younger brother and sister were called Keisuke and Setsuko.

Initially raised by servants, she first met her father in San Francisco when she was three years old. She returned to Tokyo in 1937 and her mother then took her and Keisuke back to America in 1940, settling in New York. When Yoko's mother became pregnant with Setsuko in 1941, the family returned to Japan.

The family travelled to America in 1953 and 19-year-old Yoko attended the prestigious Sarah Lawrence School. During her third year there, she left for Manhattan to live with a Japanese musician, Toshi Ichyanagi. The couple married, but were eventually divorced in 1963 and Yoko then married avant-garde film-maker Tony Cox and gave birth to their daughter, Kyoko.

At the time she was part of an artistic set in Greenwich Village called Fluxus and involved herself in concerts, exhibitions and 'happenings'.

Yoko, Cox and their daughter moved to London in September 1966 and her activities began to attract media attention – in particular her film *Bottoms*, which featured the bare backsides of a number of London celebrities, including the Beatles' biographer Hunter Davies.

Several people who knew Yoko at the time claim that she actually planned to get to know the Beatles – and Lennon in particular. In New York she told 'Happenings' artist Allan Kaprow: 'I'd like to marry John Lennon.'

On 9 November 1966 her exhibition opened at the Indica Gallery in London, run by Barry Miles, John Dunbar and Peter Asher, who were all friends of the Beatles. In fact, Paul McCartney had made financial contributions to the gallery. Yoko asked the organizers to make sure that John Lennon and Paul McCartney attended the exhibition. John arrived at the preview with Terry Doran and Yoko feigned not to know who he was.

When John wanted to knock a nail into a canvas, Yoko demurred, then said he could do so if he paid her two shillings. John said: 'I'll give you an imaginary two shillings and hammer an imaginary nail.'

Yoko then began her pursuit of John, sending him her book *Grapefruit*, which he used to keep in his bedside table. At another meeting with him she mentioned she needed a sponsor for her next exhibition, 'The Half-Wind Show', at the Lisson Gallery. John then gave her his financial support.

During 1967 Yoko was omnipresent. She'd call John on the telephone, write him notes, turn up at his home unannounced and jump into his car outside the recording studio, even when Cynthia was in it. Her constant attempts to contact John didn't go unnoticed by Cynthia, who asked John about Yoko and was told: 'She's crackers.'

In May 1967 Cynthia was on holiday in Greece and Yoko had suggested to Tony that he take Kyoko to the South of France. She then went to John's house in Weybridge and the two began to make some experimental tapes in John's home studio. Yoko commented: 'It was midnight when we started and it was dawn when we finished and then we made love.' The next morning Cynthia arrived home to find John and Yoko drinking tea – with Yoko wearing Cynthia's kimono. Nervous and embarrassed, Cynthia suggested that they have dinner in London. John said: 'No, thanks.'

There was a brief attempt at a reconciliation, but John had made up his mind to divorce Cynthia and marry Yoko. The two settled into Ringo Starr's Montague Square flat.

Yoko was determined to involve John in her works, the first of which was an 'acorn sculpture event' at Coventry Cathedral. For the rest of John's life he was drawn into Yoko's world of conceptual ideas and avant-garde events. Rather than draw out John's talent, Yoko swamped him with her own ideas and concepts, and used him as a vessel for them.

The affair became public knowledge in June 1968, when the couple attended the performance of the play *In His Own Write*, based on John's book. The following month John held an exhibition 'You are Here – to Yoko from John, with Love'.

Yoko became pregnant and was admitted to Queen Charlotte's Hospital, where she miscarried. She was to have two further miscarriages before their son, Sean, was born.

By the end of the year the couple had released the *Two Virgins* album, tele-recorded for 'The Rolling Stones' Rock & Roll Circus' and appeared at the 'underground' event, 'The Alchemical Wedding'.

For a number of years, experimental albums, films and happenings became a joint venture – mainly at Yoko's instigation. None of the events displayed the genius of John's solo ventures.

Soon after Paul and Linda got married, John and Yoko, now divorced from their respective spouses, were married in Gibraltar, John officially changed his name to John Ono Lennon, and the two settled into a large estate in Ascot called Tittenhurst Park.

There is no doubt that John was passionately in love with Yoko and was genuinely excited by her ideas. He was also angry at the constant sniping by the media at the woman he loved. He also felt betrayed by the attitude of his fellow Beatles and said that Ringo and his wife, Maureen, were the only ones to treat her in a friendly fashion. Even fanatical Beatles fans seemed to hate Yoko and John resented the attitude the staff at Apple had towards his wife.

John was drifting away from the group and he and Yoko formed the Plastic Ono Band. She involved him in widely publicized events for world peace which she called 'Bed-Ins'. They both became involved in Primal Therapy and then relocated to New York, where John began his battle to obtain a green card.

Yoko continued to swamp him with her ideas, involving him in American politics and an association with radicals such as Abbie Hoffmann and Jerry Rubin, resulting in the double album *Sometime in New York City*, with its half-baked political ideas indicating just how much John had been manipulated. It also contained several of Yoko's compositions such as 'Sisters O Sisters' and 'We're All Water'. Lennon fans now found that if they wanted to buy any of John's recordings they'd have to accept B-sides by Yoko.

She also involved him in attempts to take her daughter, Kyoko, away from her former husband.

The couple settled in the Dakota Building in New York, but for a period of 18 months John left Yoko for the company of their secretary, May Pang, and moved to the West Coast, with Pang declaring that Yoko had deliberately thrown them together.

John and Yoko were reunited and she gave birth to their son, Sean, on 9 October 1975. For the next five years John became something of a recluse, dedicating himself to rearing the child, while Yoko took charge of their business affairs.

She proved to be an astute and very successful businesswoman, building their fortune with numerous lucrative ventures, including buying real estate and breeding prize cattle.

She also had various record releases in her own right, including albums such as *Fly*, *Approximately Infinite Universe* and *Feeling the Space*.

Following John's murder, she sent out an official message: 'Bless you for your tears and prayers. I saw John smiling in the sky. I saw sorrow changing into clarity. I saw all of us becoming one mind. Thank You. Love. Yoko.' She remained in the Dakota and launched the Spirit Foundation, a charity in John's honour. She also arranged for a two-and-a-half-acre garden memorial to John in Central Park called Strawberry Fields, which opened in 1984, the year she took Sean to Liverpool to visit John's childhood home in Menlove Avenue. She was also to embark on an international tour which she called 'Starpeace'.

Her name was also linked to Sam Havadtoy, a Hungarian she had employed to redecorate her apartments.

Yoko released a number of albums, including *Season of Glass*, *Milk & Honey* and *Every Man Has a Woman Who Loves Him*, her fortune grew and she was named by *Forbes* magazine as one of the richest individuals in the world, with a fortune of at least $150 million.

She also began to promote the relationship she had with John as one of the 'great love stories of the century', with the three-hour teleplay *John & Yoko: A Love Story* and *Imagine: The Movie*.

There was also a great deal of criticism when she began to commercially market merchandise in John's name, some of it regarded as rather tacky.

However, no one can ignore the fact that Yoko has pursued her belief in her artistic talent with the utmost zeal, has become one of the richest women in the world and has achieved a degree of international recognition in her own right.

O'RAHILLY, Ronan Irish entrepreneur who began the pirate radio boom in Britain when he launched Radio Caroline. In 1958, after the Marine Offences Bill had banned the pirates from the airwaves, the Beatles hired O'Rahilly as a business adviser to Apple.

ORBISON, Roy Although the Beatles admired Roy Orbison, he wasn't one of the main influences on their music in the way that Chuck Berry or Carl Perkins was. In fact, they only ever included one of his numbers in their repertoire, and that not until 1962 – 'Dream Baby', which Paul sang. However, it was 'Dream Baby' which was the first song the Beatles ever broadcast. They performed the number on *Teenagers' Turn* in Manchester on 8 March 1962, only a month after the original Orbison release.

The singer also provided inspiration for their first No. 1 record. When John was composing an early, slow version of 'Please Please Me' in his bedroom at Menlove Avenue, he imagined Roy Orbison singing it as he'd just been listening to 'Only the Lonely'. Later he was to say: 'It was my attempt at writing a Roy Orbison song.'

It was only a few months after the release of 'Please Please Me' that the Beatles found themselves touring with Orbison.

Their third tour was the only British tour not promoted by Arthur Howes. The Manchester promoters Kennedy Street Enterprises had originally booked Duane Eddy as a bill-topper, but he became indisposed. They also considered Ben E. King, then the Four Seasons, before selecting Roy, who had had nine chart hits, including a No. 1, in less than three years.

When he was contacted by phone in America, he was told that the Beatles were to be second on the bill. He was later to say: 'I had never heard of the Beatles, and it seemed to me at first like it was just a rehash of rock 'n' roll that I'd been involved with for a long time, but what it turned out to be was these four guys, their particular spirit, putting out rock 'n' roll as they saw it and it turned out to be very fresh and full of energy and vitality. So I recognized it at the time.'

Also on the tour bill were Gerry & the Pacemakers, Tony Marsh, stand-up comedian Erkey Grant, singer David Macbeth and Louise Cordet, all backed by the Terry Young Six.

Roy had arrived in England sans his clear glasses, which he'd left behind on the plane, and took to wearing prescription sunglasses, which soon became part of his image. Still recovering from jetlag, he arrived at the Adelphi Cinema, Slough, to rehearse in the afternoon with the Terry Young Six, who were backing him. Then he retired to his dressing room, where he was visited by John Lennon and Brian Epstein.

John said: 'How should we bill this? Who should close the show? Look, you're getting all the money, so why don't we close the show?'

Orbison recalled: 'I didn't know whether that was true or not, whether I was getting that much more than they were. It wasn't that much – and the tour had sold out in one afternoon.'

Due to their amazing success in Britain, it was inevitable that the Beatles should be the headliners and new programmes to this effect were printed a week later.

Yet, Orbison's performances and the audience reactions to them were phenomenal. He was booked to appear for 15 minutes, but on that first night he played a full half-hour set, performing 'Only the Lonely',

'Candy Man', 'What'd I Say?', 'Cryin'', 'Running Scared' and 'In Dreams'.

He was greeted by a standing ovation, the first standing ovation ever at a concert at that particular theatre. Orbison remembered Paul and John 'grabbing me by the arms and not letting me go back to take my curtain call'. The audience were yelling out for him 'and there I was, held captive by the Beatles saying, "Yankee Go Home," so we had a good time'.

Ringo was also to say that Orbison would slay the audience, who would scream for more. He told Beatles biographer Hunter Davies: 'It was terrible following him ... In Glasgow we were all backstage, listening to the tremendous applause he was getting. He was just standing there singing, not moving or anything. As it got near our turn, we would hide behind the curtain whispering to each other, "Guess who's next, folks, it's your favourite rave." '

The tour ran from 18 May to 9 June 1963.

Orbison remained a lifelong friend of the Beatles and his later career was given a new lease of life when George Harrison invited him to become part of a supergroup the Traveling Wilburys, along with Bob Dylan, Tom Petty and Jeff Lynne.

Roy died of a heart attack in Nashville on 6 December 1988 at the age of 52.

ORMSBY-GORE, Sir David During the Beatles' first trip to Washington, Brian Epstein had arranged for them to attend an event at the British Embassy following their Washington Coliseum appearance.

Sir David Ormsby-Gore was the British ambassador at the time and the event was a formal staff dance to raise money for the National Association for the Prevention of Cruelty to Children. Ormsby-Gore had requested that the Beatles present the raffle prizes at the gala.

News of their appearance had circulated by word of mouth and a cordon of police had to circle the embassy. The Beatles, together with Brian, had a private meeting with Sir David and Lady Ormsby-Gore. Lady Ormsby-Gore then escorted them into the embassy rotunda, announcing: 'Attention! Beatles are now approaching the area.'

No one in their party was prepared for the behaviour from guests and staff, many of whom had had more than their fair share of punch that evening.

They were jostled and pushed around. There were condescending remarks such as 'those darling little baby boys', and one woman put her arm around Paul and asked: 'Which one are you?' 'Roger,' he told her. 'Roger what?' she asked. 'Roger McCluskey the Fifth,' he said.

John Lennon was furious at the treatment and wanted to leave. When an embassy official told him, 'Come on, now, go do your stuff,' he said, 'I'm getting out of here,' but Ringo took hold of his arm and suggested that they get it over with.

When reports of the rude behaviour filtered out, the British press were incensed and Conservative MP Joan Quennell asked the Foreign

Secretary, R.A. Butler, to look into the affair.

However, the real diplomat turned out to be Brian Epstein, who, not wishing to make a fuss of the situation, sent a thank-you note to Lady Ormsby-Gore.

When his brother was killed in a car crash, Ormsby-Gore then inherited the title Lord Harlech. After his wife was killed in a car crash in 1967, there was talk that he would marry his close friend Jackie Kennedy. Instead, he married a New York journalist, Pamela Colin, who was 18 years his junior.

In 1974 Lord Harlech's son Julian shot himself while suffering from depression. His daughter Alice fell in love with Eric Clapton and the two began to live together.

Lord Harlech was killed in a car crash in 1985. Death duties of more than £1 million caused severe financial hardships for the family. Eric Clapton left Alice and she was to become a drug addict and was found dead in a squalid bedsit in a rundown area of Bournemouth in April 1995. A needle was stuck in her arm. She was 43 years old.

ORNSTEIN, Bud Production head of United Artists in Britain in 1963 when he negotiated a three-picture deal for the Beatles. Ornstein was primarily interested in obtaining the rights to Beatles albums and decided that offering them a film deal gave United Artists the opportunity of releasing Beatles film soundtracks.

Although he was prepared to offer the group 25 per cent of the deal, Epstein pre-empted him by asking for seven and a half per cent. Later, it was decided to give the Beatles the 25 per cent.

Ornstein left United Artists in 1964 to go into partnership with Brian Epstein in a new company, Pickfair Films, ostensibly to produce further Beatles movies, beginning with *A Talent for Loving*, but nothing more came of it.

Neil Aspinall was to marry Ornstein's daughter.

ORTON, Joe Controversial British playwright who wrote a film script for the Beatles called *Up Against It*, which Brian Epstein considered too outrageous for them to do. Orton was brutally murdered by his lover, Kenneth Halliwell, in August 1967.

OVERLANDERS, The The group originally formed in 1961 as Pierce Rodgers & the Overlanders and made their recording debut on Parlophone. By 1963 they'd become a folk trio comprising Laurie Mason (who'd previously used the pseudonym Pierce Rodgers), Paul Arnold (whose real name was Paul Friswell) and Peter Bartholomew. That year they signed to Pye and their recording manager was Tony Hatch.

They released a number of folksy singles and covered the Chad and Jeremy number 'Yesterday's Gone'. Although the Chad and Jeremy version hit it big in America, the Overlanders had a minor hit there with their release in 1964.

With the addition of Terry Widlake on bass and David Walsh on drums in December 1965 they recorded one of the 20 versions of 'Michelle' from the newly released *Rubber Soul* album and within three weeks they'd topped the British chart.

Although they beat David and Jonathan's version in the British charts, the British duo had a bigger hit in the States with 'Michelle' than the Overlanders.

Pye also issued an Overlanders EP and album which featured 'Michelle'.

Their next release, 'My Life', failed to hit the charts and Paul Arnold left for a solo career. He was replaced by Ian Griffiths, although the group were never to repeat their chart success.

OWEN, Alun Playwright, actor and director, born on 24 November 1925 in, according to some sources, Menai Bridge, North Wales, and according to others Liverpool. He certainly always regarded himself as a Liverpool-Welshman and was to comment: 'Liverpool and Wales, they're the two things I really know, and yet I'm not completely at home in either place.'

Alun, son of Welsh-speaking parents whose father was a merchant seaman, was initially educated at Cardigan County High School prior to his family's move to Liverpool.

He married Mary O'Keefe at the age of 16 in 1942 and the couple were to have two sons. His first stage play, *Progress to the Park*, was broadcast on the radio in 1958 and his first broadcast television play was *No Trams to Lime Street* in 1959.

Composer Lionel Bart contacted him to write a musical based on the Liverpool folksong 'Maggie May'. Alun told him: 'You've got to learn a whole new language. The Liverpool dialect, the real, pure Scouse is part-Irish, part-Welsh, part-catarrh.' He suggested Bart move to Liverpool to soak up the atmosphere.

It was during this time that he was approached to write the screenplay for *A Hard Day's Night*, apparently on the suggestion of Paul McCartney.

Brian Epstein wrote to Owen and then met him after the performance of one of his plays in Liverpool, telling him: 'Whatever you think, you must meet the boys. They're keen to see you – they admire your work.'

Owen then met up with the Beatles on a number of occasions, getting together with all four of them for the first time in October 1963 following their *Sunday Night at the London Palladium* appearance and travelling with them to Dublin and Belfast in November. He also joined them in Paris in January 1964, along with the film's producer, Walter Shenson.

He actually began writing the script in November 1963 and was given a virtually free hand. The only thing he was specifically asked to do was include a scene that would give them an opportunity to sparkle like they did at the press conference in New York in February 1964, so he introduced a press conference scene in a theatre lounge.

He was to say: 'I write by the minute not the page. I had a couple of false starts trying to write a fantasy film, but quickly realized that nothing could compare with their own fantastic lives. They are always on the move, usually from one box to another, hotels, cars, dressing rooms, but they know what they want. Where they are going.'

He also commented: 'In the film we see the boys in a world which has no future and no past and I've tried to incorporate into the script some of the fantastic and curious things which happen to the boys, the world they carry in them, by just being themselves. What I am doing is taking what I see in them and putting it down on paper. In fact, they emerge as four very different people.'

'I want to give them things they want to do. They have a terrific joy in being alive and there is a great sense of fantasy in their humour. There is a conflict in the script and there is conflict in the way the boys send each other up. I'm sure the film will do very well in America. Americans will find the Liverpool accent easier to understand than, say, a Cockney one. Liverpool people hit their words when they talk, it's part of their aggressiveness.'

He was also to point out that because the dialogue was in short sentences and naturalistic, many people thought it was ad-libbed. It wasn't – he pointed out that the only member of the Beatles who ad-libbed in the film was John Lennon.

Alun tried to ensure that all four received an equal share of the action, although it was Ringo's role which attracted the attention of the critics. Owen wrote individual scenes for each member, but the scene featuring Paul ended up on the cutting-room floor.

In it, he wanders around the Notting Hill area and enters a church hall where he meets and talks to a young actress. He has to utter such lines as: 'I know your sort – two Cokes and a packet of cheese and onion crisps suddenly it's love and we're stopping in an empty street doorway. Gerrout of it! Ah, you're lovely all right, you're smashin', but come round here and tell all that to me mum – you won't, will you? You're just after me body and you can't have it, so there!'

Allegedly, Paul didn't carry it off and the scene proved too embarrassing to include in the finished print.

Alun was nominated for an Oscar for his script and, since the critical reaction had been so enthusiastic, he believed that he'd have the opportunity of penning their second film. Unfortunately, this wasn't the case. Epstein told him that Richard Lester had already employed another scriptwriter for their next project, which may have been why Owen, perhaps ungenerously, commented: 'I don't get on very well with John, Ringo is fine, but not the greatest intellectual in the world. We had trouble with one scene with Paul ... mind you, I like George very much.'

When Epstein heard that, he told Owen: 'What would you say if I told you that the one person who doesn't want you to work on this film is George Harrison?'

Owen went on to complete *Maggie May*, which he set in contemporary times, featuring Mersey Beat music, and he booked a Liverpool group called the Nocturnes to appear in it.

The stars of the musical were Kenneth Haigh and Rachel Roberts. Interestingly enough, Haigh had appeared as an advertising executive in *A Hard Day's Night*. It was rumoured that he wanted his name kept from the credits, but as the reputation of the film grew he cited it as giving him one of his best cameo roles.

Sadly, Alun died at the age of 69, following a short illness, on 6 December 1994.

PAAR, Jack American television celebrity who hosted his own show. On 3 January 1964, he became the first person to present the Beatles to the American viewing public when a film of them performing 'Love Me Do' was screened during his show. Paar made some rather derisory comments about the Beatles' appearance at the time.

PADDY, KLAUS & GIBSON An interesting trio because it brought together two prominent members of Liverpool bands and one of the Beatles' friends from Hamburg.

Paddy, Klaus & Gibson formed in 1965 and comprised Paddy Chambers (lead guitar), who'd been in several Mersey Beat bands, including Faron's Flamingos and the Big Three, Klaus Voormann (bass guitar), who'd been inspired by Stuart Sutcliffe, and Gibson Kemp (drums), the young Liverpudlian who'd replaced Ringo Starr in Rory Storm & the Hurricanes. Kemp had been a member of Kingsize Taylor & the Dominoes and had married Klaus's former girlfriend and Stu Sutcliffe's fiancée, Astrid Kirchherr.

The trio actually formed in Hamburg, moved to Liverpool and then settled in London, where they were initially managed by Don Paul, a former member of the vocal group the Viscounts. Paul approached Tony Stratton-Smith and agreed to give him 10 per cent of his 25 per cent management commission in exchange for £250, which he urgently needed to buy equipment for the group.

'Stratters' agreed and set to work on the first of the several groups he was to manage, immediately securing them a residency at London's Pickwick Club, a haunt of celebrities, including Paul McCartney and Jane Asher.

Stratton-Smith began to work hard to gain recognition for the band, entertaining disc jockeys and journalists at the club while the group were performing.

It was probably a pity that John Lennon became so enthusiastic about the band that he encouraged Brian Epstein to take an interest. Once Epstein declared an interest in managing the trio, Stratton Smith and Paul reluctantly allowed the transfer, accepting a settlement of £5,000, although 'Stratters' felt they were making the wrong move, commenting: 'I had regrets because I think they should have made it. They weren't a Top 20 band but they had a marvellous live feel. I think the way I was handling them, building them through the clubs and delaying a record debut was, with hindsight, the best way. With NEMS, record after record came out and they were put on tours and I don't think they really had time to develop.'

Epstein signed Paddy, Klaus & Gibson on 6 June 1965, securing them a contract with Pye Records, and the group were to release a total of three singles, beginning with 'I Wanna Know', flipside 'I Tried' on 9 July.

As with a number of the acts signed by Brian following his initial Liverpool successes, they vanished without a trace.

There were plans at one time, suggested by Pete Townshend, to amalgamate the trio with the Who. However, when internal disputes within the Who were settled, the scheme was dropped and Paddy, Klaus & Gibson disbanded on 13 June 1966.

In interviews with music biographer Ray Coleman, Paddy was to comment that although he paid them £50 a week, Epstein got them very little work and 'to be honest the management side of things he completely cocked up'. He also told Coleman: 'I basically don't think he gave the band anything in management. I don't think he had a clue. But it was obvious after a while that he was getting emotionally very hung up on me and I tried my best to cope with it. I actually ended up in bed with him one day but after about five minutes I said, "Brian, I just can't handle this," and I got up and walked out.'

Paddy returned to Liverpool, where he joined the Escorts for a while and later teamed up with another former Stratton-Smith artist, Beryl Marsden, in a soul band called Sinbad. He then began managing local clubs.

Gibson became a prominent record executive for Polygram. Klaus continued his association with the Beatles, was a member of the Hollies, Manfred Mann and the Plastic Ono Band, and eventually returned to Hamburg.

PANG, May Girl who first met John and Yoko while working in Allen Klein's office in New York in late 1970. John and Yoko hired her to work in their movie production company. She then became the couple's secretary.

When John turned 33 years of age he suddenly fled to Los Angeles with May and for the period described as his '18 months long weekend' she became his mistress.

She also continued to act as his secretary and helped to organize some of his West Coast recording projects. She was credited as production coordinator on the *Walls and Bridges* and *Rock 'n' Roll* albums.

When John returned to Yoko, May resettled in New York, where she became professional manager of United Artists Music. Following John's death, she became friendly with Cynthia Lennon and accompanied her to some Beatles conventions.

Her book *Loving John – the Untold Story*, written in collaboration with Henry Edwards, was published in 1983.

May was to marry record producer Tony Visconti, Mary Hopkin's ex-husband, on 25 February 1989.

PANTHERS, The Group who appeared with the Beatles at the Cavern on Friday 12 March 1962.

PAOLOZZI, Eduardo Noted British sculptor, born in Edinburgh, who sponsored Stuart Sutcliffe at Hamburg's Staatliche Hochschule, where he was a visiting professor. Stuart was able to enter the Master Class in June 1961 because Paolozzi approached the Hamburg authorities to give Stuart a grant.

▲ **ACKER BILK.** He shared a
'Riverboat Shuffle' bill
with the Beatles and
invited them to partake
of his crates of ale!

► **LONNIE DONEGAN**, the man behind Britain's skiffle boom and an inspiration to Paul McCartney and George Harrison.

◄ **BRIAN EPSTEIN**, hosting the American television pop show *Hullabaloo*.

▼ **ALMA COGAN.** Rumours that John Lennon fell in love with her are greatly exaggerated.

◄ **JIM GRETTY,** Liverpool entertainer who booked the Beatles in variety shows.

▲ **BERT KAEMPFERT,** the first A&R man to 'discover' the Beatles.

▶ **THE BIG THREE,** another of Liverpool's legendary bands: Adrian Barber, Johnny Hutchinson and Johnny Gustafson.

◀ **DICK JAMES,** the Beatles' publisher.

▼ The Star Club in 1963: Bill and Virginia Harry, Manfred Weissleder and Ray McFall and his wife.

▼ **JULIAN LENNON.** The shadow of his father loomed over his musical career.

▲ **BOB WOOLER** and **ALLAN WILLIAMS** at the Adelphi Hotel, Liverpool.

▲ **THE KUBAS,** a Mersey band who toured with the Beatles.

◄ **ELVIS PRESLEY.** Following his historic meeting with the Beatles, he harboured a resentment of John Lennon.

▲ **BUDDY HOLLY.** The name of his backing group, the Crickets, inspired the Beatles' name.

▲ **CYNTHIA LENNON** at the 'Art of the Beatles' exhibition.

▶ **LITTLE RICHARD,** who featured on bills with the Beatles in Liverpool and Hamburg.

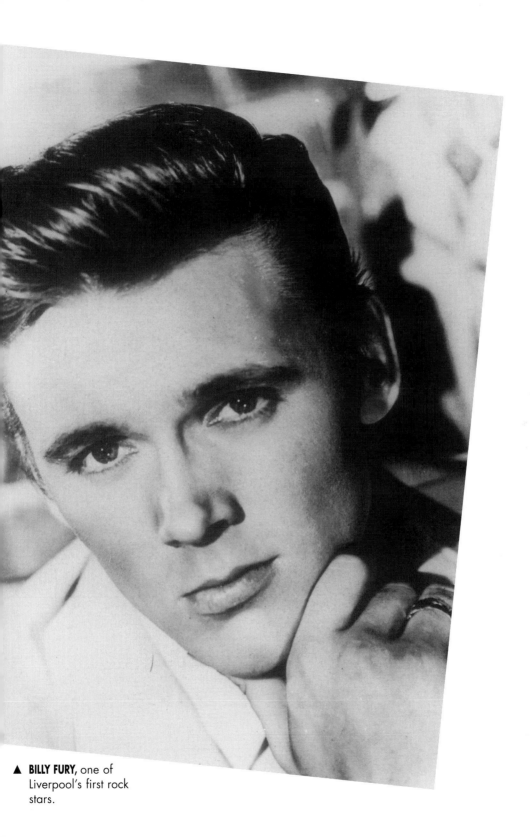

▲ **BILLY FURY,** one of Liverpool's first rock stars.

▲ **THE SWINGING BLUE JEANS:** the hit team of Ralph Ennis, Norman Kuhlke, Ray Ennis and Les Braid.

◀ **ROY ORBISON.** When he headlined a tour above the Beatles, the billing had to be changed as they were No. 1 in the charts.

▶ **DAVID HAMILTON,** one of several disc jockeys who introduced the Beatles in a live show.

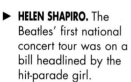

▶ **HELEN SHAPIRO.** The
Beatles' first national
concert tour was on a
bill headlined by the
hit-parade girl.

▼ **THE RUTLES,** the Pre-Fab
Four, stars of the hilari-
ous television parody of
the Beatles.

PARAMOUNTS, The Group from Southend who were signed to NEMS in 1965, leading to their inclusion in the Beatles' last British tour in December of that year. At the time the group comprised Gary Brooker (keyboards/vocals); Robin Trower (guitar) Chris Copping (bass) and Barrie Wilson (drums). After leaving NEMS they evolved into Procol Harum.

PARKINSON, Norman A leading British fashion photographer who took photographs of the Beatles at the Abbey Road Studios in 1963 which were published in a book, *The Beatles Book*, the following year. He died in 1991.

PARNES, Larry Arguably Britain's top pop impresario of the 1950s. Following his discovery of Tommy Steele in 1956, he built a school of young pop artists and became known as 'Parnes, Shillings and Pence' for his reputed tight-fistedness. He was also noted for the colourful stage names he coined for his artists – Marty Wilde, Duffy Power, Johnny Gentle, Billy Fury, Dickie Pride and Lance Fortune.

Parnes co-promoted a Gene Vincent bill at Liverpool Stadium with Jacaranda Enterprises and was impressed by the local groups on the bill. He asked Allan Williams to set up an audition for Liverpool groups with a view to finding backing bands for his acts. He booked the Silver Beatles to back Johnny Gentle on a tour of Scotland.

Parnes became friendly with Brian Epstein, although they never entered into any business deal together following Parnes's refusal to book the Beatles for various concerts – he wouldn't pay the amount Epstein requested.

He died at the age of 59 on 30 July 1989.

PARSONS, Alan A tape engineer at Abbey Road Studios who was contacted by George Martin to bring Abbey Road equipment down to the Apple Studios in Savile Row when Martin discovered that the equipment Alexis Mardas had built for Apple was useless. Parsons then remained as a second engineer on the Beatles 'Get Back' sessions until October 1969 and the album was eventually issued as *Let It Be*. Parsons later created a successful outfit called the Alan Parsons Project.

PATHFINDERS, The A group who appeared with the Beatles at the Cavern on Thursday 19 February 1963.

PEASE, Gayleen One of two Beatles fans – the other was Lizzie Bravo – to be invited to sing on a Beatles record. The two were among the fans gathered outside Abbey Road Studios on Sunday 4 February 1968 when Paul McCartney came out and picked them because some falsetto voices were needed on the recording of 'Across the Universe' to sing 'nothing's gonna change our world'. A Londoner, Gayleen was 17 years old at the time.

PENNER, Peter One of the group of Hamburg students, along with Astrid Kirchherr, Klaus Voormann and Jurgen Vollmer, who used to drop into the Kaiserkeller club in October 1960 to watch the Beatles. Peter had his hair styled by Astrid, who also styled Stuart Sutcliffe's hair in the same way, leading to the famous 'moptop' image.

PEPPI & THE NEW YORK TWISTERS Singer, dancer, mime artist, comedian and impressionist, born in Sarasota, Florida. He originally intended joining the circus, where his parents had a high-wire and trapeze act, but decided to become a dancer instead. He turned professional at the age of eight and teamed up with his sister Nita.

He was highly successful in America, appearing five times on *The Ed Sullivan Show* and on the Jackie Gleason and Steve Allen shows.

Sammy Davis Jr brought him over to England early in 1962 to appear with him at the Prince of Wales Theatre in London. Peppi then formed the New York Twisters and toured Britain.

During that year he appeared on two Cavern bills with the Beatles, on Thursday 22 March and Sunday 19 August.

PERKINS, Carl A major early influence on the Beatles. Born 9 April 1932 in Ridgely, Tennessee, he made his recording debut on the Sun label in 1955. He supported fellow Sun artist Elvis Presley on tour and, when Presley left Sun to join RCA, record head Stan Phillips decided to build Perkins as Presley's replacement on the label. Perkins's record 'Blue Suede Shoes' hit the American charts at the same time as Elvis's 'Heartbreak Hotel'. Then Perkins and his brother were in a road accident and hospitalized. Promotion for Perkins's version of 'Blue Suede Shoes', although it was a million-seller, slipped. Elvis rushed out his version and had a major hit, stealing Carl's thunder and perhaps dimming what could have been a far brighter future for the artist.

George Harrison, in particular, was strongly influenced by Perkins and when the Beatles toured Scotland called himself Carl Harrison in deference to his hero.

There were a considerable number of Perkins's numbers in the Beatles early repertoire, including 'Lend Me Your Comb' and 'Gone Gone Gone'. Ringo sang 'Honey Don't', Paul sang 'Sure to Fall', George sang 'Your True Love', 'Glad All Over' and 'Everybody's Trying to be My Baby', while John sang 'Matchbox', 'Tennessee', 'Boppin' the Blues' and 'Blue Suede Shoes'.

George was introduced to Perkins at Alma Cogan's flat and the two became good friends.

Good fortune came when the Beatles recorded three of his numbers, 'Matchbox', 'Honey Don't' and 'Everybody's Trying to be My Baby', enabling him to buy his parents a farm with the royalties. Carl was actually at the recording sessions. He'd been touring Britain with Chuck Berry in 1964 and at the end of the tour was about to fly back to the States when the Beatles threw a party in his honour. They then invited him to

Abbey Road while they recorded his songs.

Perkins also struck up a friendship with Paul McCartney and composed a number, 'My Old Friend', as a tribute to him.

At the age of 53 Carl set up a television show, *Carl Perkins & Friends: A Rockabilly Special*, in which he was joined by George and Ringo.

PETER AND GORDON Pete Asher and Gordon Waller, both sons of doctors, met at Westminster Boys' School, where they formed a folk duo. They had a residency at the Pickwick Club, frequented by Paul McCartney and his girlfriend Jane Asher, Peter's sister, where they were spotted by record producer Norman Newall.

They had an undoubted advantage in the association with Paul and he provided them with their first number, 'World Without Love', which topped the charts. They continued their chart run with two further McCartney compositions, 'Nobody I Know' and 'I Don't Want to See You Again'.

Paul also penned 'Woman' for them, using the pseudonym Bernard Webb.

The duo had further hits, including 'True Love Ways' and 'Lady Godiva', before Peter suggested to Gordon in 1967 that they split up.

PETER JAY & THE JAYWALKERS Group who toured with the Beatles during November and December 1963. From East Anglia, the band comprised Peter Jay (drums), Pete Miller (lead), Tony Webster (rhythm), Mac McIntyre (tenor sax/flute), Lloyd Baker (baritone sax/piano), Geoff Moss (acoustic bass) and Johnny Lake (bass). They disbanded in 1966.

PETERS, Lee Disc jockey/compère on the first four *Pop Go the Beatles* radio programmes. The group nicknamed him Pee Litres. He was replaced by Rodney Burke when the show was renewed for a further 11 programmes.

PHANTOMS, The Melbourne group who appeared on the Beatles Australasian tour. An instrumental quartet, they also provided backing for singers Johnny Chester and Johnny Devlin during the tour. The group were later to transform themselves into a Beat group using the name MPD Ltd and enjoyed a degree of success in Australia.

PHILLIPS, Esther Singer who impressed the Beatles with her version of 'And I Love Him'. Paul McCartney considered it the best cover version of a Lennon and McCartney number up to that time and invited her to perform the number on their *The Music of Lennon and McCartney* television special.

PHILLIPS, Percy The man who made the Quarry Men's first record. Phillips converted the ground floor of his terraced house at 58 Kensington, Liverpool, into a recording studio. The front room served as a waiting room for prospective clients and the large back room housed the studio, which was relatively primitive compared to the professional studios of the time. It featured two large twin-track tape recorders, one microphone, which hung from the ceiling, a stand-up piano and a disc cutter which produced a metal core 78rpm shellac disc.

John Lennon, Paul McCartney, George Harrison, Colin Hanton and Charles Duff Lowe recorded two numbers there in the summer of 1958: 'That'll be the Day' and 'In Spite of All the Danger'.

The lads produced the required 18s for a single disc of the recording as they couldn't afford the extra 1s 1d which would have provided a tape of the numbers.

PILBEAM, Peter BBC radio producer who booked the Beatles for their first major appearance. He produced them performing on the show *Teenagers' Turn* and *Here We Go*.

PILCHER, Norman A police sergeant with the drug squad who raided Ringo's flat at 34 Montague Street, London, on 18 October 1968 when John and Yoko were in residence. Pilcher alleged he found 219 grains of cannabis, and, although John denied it, he then decided to plead guilty to save a pregnant Yoko from the strain of the charge. Pilcher also raided George's and Pattie's house on 12 March 1969 and was the person behind the raid on Keith Richard's house, which led to charges against the Rolling Stones. Pilcher was jailed for six years in October 1972 after being found guilty of planting dope in several people's homes.

PINKY AND PERKY Highly popular pig puppets, created by Jan and Vlasta Dalibar, two Czechs who smuggled themselves into Britain in 1948. Their creations, Pinky and Perky, first appeared on BBC TV in 1957 and proved so successful they were placed in an adult viewing slot and became a major cult of the 1960s.

Their speeded-up voices proved ideal to utilize in pop songs, in a similar fashion to the Chipmunks in the States. Pinky and Perky introduced their own television station, PPC TV, in which they featured a group called the Beakles, a fab four with large beaks.

Their following was huge and they issued several discs, including 'Beat Party', an EP issued in March 1965 which featured the numbers 'She Loves You', 'All My Loving' and 'Can't Buy Me Love'. They were also to cover 'When I'm 64' and 'Yellow Submarine'.

Pinky and Perky retired from television in 1970.

PINSKER, Harold In 1968 the chief financial adviser to Apple. During the 'Get Back' sessions which resulted in *Let It Be*, Paul sang a mock version of 'Hare Krishna' in which he mentioned Pinsker.

PLASTIC ONO BAND, The When Yoko Ono began to loom large in John Lennon's life, they began an artistic collaboration which included the formation in 1969 of the Plastic Ono Band to perform and record.

For the Toronto Rock 'n' Roll Revival Concert, the line-up comprised John and Yoko, Eric Clapton (lead guitar), Klaus Voorman (bass) and Alan White on drums. They were also among the members of the Plastic Ono Supergroup who performed at the Lyceum, London, on 15 December 1969.

The group's first single was 'Give Peace a Chance', recorded during John's and Yoko's Bed-In in Montreal, Canada. This was followed by 'Cold Turkey' and the album *The Plastic Ono Band – Live Peace in Toronto 1969*. The next single was 'Instant Karma', followed by the album *John Lennon/Plastic Ono Band*. Other releases also included variations of the name: 'Power to the People'; 'God Save Us', the Elastic Oz Band; 'Imagine', John Lennon and the Plastic Ono Band, with the Flux Fiddlers; 'Some Time in New York City', John and Yoko/Plastic Ono Band with Elephants Memory plus Invisible Strings; 'Happy Xmas (War is Over)', John and Yoko/Plastic Ono Band with the Harlem Community Choir; 'Mind Games', John Lennon with the Plastic UF Ono Band; 'Whatever Gets You Thru the Night', John Lennon with the Plastic Ono Nuclear Band; and 'Walls and Bridges', John Lennon with the Plastic Ono Nuclear Band.

POBJOY, William Ernest Headmaster of Quarry Bank School when John Lennon was in attendance. Pobjoy suggested to John's Aunt Mimi that he should develop his talents as an artist and enrol at Liverpool College of Art. He then arranged for John to enter the college without having to take an examination.

POWER, Duffy It was producer Ron Richards who told singer Duffy Power: 'The Beatles think you're the best R&B singer in the country.'

Power, real name Ray Howard, was discovered by entrepreneur Larry Parnes, who signed him to his stable of acts. Parnes concocted names for each of his artists and took the name Duffy from actor Howard Duff and Power because actor Tyrone Power had just died that week.

He became one of the first artists to record a Lennon and McCartney number when 'I Saw Her Standing There' was issued on the Beatles' own Parlophone label in May 1963.

On the recording he's backed by the Graham Bond Quartet.

PRECHT, Bob Son-in-law of Ed Sullivan who also produced *The Ed Sullivan Show*. Once Sullivan had decided he wanted the Beatles to appear, negotiations had to be conducted with Precht, who originally offered them only one spot. Epstein negotiated for three appearances, with the Beatles headlining.

PRESLEY, Elvis The greatest solo star of rock 'n' roll, born Elvis Aaron Presley on 8 January 1935 in East Tupelo, Mississippi.

Brian Epstein was to claim that the Beatles would become 'bigger than Elvis', and he was right.

John Lennon was the main Elvis fan and was to say: 'Nothing really affected me until I heard Elvis. If there hadn't been Elvis, there would not have been the Beatles.' However, John became disenchanted with Presley's music in the 1960s and when he made his appearance on *Juke Box Jury* on 22 June, 1963, he criticized the Elvis record 'Devil in Disguise' and called Elvis 'today's Bing Crosby', suggesting that he return to his rock 'n' roll roots.

Journalist Chris Hutchins arranged for the historic meeting between Elvis and the Beatles at 565 Perugia Way, Bel Air, on Friday 27 August 1965. The meeting lasted for three hours.

Hutchins was to detail it in his 1994 book *Elvis Meets the Beatles* and says that during the meeting a feud began between John Lennon and Elvis, because of Lennon's anti-Vietnam war stance and Elvis's right-wing views. Elvis later became a federal agent and urged the FBI to have John deported from the States.

During the meeting at Elvis's Hollywood home, Lennon made various remarks which needled Presley and the two were never to meet again.

However, in public, John continued to praise Elvis, commenting: 'There's only one person in the United States of America that we ever wanted to meet – not that he wanted to meet us!' In private, he was to tell a friend: 'It was just like meeting Englebert Humperdinck.'

During their Quarry Men days, the group introduced several Elvis numbers into their repertoire, including 'All Shook Up', 'Blue Moon of Kentucky', 'Hound Dog', 'Jailhouse Rock', 'Mean Woman Blues', 'I Forgot to Remember to Forget', 'I'm Gonna Sit Right Down and Cry Over You', 'It's Now or Never' and 'That's All Right, Mama'.

Elvis was also to perform and record several Beatles numbers, including 'Hey Jude', 'Yesterday' and 'Something'.

His body was discovered on the floor of his bathroom in Graceland on 16 August 1977. He had died of heart failure.

PRESSMEN, The Mersey group who formed in 1961, when the line-up was Ritchie Press (lead), Bob Pierce (bass), Tom Bennett (drums) and Phil McKenzie (sax).

They appeared at three Cavern gigs with the Beatles in 1961: Wednesday 19 July, Wednesday 16 August and Wednesday 13 September.

For a while they acted as backing band to singer Derry Wilkie. After a season at the Tanz Club in Hamburg, where they were billed as the Flamingos, they returned to Liverpool in March 1964 and changed their name to the New Pressmen, as there had been some personnel changes. Their line-up was now Tom Bennett (drums), Howard Morris (rhythm), Willie Van Gellen (lead) and Al Flowerday (lead).

PRESTON, Billy American musician, born in Houston, Texas, on 9 September 1946, who originally met up with the Beatles in Hamburg when he was appearing with Little Richard at the Star Club.

A keyboards player, he was only 15 at the time and initially formed a friendship with George Harrison (ironically, George was older than Preston when he was deported from Hamburg for being under-age).

When Preston toured Britain as a member of Ray Charles's backing band, George met up with him again and arranged for his fellow Beatles to join him in buying Billy's contract from Vee Jay Records and signing him to Apple.

He performed with them on the 'Get Back' single, issued with the credit 'The Beatles with Billy Preston', earning him the distinction of being the first musician to be credited on a Beatles record.

Preston also appeared on other Beatles tracks: 'Let It Be', 'I, Me, Mine', 'I've Got a Feelin'', 'Dig a Pony' and 'One After 909'.

George Harrison co-produced both of Billy's Apple albums, *That's the Way God Planned It* and *Encouraging Words*.

After the Beatles' break-up, he was in demand for their solo albums and played on George's *The Concert for Bangladesh*, *All Things Must Pass*, *Extra Texture*, *Dark Horse* and *33⅓*, John's *Sometime in New York City* and Ringo's *Ringo* and *Goodnight Vienna*.

In 1991 he was accused of assaulting a teenage boy and the following year accused of sexually assaulting a handyman who refused to have sex with him. The sex charges were dropped when he agreed to plead guilty to cocaine and assault charges and he received a suspended sentence, although he had to spend nine months at a Drug Rehabilitation Centre.

PRITCHARD, Jill A member of the Apple Scruffs. A former hairdresser, she left her job to travel to Marylebone Register Office to watch Paul and Linda get married, then stayed in London as one of the Scruffs, fanatically devoting herself to Beatle-watching 24 hours a day. In 1979 she was to join Abbey Road Studios as a receptionist.

PROBY, P.J. Born James Marcus Smith in Texas, Proby was brought to Britain by Jack Good to appear in the *Around the Beatles* TV special. He became an instant star and began to tour the country. His version of Lennon and McCartney's 'That Means a Lot', a number originally planned for *Help!* but left out of the film, was issued in July 1965, but Proby's career at the top was to be short-lived due to the controversy caused when his trousers split on stage.

QUARRY MEN, The A skiffle group originally formed by John Lennon in March 1957, when he was at Quarry Bank school. For one week only they were dubbed the Blackjacks, then John decided to name them after the school, probably inspired by a line in the school song which read 'quarry men, old before our birth'.

Having recently talked his Aunt Mimi into buying him a £15 guitar at Frank Hessy's, John was keen to lead a group and he immediately enlisted his closest friend, Pete Shotton, as washboard player. After the first week and the name change, the third member to be enrolled was another boy in the same class, Bill Smith, who was asked to play tea-chest bass. Smith remained with the Quarry Men for only a matter of weeks and for the next year the tea-chest bass was shared between Ivan Vaughan, Nigel Whalley and Len Garry. Other members included Rod Davis on banjo and Colin Hanton on drums.

Initial gigs included private parties and local skiffle contests. On 9 June 1957 they entered the qualifying audition for the Carroll Levis 'TV Star Search' show at the Empire Theatre, but failed the audition.

The group's initial repertoire comprised popular skiffle hits of the time: 'Rock Island Line', 'Freight Train', 'Railroad Bill', 'Lost John', 'Cumberland Gap', 'Midnight Special', 'No Other Baby' and 'Worried Man Blues'. They also performed the Liverpool sea shanty 'Maggie May'.

The group's next major engagement was at an outdoor party in Rosebery Street on 22 June. One of the main organizers of the event was Mrs Marjorie Roberts, whose son Charles was a friend of Colin Hanton.

The occasion was the anniversary of the granting of Liverpool's charter by King John and the 550th anniversary of the event was celebrated throughout Liverpool.

The Quarry Men performed on the flatbed of a stationary coal lorry belonging to the resident at No. 76, who also provided the group with a microphone. There was a day-long party during which the Quarry Men performed twice.

Charles Roberts, who also took the famous photograph of the group performing in the street, related how two black boys from neighbouring Hatherley Street began to heckle the group and threatened to beat up John. John jumped off the back of the truck and fled to No. 84, the Roberts' house, followed by the rest of the group. Mrs Roberts provided them with refreshments while a policeman was called and he escorted the boys to the bus stop, where they caught a bus home to Woolton.

Their next gig, on Saturday 6 July, was at the garden fête of St Peter's Church in Woolton. This was historically one of the most important events because it was here that John met Paul.

The Quarry Men that day featured John, Griffiths, Hanton, Davis, Shotton and Garry, while Geoff Rhind, a schoolboy with a Box Brownie, took a photograph of them for posterity.

As Ivan Vaughan wasn't playing tea-chest bass that day, he'd invited along a friend from the Liverpool Institute, Paul McCartney, who cycled to the event.

After the Quarry Men had performed, they took their gear over to the church hall, where they were performing that evening. Ivan took the 15-year-old Paul across to meet them.

The young lad made an impression because he showed them how to tune a guitar, which none of them could do, and he particularly impressed John with his knowledge of the lyrics of rock 'n' roll songs. He even wrote out the words of 'Twenty Flight Rock' and 'Be-Bop-A-Lula' for John. He also borrowed a guitar and began to play some Little Richard numbers, including 'Long Tall Sally' and 'Tutti Frutti'.

After Paul had left, John considered asking him to join the Quarry Men and the message was relayed to Paul by Pete Shotton two weeks later.

In the meantime, the group made their Cavern club debut on a special skiffle night on 7 August on a bill with Ron McKay, the Dark Town Skiffle Group, the Deltones and the Demon Five. It was during this gig that John sang two Presley numbers, causing the Cavern owner Alan Sytner to send him a curt note; 'Cut out the bloody rock!'

Paul had been away at a summer camp with his brother, Michael, and on his return to Liverpool made his debut with the group at the New Clubmoor Hall, Back Broadway, on Friday, 18 October.

The Quarry Men had been booked by local promoter Charlie McBain and they wore matching outfits with long-sleeved cowboy shirts, black string ties and black trousers. John and Paul wore white sports coats.

The line-up that night comprised Hanton on drums, Garry on tea-chest bass, Griffiths on guitar and John and Paul. On this occasion, Paul played lead guitar for the first and only time – and it was a disaster.

Paul played the old Arthur Smith hit 'Guitar Boogie', but ruined the guitar solo because he was playing his guitar upside-down and backwards, as he still didn't know how to restring a guitar for a left-handed person.

After the show, aware that his debut as lead guitarist hadn't gone down too well, Paul tried to impress John by playing him an original number he'd written called 'I've Lost My Little Girl'. John responded by trying out a few tunes he'd written, and the Lennon and McCartney songwriting team was soon to develop.

On Thursday 7 November they were booked by McBain to appear at Wilson Hall, Garston. They had three other gigs that year – at Stanley Abattoir Social Club on 16 November, New Clubmoor Hall on 23 November and Wilson Hall on 7 December.

It was obvious from the time of their Cavern debut that John was becoming increasingly interested in rock 'n' roll and was moving away from skiffle music. This displeased the group's music purist Rod Davis, with the result that he left in February 1958.

Rock numbers they selected in their early repertoire included 'All Shook Up', 'Be-Bop-a-Lula', 'Blue Moon of Kentucky', 'Bony Moronie',

'Lawdy Miss Clawdy', 'Mailman Blues', 'Mean Woman Blues', 'Roll Over Beethoven', 'Searchin'', 'Short Fat Fanny', 'Sure to Fall (in Love with You)', 'That's All Right Mama' and 'Twenty Flight Rock'.

In 1958 a new member, John Charles Lowe, nicknamed 'Duff,' joined them occasionally on piano. He was in the same form at Liverpool Institute as Paul and Paul asked him to his house in Allerton to meet John. George Harrison joined two weeks later.

The Quarry Men appeared at the New Clubmoor Hall on 10 January and the Cavern on 24 January. Their appearance for Charlie McBain on 6 February at Wilson Hall is when George saw them for the first time.

On 13 March they appeared at the opening night of Alan Caldwell's (later to become Rory Storm) cellar club the Morgue in Broadgreen. Among their other appearances that year was at the wedding reception for George's brother Harry in Speke on 20 December.

During the first two years of the group's existence, their repertoire changed dramatically. Paul's influence in the group brought in the Little Richard numbers 'Long Tall Sally' and 'Lucille', but one of their major influences was Buddy Holly and they performed several of his hits, including 'It's So Easy', 'Maybe Baby', 'Peggy Sue', 'That'll Be the Day', 'Think It Over' and 'Words of Love'.

John and Paul also began to write songs, individually and together, which were performed by the group. These included 'Hello Little Girl', 'I Lost My Little Girl', 'Just Fun', 'Keep Looking That Way', 'Like Dreamers Do', 'Love of the Loved', 'The One After 909', 'That's My Woman', 'Thinking of Linking', 'Too Bad About Sorrows' and 'Years Roll By'.

George Harrison sang 'Youngblood', 'Your True Love' and 'Three Cool Cats'. He also co-penned a number with Paul, 'In Spite of All the Danger'.

The group also performed some instrumentals, including 'Guitar Boogie', 'Ramrod', 'Raunchy', the McCartney compositions 'Catswalk' and 'Hot As Sun', John's 'Winston's Walk' and the Lennon and McCartney instrumental 'Looking Glass'.

During the summer of 1958 a historic record was made. The Quarry Men decided on cutting a demo disc, using Percy Phillips's studio at 58 Kensington. The five members at this time were John, Paul, George, Hanton and Lowe, who each contributed 3s 6d to the fee for making the record, which featured 'That'll Be the Day' on the A-side and the Harrison/McCartney 'In Spite of All the Danger' on the flipside. The original tape was later wiped by Philips, but Lowe, who left the group in 1958, retained a copy.

The Quarry Men played only two minor gigs at the beginning of 1959, at a Speke Bus Depot Social Club Party, organized by George's father at Wilson Hall on 1 January, and at another party at Woolton Village Club on 24 January.

The group then drifted apart and it seemed as if the career and the musical aspirations of the Quarry Men were over. John and Paul continued to meet and write songs together and George joined an outfit called the Les Stewart Quartet.

The Quartet were to become resident band at a new coffee club opening on 29 August. Launched by Mrs Mona Best, it was called the Casbah, and a live group was to be presented each Saturday evening.

Another member of the Quartet, Ken Brown, arranged the residency, but Les Stewart was annoyed because Brown missed rehearsals to help with the decorating of the Casbah and he refused to play. Brown and George decided to go ahead with the residency and within a matter of hours George had recruited John and Paul, who decided to keep the name the Quarry Men. But for this incident in August, the Quarry Men would probably have never played again and there wouldn't have been the Beatles!

The Casbah residency came to an end on Saturday 10 October, when there was a dispute with Ken Brown and the group walked out.

Their next appearances were at the Carroll Levis auditions at the Empire Theatre, Liverpool, during which they used the name Johnny & the Moondogs. Several other name changes were to occur before the group settled on the Beatles for their appearances in Hamburg in August 1960, when their line-up comprised John Lennon, Paul McCartney, George Harrison, Pete Best and Stuart Sutcliffe.

QUICKLY, Tommy Merseyside singer who appeared with his group on a bill with the Beatles at the Majestic Ballroom, Birkenhead, on Thursday 31 January 1963, advertised as Johnny Quickly & the Challengers. Brian Epstein noticed him when he opened the show at a NEMS Enterprises Beatles promotion at the Queen's Hall, Widnes. The 17-year-old telephone fitter didn't get to sign with Epstein until the following year, when Brian changed his name to Tommy Quickly, taking him on as a solo artist and dispensed with his backing band, the Challengers.

Epstein then embarked on a massive promotional campaign to establish his new signing. As George Martin had enough acts to handle at that time, Brian contacted Ray Horricks of Pye, via Dick James, and Tommy was signed to the label. Brian then gave him a new backing band, the Remo Four, and a Lennon and McCartney number 'No Reply', to record. Slightly drunk, he found it almost impossible to record and after 17 takes it was abandoned. This frustrated the Remo Four, who believed that a proper interpretation of the number would have brought them a hit. Tommy then made his record debut with another Lennon and McCartney number, 'Tip of My Tongue,' which was arguably not as strong as 'No Reply'. Epstein spent $30,000 on a promotional tour of America. Tommy was included on three Beatles tours, a Beatles Christmas show, plus a Gerry & the Pacemakers Christmas show, a Gerry & the Pacemakers tour and a Billy J. Kramer tour. On the 1963 Beatles Christmas show he performed 'Winter Wonderland' and 'Kiss Me Now'. Yet, despite the major exposure, all five singles by Quickly failed to register and the singer left NEMS in February 1966.

His lack of success was puzzling, as he was an appealing young vocalist with a cheery personality, not unlike Peter Noone of Herman's Hermits. Perhaps it had something to do with his record product.

RADHA KRSNA TEMPLE A sect established in London in 1966 by his Divine Grace A. C. Bhakjtivedanta Swami Prabhupada. George Harrison produced some recordings by members of the sect for Apple, using the name Radha Krsna Temple. Two singles, 'Hare Krsna Mantra' and 'Govinda', entered the charts and George also released an album, *The Radha Krsna Temple*.

RAMON, Paul Alias used by Paul when the Silver Beatles toured Scotland with Johnny Gentle in 1960. He used the name again on the 'My Dark Hour' track for the Steve Miller Band in 1969. The American band the Ramones took their name from the alias in tribute to Paul.

REBELS, The Erstwhile skiffle group formed by George Harrison and his brother Peter. George's friend Arthur Kelly completed the three-guitar line-up and two other friends played mouth organ and tea-chest bass. The group played a single gig at the British Legion Club in Speke.

REMAINS, The Boston group who appeared on the Beatles last tour of America in 1966. They comprised Barry Tashian (vocals/guitar), Bill Briggs (keyboards), Vern Miller (bass) and Chip Damiani (drums). Chip left immediately prior to the tour and had to be replaced.

REMO FOUR, The They first formed as a vocal group, the Remo Quartet, in 1958 and played at social clubs and weddings. They changed to rock 'n' roll music at the beginning of 1960 and were nicknamed 'Liverpool's Fendermen' because they were the first group on Merseyside to have a complete line-up of Fender guitars.

As the Remo Quartet they appeared on a number of Cavern bills with the Beatles, including the Beatles' first evening appearance on Tuesday 21 March 1961. Other 1961 appearances included Wednesday 19 July and Tuesday 25 July.

When they next appeared with the Beatles, on Saturday 5 August, they'd changed their name to the Remo Four and under their new name appeared with them on Wednesday 8 November, Tuesday 14 November, Tuesday 21 November, Wednesday 29 November, Wednesday 6 December and Saturday 23 December, all in 1961. Their 1962 Cavern appearances with the Beatles included Wednesday 17 January, Wednesday 31 January and Tuesday 20 January.

They appeared with the Beatles on various other gigs, including the 'Rock Around the Clock' all-night session at the Iron Door on 11 March 1961 and as Johnny Sandon & the Remo Four at the Scala, Runcorn, on Tuesday 11 December 1962.

The group comprised Keith Stokes (rhythm/vocals), Colin Manley, who was rated as Liverpool's top rock 'n' roll guitarist and was the first to play a Fender (lead), Don Andrews (bass) and Harry Prytherch (drums).

In December 1962 they became Johnny Sandon & the Remo Four in order to embark on a tour of US bases in France, when Roy Dyke replaced

Prytherch and they were joined by Johnny Sandon. They made several further appearances on Beatles Cavern bills under the name Johnny Sandon & the Remo Four.

The group performed some original numbers, including an instrumental 'The Rat Race' and a number sung by Johnny Sandon, 'Spanish Main'. Their single 'Yes', flipside 'Magic Potion' was issued by Pye Records on 27 August 1963, but Johnny left on 18 December, after two years, to turn solo.

They turned down the offer of becoming Billy J. Kramer's backing band but seemed fated to be cast in such a role. They accepted the offer of backing Tommy Quickly.

The Remo Four felt that they were on the brink of success when they teamed up with Tommy Quickly. Managed by Brian Epstein, they were included on the Beatles Christmas show at the Finsbury Park Astoria and also joined the Beatles on their autumn tour of Britain in 1964.

The group were excited when the Beatles provided them with 'No Reply' to record and felt that it would be the single to take them and Tommy to the top of the charts. The Remo Four recorded the backing track, then double-tracked the guitars and added extra percussion, with Paul McCartney joining them on tambourine and John Lennon clinking Coke bottles in the background. Unfortunately, Quickly was slightly drunk and very nervous at the session and the single was never released.

The group then began to back a variety of singers, including Georgie Fame, Billy Fury and Billy J. Kramer. By this time Tony Ashton had joined the group.

The personnel of the band comprised Manley, Ashton, Dyke and Phil Rogers in 1968, when George Harrison used them on the recording of his *Wonderwall* album.

Bass guitarist Kim Gardner teamed up with Roy Dyke and Ashton in the trio Ashton, Gardner & Dyke and they were later to have a chart hit in 1971 with 'Resurrection Shuffle'. George Harrison was to play guitar on the 'I'm Your Spiritual Breadman' track on their album *The Worst of Ashton, Gardner & Dyke*.

When the group broke up, Colin began to back singers such as Clodagh Rodgers and Freddie Starr, before becoming a member of the Swinging Bluejeans.

REYNOLDS, Gillian A Liverpool-born journalist who was a columnist with the *Daily Telegraph* when the Beatles came to her attention. She got on particularly well with John Lennon, who was five years her junior, and recommended to journalistic colleague Maureen Cleave that she travel to Liverpool to write a feature on the group. At the time Gillian was married to an American writer, Stanley Reynolds, who worked for the *Manchester Guardian*, and he was also to write about the group.

RICKY GLEASON & THE TOP SPOTS Group comprising Ricky Gleason (vocals), Graham Little (rhythm), Tommy Limb (drums), Keith Dodd (lead) and Kenny Rees (bass). They hit the headlines when they went to London to see 'The Beatles Show' at the Finsbury Park Astoria at Christmas 1963.

They turned up outside the theatre on a lorry, complete with amps and equipment, and began to play. They were mobbed by the 2,000 youngsters in the crowd and the police had to be called. An inspector moved them on.

Ricky commented: 'We wanted to show people that the Mersey groups are proud of the Beatles and are in no way envious of their success. It was a "Tribute to the Beatles" and, we are pleased to say, enjoyed by all.'

The group composed original material, including a science-fiction Beat number, 'The Gobblies', about an invasion from outer space.

RHONE, Dorothy Paul McCartney's first serious girlfriend. He began going out with the blonde-haired Dot in the late 1950s and the romance lasted until 1962.

During the Beatles season at the Top Ten Club in April 1961, both Dot and Cynthia Powell travelled over to Germany to be with them.

Cynthia talked Dot into taking a room in the house where she was lodging, and it was while she was there that Paul arrived to tell her their affair was over.

She moved back to her parents' house in Childwall, but within a year had gone to live in Canada and later married, naming one of her daughters Astrid, in memory of Astrid Kirchherr, whom she had met in Hamburg.

RICHARDS, Ron Recording manager who became George Martin's assistant in 1962. Richards usually recorded the rock 'n' pop acts, while Martin concentrated on the comedy and variety artists. When the Beatles turned up for their recording audition on Wednesday 6 June 1962, it was Richards who initially recorded the session, while George Martin left the studio to go to the canteen. Richards recorded the Beatles performing 'Besame Mucho', 'P.S. I Love You', 'Ask Me Why' and 'Love Me Do'. There was some excitement about the number 'Love Me Do' and Martin was called up from the canteen.

For the session later that year, on Tuesday 4 September, Richard rehearsed the Beatles in the afternoon and Martin recorded two numbers with them that evening. Norman Smith, present at the session, remarked: 'I've a feeling that Paul wasn't too happy with Ringo's drumming, and felt it could be better.' Apparently, this was also the feeling of Richards and Martin.

The next session, on Tuesday 11 September, was produced solely by Richards, who said: 'We weren't happy with the drum sound on the original "Love Me Do" so I booked Andy White for the remake. I used him a lot at that time – he was very good.'

The sequence of events seems to disprove the allegations about Pete Best and his drumming. White was booked because of disenchantment with Starr, not Best.

While the session took place, Ringo was initially asked to join Richards in the control box, then Richards, possibly taking pity on him, asked him to play maracas on 'P.S. I Love You'. He then asked him to play tambourine on 'Love Me Do'.

The succeeding sessions were taken over by Martin and it has never been made clear why he became the Beatles' recording manager rather than Richards, who, as already mentioned, handled Parlophone's pop and rock 'n' roll acts and was credited on the Beatles' initial recording sheets as the 'Artistes' Manager', meaning he was their A&R man.

RIGHTEOUS BROTHERS American vocal duo comprising Bill Medley, a baritone, and Bobby Hatfield, a tenor. They'd already received acclaim with records such as 'Little Latin Lupe Lu' when Phil Spector signed them to his Philles label.

The duo were booked to support the Beatles for 25 concerts as they began their American tour at the Cow Palace, San Francisco, on 19 August 1964. They were paid $750 per week during the tour and a few months later Spector produced them performing the classic single 'You've Lost That Lovin' Feelin'', which topped both the American and British charts.

They had several further hits before they split up in 1968.

ROADRUNNERS, The A Liverpool R&B group who formed in mid-1962. They initially played Chuck Berry numbers. The original line-up comprised Pete Cook, ex-Kansas City Five, John Bedson, ex-Four Clefs (drums), Brian (?), ex-Caribbeans (vocals) and Kenny Colly, ex-Columbians (rhythm).

Mike Hart on lead/vocals and Pete Mackey on bass guitar joined the band and the Roadrunners soon became acknowledged as Liverpool's leading R&B band, following the usual path of top local groups by appearing at the major venues such as the Cavern and performing at the Star Club, Hamburg.

When George Harrison was telling Dick Rowe about the Rolling Stones in the conversation which directly led to Decca signing the group, he said: 'We've seen a great band down in London called the Rolling Stones who are almost as good as our own Roadrunners.'

Incidentally, Mackey had become president of the Student's Union at the Liverpool College of Art and was assigned to recover the art college PA equipment lent to the Beatles, which was needed for the college dances. He travelled to Manchester on the fan club coach and approached John Lennon, who said: 'We've hocked it in Hamburg. If you need to know anything about it, just contact our manager.'

The group recorded a charity record, issued locally on 'Panto Day'. The 'Pantomania' EP, featuring 'Cry Cry Cry,' 'Fun at Twenty-One', 'If You

Want to Know the Time' and 'The Leaving of Liverpool', was recorded at Cavern Sound and the proceeds went to Liverpool charities.

The Roadrunners appeared on three Cavern bills with the Beatles during 1963, on Sunday 3 February, Friday 12 March and on the Beatles' final Cavern appearance, on Saturday 3 August.

ROBINS, Jesse Stout actress who portrayed Ringo's Aunt Jessie in *Magical Mystery Tour*, during which a gentleman by the name of Buster Bloodvessel, played by Ivor Cutler, falls in love with her.

ROBBINS, Mike Uncle to Paul and Mike McCartney and a former Butlin's redcoat who encouraged Paul and Mike to enter a talent contest at the holiday camp. When he opened a pub, the Fox and Hounds, in Berkshire with his wife, Betty, John and Paul visited them and performed as a duo there in April 1960 using the name the Nurk Twins.

ROE, Tommy American singer, born Thomas David Roe in Atlanta, Georgia, on 9 May 1942.

He formed his own group, the Satins, at the age of 16 and enjoyed his first hit with 'Sheila' in 1962. The million-seller topped the charts in America and reached No. 3 in Britain. The Beatles liked the number so much they included it in their own repertoire, with George Harrison as lead vocalist.

Despite spending two years in the Army, Roe had a total of 11 chart singles in America between 1962 and 1971, including another chart-topper, 'Dizzy'. He also had six chart hits in Britain, where he was very popular.

From 9 March 1963, Roe began a month-long tour of Britain, co-headlining with fellow American Chris Montez, and the Beatles were the main support band.

Roe also appeared on the bill of the Beatles' first American concert at the Coliseum, Washington DC, on 11 February 1964.

ROLAND, Cheniston K. Mersey photographer who took a set of photographs at the Larry Parnes audition at the Wyvern Club in May 1960, including the famous photograph of the Silver Beatles performing with John, Paul, George, Stuart and substitute drummer Johnny Hutchinson. The shoot also included what is probably the only photograph of the group with Tommy Moore on drums.

RONETTES, The American girl group, discovered by Phil Spector. Their hits included 'Be My Baby' and 'Baby I Love You'. The trio, which comprised Ronnie and Estelle Bennett and Nedra Talley, visited the Beatles at the Plaza Hotel, New York, in February 1964. They also featured on the Beatles' final American tour in 1966.

Ronnie married Spector and recorded for the Apple label in 1971 on a record co-produced by George Harrison and Phil Spector with a number penned by George, 'Try Some, Buy Some'.

ROLLING STONES, The The group with an image deliberately constructed to contrast with that of the Beatles.

When Andrew Loog Oldham, who had been involved in the publicity for the Beatles' first single, saw the Beatles perform, he realized that there was an opening for a group with an image the complete opposite to that of the 'lovable moptops'.

He created a rebellious one for the group, leading a contemporary critic to comment: 'The Beatles became the kids who charmed a nation. The Stones were the louts who kicked it in the bollocks.'

Yet it was the Beatles were were originally the savage young group, performing wild rock 'n' roll and R&B, coming from working-class backgrounds, swearing and smoking on stage. While they were performing in the riotous clubs in Hamburg, insulting audiences and associating with prostitutes, the Stones were enjoying a much more genteel existence, cosseted in a middle-class environment and education.

It was Brian Epstein who changed the Beatles' image from the savage to the soft, dressing them in mohair suits, instructing them on how to behave, and even taming their music. It proved a successful formula, although John Lennon always hated it and considered that the Stones had stolen their image. In the years up to 1962, the Beatles would be more likely to hold the title 'the greatest live rock 'n' roll band in the world' than the Stones. John was to say: 'Our best work was never recorded, you know. We were performing in Liverpool, Hamburg and around the dance halls, you know, and what we generated was fantastic.'

Georgio Gomelski, who was unofficially managing the Stones, approached the Beatles and invited them to the Crawdaddy Club in Richmond to see his group. They turned up at the gig and later went back to the Stones' flat, beginning a long and friendly relationship.

It was George Harrison who tipped Dick Rowe off about the Rolling Stones and Rowe immediately signed them to Decca. They made the breakthrough with a song the Beatles gave to them, 'I Wanna Be Your Man'.

An agreement was also made between the two groups that they would coordinate their releases so that they did not conflict and thus affect each other's sales.

Their line-up at the time was Mick Jagger (vocals), Brian Jones (guitar/vocals), Keith Richard (guitar/vocals), Bill Wyman (bass) and Charlie Watts (drums).

RORY STORM & THE HURRICANES A legendary Merseyside group, whose blond-haired leader, standing at six foot two, was acknowledged as one of the most entertaining performers on the Mersey scene, where he was dubbed 'Mr Showmanship' and 'The Golden Boy'.

His real name was Alan Caldwell. A former cotton salesman, he decided to form a skiffle group, which he called Al Caldwell's Texans, although he suffered from the impediment of a stutter. Surprisingly, although the stutter was apparent whenever he spoke, he never stuttered on stage.

In January 1959 he changed the name of the group to the Raving Texans and their line-up comprised Al Caldwell (guitar/vocals), Johnny Byrne (guitar/vocals), Paul Murphy (guitar/vocals), Reg Hales (washboard) and Jeff Truman (tea-chest bass). Spud Ward, a former member of the Swinging Bluejeans, took over from Truman on bass guitar and the group continued as the Raving Texans until July 1959.

By this time Rory had met Ritchie Starkey at a talent contest called '6.5 Special'. Ritchie had left the Eddie Clayton Skiffle group and was playing with the Darktown Skiffle. Rory told him that he was looking for a drummer. Ritchie was interested in joining them and first appeared with the group on 25 March 1959 at the Mardi Gras in Mount Pleasant.

There were a number of changes to the group's name during 1959, first to Al Storm & the Hurricanes, then Jett Storm & the Hurricanes and finally, by the end of the year, Rory Storm & the Hurricanes. The new name came about after he and Johnny had appeared on a show with singer Rory Blackwell at Butlin's in August 1959.

In October 1959 the Hurricanes entered a Carroll Levis 'Search for Stars' competition at the Empire Theatre, passing the various heats, and on Saturday 31 Johnny was able to write in his diary: 'Played final and came out 2nd out of 150 acts. Winner, singer, 26 points. Al Storm & the Hurricanes – 22 points (recount 16 points, but still second).'

During the group's first few years, Rory evolved several changes in stage wear and at one time they wore sunglasses and shirts with a palm tree motif. They then donned red suits, with Rory wearing a pink suit, and Rory also got himself an Elvis-style gold lamé suit. When they appeared for their first season at Butlin's, Rory wore a turquoise suit and gold lamé shirt and the Hurricanes wore fluorescent suits.

The line-up now became Rory Storm (vocals), Johnny Byrne (rhythm guitar), Charles O'Brien (lead guitar), Wally Eymond (bass guitar/vocals) and Ritchie Starkey (drums). It remained this way until August 1962 when Ritchie became a member of the Beatles.

Despite changing the name from the Texans, Rory was obviously still fond of a Western theme – at that time there were numerous Western series on television. He decided to call Byrne Johnny Guitar, after the title of the 1954 Joan Crawford Western, Ritchie became Ringo Starr and Charles was renamed Ty, after Ty Hardin, star of the *Bronco* series. Rory also thought that Lou Walters was a more suitable name for Wally.

Changing from a skiffle group to a rock 'n' roll band caused problems at the Cavern club, where rock 'n' roll was banned. In January 1960 the group were still including a number of skiffle songs in their repertoire and appeared at the Cavern on a bill with the Cy Laurie Jazz Band on Sunday 2 January, and the following Saturday were appearing there again supporting the Saints Jazz Band and Terry Lightfoot's New Orleans Jazz Band. On Sunday 10 January Ray McFall began his Liverpool Jazz Festival in an attempt to put Liverpool and jazz on the map. During that week top trad bands such as Acker Bilk's appeared, together with modern jazz outfits, country music bands and skiffle groups. When Rory Storm & the Hurricanes appeared again on Sunday 17 January, on a bill with Micky Ashman's Jazz Band and the Swinging Bluegenes, they began their set with 'Cumberland Gap'. Then they decided to switch to a rock 'n' roll set and played 'Whole Lotta Shakin' Goin' On'. The jazz fans became furious and started pelting the group with copper coins. The Hurricanes continued the show but were drowned out by a booing audience. When they came offstage, a furious McFall fined them 6s for daring to play rock 'n' roll music. The group were able to collect all the coins off the stage, which more than compensated for the fine.

Lou Walters's voice produced a contrast to Rory's and he performed numbers such as 'Fever', 'Let It Be Me', 'Summertime' and 'Mailman', Rory performed numbers such as 'Brand New Cadillac', 'I'll Be Your Hero', 'Roll Over Beethoven', 'Down the Line', 'Dr Feelgood' and 'Whole Lotta Shakin' Goin' On'. Johnny duetted on 'Since You Broke My Heart' with Lou and played the instrumental 'Green Onions'.

The group appeared at the Liverpool Stadium on 3 May 1960 on the bill with Gene Vincent. This is the show which aroused Larry Parnes's interest in Liverpool groups and led to the Wyvern Club auditions. Rory actually turned up at the auditions, not to perform but just to have his photo taken with Billy Fury! That summer the group began their season at Butlin's in Pwllheli in the Rock 'n' Calypso Ballroom, from July to September.

Despite the Butlin's offer of £25 each per week, some members of the group had to consider the risks they were taking in becoming fully professional. Ritchie was the most reluctant member: he was an apprentice at Henry Hunt's, making school climbing frames at the time. He didn't want to go to Butlin's, but Rory decided to convince him.

It was during this period that Rory insisted on Ringo having his own five-minute spot, 'Starrtime', during which he sang numbers such as the Shirelles 'Boys' and 'Alley Oop'.

They were Allan Williams's first choice for a group when he wanted to send a Liverpool band to the Kaiserkeller in Hamburg. As they were committed to Butlin's, he sent over Derry & the Seniors instead.

Back at Butlin's, the act began to shape up far more professionally and they were playing for 16 hours a week.

In October 1960 they were off to Hamburg, replacing Derry & the Seniors at the Kaiserkeller. They were paid more than either the Seniors or the Beatles.

They were billed above the Beatles and alternated with them on the daily 12-hour stretch which the groups had to play. So each band did 90 minutes on and 90 minutes off.

It was during this eight-week season, on Saturday 18 October 1960, that the recording session took place at the Akustik Studio. Three of Wally's ballads were recorded: 'Fever', 'September Song' and 'Summertime'.

Rory also sang at the Top Ten, accompanied by Tony Sheridan.

Rory Storm & the Hurricanes became the star band on the first Beat night at the Orrell Park Ballroom in March 1961 and they began their second Butlin's season at Skegness in Lincolnshire, 161 miles from Liverpool.

When local promoter Sam Leach decided to publicize Mersey groups in the London area in order to give top agents the opportunity of seeing them perform live, he booked a series of Saturday evenings at the Palais Ballroom, Aldershot. The first, on Saturday 9 December, featured the Beatles. The planned advertisement for the gig didn't appear in the local paper and eventually only 18 people turned up. Rory Storm & the Hurricanes appeared the following week and drew an audience of 210.

At one time Ringo considered joining the Seniors, but on 30 December 1961 he left for Germany to back Tony Sheridan at the Top Ten Club in Hamburg, enticed by the lure of a large fee, a flat and the use of a car. However, he found Sheridan's eccentric style of performing too hard to cope with (he'd often change songs in a middle of a performance without telling his backing band) and returned to the Hurricanes. While he was absent from the group, he was replaced by Derek Fell from the Blackpool group the Executioners.

The band also toured American bases in France and appeared at a club in Marbella, Spain, before their third season at Butlin's, again in Skegness. One of their bookings was for a one-month season at an American base in Fontenet, when they had to be accompanied by a female vocalist. They took Vicki Woods, who'd appeared regularly in Liverpool clubs in a double act with her mother. The group performed from seven to ten forty-five each night, with four 15-minute breaks. It was also during this year that Lou left the group for a while when he joined the Seniors.

During the Skegness season, Ringo received a letter from Kingsize Taylor offering him £20 a week if he would join them in Germany as a replacement for Dave Lovelady, who was leaving the group to complete his studies. Ringo agreed. Then, one day, John Lennon and Paul McCartney turned up at the camp and offered Ringo £25 a week if he'd join them. The extra £5 sealed it and Ringo agreed to become a Beatle as from August 1962.

Johnny Guitar says that John and Paul turned up at ten one morning and knocked on their caravan door, saying they wanted Ringo to join them. Rory told them that the Hurricanes couldn't work without a drummer and they hadn't finished their season. Paul told him that Brian Epstein said they could have Pete Best. Rory went to Liverpool but Pete Best was too upset. Rory then returned to Skegness and used relief drummers.

Once Ringo left the band, the Hurricanes fell into a pattern of losing drummers on a regular basis. In the 23 May 1963 issue of *Mersey Beat*,

Virginia Harry wrote in her 'Mersey Roundabout' column:

> Hurricanes drummer Brian Johnson is joining Mark Peters & the Silhou-
> ettes. Says Brian: 'Any drummer who wants to get anywhere should join
> the Hurricanes. Young drummers will find the group an ideal training
> ground – I have improved tremendously since joining them – and look
> how their former drummers have fared: Ringo Starr is now with the
> Beatles and Gibson Kemp is with Kingsize Taylor & the Dominoes.'

On 2 January 1964, *Mersey Beat* ran a story called 'The Ghost of Ringo
Haunts This Group':

> Virtually every night of the week, Rory Storm & the Hurricanes perform at
> venues in the North. But something seems to be missing. Rory, Ty, Lu and
> Johnny seem to swing together, but the drummer always seems to be the
> odd one out.
>
> It has been this way since August 1962 when Richard Starkey left the
> group.
>
> Says Rory: 'Ringo was with us for more than four years. When the group
> first started, only ourselves and the Bluejeans were known on the Mersey
> scene – we were the first rock group to do the rounds.'
>
> At the time Ringo was a member of the group, the Hurricanes were
> regarded as one of Merseyside's leading outfits, and in the first *Mersey Beat*
> poll they were placed 4th.
>
> 'During the four or five years Ringo was with us he really played drums
> – he drove them. He sweated and swung and sung.
>
> 'Ringo sang about five numbers a night, he even had his own spot – it
> was called "Ringo Starrtime". Now he's only a backing drummer. The
> Beatles' front line is so good he doesn't have much to do. This is not the
> Ringo Starr who played with us.
>
> 'When Ringo first joined the Hurricanes (we were called the Raving
> Texans then) he didn't have any rings and we just called him Ritchie.
>
> 'During our first year at Butlin's we all chose fancy stage names and
> that's when he became Ringo Starr.'
>
> Since August '62 the group has had a great deal of bad luck as far as
> finding a suitable replacement is concerned. Drummers from Preston,
> Newcastle, London and numerous Merseyside musicians have occupied
> the drum seat with the group – yet Ringo's place remains vacant.
>
> Gibson Kemp, Brian Johnson, Keef Hartley, Ian Broad, Trevor Morais –
> the names of the drummers who have appeared with the Hurricanes
> continues to lengthen.
>
> Without a suitable regular drummer the group can't practise or rehearse,
> and they can't regain the enthusiasm they once had.
>
> But whatever happens, Liverpool's 'Golden Boy' has been on the local
> scene for seven years – and he'll be around for some years to come.

Keef Hartley joined the Hurricanes in August 1963. He'd formerly been
with Preston's Thunderbeats. Then he joined Freddie Starr & the Midnighters, later leaving Liverpool to join the Artwoods and then John
Mayall's Bluesbreakers.

Rory Storm & the Hurricanes appeared on scores of bills alongside the Beatles, particularly at the local ballrooms and town halls, ranging from Lathom Hall and Litherland Town Hall to the Hambleton Hall and Knotty Ash Village Hall. Initially they were the bill-toppers, then they shared bills, then they were billed second to the Beatles. Several Beatles books seem be under the impression that the Beatles got to know Ringo only in Hamburg, but they were appearing regularly at local 'jive hives' together and knew each other well. A selection of the gigs in which Rory Storm & the Hurricanes appeared with the Beatles follows.

In 1961 dates included the St Valentine's Night 'Rock Ball', Cassanova Club, Tuesday 14 February; Hambleton Hall, Wednesday 15 February; Cassanova Club, Saturday 18 February; all-night session, Liverpool Jazz Society, Saturday 11 March; Liverpool Jazz Society (billed as Rory Storm & the Wild Ones), Wednesday 15 March; Litherland Town Hall, Thursday 21 September; Operation Big Beat II, Tower Ballroom, Friday 24 November; Tower Ballroom, Friday 1 December; 'The Davy Jones Show', Tower Ballroom, Friday 8 December.

In 1962 dates included 'Twist Around the Tower', Tower Ballroom, Friday 12 January; St Patrick's Night Rock Gala, Knotty Ash Village Hall, Saturday 17 March; 'A Night to Remember', Tower Ballroom, Friday 6 April; Queen's Hall, Widnes, Monday 3 September; Queen's Hall, Widnes, Monday 10 September; 'The Beatles Show', Rialto Ballroom, Thursday 6 September; 'Rory Storm's Birthday Night', Tower Ballroom, Friday 21 September; 'Little Richard at the Tower', Friday 12 October.

Rory Storm & the Hurricanes remain a Liverpool legend and there have been no fewer than three stage plays about Rory. Cilla Black has said: 'Rory Storm & the Hurricanes was the very first group I sang with.'

Drummer Dave Lovelady of the Dominoes said: 'One night at St Luke's Hall was an absolute sensation. Rory Storm came in with Wally, who had got the first bass in Liverpool. There was always a bass on American records, but we'd never seen one, and here was Wally with a Framus four-string bass guitar. The groups crowded round in amazement, and when they opened with "Brand New Cadillac", this deep, booming sound was tremendous.'

In the first *Mersey Beat* poll, Rory Storm & the Hurricanes received more votes than any other group, but Virginia and I disqualified a number of the entries because they were all written in green ink and posted from the same place at the same time, which meant that the Beatles became No. 1 instead and the Hurricanes stood at No. 4. The following year they had dropped to the No. 19 position. This was probably due to the fact that they were absent from Liverpool for most of the year with their season at Butlin's, their tour of American bases in France and their spell in Hamburg.

As befitted his local star status, Rory was featured regularly in *Mersey Beat*. There were photographs of him leaving hospital with nurses after breaking a limb at a gig, signing autographs for fans at the airport, leading the *Mersey Beat* XI soccer team and so on. He was also renowned for his exuberant stage act. At a 'Beat & Bathe Show' at New Brighton swimming baths on August Bank Holiday 1963, attended by 1,600 people, he twisted his way to the high-diving board, stripped to his trunks, climbed to the top board, diving as he finished the song. In January 1964, during an appearance at the Majestic Ballroom, Birkenhead, he scaled one of the columns from the stage to the balcony, slipped and fell 30 feet, fracturing his leg, necessitating a short stay at Broadgreen Hospital. While performing at New Brighton Pier, he climbed on to the roof of the Pavilion, started twisting, and fell through the glass skylight! During one of his shows at the Majestic he played five-a-side football with a team from the ballroom, the Top Rank Ravers – the result was a five-all draw!

Once he'd decided to become a singer, Rory turned professional with total dedication. He changed his name to Rory Storm by deed poll, christened the family home in Broadgreen 'Stormsville' and, when some members of his band couldn't play lunchtime sessions at the Liverpool Jazz Society because they had jobs, he formed Rory Storm & the Wild Ones to perform during lunch hours.

A superb athlete, apart from being an exceptional swimmer (he swam the $12\frac{1}{2}$-mile length of Windermere) and golfer (he would go round Allerton golf course dressed only in shorts and golf shoes), he was captain of the *Mersey Beat* soccer team and also ran for the Pembroke Harriers.

When A&R men began to take an interest in Liverpool in 1963, Rory and the group were among a number of bands who recorded for Oriole's two *This is Mersey Beat* albums, and Oriole also released a single, 'Dr Feelgood', flipside 'I Can Tell', in December 1963. The mobile unit recorded them in primitive conditions at the Rialto Ballroom and they missed the opportunity of proper recording facilities in a studio. However, for some reason they were overlooked by the major record companies, perhaps because they lacked a manager.

Rory actually approached Brian Epstein and asked him to manage them, but he refused. Later on, Arthur Howes, the promoter of the Beatles' tours, took over as their manager, but he was based in London and they remained in Liverpool.

It seemed that their luck had changed in 1964, when Rory met Epstein at the Blue Angel club one evening and Epstein agreed to personally record the group. This was a coup and they travelled to London, where Brian produced their record at IBC Studios. They selected the number 'America' from the musical *West Side Story*. As Rory explained to *Mersey Beat*:

We first heard this number when we played in Spain. Everyone seemed to be playing it. We liked it a lot and when we came back to Liverpool we did our own arrangement and added it to our repertoire. We shortened it, used some of our own words, and it goes down a bomb!

At the recording session we played one number after another to Brian Epstein. He kept saying 'No' until we played this and then he gave an emphatic 'Yes.'

The B-side was the old Everly Brothers number 'Since You Broke My Heart', with the vocals handled by Lou and Johnny.

'America' was released by Parlophone on 20 December 1964, but didn't reach the charts. Epstein only ever recorded one other band – the Rustiks.

The record did sell well in Florida, where the group had an active fan club, and it became the No. 1 record on the Florida WL05 radio station chart.

Ringo had offered his support to his old group and gave them further chances to record, but they didn't take them. Ringo said that he'd fix for them to record whenever they wanted to, but Rory couldn't be bothered finding new material and seemed content to just play rock 'n' roll standards. Perhaps he didn't really want to make the big time. His sister Iris said: 'He was happy to be the King of Liverpool; he was never keen on touring, he didn't want to give up running for the Pembroke Harriers ... and he'd never miss a Liverpool football match!'

For a time they were joined by Vince Earl, former leader of bands such as the Zeros and the Talismen. Then, in 1967, Ty Brien collapsed on stage and was rushed to hospital. There were complications resulting from a recent appendicitis operation and he died at the age of 26.

The group then broke up for a short time, before Rory and Johnny tried to revive it with three new members, but it didn't work out. After that Rory became a disc jockey in Benidorm and Amsterdam – a strange profession for a man with a noticeable stutter.

It was while in Amsterdam that Rory received the news that his father had died. He returned to Liverpool to console his mother, Vi, but neither recovered from the shock. Rory was suffering from a chest condition and took sleeping pills to ease it.

On 28 September 1972, both Rory and his mother were found dead in Stormsville. Their deaths remain a mystery, although Shane Fenton, his brother-in-law at the time, commented: 'Rory became very ill. He had a chest condition which meant he couldn't breathe properly. He found it difficult to sleep so he'd take his pills with a drop of Scotch which doped him completely. At the post-mortem it was established that he hadn't taken enough pills to kill himself ... It had been nothing more than a case of trying to get some kip, but because he was so weak, his body couldn't handle it. He died in the night and his mother found him. She must have felt that she'd lost everything. I think she took an overdose, but I'm convinced that Rory didn't. When you've known somebody long enough, you know whether they're going to do it or not. The whole thing was an accident.'

No member of the Beatles attended Rory's funeral. When asked about this, Ringo said: 'I wasn't there when he was born either.'

Rory Storm & the Hurricanes were to become Liverpool icons, affectionately remembered on Merseyside but virtually unknown outside the area. They were the classic group who didn't make it, the favourite local group with the golden-boy singer who were left behind when the recording moguls trawled the Mersey scene.

Johnny Guitar became an ambulance driver. In the 1990s he joined Mersey Cats, a group of original Mersey bands who perform in aid of local charities, and he launched his own band, Johnny & the Hurricanes. Lou Walters became a psychiatric nurse, while Vince Earl found success as a comedian and later became one of the stars of the television soap *Brookside*.

ROSA The Hamburg woman, surname unknown, whom the Beatles used to call 'Mutti'.

She was the Toiletten-Frau at the Indra club and befriended the group when they first arrived in Hamburg. Rosa, who was 67 years old at the time, discovered that they'd spent all their money on travel expenses and were hungry, so she gave them some marks and sent them to Harold's Café, nearby, for some potato fritters, cornflakes and chicken soup.

Rosa regularly provided the lads with soap and towels, gave them chocolate bars and would wash their shirts and socks. She also let Paul stay at her bungalow by the docks, and was later to comment: 'I remember when young Paul used to practise guitar on the roof of my little place. We used to get crowds of burly old Hamburg dockers, just listening. They shouted out things in German, but Paul couldn't understand them.'

She moved to the Top Ten when the Beatles began to play there and was also given the job as WC attendant at the Star Club when the Beatles made their debut there.

The St Pauli district in those days was not as seedy as has been made out and was visited by lots of respectable couples in much the same way as visitors flock to Soho in London. The area changed into a more sinister place many years later, with the introduction of hard drugs. Still, amphetamines such as Preludin and Captogen were available over the pharmacist's counter, and the groups used to take 'uppers' regularly, to keep them going through their long sessions and the unsociable hours. When Henry Henroid heard that the police were about to raid the club for drugs, he was baffled – no drugs were allowed to be sold at the club. He was then told that the Beatles (with the exception of Pete Best) and other musicians were being supplied with tablets by Rosa, who had a big sweet jar full of 'Prellies' in the toilet.

Henry called her to the office and sacked her – until the doorman, Ali, intervened and told him that Rosa didn't get any money for the pills. The financial rewards from the selling of the pills went to an English road manager who, as a result of the incident, was dubbed 'Terry the Pill'.

Rosa died in 1991.

ROSS, Alan Cabaret artist who had been performing semi-professionally on Merseyside before making his professional debut at the Odeon, Manchester, in 1958. He later featured in several cabaret clubs in London and in a TV series and film, before returning to Liverpool for a week of appearances during which he was backed by the Beatles.

He was also to make several local appearances as a compère including the Beatles' appearance at the Tower Ballroom, New Brighton, on Friday 8 December 1961.

ROSSINGTON, Norman Actor, born in Liverpool in 1928, who appeared in the popular television comedy series *The Army Game* and followed with appearances in over 40 feature films, ranging from *Carry On* movies to blockbusters such as *Lawrence of Arabia*.

He is the only actor to appear in films with the Beatles and with Elvis Presley, featuring in *A Hard Day's Night* in 1964 and *Double Trouble* in 1966.

Writer Alun Owen specifically wrote the part of the road manager, Norm, for Norman, who'd appeared in Alun's play *Progress in the Park* in 1961.

Norman was also the actor who proposed the Beatles for an Equity card, which they had to have before being allowed to appear in their debut film.

He was also one of the celebrities introduced to the audience at the northern première of *A Hard Day's Night* at the Odeon, Liverpool, on Friday, 10 July, 1964.

In addition, Norman took Joe McGrath, director of the Peter Cook and Dudley Moore TV series *Not Only . . . But Also*, to meet the group during an appearance at Dunstable to see if John would agree to appear on the programme, reading his poetry.

As a result of *A Hard Day's Night*, Norman was hired to appear in *Tobruk* and while in Hollywood he was also cast as Arthur Babcock in the Elvis film *Double Trouble*.

In 1994 he appeared in a documentary film about the making of *A Hard Day's Night*: *You Can't Do That! The Making of 'A Hard Day's Night'*.

ROWE, Dick Recording manager at Decca Records who had to live with the stigma of being known as 'The Man Who Turned Down the Beatles', which was the title of his unpublished autobiography.

This was rather unfair on Rowe, who did have an ear for talent and signed up some of the biggest pop artists of the decade for his company. When George Martin turned down Tommy Steele, for example, Rowe immediately snapped him up and he became the biggest British pop hit-maker of the 1950s. The actual person who turned down the Beatles at Decca was probably Mike Smith, the man who recorded them.

Unlike EMI and the other record companies, Decca decided to give the Beatles a chance by arranging a recording audition. It was Epstein who tried to talk the group into not using any of their original material for this session. John wanted to perform a strong rock 'n' roll set, just like they played at the Cavern, but Brian insisted that they perform as few of their original numbers as possible and concentrate on standards such as 'Till There Was You'.

Both John and Paul were unhappy about this advice, but acceded to Brian's wishes. Had he not interfered, perhaps the outcome of the audition would have been different.

Recording manager Mike Smith conducted the Beatles' recording audition and during the same afternoon he recorded another band, Brian Poole & the Tremeloes, who were from Dagenham.

Apparently, Rowe told Smith he could pick one of the two groups he recorded that day and Smith opted for the Tremeloes, reputedly because they lived relatively close to London and not almost 300 miles away, as was the case with the Beatles.

Decca was also to act generously by letting Epstein have the tapes of the recording audition for use in promoting the group.

The stigma Rowe suffered is probably the result of Brian Epstein's account, related in his autobiography, *A Cellarful of Noise*, which was taped in a single weekend. In it he accused Rowe of saying: 'Not to mince words, Mr Epstein, we don't like your boys' sound. Groups are out: four-piece groups with guitars particularly are finished.'

This would be a strange attitude for Rowe to take as the very month Decca agreed to audition the Beatles he had become part of a new team spearheading the search for new talent, and he was to sign up several guitar groups who became hit artists.

Rowe also actively went out in search of talent, participating in the judging of many competitions – unlike a lot of other recording managers, who stayed put and made the artists come to them.

When Rowe was judging a group competition in Liverpool a fellow judge, George Harrison, told him about a London band called the Rolling Stones. Rowe rushed back to London and signed them up.

For the rest of the decade the groups he signed up were responsible for many major hits, but he could never escape the charge levelled at him in Epstein's book, which probably owed more to imaginative licence than the truth. History then began to be rewritten, when the alleged quote was altered to: 'Groups of guitars are on the way out, Mr Epstein – you really should stick to selling records in Liverpool.'

Rowe had been suffering from diabetes for some time when he passed away at the age of 64 on 6 June 1986.

ROY PURDON & THE TELSTARS Group who appeared on a bill with the Beatles at the Museum Hall, Bridge of Allan, on Saturday 5 January 1963.

RUDY, Ed American columnist and radio reporter who joined the Beatles on their American tour in 1964. He later released some albums featuring his interviews with them.

RUSSEL, Ethan Photographer whose shots of the Beatles' recording were included in a limited-edition book issued with the *Let It Be* album.

RUSTIKS, The A group from Paignton, Devon, who made their performing debut at a hotel in Torquay. Initially an instrumental outfit because, they said, they were too nervous to sing, they were first called the Vibros and then the Fireballs, before becoming the Rustiks.

They entered a talent contest organized by Westward Television, which they won. The judges included Decca A&R man Dick Rowe and Brian Epstein. When Brian presented the group with their prize, he announced that he would sign them to NEMS Enterprises.

The group comprised Joe Romane (drums), Tony Mant (rhythm), Rob Tucker (lead) and Dave Gummer (bass). Epstein took them into the studio and produced their first single, 'What a Memory Can Do', which was released in September 1964, the same month they made their Liverpool debut. The following month they were included on the bill of the Beatles' concert tour.

As a group the Rustiks had no success and when their contract ran out Epstein didn't renew it.

RUTLES, The A Beatles parody, conceived by Eric Idle, which began life as a comedy sketch in a TV show and was enlarged into a full-scale project, *All You Need is Cash*, first broadcast in 1978. Neil Innes composed the music. The featured players were Eric Idle as Dirk McQuickly (the Paul figure), Neil Innes as Ron Nasty (the John figure), John Halsey as Barry Wom (the Ringo figure) and Rikki Fataar as Stig O'Hara (the George figure).

SANDON, Johnny Liverpool singer, real name Bill Beck. He began singing at the age of 12 and in 1958 entered Hughie Green's 'Opportunity Knocks' contest at the Adelphi Hotel. He was spotted by the Searchers, who asked him to join them, and their first gig together was at St Luke's Hall, Crosby. As Johnny Sandon & the Searchers he appeared with the Beatles on several Cavern bills: 1961 appearances were on Wednesday 26 July, Wednesday 6 September and Wednesday, 15 November; 1962 appearances were on Wednesday 3 January and Wednesday 14 February.

He joined the Remo Four in February 1962 and as the Remo Four with Johnny Sandon he also appeared on several Cavern bills with the Beatles during 1962, on Wednesday 28 March, Wednesday 17 October, Wednesday 28 November and Wednesday 6 December, and on Wednesday 30 January 1963. There were several other bills the group shared with the Beatles, including an appearance at La Scala, Runcorn, on Tuesday 11 December 1962. Billed simply as Johnny Sandon, he appeared at the Cavern with the Beatles on Tuesday 20 March 1962.

He recorded two singles with the Remo Four, both released in 1963: 'Lies', flipside 'On The Horizon' and 'Yes', flipside 'Magic Potion'. As a solo artist he continued recording for Pye and had three further singles released in 1964: 'Sixteen Tons', flipside 'The Blizzard', 'Donna Means Heartbreak', flipside 'Some Kinda Wonderful' and 'The Blizzard', flipside '(I'd Be) A Legend in My Time'.

As Johnny Sandon he continued performing on Merseyside until the 1970s, when he reverted to the name Bill Beck and appeared on the club circuit as a comedian. He was later to restart his singing career as Johnny Sandon.

SAPPHIRES A Mersey group who appeared on the Beatles' final Cavern appearance on Saturday 3 August 1963.

SAVILE, Jimmy Major British disc jockey who introduced the Beatles performing 'Please Please Me' on *Top of the Pops* with the words: 'Well, here it is, the big new record from Liverpool's Beatles. I sure hope it pleases somebody out there, 'cause it sure isn't me.' He was soon to change his tune and appeared as compère of their 1964 Christmas show at the Hammersmith Odeon, where he also took part in a variety sketch with them.

SCAFFOLD, The Satirical pop group from Liverpool, indicating the wide variety of musical styles which developed on Merseyside. Local teacher and poet Roger McGough teamed up with hairdresser Mike McGear (Paul McCartney's younger brother, who used the pseudonym as he didn't want to capitalize on his brother's fame) and post office engineer John Gorman in 1962 and the trio were featured regularly on the TV magazine show *Gazette*, appeared at the Edinburgh Festival and enjoyed a successful residency at the Establishment Club in London.

In 1965 the trio signed with NEMS and began a recording career, making their debut with '2 Day's Monday', a surreal effort, recorded by

George Martin. The Scaffold were to break away from NEMS soon after, with even Epstein agreeing that his organization was not the best one to manage such an offbeat group. They then found huge success with five hit records, including 'Thank U Very Much', 'Do You Remember?', 'Gin Gan Goolie' and their chart-topper 'Lily the Pink'.

The Scaffold were together for more than ten years, although there were some hiccups in their career. They merged with the Liverpool Scene to become Grimms in 1970. Then Mike went solo and recorded 'Woman', before teaming up with Roger for an album, *McGough & McGear*, recorded by Paul McCartney.

Mike then decided to revive Scaffold with the inclusion of Zoot Money on Keyboards, Ollie Halsall on guitar and the horn section from the Average White Band – which resulted in 1974 in the final Scaffold chart entry, 'Liverpool Lou', which was also produced by Paul.

After the group's final demise, Mike McGear found success as a photographer and remained on Merseyside, Roger became a renowned and best-selling poet after moving to London and John became a TV personality on children's shows and was one of the Four Bucketeers, who had a hit with 'The Bucket of Water Song' in 1980, before he moved on to settle in France.

SCHACHT, Alfred German publisher who suggested that producer Bert Kaempfert join him on a visit to see Tony Sheridan perform at the Top Ten Club in Hamburg. As the Beatles were backing Sheridan, they were engaged to join him on a recording session.

SCHWARTZ, Francie American girl who had a brief affair with Paul McCartney in 1968, causing the split with Jane Asher. She was to pen a book about the affair called *Body Count*.

SEARCHERS, The Arguably, the next best Liverpool band to the Beatles.

The group had its origins in the Liverpool district of Bootle (from where Billy J. Kramer originated), and John McNally and Mike Prendergast were in different skiffle groups in that area. They teamed up as a duo in 1959 and were then joined by Tony Jackson. They became a quartet when drummer Norman McGarry joined them, but his period with the band was brief and they were joined by Chris Crummy, a schoolfriend of Mike's.

When Buddy Holly saw *The Searchers*, he penned 'That'll Be The Day', which is a phrase John Wayne used throughout the film. When the group saw the John Ford western, they decided on adopting the name 'The Searchers' for themselves. Chris changed his name to Chris Curtis and Mike became Mike Pender.

They were joined by vocalist Bill Beck, using the name Johnny Sandon, and became known as Johnny Sandon & the Searchers, building a reputation which placed them at No. 5 in the first *Mersey Beat* poll.

Johnny left the group to team up with the Remo Four and the group decided to remain a quartet.

John McNally was to tell broadcaster Spencer Leigh:

One of my regrets is not having been managed by Brian Epstein. We'd have been a better band for it and he always wanted to sign us. He came to the Cavern to see us just before Johnny Sandon left and we knew that he was coming with a view to managing us. We took our gear down the steps and then went to the Grapes for a drink. That was fatal because Johnny got drunk. Tony got drunk and when we went on stage, it was chaos. Johnny pulled all the wires out. Everything went flat. We died a death and Epstein wasn't interested.

Oddly enough, in the first issue of the magazine *Fabulous*, Brian Epstein said: 'If I could retrace my footsteps and add just one more Liverpool group to my list of recording artists, I would choose to have the Searchers on my books.'

The Searchers appeared at the Cavern on a number of bills with the Beatles, including Saturday 23 December 1961 and on Wednesday 28 February and Wednesday 4 April 1962. The group played a season at the Star Club, Hamburg, where they first met Frank Allen, guitarist with Cliff Bennett & the Rebel Rousers.

Back in Liverpool, the group were managed by Les Ackerley, a local accountant, who also had ties with the Iron Door and the Odd Spot clubs. They signed with Pye Records, Tony Hatch became their recording manager and their debut disc, 'Sweets For My Sweet', hit the top of the charts. They appeared with the Beatles on the all-Merseyside edition of *Thank Your Lucky Stars*, promoting the song. John Lennon was to say that he considered it to be the best record to come out of Liverpool.

Brian Epstein gave them an original Lennon and McCartney number to record, 'Things We Said Today'. Management complications meant they couldn't record it and the Beatles used it as the flipside to 'A Hard Day's Night'. Their next hit, 'Sugar & Spice', was penned by their recording manager, under the name Fred Nightingale. The group's third hit, 'Needles And Pins', introduced a jangly guitar sound which inspired the American band the Byrds.

The Searchers had seven further British hits: 'Don't Throw Your Love Away', 'Someday We're Gonna Love Again', 'When You Walk In The Room', 'What Have They Done To The Rain', 'Goodbye My Love', 'He's Got No Love' and 'Take Me For What I'm Worth'. Their biggest hit in America was 'Love Potion No. 9', which was not issued as a single in Britain.

With success came musical differences. Chris, who chose most of the group's songs from his collection of American discs, felt that the group should direct themselves towards slower, melodic material, while Tony wanted more rip-roaring rock numbers. Tony left and was replaced by Frank Allen. In the mid-1960s Chris left the group and was replaced by John Blunt, who was replaced by Billy Adamson in 1969.

Although their run of hits ended in the late 1960s, they received critical acclaim for two albums on the Sire label, *The Searchers* in 1979 and *Play For Today* in 1980.

Mike left the band in 1985 to form Mike Pender's Searchers and he was replaced by vocalist Spencer James.

By 1995 there were three groups actively performing in Britain which contained members of the original band, all performing the early hits such as 'Sweets For My Sweets' and 'Needles And Pins'. Tony Jackson had his own outfit, John McNally continued to lead the Searchers, with Frank Allen and Mike Pender's Searchers were still active. The distinctive voice remembered from early hits, such as 'Sweets For My Sweet', is that of Tony Jackson.

SEGAL, Erich One of the four scriptwriters who contributed to the screenplay of *Yellow Submarine*, the others being Al Brodax, Jack Mendelsohn and Lee Mintoff. Segal became a best-selling author with his novel *Love Story*, which was a box-office smash when filmed with Ali McGraw and Ryan O'Neal.

SELLERS, Peter Film comedian and former member of the Goons, who were a Beatles favourite. He appeared on *The Music of Lennon and McCartney* performing 'A Hard Day's Night' in Shakespearian style, which provided him with a chart hit in December 1965. Sellers presented the Beatles with a Grammy Award on the set of *Help!* and appeared with Ringo Starr in *The Magic Christian*. He died in 1980.

SHADOWS, The Britain's leading instrumental group of the 1960s, who were also backing band to Britain's most popular singer, Cliff Richard.

They adopted the name the Shadows in 1958 and comprised Hank B. Marvin (guitar), Bruce Welch (rhythm), Jet Harris (bass) and Tony Meehan (drums).

The Shadows influenced groups all over Britain, but few in Liverpool, where a rough, aggressive rock 'n' roll scene had developed. There were a couple of instrumental groups such as the Remo Four, but even they performed a more powerful instrumental set.

Rory Storm & the Hurricanes challenged the Beatles to produce a Shadows spoof, and George Harrison obliged with 'Cry for a Shadow', which became the first original Beatles number to be recorded when they undertook a session with Bert Kaempfert in Hamburg.

There were various line-up changes before the group split up in 1968, but there were to be occasional revivals of the name with various original members joining Hank for concerts and record sessions.

SHANKAR, Ravi Indian musician, born in Benares on 7 April 1920.

Shankar first met George Harrison in 1966. George requested that Shankar teach him to play sitar and travelled to India with him to study for a six-week period. As a result of the trip, George became deeply involved in Indian musical influences, which led to his playing sitar on his track 'Within You, Without You' on the *Sgt Pepper* album. He also wrote the 'Inner Light' in 1968, recording it with Indian musicians, and the following year he began recording the *Radha Krsna Temple*.

Ravi was to comment: 'The Beatles scene and the sitar explosion brought me immediately into a position of immense popularity with the young people, and I now find myself adored like a movie star or a young singer.'

When the Apple Records label was launched, George signed up Ravi and issued his single 'Joi Bangla'/'Oh Bhaugowan' in August 1971. An album, *Raga*, was issued later that year and George appeared in a documentary about Shankar, also called *Raga*.

George was to produce further records by his sitar mentor and it was due to a suggestion by Ravi that he organized *The Concert for Bangladesh* on 1 August 1971. Ravi opened the concert by performing 'Bangla Dhum'.

The close friendship continued and in 1995 George and Olivia joined Ravi for a holiday in Italy. George also arranged for the publication of a limited edition of 2,000 copies of *Ravi Shankar: The Autobiography*, by Genesis Books in addition to assembling a four-CD set, *Ravi: In Celebration*, in honour of Ravi's seventy-fifth birthday.

George then went to India with Shankar in January 1996 to produce more material for a new album due to be released in August 1996.

SHANNON, Del American singer, real name Charles Westover, born in Grand Rapids, Michigan, on 30 December 1939.

It was while he was playing a Del Shannon record, probably 'Runaway', that John Lennon found a chord variation which he used in composing 'I'll Be Back', one of his numbers on the *A Hard Day's Night* album.

Shannon was very popular in Britain, where he had 13 chart singles between 1961 and 1965. His first million-seller was the number which inspired John Lennon, 'Runaway', which was No. 1 in the American charts for five weeks and No. 1 in the British charts for four. His other hits in 1961 and 1962 included 'Hats off to Larry', 'So Long Baby' and 'Hey Little Girl'.

It was soon after his new hit 'Little Town Flirt' in 1963 that he appeared on 'Swingin' Sound '63' at the Royal Albert Hall, London, on a bill with the Beatles on Thursday 18 April.

This was broadcast on the Light Programme of the BBC and there was a dispute about billing. The Beatles were obviously the most popular act in Britain at the time, with their new single, 'From Me to You', which they performed on the show, soon to top the charts.

However, this didn't prevent Shannon's manager insisting that his artist be given top billing. His demands that Shannon appear after the Beatles and close the show were accepted.

During the day Shannon, impressed by the Beatles, suggested to John that he could help expose their work in America if he covered one of their songs. Initially, John seemed pleased, but then he changed his mind.

Shannon went ahead anyway and speedily recorded their current hit, 'From Me to You', in Britain with a British backing band. The number was issued in the US on Bigtop Records with 'Two Silhouettes' as the flip and entered the *Cashbox* charts at No. 86 on 6 July. It reached only No. 77 in the charts, but was the first Lennon and McCartney number to become an American hit.

The *Cashbox* review read: 'Shannon, who recently did chart business with "Two Kinds of Teardrops", can have another big one in "From Me to You". It's an infectious, thump-a-twist version of the tune that's currently riding in the number one slot in England – via the Beatles stand (available here on VJ).'

He was undoubtedly one of the first Americans to appreciate their potential in the American market and when they were touring the States he dropped in to see them on 19 August 1965.

Shannon, also a songwriter and producer, penned the Peter and Gordon hit 'I Go to Pieces'.

When he appeared in the Beatles' home town on a bill with Johnny Tillotson, the two performed a duet of 'From Me to You' on stage at the Empire Theatre.

The singer was also booked to appear at Brian Epstein's Saville Theatre in London, on a bill with Chuck Berry. John and Ringo attended the show on 19 February 1967.

In 1987 Shannon made some recordings with George Harrison. Mysteriously, Shannon was found dead at his home in Santa Clarita, California, on 8 February 1990. He had died of gunshot wounds, said to have been self-inflicted.

SHAPIRO, Helen British singer, born in Bethnal Green, east London, on 28 September 1946. She reached No. 3 in the charts with 'Don't Treat Me Like a Child' in 1961 at the of 14 and swiftly followed with two chart-toppers, 'You Don't Know' and 'Walkin' Back to Happiness'.

Her success continued the following year with 'Tell Me What He Said' and 'Little Miss Lonely', and she was voted best British Female Singer and Best Newcomer.

She starred in the film *It's Trad, Dad!*, directed by Dick Lester, and the Beatles were booked to appear with her on her first headlining tour. She preferred travelling on the tour bus with the other acts and John and Paul offered her their song 'Misery', but her recording manager, Norrie Paramor, turned it down.

Helen was later to enjoy a career as a jazz singer and, for a short time, was managed by former Beatles publicist Tony Barrow.

SHENSON, Walter American film-maker, born in San Francisco, who moved to London in the 1950s to make a series of low-budget comedies such as *The Mouse That Roared* and *Mouse on the Moon*.

In 1963, when United Artists decided to make a three-picture deal with the Beatles, primarily in order to obtain soundtrack album rights, they approached the 45-year-old Shenson because of his reputation for working on a small budget. He was able to bring in their debut film, *A Hard Day's Night*, on a budget of only $200,000.

During negotiations, Shenson's accountant proposed a clause in the contract allowing for the Beatles' films to revert to Shenson's ownership after 15 years. As UA considered the Beatles would have only a short lifespan, they agreed.

After he'd produced *Help!* Shenson had difficulty persuading the group to make a third film with him. He'd had about 40 different scripts submitted, including *Shades of a Personality* and *A Talent for Loving*, but the Beatles were no longer interested in a film career.

They resolved their contractual obligation to United Artists by filming *Let It Be* and Shenson received a small percentage of the profits.

The producer remained in England, making movies such as *Thirty is a Dangerous Age, Cynthia, Don't Raise the Bridge, Lower the River* and *Digby, the Biggest Dog in the World*.

Together with his wife, Gerry, he decided to return to America in 1973 after spending 14 years in Britain.

The rights to *A Hard Day's Night* and *Help!* reverted to him after 15 years and he was able to re-record them with a stereophonic soundtrack.

In 1995 he produced a documentary, *The Making of 'A Hard Day's Night'*, hosted and with a narration by Phil Collins.

SHERIDAN, Tony Musician who became known to Liverpool bands as 'The Teacher' because of his influence on such groups as the Beatles. He was born Anthony Esmond Sheridan McGinty in Cheltenham in 1940.

Sheridan's first outfit was a skiffle group, the Saints, and he was to join a series of bands and appeared on the TV shows *Oh Boy!* and *Boy Meets Girl*. He was also one of the musicians on the bill of the 'Gene Vincent Show' at Liverpool Stadium on 3 May 1960.

Sheridan was at the 2 I's coffee bar in Soho when Bruno Koschmider came looking for musicians for his Hamburg club and was recruited by Iain Hines, in a group they called the Jets, to appear for a season in Hamburg. Sheridan was to remain in the city for a number of years.

Following the Kaiserkeller season, he took up a residency at the Top Ten Club, where the Beatles joined him on stage. When the Beatles returned to Hamburg for their own Top Ten residency in 1961, they were hired to back Sheridan for a three-day recording session at the Harburg Friedrich Ebert Halle from 22 May. They provided backing for Sheridan on 'My Bonnie Lies Over the Ocean', 'When the Saints Go Marching In' and 'Why?'.

They were credited as the Beat Brothers on the record and it was a name Sheridan used for the various musicians who backed him on stage and record.

Ringo Starr was also to join Sheridan's backing band for a period, from January 1962.

He continued appearing in Germany until 1967, when he left to entertain American troops in Vietnam. A British music paper reported he had been killed there and for several years many people believed that he was dead, but he'd returned to Germany in 1969.

In 1995 he teamed up with Howie Casey and Roy Young in Bournemouth to rehearse as the Beat Brothers. They attempted to enlist Pete Best as drummer, but he had his own band, so they engaged another drummer and set off for Hamburg

SHIMMY SHIMMY QUEENS, The In August 1961 Bob Wooler noticed two girls dancing in rhythm at Aintree Institute. He considered them so good he invited them to dance on stage and suggested they form an act. Bob coined the name the Shimmy Shimmy Queens for them and with specially styled dresses and the addition of another girl dancer they made their debut at Litherland Town Hall. They next appeared on a bill with the Beatles at Aintree Institute on 19 August and danced at other venues, such as Hambleton Hall.

The girls were Marie Williams, Joan Pratt and Maureen O'Donnell.

'Shimmy Shimmy' was a number the Beatles included in their repertoire in 1960, after the US hit the same year by Bobby Freeman.

SHIRELLES, The American girl vocal group, originally formed in 1957, who comprised Shirley Owens, Addi 'Micki' Harris, Doris Coley and Beverley Lee. They had several million-sellers, including 'Will You Still Love Me Tomorrow?' in 1960. The flipside of that release was 'Boys', a number which Pete Best sang with the Beatles and Ringo Starr performed with Rory Storm & the Hurricanes. When the Beatles came to record their debut album, Ringo provided lead vocal for 'Boys'. The group also recorded a second Shirelles hit on the album, 'Baby It's You'.

SHORT, Don Show-business correspondent for the *Daily Mirror* in the 1960s who provided extensive coverage of the Beatles and wrote the first national news story about them when he reported on the incident in which John Lennon attacked Liverpool disc jockey Bob Wooler at Paul's twenty-first birthday party.

SHOTTON, Pete One of John Lennon's closest friends. They attended the same primary school together and Shotton became a member of John's gang. They were at their closest during John's early years and also attended Quarry Bank School together. When John decided to form the Quarry Men, his first recruit was Pete – on washboard.

He was only with the group for a short time and when John attended art college Shotton became a police cadet.

John arranged for him to receive money to set him up in business. When this failed, John financed him again, enabling him to buy a supermarket. Following the formation of Apple Corps, John asked him to run the Apple Boutique, but it proved to be a failure.

Written in collaboration with Nicholas Schaffner, Shotton's biography, *John Lennon: In My Life*, was published in 1983.

Pete currently runs a chain of restaurants in Britain.

SILKIE, The Folk group, heavily influenced by Bob Dylan, who originally formed at Hull University and comprised Sylvia Tatler (vocals), Mike Ramsden (guitar/vocals), Ivor Aylesbury (guitar/vocals) and Kevin Cunningham (double bass).

Kevin, who was born in Liverpool, was to tell *Mersey Beat*: 'We began playing in Leeds but after leaving Hull University decided to move to Liverpool. The scene was unfortunately not ripe for a group of our kind, so we decided to write to Brian Epstein. Included with our letter was a demo disc and tapes and we were astounded to received a reply.'

Brian signed them to NEMS in July 1965 and appointed Alistair Taylor as their manager. The group made their debut on the Fontana label with 'Blood Red River', which failed to register. So Brian decided to raise their profile by associating them with the Beatles. He asked John and Paul whether they'd write a number specially for the group. They refused, but John said they could record his Dylanesque 'You've Got to Hide Your Love Away'.

John also produced the single for them on 9 September 1965. Paul McCartney played piano and George Harrison tambourine on the disc, which was released in October and reached No. 28 in the British charts. It was their only UK hit.

The record was also issued in the States, where it reached No. 10. While it was still hot in America, Alistair Taylor arranged for them to appear on nine American TV shows, including *The Ed Sullivan Show*, for which they'd receive fees of $9,000. The bad news was that they didn't have a work permit. However, Alistair discovered how he could obtain one by paying $1,000 for greasing someone's palm.

He asked Epstein for permission to spend the $1,000, but Epstein refused. This would have been more than compensated for by the $9,000 in fees for the shows, plus the move could well have established them in America and pushed the record even further up the charts.

The Silkie were waiting at the airport, ready to fly to New York, when they were told that Epstein's refusal to allow the deal to go through meant their trip had to be cancelled. They never forgave him and they broke up soon afterwards.

SISSONS, Peter Classmate of Paul McCartney at Liverpool Institute. The two used to travel to school together by bus. Peter was to tell writer Chris Salewicz: 'Paul stood out as a bright lad, but a cheeky lad. It was much more than just the proverbial Liverpool wit, though. I mean, George Harrison had the wit, but not the brain. George was in one of the lower classes when I was head boy – I remember George giving cheek and my hitting him over the head with a rolled-up newspaper, which the prefects were allowed to do to the cheeky lads in the yard.' Sissons became a prominent newscaster, presenter and interviewer at ITV, and also became the host of the BBC TV programme *Any Questions* for a time.

SMITH, Alan Merseyside journalist who worked for the *New Musical Express* in London and interviewed the Beatles on several occasions. He wrote for *Mersey Beat* under the pseudonym George Jones.

SMITH, George John's uncle and husband to Mimi. He died of a haemorrhage in 1953.

SMITH, John Promoter who booked the Beatles for several concerts in the south of England during 1963, beginning with a show in Oxford on Saturday 16 February. His other Beatles bookings took place in April, June and September. He died in 1988.

SMITH, Mary Elizabeth John Lennon's aunt, affectionately known as Aunt Mimi. She was one of Julia Lennon's four sisters. She married dairy farmer George Smith, but the couple had no children of their own and Mimi insisted that Julia let her take care of John, as she believed that Julia was neglecting him. Julia agreed and John went to live with his aunt from the age of five.

She took care of him, although she was very strict, particularly when her husband died and she had to raise John on her own. Although she bought him his first guitar, she told him: 'The guitar's all right as a hobby, but you'll never make a living out of it.'

When the Beatles became successful, John bought her a bungalow in Poole, Dorset, where she remained for the rest of her life.

She died at the age of 88 on 6 December 1991 and her funeral was attended by Yoko, Sean and Cynthia, while Paul, George and Ringo sent bouquets.

SMITH, Mavis Former dancer who worked with Derek Taylor in the Apple press office. She was married to *New Musical Express* journalist Alan Smith.

SMITH, Mike Decca A&R manager who was the actual person who made the decision not to sign the Beatles to the label, although writers continue to lay the blame at the door of his boss, Dick Rowe.

Due to Brian Epstein's influence as a record store manager, Decca Records felt that someone had to take an interest when he was pressing them to sign the Beatles. As a result Smith went to see them perform live on stage at the Cavern in Liverpool on 13 December 1962 and was impressed enough to book them for a recording audition at Decca's West Hampstead studios on New Year's Day.

He was disappointed with the session, at which he recorded them performing 15 numbers, and when he presented the tape at a meeting in

Decca House was told that they sounded like the Shadows. However, he was given the option of signing one of the two groups he'd recorded that day. He opted for the second group, Brian Poole & the Tremeloes, because he considered they were a better band in the studio.

When he met the Beatles at a later date they gave him a two-fingered salute!

In hindsight, he claimed he should have gone ahead with his initial instinct when he saw them perform live and signed them. Actually, immediately following the session he gave them the impression that they'd passed the audition. He even sang their praises to such an extent that Tony Barrow was to write in his review column in the *Liverpool Echo*: 'Decca disc producer Mike Smith tells me he thinks the Beatles are great. He has a continuous tape of their audition performance, which runs for over 30 minutes, and he is convinced that his label will be able to put the Beatles to good use.'

On 7 February 1964 he travelled to Liverpool to watch the Pete Best Four perform at the Downbeat Club in Victoria Street and signed them. However, their Decca release 'I'm Gonna Knock on Your Door' was unsuccessful.

Smith himself did have a number of hits with Brian Poole & the Tremeloes and also with other artists, such as the Bachelors, Billy Fury and Georgie Fame. He also recorded the Applejacks' 'Like Dreamers Do', a Lennon and McCartney number.

Smith eventually left Decca in 1979 to join GTO Records as General Manager.

SMITH, Norman Born in Edmonton, north London, Norman began working in Abbey Road Studios as a tape engineer in 1959. He was brought in on the Beatles' first recording session by George Martin and was their recording engineer up to the *Rubber Soul* sessions in December 1965. He was later to record in his own right under the name Hurricane Smith and had a chart topper in the States with 'Oh Babe, What Would You Say?'.

SOMERVILLE, Brian At the age of 32, Somerville became publicist for the Beatles for a ten-month period. He had spent 14 years in the Royal Navy, where he rose to the rank of lieutenant commander. On leaving the navy he joined the Theo Cowan publicity agency and worked with such artists as Peter Sellers and Judy Garland, and later worked in the publicity department of the *Daily Express*. He first met Brian Epstein in a Liverpool pub. Back in London Brian offered him the job as the Beatles' press officer for a fee of £100 per month. Somerville agreed, on condition that he could own his own limited company rather than be a member of NEMS staff.

Nicknamed 'Old Baldie' by the group, he seemed to get on well with John, Paul and Ringo, but not with George. The matter came to a head in Paris, after Somerville had set up an interview with an important journalist. George told him the journalist would have to wait an extra hour before he'd give an interview. When Somerville tried to reason with him, George threw orange juice over him and Somerville clipped him on the ear!

Brian Epstein began to place increasing pressure on Somerville, criticizing him, haggling over his expenses and berating him in public. When his term of ten months had expired, Epstein refused to renew the contract unless Somerville became a member of staff, which he refused to do. Somerville believed that Epstein wanted him out in order to replace him with Derek Taylor.

He then took an advertisement in *The Times*: 'Ex-Beatles Publicity Manager looking for a job'. It brought him a host of acts, including the Who, the Kinks and Manfred Mann.

Somerville continued to resent the manner in which he was treated by Brian and told Epstein biographer Ray Coleman: 'He was very bad at arranging financial matters. He allowed his heart to rule his head far too many times in too many areas. He wasn't honest. He didn't have integrity. I couldn't trust his word.'

Eventually, Somerville tired of public relations and became a stipendiary magistrate in London.

SOUNDS INCORPORATED   A six-piece instrumental outfit, formed in Kent in 1961. They comprised Alan Holmes (flute/sax), Griff West (sax), John St John (guitar), Barrie Cameron (keyboards), Wes Hunter (bass guitar) and Tony Newman (drums).

Being an instrumental band, they found themselves in demand for backing visiting American artists on the popular package of shows of the time, and they provided backing for Little Richard and Gene Vincent.

The group originally met the Beatles at the Star Club, Hamburg in April 1962. Later that year on Sunday 28 October, they appeared on a bill with the Beatles, backing Little Richard at the Empire, Liverpool.

They became one of the eight acts that Brian Epstein had on his books when he signed them to an agency and management contract on 24 January 1964, and they were the first group from the south of England to join NEMS Enterprises.

Epstein was able to place them on the numerous package shows with his artists and they were to appear regularly with the Beatles. Sounds Incorporated were one of the acts booked to appear on *Around The Beatles*, the TV special screened on 6 May 1964 and in October of that year they also appeared with the Beatles on the all-British edition of the NBC television show, *Hullaballo*, produced by Jack Good in London.

They were also featured on the Beatles' autumn tour of Britain in October and November 1964 and 'The Beatles Christmas Show' at the Odeon, Hammersmith.

Sounds Incorporated also travelled to America for the Beatles' autumn tour of the US in 1965, appearing with them at Shea Stadium on Sunday 15 August, which was filmed as a TV special.

In March, 1967 they performed on the 'Good Morning, Good

Morning' track during the 'Sgt Pepper' sessions.

The group, who abbreviated their name to Sounds Inc in 1967, began their act with their signature tune, 'The William Tell Overture', which they recorded. Other record releases included 'The Spartans', 'Spanish Harlem' and 'Little Red Book'.

When the group disbanded, a number of them became session men. Tony Newman was to join the Jeff Beck Group and backed David Bowie in the 1970s before forming Boxer in 1975.

SOUTHERN, Terry American author. Ringo Starr featured in two film adaptations of his books, *Candy* and *The Magic Christian*. He is one of the figures appearing on the *Sgt Pepper* tableau.

SPECTOR, Phil Noted American record producer, born Philip Harvey Spector in New York on 26 December 1940.

He formed his first group, the Sleepwalkers, while still at high school and at the close of 1958 formed an outfit called the Teddy Bears. He composed the song 'To Know Him is to Love Him', which took the Teddy Bears to No. 1 in the charts.

Spector then became a record producer and formed his own record label, Phille. He recorded acts such as the Crystals, Darlene Love and Bob B Soxx & the Bluejeans, producing a string of hits, including 'He's a Rebel', 'And Then He Kissed Me' and 'Be My Baby'.

Spector was invited to join the Beatles on their first flight to New York in February 1964 and he also produced a record, 'I Love Ringo', by Bonnie Jo Mason, a pseudonym for Cher.

His major involvement with the Beatles came when he was brought in to handle the mass of tapes George Martin and Glyn Johns had been working on for the projected 'Get Back' album.

Spector had initially produced the Plastic Ono Band's 'Instant Karma' single and was given the opportunity of working on the 'Get Back' tapes, which he finally produced as *Let It Be*.

Paul McCartney in particular was horrified by what Spector had done with their work, especially his overproduction on Paul's song 'The Long and Winding Road'.

Apple were to release Spector's famous *Christmas Album*, which he originally produced in 1963, and he was later to produce some further records by John Lennon, most notably the *Rock 'n' Roll* album.

SPENCER, Graham Young Liverpool photographer commissioned to take photographs of the Beatles and other local groups for *Mersey Beat*. His studio was situated in Queen's Drive and he even took to managing groups. He died in 1982.

SPENCER, Terence A photographer, formerly a Second World War Spitfire pilot, who spent four months on the road with the Beatles in 1963.

At the time Spencer was a war photographer who had returned to

Britain after working in various trouble spots around the world for *Life* magazine. He noted: 'Everyone was talking about this great new group which was setting new trends, not only musically but culturally – at least as far as the young were concerned. Yet they were virtually unknown outside the UK.'

After seeing them perform on the *Royal Variety Show*, Spencer travelled to the Winter Gardens, Bournemouth, on 16 November, found where they were staying, the Branksome Towers Hotel, introduced himself and spent the next few months travelling with them, taking photographs on stage and off.

Only a few of his photographs were printed in a story in *Life* magazine to coincide with their first tour, in 1964.

In 1992 Spencer discovered the photographs in his attic and put them up for auction in order to buy his daughter a flat. The 5,000 black-and-white pictures were bought by Bloomsbury Books plc for £82,000 in the July 1993 auction at Sotheby's and the company published a portfolio in book form, *It was Thirty Years Ago*, on 27 October 1994. They also utilized pictures from the vast collection as postcards and posters.

SPIDERMEN, The Mersey group formed in 1961 comprising Norman Dunn (vocals), Ray Binnion (drums), Glyn Jones (rhythm), Pete Malloy (lead) and Phil Roberts (bass). Norman left due to ill-health in 1962 and was replaced by Vic Wright, and the group became Vic & the Spidermen.

They appeared on five Cavern bills with the Beatles in 1962: on Friday 15 June, Wednesday 4 July, Wednesday 18 July, Wednesday 12 September and Wednesday 26 September.

SPIEGL, Fritz Musician based in Liverpool who recorded an album of Beatles music in classical style called *Eine Kleine Beatlemusik*. He also appeared on *The Music of Lennon and McCartney* TV special, performing some of the numbers with the Royal Philharmonic Orchestra.

SPINETTI, Victor Actor, director, writer and producer, born in Cwm, near Ebbw Vale, Gwent, who was the only person, apart from the Beatles themselves, to appear in all three of their 'acting' films: *A Hard Day's Night*, *Help!* and *Magical Mystery Tour*.

Spinetti's association with the Beatles began when 'The lads saw the production I was in, *Oh! What a Lovely War*, and they said, "We want you in our film!" and that was that.'

In *A Hard Day's Night* he played the neurotic director of the television show they were in. He next appeared as Professor Foot in *Help!*. The Beatles then asked him to appear in *Magical Mystery Tour*.

He commented: 'They wanted me to play the courier on the bus in *Magical Mystery Tour* so I would be travelling with them all the time. But I couldn't, because I was doing a show in London, so I could only join them from London and go back there to do the show. Otherwise I would have loved to have gone on that whole trip, it would have been marvellous.

'I had to write my own script. I've got a letter from John somewhere saying, "We want you to be in this," and I said, "What can I do?" and he said, "Well, write it yourself. You know, just do your own bits." I said, "OK," so I did the drill-sergeant thing that I had done in *Oh! What a Lovely War*, where I was portraying the kind of establishment figure who was telling them to get their hair cut, pull themselves together and behave like responsible people. In other words, be killers!'

He dropped in to see the Beatles recording in November 1967, ostensibly to discuss with John the new play they were doing together. The group were recording their fifth fan club record and Victor joined them during a rendition of 'Christmas Time (is Here Again)'.

Victor produced and co-authored a special stage version of John's two books. He said: 'A girl from Detroit called Adrienne Kennedy who wrote a play which was put on at the Royal Court Theatre came to see me when I was in London doing *The Odd Couple* and asked me to be in it. And I read it and said, "Well, you know, if you are going to put this on stage you will have to do more than you have done." And I told her what I felt about the person growing up and his own reactions to family situations, schools etc. Because it's very autobiographical, the whole thing.

'And so she said, "Come and tell Ken Tynan," and I told Ken Tynan and he said, "Come and tell Laurence Olivier," and I told Laurence Olivier, and he said, "My dear baby, direct it for us!" So then I said to Adrienne, "Have you had permission from John to do this, turn it into a play?" and she said "No!"

'I said, "But you have to!" So I rang him up and asked him, and he said, "Yeah, OK. You got permission." And then he came to a rehearsal and became interested, and then we worked together on the script.

'At the rehearsal he in fact cried and said, "These were all the things that I was thinking about when I was 16,"· and he got involved in it and eventually we spent quite a bit of time together working on the script, writing out those little extra things that one needed for it.'

To promote the play, Victor and John appeared on the BBC 2 programme *Release* and discussed it. A book of the play, credited to Victor, Adrienne and John, was published in 1968. The production originally appeared in a single performance in December 1967, then opened as a one-act play at the Old Vic on 18 June 1968.

Victor was also to appear in a cameo role in Paul's video of 'London Town'.

STARKEY, Jason Second son of Ringo Starr and Maureen Cox. Jason was born at Queen Charlotte's Hospital in London on 19 August 1967 and it was his mother who chose his name.

With less of a public profile than his older brother, Zak, he became a road manager for a time and then took up drums in the footsteps of his father and brother, although he was not as successful as either. He was once to comment: 'Being Ringo's son is the biggest drag in my life. It's a total pain.'

In 1987 he was caught stealing a car stereo and fined £125 and in 1989 appeared in court twice on drugs charges.

In 1995 he was playing drums in a pub band.

STARKEY, Lee Parkin Only daughter of Ringo Starr and Maureen Cox. Her middle name, Parkin, was the reintroduction of a former Starkey family name. Lee was born at Queen Charlotte's Hospital, London, on 11 November 1970.

After leaving King Alfred's School in Hampstead at the age of 16 with no qualifications, she worked for a time at Tower Records and enrolled briefly in drama school. She didn't like drama school and left before completing the course, next entering a make-up school. Although she received her diploma she said she didn't like that profession either.

She was to comment: 'I want to make my mark. I don't want to make a point of saying who my dad is. I really don't know much about the Beatles. They had almost split up when I was born.'

Lee next became co-owner with Christian Paris of a boutique, Planet Alice, in Portobello Road, which specialized in 1960s clothes.

Her mother married Isaac Tigrett and moved to Los Angeles, prompting Lee to ask her partner if they could relocate their boutique there, which they did in 1991, when Lee was 20.

At the official opening of the store, situated on Melrose Avenue, Ringo and Barbara and Maureen and Isaac were in attendance.

Lee moved into a house in Beverly Hills which she shared with her brothers, Jason and Zak, but her boutique closed within a year and she moved back to Britain, into the flat next to Warwick Avenue tube station where Ringo used to live in the 1970s.

During 1994 she spent a great deal of time caring for her mother, who died of leukaemia in December. In August 1995, Lee was rushed to a London clinic for an emergency operation to drain fluid from her brain. Ringo cancelled his All Starr Band tour of America to be at her bedside. Within three weeks she was undergoing a second operation at Brigham Women's Hospital, Boston, this time for a tumour. She was then given radiation treatment.

Lee moved into her stepfather's house in Mulholland Drive in the San Fernando Valley to recuperate. Her maternal grandmother, Flo Cox, also lived there, together with Lee's half-sister, Augusta.

She returned to Britain in December 1995 to spend Christmas with the family.

STARKEY, Richard Liverpool dockworker who later became a baker. While working in the bakery he met Elsie Gleave and the two were married in 1936. Their son, Richard, was born in 1940.

When the child was three years old, Starkey senior left the family home and the couple were soon divorced. He remarried and moved to another town, where he became a window-cleaner.

When the *Daily Express* newspaper tracked him down in 1980 he was to comment about his son: 'He's done well, the lad, and good luck to him, but he owes me nothing.'

STARKEY, Zak   Oldest son of Richard and Maureen Cox, born on 13 September 1965 at Queen Charlotte's Hospital, London.

Since their first child was a boy, Ringo had the choice of name and decided on Zak, because it was what he wished he'd been called as a youth. He commented: 'It's a nice strong name and it can't be shortened – that was something I didn't want at all.'

Although Ringo told the press, 'I won't let Zak be a drummer,' he bought him a drum kit for his ninth birthday. He gave him only one lesson, when he was ten, telling him that as he'd been self-taught, he suggested Zak simply listen to records and play along with them. However, he did hire a piano teacher for his son.

Zak was five years old when the Beatles split, but being the son of a famous father caused problems and he had a serious drinking problem by the age of 15. For a time Ringo kicked him out of the family home, Tittenhurst Park.

The estrangement deepened when Ringo and Maureen divorced, as Zak blamed Ringo for the break-up of the marriage.

He was married himself on 24 January 1985, at the age of 19, to 25-year-old Sarah Menikides. The wedding was kept secret, even from his parents.

When Zak and Sarah had a baby daughter, Tatia Jayne, the father and son relationship became close once again when Ringo saw his granddaughter for the first time. Zak said: 'The look of joy on his face is one I'll never forget.'

Zak had a degree of success in his own right as a drummer, appearing in bands such as the Next, Nightfly and Ice, spending ten years as a session musician and also playing with artists such as Roger Daltrey and Bobby Womack. His major influence was Keith Moon, who bought him a drum kit for his birthday and encouraged him to play. Zak commented: 'My old man's a good timekeeper but I've never thought of him as a great drummer.'

He joined his father in the All Starr Band on world tours in 1992 and 1995 and for a time settled in Los Angeles, sharing a house with his brother and sister.

After his mother contracted leukaemia, he donated some of his bone marrow to save her, but she died as a result of the operation in December 1994.

In 1995 he moved back to England with his wife and daughter and in September 1995 formed a band called Face with Ronnie Thomas, Gary Nuttall and Danny Burton.

STARR, Freddie Freddie, real name Freddie Fowell, made his first public appearance in 1950 at the Huyton UDC Club and won first prize in a talent contest, imitating Al Jolson and Ruby Murray, at the Scala Theatre, Southport, in 1952. He joined the Hilda Fallon Road Show, a song and comedy act, in 1954 and remained with them for four years.

In 1958 he teamed up with Johnny Fallon in an act miming at local clubs and during the year appeared as a young teddy boy in the film *Violent Playground*.

In January 1961 he became second vocalist with Howie Casey & the Seniors – the other singer was Derry Wilkie. The band was the first from Liverpool to appear in Hamburg when they were booked for a season at the Kaiserkeller.

They auditioned for Fontana, who suggested that they record some twist numbers, and the group were to record an entire album in one afternoon. Their debut single, 'Double Twist', was penned by Freddie and Derry Wilkie, and Freddie penned the title track of their album *Twist at the Top*. Because they were let down financially by promoters, Derry Wilkie left the band and they broke up soon after, in the summer of 1962.

Freddie considered going to Germany and intended to simply be known by his first name. When he found that there was a German singer called Freddie, he thought of Ringo Starr and then changed his name to Freddie Starr. He led a group called the Ventures until November 1962, when he replaced Gus Travis as lead singer with the Midnighters, a group he led until April 1964.

They appeared twice with the Beatles at the Cavern in 1963: on Wednesday 23 January and Tuesday 19 February.

The group also recorded three singles with Joe Meek, although they all failed to make any impact in the charts. Freddie was disenchanted with the records, as they weren't the type of material which suited him, and he called them 'commercial rubbish'. The three Decca releases were 'Who Told You?', 'Baby Blue' and 'Never Cry on Someone's Shoulder'.

Freddie was due to appear in the Lionel Bart/Alun Owen musical *Maggie May*, but it fell through and he teamed up with the Delmonts, in August 1965, mainly to appear in cabaret.

He then became a solo act, performing impressions and comedy. An appearance on *Sunday Night at the London Palladium* established him as a leading comedian and he has steered himself through a controversial but successful career as a comic ever since.

Freddie did, however, finally have a hit record as a singer with 'It's You', which reached No. 9 in the British charts in February 1974.

STATESMEN, The Mersey group who appeared with the Beatles at the Cavern on Wednesday 11 July and Wednesday 5 December 1962.

STEELE, Tommy Pioneer of British rock 'n' roll. Tommy appeared on the bill with the Beatles at the *Royal Variety Show* on 4 November 1963. His hobby is sculpture and his statue of Eleanor Rigby, which he donated to Liverpool, sits on a bench in Stanley Street.

STEVE MILLER BAND Band led by American singer/guitarist Steve Miller, whom Paul originally met at the Monterey Festival in 1967. Inspired by *Sgt Pepper*, Miller decided to bring his band to London and record a concept album, *Children of the Future*. Glyn Johns, who was working as an engineer on the Beatles' 'Get Back' project, was producing the album for Miller. On Friday 9 May 1969 the Beatles had been recording at Olympic Sound Studios. There was tension at the time, as John, George and Ringo were about to sign a management contract with Allen Klein. Paul decided to stay behind in the studio and that evening he played drums, bass guitar and provided backing vocals for Miller on the track 'My Dark Hour'. When the single was issued in America in June, Paul used his old pseudonym Paul Ramon.

STERNER, George German waiter who acted as an interpreter for Bruno Koschmider. He also travelled with the Beatles on their first trip to Hamburg.

STEVENS, Margo Leader of a determined group of Beatles fans who called themselves the Apple Scruffs. They launched their own magazine in 1970 and members of the group once broke into Paul McCartney's Cavendish Road house.

STIGWOOD, Robert Australian-born impresario who based himself in Britain at the beginning of the 1960s, initially managing artists such as John Leyton and Mike Sarne.

Together with accountant David Shaw, Stigwood formed the Robert Stigwood Organization. Brian Epstein had several meetings with him and eventually bought the Robert Stigwood Organization, making Stigwood joint managing director of NEMS.

Strangely, despite having rejected an offer of $20 million for his organization two years previously, Brian offered Stigwood and Shaw a 51 per cent controlling interest in NEMS for only £500,000. Acts which Stigwood brought into NEMS included Cream, Jimi Hendrix, the Moody Blues and the Who.

When the Bee Gees approached NEMS, they were referred to Stigwood, who was now responsible for signing all new acts to the company.

After Brian's death, the Beatles made it plain that they did not wish to have any involvement with Stigwood, so Clive Epstein suggested that Stigwood should leave NEMS, taking with him his own artists and a substantial severance payout. Stigwood also took the Bee Gees, who proved to be his biggest success.

He became a film and theatre impresario, enjoying tremendous success with *Saturday Night Fever* and *Grease*. His flops included a film version of *Sgt Pepper's Lonely Hearts Club Band* in 1978.

STRACH, Dr Walter Czech financial expert who was appointed by Brian Epstein to handle the Beatles' affairs. He suggested that they buy houses in Weybridge – advice which John and Ringo took. The group called him Uncle Walter.

STRANGERS, The A much underrated Mersey band. Very popular locally, they were featured on a front cover of *Mersey Beat* and placed in both *Mersey Beat* popularity polls: No. 8 in 1962 and No. 12 in 1963.

The Strangers performed at most leading Liverpool venues and made their first appearance with the Beatles on Thursday 27 July 1961 at St John's Hall, Bootle (called the Jive Hive), and the following evening appeared on a special Aintree Institute gig, which was one of the 'Battle of the Groups' promotions in which two Mersey bands competed against each other. Bob Wooler took out an advertisement in the Liverpool Echo announcing:

> Beatles vs. Strangers
> Referee: Bob Wooler
> Never before have these two great groups appeared together.

The Strangers were to perform on various other bills with the Beatles and during 1961 they appeared with them at the Cavern on Wednesday 30 August, Wednesday 25 October, Wednesday 1 November, Wednesday 6 December and Wednesday 20 December. In 1962 they appeared with them on Friday, 12 January, Saturday 14 July and Wednesday 14 December, and during the two-week Star Club season in late December.

After the group disbanded, lead vocalist Joe Fagin embarked on a solo career and reached No. 3 in the British charts in February 1984 with 'That's Living Alright'.

STRATTON-SMITH, Tony When Ernest Hecht, head of Souvenir Press, approached Brian Epstein for rights to his autobiography, Brian had to seek a ghost writer. Hecht suggested Tony Stratton-Smith, former *Daily Express* journalist turned author.

Hecht paid for Stratton-Smith to fly to Amsterdam to meet Epstein at his Penthouse Suite in the Amsterdam Hilton. They went out to dinner and Epstein asked him when he could start work on the book. 'Stratters' told him that he was currently working on a book called *The Rebel Nun*, but would be able to start on Brian's biography in six months' time.

Epstein wouldn't accept this and phoned Hecht to tell him so. He eventually paid Derek Taylor to write *A Cellarful of Noise* for him.

Stratton-Smith was impressed with Epstein's lifestyle and decided to become a manager himself, beginning in 1966 with Paddy, Klaus & Gibson. As fate would have it, the Beatles recommended them to Epstein, who talked Stratton-Smith into transferring them to NEMS.

The next signing was another Liverpudlian – singer Beryl Marsden. She was so undisciplined that Stratton-Smith had severe problems with her which led to his temporary hospitalization.

He then signed up another Liverpool outfit, the Koobas, who, like Beryl, had toured with the Beatles. Another act he signed at the time was Creation.

The Koobas almost brought him to financial ruin. He said: 'I think that was the only band I ever spoiled and I regretted it. Their career became more important to me than was healthy. I was putting far too much time into this one band in an attempt to crack them and I think you lose your objectivity if you do that.'

Their failure caused him to return to journalism, but within months he had signed Nice. He then began to enjoy success and achieved his ambition of becoming a millionaire manager with a lavish lifestyle, also forming Charisma Records and establishing the careers of bands such as Genesis and Lindisfarne.

Stratton-Smith sold Charisma in 1986, but sadly died of cancer in March 1987, at the age of 53.

SULLIVAN, Ed Host of one of America's leading entertainment shows, *The Ed Sullivan Show*, which was a major factor in establishing the Beatles in America.

The booking came about virtually by accident. Sullivan happened to be at London's main airport when the Beatles returned from a short Swedish tour on 31 October 1963. He said: 'My wife, Sylvia, and I were in London, at Heathrow Airport. There was the biggest crowd I'd ever seen in my life! I asked someone what was going on, and he said, "The Beatles." "Who the hell are the Beatles?" I asked. But I went back to my hotel, got the name of their manager, and arranged for them to do three shows.'

When the Beatles appeared on 9 February 1964, the show drew the biggest audience for an entertainment programme in the history of television. An estimated 73 million viewers saw the performance and it was reported that the crime rate among teenagers throughout America dropped to virtually zero that night.

Sullivan opened the show with the words: 'Now, yesterday and today, our theatre's been jammed with newspapermen and hundreds of photographers from all over the nation, and these veterans agree with me that the city never has witnessed the excitement stirred by these youngsters from Liverpool, who call themselves the Beatles. Now, tonight, you'll twice be entertained by them – right now and in the second half of the show.' Sullivan also read out a telegramme from Elvis Presley (actually sent by Colonel Tom Parker using Elvis's name).

They next appeared on a Sullivan show later that month, on 16 February, telecast from the Deauville Hotel, Miami Beach, Florida. Their third appearance, on 23 February, had been pre-recorded before they'd returned home to Britain.

The Ed Sullivan Show finally went off the air on 6 June 1971 and Sullivan died on 13 October 1974.

SUTCLIFFE, Martha (Millie) Scots-born Martha Cronin, more commonly known as Millie, entered a Franciscan convent, intending to become a missionary, but ill-health prevented her taking her final vows and she began training as a school teacher.

She met Charles Fergusson Sutcliffe, a married man with a daughter and three sons. They fell in love, he divorced and the couple were married.

In 1940, at the age of 33, she gave birth to her first child, Stuart, followed by daughter Joyce in 1942. Their second daughter, Pauline, was born in 1944 in Huyton, Merseyside, after the family had moved south from Edinburgh.

Charles joined the Merchant Navy in 1947 and was away at sea for long periods of time.

Although the Sutcliffes changed their address several times, Huyton wasn't technically within Liverpool's city limits at the time Stuart enrolled at Liverpool College of Art and he was therefore unable to obtain a grant when he began to take the National Diploma in Design Course in 1956, at the age of 16.

His father wasn't too pleased with Stuart's choice, having wanted him to become a doctor. However, Millie was completely supportive as Stuart was the apple of her eye.

She agreed to his leaving home to move into student flats, although she continued to fuss over him, visiting him regularly, cleaning his clothes, checking that he ate regularly and supporting him financially as best she could.

Millie and her daughters moved into Liverpool, settling at 37 Aigburth Drive. At the time she worked as a teacher at a local school for the blind. Although she had given her tacit approval when Stuart joined his friend John Lennon's group, Millie was so appreciative of her son's talent as an artist that she was bitterly disappointed when he set off for Hamburg as a member of the Beatles.

Despite Stuart professing to earn good money in Hamburg, Millie still had to involve herself in a degree of financial support for her son, ensuring that the hire purchase payments on his guitar were paid regularly to Frank Hessy.

She also received a call from Stuart's former flatmate in Gambier Terrace, Rod Murray, claiming that he had to move out of the flat but owed money on the rent, some of which was the responsibility of Stuart and John. He mentioned that if Millie could pay off some of Stuart's debt she could collect his personal possessions from the flat.

Millie did so, hiring a van to collect the belongings, which included Stuart's camp bed. In later years she was to point out the silliness of some books which suggested that Stuart had slept in a coffin while at Gambier Terrace.

Among the other items she packed away in the van was a chest of drawers which contained John's clothes. She stored these for a time in Aigburth Drive, until her husband arrived home from one of his trips and threw them out.

Stuart was an inveterate letter writer and kept his mother in touch with his activities in Hamburg, although judiciously omitting some of the wilder antics. He also contacted her regularly by telephone.

Time passed and he left the Beatles to enrol in the Staatliche Hochschule, Hamburg's equivalent of the Liverpool College of Art. Millie was very proud. Then something occurred which will perhaps always remain a mystery: the reason behind Stuart's premature death.

Millie began to tell her friends that she was very concerned about Stuart, who had been suffering from intense headaches and blackouts. She said that he'd fallen down the stairs leading from his attic flat in Astrid Kirchherr's house and damaged his head. The headaches began to occur soon after.

Years later, Allan Williams attributed the death to a head injury Stuart allegedly suffered in a battle with Teddy Boys at Litherland Town Hall. Another report stated that he was involved in a fight at Lathom Hall, yet the witnesses to this incident, Pete Best and Neil Aspinall, denied that Stuart was physically hurt. American writer Albert Goldman even said the injury arose when John Lennon kicked Stuart in the head in Germany.

Millie became distraught at her son's suffering and she tried to talk him into attending Sefton General Hospital when he was in Liverpool. Stubbornly he refused, and he also insulted a consultant she brought to the house.

When Stuart collapsed on 10 April 1962, Astrid sent Millie a telegram saying that he was very ill. He died the same afternoon and she sent a second telegram to say that he was dead. Millie opened the second telegram first.

The Beatles were due to appear at the Star Club, and Brian Epstein was able to take Millie to the airport and sit with her during the flight to Germany. She identified the body and signed all the necessary forms, arranging for the corpse to be sent back to Liverpool. She also agreed to aid medical research by allowing the pathologist to remove the brain.

For the rest of her life Millie dedicated herself to promoting Stuart's work and arranged a posthumous exhibition at the Walker Art Gallery in Liverpool. She was always surprised that not a single member of the Beatles ever attended an exhibition or offered to help her in any way in bringing Stuart's art to a wider audience, even though, for example, John and Paul had financed and promoted an exhibition by Jonathan Hague, another ex-student of Liverpool College of Art, and Paul, who was to collect works of art, never bought any of Stuart's pieces.

However, on Sunday 8 November 1964 my wife and I visited the Beatles backstage at the Empire Theatre, Liverpool, and suggested to John that we all make a surprise visit to Millie. Together with Pete Shotton and his wife, we went to Aigburth Drive. Millie was thrilled. She gave John a clipping of one of their first-ever write-ups, headed: ' "Rock" group at Neston Institute' and a book, *How to Draw Horses*, which John had won as a prize at school many years before and had lent to Stuart.

She then took us round the rooms where Stuart's paintings were displayed and invited John and me to take our pick of any work we wished. John selected a blue abstract oil painting and said: 'This will take pride of place in my living room.'

Despite ill-health, Millie persevered in her dedication and, when her daughters had left the parental nest, went to live in Sevenoaks, Kent.

She would have been delighted to know that Stuart finally achieved the recognition she had always sought for him, but she died before he became posthumously famous – with a Granada TV film, *Midnight Angel*, in 1990, international exhibitions of his work and a major feature film of his brief life, *Backbeat*.

Before she died, however, she did manage to attend the stage play *Stu – Scenes from the Life of Stuart Sutcliffe*, by Hugh O'Neill and Jeremy Stockwell.

Millie died on 8 December 1983 in a hospital in Tunbridge Wells.

SUTCLIFFE, Stuart Fergusson Victor   Stuart was born on 23 June 1940 at the Simpson Memorial Maternity Pavilion, Edinburgh. The son of Charles Fergusson and Martha (referred to as Millie) Sutcliffe, he was to have two sisters, Joyce and Pauline.

During the war the family moved to Huyton, a Liverpool suburb, but returned to Edinburgh at the war's end. They then went back to Lancashire, where Stuart attended Prescot Grammar School in September 1951.

By that time Charles had joined the Merchant Navy and Millie was working on Merseyside as a teacher.

In 1956 the 16-year-old Stuart enrolled at the Liverpool College of Art, taking the National Diploma in Design course. There he became friends with me, John Lennon and Rod Murray. He took to art college life, participated in the social events and, along with me, became a member of the Students' Union committee. At the time he identified with the Polish actor Zbigniew Cybulski, the 'Polish James Dean', and began to emulate him by wearing tinted glasses.

He'd left the family home to move into a flat in Percy Street, close to the college, and was then invited by Rod Murray to join him in a flat at 8 Gambier Terrace. Later, John Lennon was to stay there on a regular basis.

It was John who independently invited both Stuart and Rod to become bass guitarist with his group, the Quarry Men. All they needed was a guitar. Rod began to make one, but Stuart beat him to the punch when a painting of his which he'd entered in the John Moores Exhibition at the Walker Art Gallery was bought by millionaire Moores himself. As a result, Stuart placed a deposit on a Hofner President bass guitar at Frank Hessy's music store and joined the group.

They began to play at art college dances, so Stuart and I proposed and seconded the motion that union funds be used to pay for a PA system which the group could use.

Stuart had had piano lessons as a child and his father had brought him an acoustic guitar from Spain when he was only 14. He'd also initially become interested in rock 'n' roll after hearing Elvis Presley.

When the group began to discuss a name change it was at a time when there were a number of Buddy Holly songs in their repertoire. Stuart, thinking of Buddy Holly's backing band the Crickets, suggested using the name of another insect – he came up with Beetles and John Lennon changed one of the 'e's to an 'a'.

The group auditioned for Larry Parnes at the Wyvern Club, which resulted in a short tour of Scotland. It was here that one of the many myths surrounding Stuart first developed. Allan Williams noticed that at one point Stuart turned his back to the audience while on stage. In Williams's autobiography he invented the story that Stuart couldn't really play his instrument. Ever since, Beatles scribes have reported that Stuart couldn't play. Although Stu wasn't as good a musician as the others, Pete Best confirms that he could hold his own on bass and was nowhere near as bad as writers who never even saw him claim. Pauline Sutcliffe also mentions that Stuart often turned his back to the audience, but this was mainly a stage style he was affecting and had nothing to do with how he played bass. He also had his own spot in Germany, performing 'Love Me Tender', which members of the audience often thought was a highlight of the show.

The other main myth surrounding Stuart also originally reared its head in Allan Williams's book. He stated that Stuart had his head kicked by a gang during a fight outside Litherland Town Hall and this, he considered, was responsible for Stuart's death. The idea was taken up and embroidered by writers such as Philip Norman, but no such fight ever took place outside Litherland Town Hall – this is confirmed by figures such as Best and Aspinall, who were present at all the gigs.

Pete Best and Neil Aspinall maintain that the only fracas that Stu was involved in took place at Lathom Hall on 14 May 1960. According to Aspinall: 'Two troublemakers followed Stu Sutcliffe into the dressing room, muttering things like, "Get your hair cut, girl!" John and Pete saw this and went after them. A fight broke out and John broke his little finger. It set crooked and never straightened.'

Millie Sutcliffe always maintained that Stu's headaches first began after he fell down the stairs leading to his attic room in the Kirchherr household in Hamburg.

Although Stuart didn't exert any musical influence on the group, his style and artistry did have an effect – from the way he wore his hair to the cut of his clothes.

In Germany, during the group's initial season at the Kaiserkeller club, he fell in love with Astrid Kirchherr and went to live in the attic room of the house in Eimsbutteler Strasse she shared with her mother.

When the others returned to Liverpool, he elected to remain in Hamburg for several further weeks. Back in Liverpool, he found that he was unable to re-enrol at the Liverpool College of Art, possibly because the Beatles hadn't returned the Students' Union equipment which they'd taken with them and sold in Germany.

The group returned to Germany for a season at the Top Ten Club, backing Tony Sheridan, in March 1962, but by this time Stuart was losing interest in performing with the band and wanted to return to art. He succeeded in getting a grant and a place at the State High School of Art Instruction in Hamburg and became engaged to Astrid.

One night at the club, Paul began baiting Stuart about Astrid. Stuart put down his guitar and attacked him. Paul was taken aback by the furiousness of Stu's onslaught and a few weeks later Stuart had left the group.

Paul was able to take over on bass guitar – Stuart even lent him his own instrument.

Early in 1962 Stuart announced that he would be marrying Astrid as soon as he'd completed his course at college, but by this time he'd begun to suffer from painful headaches, blackouts and temporary blindness. Astrid commented: 'For days at a time he would not come down from his attic studio to eat or sleep, and the headaches became violent, and they seemed like fits.' X-rays were taken, several doctors examined him, but they could find nothing wrong.

When Astrid found Stuart unconscious in his bed on 10 April 1962, she called an ambulance, but he died in her arms at 4.30 p.m. He was only 21 years old. The cause of death was given as 'cerebral paralysis due to bleeding into the right ventricle of the brain'.

He was buried at Huyton Parish Church Cemetery in Stanley Road, Huyton.

An exhibition of his work was held at the Walker Art Gallery in 1964 and on Sunday 13 May 1990 Granada Television screened *Stuart Sutcliffe – Midnight Angel (The Story of the Fifth Beatle)*, in their *Celebration* series.

The biggest posthumous boost came in 1994 with the release of the feature film *Backbeat*, a romanticized version of his short life. American actor Stephen Dorff portrayed Stuart in the film – and even took the trouble to develop a Liverpool accent, which Stuart never had!

SWERDLOW, Alan A student at Liverpool College of Art, who was a member of the Student Union Committee at the same time that Stuart Sutcliffe and I (who were also committee members) proposed and seconded that the Union should buy P.A. equipment.

Sutcliffe and I said that the P.A. equipment could be lent to John Lennon's group as they played regularly at the art college dances. Swerdlow was to say: 'We came back from a summer recess to find that it had been "permanently borrowed".'

Brian Epstein commissioned him to take photographs of the Beatles at the Odd Spot Club in Bold Street. Epstein also commissioned Swerdlow to design both the Beatles and Little Richard programmes for the Empire and New Brighton concerts, and he also designed all of Brian's carrier bags, labels and token vouchers for NEMS.

While he was at college, Swerdlow also took part in a Cinderella pantomime, in which he and John Lennon were the ugly sisters. Swerdlow also attended Quarry Bank School at the same time as John.

SWINGING BLUEJEANS, The   One of Liverpool's longest-serving groups.

In 1961, when compiling a personal list of the best Liverpool bands for *Mersey Beat*, Cavern disc jockey Bob Wooler placed the Beatles firmly at No. 1. Beneath his Top 10 list he added the comment: 'excluding the Bluegenes, of course, they are beyond comparison. They are in a class of their own.' Known at the time as the Swinging Bluegenes, the group originally took flight in 1957 during the skiffle boom.

They were led by Ray Ennis who, together with bass guitarist Les Braid, continues to perform with the band.

In a 1963 *Mersey Beat* interview, Les recalled the group's early career:

> During the skiffle days I used to go down to the Cavern. I was in the club one day when one of the groups appearing there – Johnny Carter & the Hi-Cats – came without a string-bass player so I just went up and asked them if I could join the group. They jumped at the chance as there weren't any bass players about in those days. During the time I was with the group the Bluegenes asked me to do jobs for them and eventually I was getting more work off the Bluegenes than the other groups, so I joined them.
>
> It was about 1959 and there weren't that many groups around – the Beatles weren't heard about in those days and there was more jazz being played at the Cavern than anything else.
>
> We used to have a three-quarter of an hour spot every Friday, Saturday and Sunday and later on we had a guest night on Tuesday evenings. The Cavern had been closed on Tuesdays and we made arrangements with Ray McFall about playing on those nights and Ray suggested we had guest groups. This was in 1961 and the groups we had as guests included Gerry, the Searchers, Billy Kramer and the Coasters and, of course, the Beatles.

When Ray Ennis recalled the night the Beatles made their debut as their guests at the Cavern, on 21 March 1961, he said: 'I thought they were German. It was the old leather gear which I'd never seen before. It wasn't till they actually spoke that I realized they were from Liverpool. I thought they were awful and I only listened to two numbers and went to the White Star for a drink.'

Les noticed that their average audience of 60 had swelled to almost 200 for that first Beatles performance and was quite impressed by their local fan following.

The Bluegenes were a quintet at the time but John Carter left two months later and they decided to remain a quartet.

Other Bluegenes guest nights at which the Beatles appeared included 25 July 1961 and 28 August 1962. The Beatles also appeared on the bill with the Bluegenes, Gene Vincent and Sounds Incorporated on Sunday, 1 July 1962, which was the first Sunday at the Cavern which wasn't headlined by a jazz band.

Their original line-up had been washboard, tea-chest bass, guitar and banjo. Washboard player Norman Kuhlke became their drummer and remained with the band until 1969. Banjoist Paul Moss left in 1960 and wasn't replaced. The line-up and personnel who performed on their initial hit singles lasted from 1961 to 1966 and comprised Ray (rhythm), Les (bass), Norman (drums) and Ralph Ellis (guitar).

Ralph was replaced in 1966 by Terry Sylvester, former member of the Escorts, and the quartet became a quintet the following year with another ex-Escort, Mike Gregory, on bass (Les became organist for a time). Terry left to join the Hollies and Mike had also left and was replaced by Billy Kinsley, former member of the Merseybeats, who was to leave and form Liverpool Express. Ray and Les were then joined by Mike Pynn on lead and John Lawrence on drums for a while. They were replaced in 1975 by Hedley Vick and Chris Mute. Garth Elliott replaced Hedley in 1975 and in 1978 Les and Ray were joined by Colin Manley, former member of the Remo Four, on lead guitar/vocals and Ian McGee on drums. Ian was replaced by John Ryan for a while and then Phil Thompson took over on drums in 1984.

Strangely enough, the group didn't receive a placing in the first *Mersey Beat* poll of the 20 most popular groups in Liverpool in 1961, despite the fact that they were firmly established locally and were always in work. The following year they entered the poll at No. 11. This could well have been because of their image at the time. They'd been regarded as a skiffle band and their stage outfits were rather 'square' compared to what the other groups were wearing. Once they'd changed Bluegenes to Bluejeans, actually wore jeans on stage and turned to rock 'n' roll, things began to happen very swiftly for them.

Brian Epstein wasn't the only local manager to have a stable of artists. Jim Ireland, who ran some popular clubs – the Mardi Gras and the Downbeat – managed the Swinging Bluejeans, the Escorts, Earl Preston's Realms and Cy Tucker's Friars.

The group signed with EMI's HMV label and their debut single, 'It's Too Late Now', was issued in June 1963, followed by 'Do You Know?' in September. It was their third disc, 'Hippy Hippy Shake', which launched them into the big time.

Many years later, Ray was to tell Radio Merseyside broadcaster Spencer Leigh: 'We had to fight like hell with EMI to get "Hippy Hippy Shake" released. They said, "No, this will never make it." We felt so strongly about it, four little humble lads from Liverpool, that we said, "If you don't release it, we won't make any more records." They released it, and Wally Ridley, the A&R man, apologized afterwards. "Hippy Hippy Shake" sold 3 million.'

When John Lennon was reviewing it on the all-Beatles edition of *Juke Box Jury* on 7 December 1963, he said: 'I prefer Bill Harry's version.' This was one of John's in-jokes as, in one of my *Mersey Beat* editorials, I had suggested that a Liverpool group would have a hit if they recorded 'Hippy Hippy Shake'.

The Swinging Bluejeans became popular nationally and in November 1963 they began their own regular Radio Luxembourg show, *Swingtime*, and the following month appeared on the Christmas edition of the popular TV series *Z Cars*, performing 'Hippy Hippy Shake', 'Angie' and 'Money'.

The following year they appeared in *Circularama Cavalcade*, a new film process in which the screen surrounded the audience, read from Shakespeare at Durham University, performed at the finishing post of a major horseracing event, participated in the famous Denby Dale pie ceremony and teamed up with Les Ballets Africains for a performance. Indeed, 1964 was their peak year and they had only one further chart hit, 'Don't Make Me Over', in 1966.

Yet the group continued to perform around the world and in a single year recently appeared in Australia, New Zealand, Germany, Denmark, Sweden, Norway, Finland, Holland, Belgium, Switzerland, Austria and the Middle East.

SYTNER, Alan   The son of Dr Joe Sytner, a Liverpool GP, Alan had a passion for jazz music and began running two Liverpool clubs, the 21 Club in Toxteth and the West Coast Jazz Club at the Temple in Dale Street.

It was while on holiday in Paris that he became fascinated by the jazz clubs on the Left Bank of the Seine, particularly one called Le Caveau Français. On his return to Liverpool he decided to use the inheritance of £400 he'd received on his twenty-first birthday to open a similar jazz club on Merseyside.

A few streets away from the Temple he discovered some warehouses at 10 Matthew Street, whose cellars had been used as air-raid shelters during the war. He immediately took over the lease and officially opened his new venue, which he dubbed the Cavern, on Wednesday 16 January 1957. The bill that night comprised the Merseysippi Jazz Band, the Wall City Jazzmen, the Ralph Watmough Jazz Band and the Coney Island Skiffle Group. He was also to introduce lunchtime sessions on Wednesday 30 January 1957.

Nigel Whalley, who was managing the Quarry Men, played golf with Dr Sytner at the Lee Park Gold Club and persuaded him to get his son to book the group at the club.

They made their debut there on 7 August 1957, although Paul McCartney didn't appear with them at the time as he was on holiday.

Sytner had a policy of allowing only skiffle to be played by groups, as he hated rock 'n' roll. Although aware of this, John Lennon, an Elvis freak at the time, launched into 'Hound Dog' and 'Blue Suede Shoes'.

An angry Sytner sent them a note stating: 'Cut out the bloody rock!' Although Paul hadn't appeared with them that night, over 30 years later he sent a note to Sytner: 'Dear Alan, I'm still playing that bloody rock.'

In 1958 Sytner got married and moved to London. Finding it impossible to run the club from his new home, he sold it to Ray McFall, the club cashier.

TAVERNER, John British composer, born in 1944. He composed 'The Whale' in 1966 and its first performance took place in 1968 with the London Sinfonietta. Ringo spotted Taverner, who then signed with Apple, and 'The Whale' was recorded at the Church of St John the Evangelist in Islington. The album was issued on Apple in 1970. The following year a second Taverner album, *Celtic Requiem*, was released. Taverner and the London Sinfonietta have since received international acclaim.

TAYLOR, Alistair Brian Epstein's original personal assistant at the NEMS White-chapel store. He accompanied Brian to the Cavern on 9 November 1961 to see the Beatles for the first time, but must surely have been aware of the band some months before as they had entered the NEMS shop regularly to listen to records and were frequently on the cover of *Mersey Beat*, the biggest-selling publication in the shop.

In fact, Alistair took over Epstein's record review column in *Mersey Beat*, although this appointment was short-lived as he kept reviewing jazz records. He was to admit that the *Mersey Beat* music of local groups was not exactly his cup of tea.

When Brian drew up his first contract for the Beatles, it was signed by Alistair and the four members of the Beatles, but not Epstein. Epstein also offered him $2\frac{1}{2}$ per cent of the group, but Alistair rejected the offer. He left Brian's employ due to the fact that his wife Lesley suffered from asthma and they were advised to move south, where he took a job at Pye Records.

When Epstein himself moved his organization to London in 1963, he offered Alistair the post of General Manager of NEMS Enterprises at £1,000 a year – and his offer was accepted.

His duties included managing a variety of Epstein's new group signings and acting as 'Mr Fixit' for the Beatles, attending to various tasks, including surveying a farm for Paul and buying an island for John.

After Epstein's death, it was John Lennon who phoned Alistair to offer him the job of Office Manager at Apple – and he is featured in an advertisement designed by Paul, in which he appears as a one-man-band, wearing a bowler hat.

He was one of the first people to be sacked from Apple when Allen Klein moved in – and he attempted to contact John and Paul, but they didn't reply to his calls. Paul was to say in an interview: 'It isn't possible to be nice about giving someone the sack.'

For several years he worked in a hotel, until he was discovered by Beatles fans and invited to be a guest at conventions. He also co-wrote the book *Yesterday: The Beatles Remembered* with Martin Roberts in 1986.

Alistair Taylor continued to be a popular guest at Beatles conventions in the early 1990s.

TAYLOR, Derek Born in Liverpool on 7 May 1934, Taylor was journalist with several local papers until he settled into the post of show-business correspondent for the northern edition of the *Daily Express* in 1962.

Derek initially reviewed the Beatles' concert at the Odeon, Manchester, on 30 May 1963 and became completely enchanted by the group. He followed with an interview with Brian Epstein and began covering other Beatles concerts, eventually ghosting a regular column by George Harrison.

When Brian Epstein sought a ghost writer for his autobiography, Derek offered his services and the two stayed for five days in a Torquay Hotel. The result was *A Cellarful of Noise*.

He was next appointed personal assistant to Epstein and travelled the world with the Beatles over a period of five months. He then had an altercation with Epstein, resigned and he was replaced by Wendy Hanson.

Derek ran his own public relations company in Los Angeles, promoting bands such as the Byrds and the Beach Boys. He became involved in the Monterey Pop Music Festival in 1967 and was the person who introduced Nilsson's music to the Beatles.

After Epstein's death, when they launched Apple Corps, the Beatles asked Derek to join them as their official company press officer. He returned to Britain, where he has lived since.

With the appearance of Allan Klein on the scene, Derek left Apple to become director of special projects at Warner Bros. Records.

He is acknowledged as a brilliant writer and his books *As Time Goes By*, *Fifty Years Adrift* and *It Was Twenty Years Ago* afford an exciting insight into the world of the Beatles.

Derek continues to work for Apple on a part-time basis, usually dropping into the office one day a week. He coordinated the publicity for the *Anthology* CD releases and television series.

TAYLOR, James One of the first Apple Records signings, a discovery of Peter Asher. On his first album, *James Taylor*, Paul McCartney played bass on the track 'Carolina on My Mind' and another track, 'Something in the Way She Moves', inspired George Harrison when he penned 'Something' the following year. After Paul and Jane Asher split, Peter's star began to wane at Apple and when Taylor decided to leave the label through lack of publicity, Asher followed him. Taylor later enjoyed chart success in America.

TEMPLE, Shirley At one time the biggest-drawing movie star in history, she received a special Oscar for bringing 'more happiness to millions of children and millions of grown-ups than any other child of her years in the history of the world'.

Born in Santa Monica in 1928, as a child she was taken around the film studios by her mother, Gertrude, and soon began appearing in shorts such as *Baby Burlesks*.

By 1934 she was the eighth biggest draw in movies after appearances in such films as *Bright Eyes*, in which she sang 'On the Good Ship Lollipop'.

In 1935 she made four films, *The Little Colonel*, *Our Little Girl*, *Curly Top* and *The Little Rebel*, which made her America's No. 1 box-office star, a position she held for three consecutive years.

20th Century-Fox refused to lend her to MGM for *The Wizard of Oz* and Judy Garland got the role. Shirley's popularity waned after that and never really recovered.

She had a much-publicized marriage to actor John Agar, but they were divorced in 1949 because of his alleged mental cruelty and alcoholism. She married again in 1950, having declared she'd make no more movies, and later unsuccessfully ran for Congress. Her husband was Charles Black, an aide to Richard Nixon. In 1969 she was appointed representative to the United Nations by President Nixon and became Ambassador to Ghana in 1974.

Shirley is represented on the *Sgt Pepper* sleeve no less that three times. There is a small doll of her made by Jann Haworth and sporting a 'Welcome Rolling Stones' shirt, which belonged to photographer Michael Cooper's son Adam. There is a cut-out figure of her between the images of Marlene Dietrich and Diana Dors on the right-hand side of the sleeve and there is another photograph of her partly seen between the waxwork figures of John and Ringo.

Whoever chose Temple to become the most represented figure on the album, it wasn't George Harrison, if events at the Cow Palace, San Francisco, were anything to go by. The Beatles appeared at the venue on 19 August 1964. Temple, Black and their eight-year-old daughter Lori attended the event and were escorted backstage by a sheriff's deputy. Neil Aspinall begged the Beatles to meet her, if only for a few minutes, but George refused, so Neil took John, Paul and Ringo to the other side of their partitioned room to meet the Blacks.

Although Brian Epstein had introduced a rule forbidding 'celebrity photographs', Derek Taylor agreed to Charles Black's request to take a picture. He went behind the partition in the room to ask George to join the others and George shouted out: 'I never liked her films, don't like her, don't want to meet her or have my picture taken.'

Derek eventually persuaded him to join the others and when the corps of press photographers heard that a photograph had been taken of the Beatles and Shirley Temple together, they began to bang on the door of the room.

Derek eventually placated them by telling them they could have Black's roll of film to pool together as long as they returned it after the show. Black was reluctant to hand over the film, but Derek persuaded him and passed the film to the photographers. After the show he was handed a roll of film by photographer Curt Gunter – but it was blank. He told Derek that the film hadn't turned out.

An embarrassed Taylor had to explain this to an angry Black. Further complications ensued when, two days later, pictures of Shirley and the Beatles began to appear in the newspapers.

Powerful Hollywood columnist Hedda Hopper ran a story criticizing the Beatles and the photographers, and someone then sent the film to Hopper, who was able to pass it over to the Blacks.

TERRY YOUNG COMBO, The An instrumental sextet who were booked to appear on the Roy Orbison/Beatles three-week British tour of May–June 1963.

They opened the show with a brief spot during which they performed two instrumentals. They then provided backing for the ten-minute spots of Louise Cordet and David Macbeth and also backed Roy Orbison.

Apart from Terry Young, other members included keyboards player Barry Booth and on bass John Rostill, who was later to join the Shadows.

Allegedly, when both Terry Young and John Lennon had too much to drink one night there were harsh words between them. As a result the Terry Young Combo were replaced on subsequent Beatles British tours by Sounds Incorporated.

However, the group were to back Orbison on other British tours, after changing their name to the Sons of the Piltdown Men.

THOMAS, Chris Assistant engineer to George Martin. Chris worked on many of the Beatles recordings, including *The Beatles* double album.

TIGRETT, Maureen Cox Born Mary Cox on 4 August 1946, she was more commonly known as Maureen and friends called her 'Mo'. The convent-educated girl lived in a Liverpool council flat at 56d Boundary Road with her mother, Mary, and her father, Joe, who was a ship's steward.

At the age of 15 she left school to become initially a manicurist's assistant, then a junior hairdressing assistant at the Ashley du Pre beauty parlour.

She had a few dates with Johnny 'Guitar' Byrne of Rory Storm & the Hurricanes, and then she met Ringo Starr, three weeks after he had joined the Beatles, and they began dating.

Although they were dating steadily, when Ringo moved to London in 1964 he started going out with other girls and his name was linked in the press with model Vicki Hodge. In the meantime, it was common knowledge in Liverpool that she was Ringo's girlfriend and the hostile attention of jealous girls who turned up at the salon forced her to give up her job.

Ringo was to reveal to *Woman's Own* magazine that he'd been told 'to pretend I didn't know Maureen and wasn't in love. Can you imagine what it must have been like for her reading in the papers that I didn't know anyone called Maureen Cox?'

In December 1964 Ringo entered University College Hospital to have his tonsils removed and Maureen took the train from Liverpool to visit him. The couple spent Christmas together and by mid-January she was pregnant.

They decided to get married and an early morning, midweek ceremony was planned to avoid the attention of fans and the media. The wedding took place at Caxton Hall, Westminster, shortly before eight o'clock on 11 February 1965, when Maureen was 18 years old.

It was a simple ceremony, with Brian Epstein as best man. In attendance were Ringo's mother and stepfather, Maureen's mother and father, John and Cynthia and George Harrison – who arrived riding a bicycle. Paul McCartney was on holiday in Tunisia at the time, but sent the couple a wedding present of a silver apple. Epstein's present was a dinner service.

A wedding breakfast was then held at Brian's Belgravia house and he had also arranged for the couple to enjoy a short honeymoon at 2 Prince's Crescent, Hove, Sussex, the home of Beatles' solicitor David Jacobs. This became even briefer than planned because the media discovered their whereabouts.

They then moved into a flat in Montague Square. When their first son, Zak, was born on 13 September 1965, Ringo bought a house in Weybridge, named Sunny Heights. Their second son, Jason, was born on 19 August 1967 and their daughter, Lee Parkin, on 11 November 1970.

An American group, the Chicklettes, released a novelty record called 'Treat Him Tender Maureen'.

The marriage seemed to be happy until an alleged incident concerning George Harrison which has been detailed in several unauthorized Harrison biographies. Apparently, George and Pattie Harrison were invited to dinner one evening. George suddenly announced that he was madly in love with Maureen. A furious Ringo strode out, a tearful Pattie locked herself in the bathroom and an embarrassed Maureen was lost for words.

In the aftermath of the declaration it was rumoured that George and Maureen had a brief affair. When George was asked, 'How could you, with your best friend's wife?' he replied, 'Incest, I guess.'

During his various trips abroad, it was clear that Ringo was seeing other women, but the most obvious affair began when he openly dated Californian model Nancy Lee Andrews, who was eight years younger than him. When he brought her over to England and was photographed escorting her to the première of *Tommy*, Maureen reluctantly applied for a divorce. After 11 years of marriage, this was granted on 17 July 1975, with Ringo admitting adultery with Andrews.

Ringo then bought Maureen a house in London's Little Venice, where she was to bring up their three children.

Ten years after the divorce, Maureen sued her solicitors, alleging that they'd underestimated Ringo's earnings when arranging the divorce settlements. The settlement had included a lump sum of £500,000, plus annual maintenance payments. Maureen lost the case and was saddled with £200,000 in legal costs.

The judge remarked that he did not sympathize with Maureen: 'Everything she ever wanted, she just had – it was charged to one of the Beatle companies. She was able to indulge her extravagances to the full.' He also mentioned that the couple had enjoyed a lavish lifestyle at the

Tittenhurst Park country mansion, and Maureen's bank account had been monitored by a secretary, who alerted Ringo when it was running low.

Maureen lived with Hard Rock Café millionaire Isaac Tigrett for a number of years and they were married in Monte Carlo in 1989, with Cynthia Lennon among the many guests. Isaac sold his interest in the Hard Rock Café chain the same year for £60 million and the couple settled in Los Angeles. They also had a house in Boston, where Isaac opened a restaurant called House of Blues.

Maureen had also given birth to a daughter, Augusta King, in 1988.

Sadly, Maureen was diagnosed as having leukaemia in 1994 and had to have a bone marrow transplant from her son Zak. She then underwent chemotherapy treatment at the Fred Hutchinson Cancer Research Center in Seattle, but died on 30 December of complications following a bone marrow transplant. She was 47 years old.

TIMON Merseyside singer and one of the artists to record for Apple in its early days. However, the numbers he recorded were never released because George Harrison didn't like them. On one track, called 'Something New Everyday', produced by Peter Asher, Paul McCartney plays piano.

TINY TIM American singer of novelty songs. The Beatles sponsored his first British concert at the Royal Albert Hall in 1968 and he also made a guest appearance on their Christmas Fan Club record that year.

TOWNSEND, Ken Now Managing Director of Abbey Road Studios, Ken originally began work at the studios as a tape engineer in the mid-1950s. When George Martin first signed the Beatles to the Parlophone label, Ken was a backroom engineer, to whom Martin was to refer to as 'our unsung behind-the-scenes technical genius.'

He assisted Martin at the group's original EMI audition on 6 June 1962 and was to work closely with them throughout the 1960s. Townsend credits the group with creating an atmosphere of experimentation which led to a revolution in recording methods. His technical expertise was to benefit the Beatles' recordings.

Following one of the 'Revolver' sessions, he was working on in April 1966, Ken went home and began to consider the amount of time and effort which was being spent on double-tracking voices and instruments. He worked out that if a signal could be taken off the recording head of the tape machine, as well as off the playback head, and delayed until it almost coincided with the signal from the playback head, then it might be possible to get two sound images instead of one. Townsend fashioned a machine to do just this, which he dubbed 'artificial double-tracking', or ADT.

When the device was first tried out in the studio (on John Lennon's voice for the track 'Tomorrow Never Knows'), John was delighted and asked Martin to explain how it worked. Martin used a typical

Lennonesque description, which was also gobbledegook: 'Well, John, it's a double-bifurcated sploshing flange.' John began to call it: 'Ken's flanger' and now the term 'flanging', is in common use in recording studios.

TRASH Glasgow group signed to the Beatles' Apple label. They comprised Ian Crawford-Clews (vocals), Fraser Watson (lead), Colin Hunter-Morrison (bass) and Tim Donald (drums). They had a minor hit in the British charts with 'Golden Slumbers/Carry That Weight' in September 1969.

TRUTH British duo comprising Steve Gold and Frankie Aiello who had a Top 20 hit with 'Girl', taken from the *Rubber Soul* album.

TROY, Doris American singer who signed with Apple Records. George Harrison produced and co-wrote her single, 'Ain't That Cute?', and musicians appearing on her only Apple album, *Doris Troy*, included George Harrison, Ringo Starr and Klaus Voormann.

TWIGGY One of the leading models of the 1960s, an international celebrity who was born in London in September 1949. Her real name was Lesley Hornby.

Twiggy and her manager, Justin De Villeneuve, originally approached John and Paul to see if they would be interested in funding a film project for her. Paul suggested she contact director Ken Russell, and Twiggy was later to star in his version of *The Boyfriend*.

When the Beatles were considering adapting *Lord of the Rings* as their third film, they intended to feature Twiggy in the movie.

In 1968, when she was due to tour Russia, Granada TV were to film the trip, but the plans fell through. Twiggy commented: 'Paul actually wrote a song for that trip to Russia that didn't come off – and it was "Back in the USSR", which went on *The Beatles* "white" album.'

It was Twiggy who spotted singer Mary Hopkin on *Opportunity Knocks* and recommended her to Paul, and Paul also penned her a number, 'Gotta Sing, Gotta Dance', for a film she intended making. The film was abandoned and Paul performed the number in his TV special *James Paul McCartney*.

U

UNDERTAKERS, The A leading Liverpool group, formed from Bob Evans & the Five Shillings (at one time also known as Bob's Vegas Five). Bob Evans, on vocals/drums, changed the group's name to the Undertakers and by 1961 they were appearing almost seven nights a week at venues including the OPB, the Jive Hive, Riverpark Ballroom, the Majestic, Bowaters and the Shell Club.

The other members were Jimmy McManus (vocals), Chris Huston (lead), Dave Cooper (bass), Geoff Nugent (solo guitar) and Brian Jones (alto/tenor). They began their performances, dressed in black, playing a rendition of the 'Death March'.

Initially they had nicknames: Chris was Shine, George was Trad, Davy was Mush, Brian was Boots, Jimmy was Spam and Bob was Big Bow.

Bugs Pemberton joined in September 1962, when Bob Evans entered hospital for an operation, and by that time Jackie Lomax, known as Max, had also joined.

The band was influenced by Fats Domino, Carl Perkins and Chuck Berry, although Chris commented: 'We have often been accused of copying the Beatles. I admit that at first we were tempted to imitate their style but now we have a style of our own which is completely original.'

They made their second trip to Germany in January 1963, to spend five weeks at the Star Club, and were known in Hamburg as Die Totengräber (the Gravediggers).

The group appeared on numerous bills with the Beatles, including 'Operation Big Beat 3' at the Tower Ballroom on Friday 29 June 1962. They also appeared with them at the Rialto Ballroom on Thursday 11 October 1962 in a 'Rock & Twist Spectacular', which was part of the ballroom's thirty-fifth anniversary celebrations, and again the following day, on the Tower Ballroom bill topped by Little Richard.

Mersey groups knew what music youngsters wanted to hear, but A&R men in London, some of them with no experience of how to appeal to teenagers, insisted on telling the groups what to record.

The Undertakers signed to Pye and were under the wing of a leading A&R man, Tony Hatch. However, although they wanted 'Mashed Potatoes' to be the A-side of their debut disc, the record company made it the B-side. They next wanted to record 'Money', but Pye insisted they record 'What About Us?'. Hatch then said they could choose their own A-side and they picked 'Just a Little Bit', which entered the Top 50.

They weren't pleased when Pye instructed them to change their image, drop the undertakers' dress and coffin-shaped amplifiers and prune their name to the 'Takers. They recorded 'If You Don't Come Back', but, once it had started to move, the annual holiday for the record plant intervened and no more copies were pressed, making it impossible for them to have a chart hit.

Disillusioned, they tried their luck in America, although Geoff Nugent remained in Liverpool.

Unreleased material by the group from that time includes 'Hold On,

I'm a-Comin'', 'My Babe', 'Watch Your Step' and 'What's So Good About Goodbye?'.

Jackie Lomax went on to become an Apple artist, but didn't find success on record and moved to Los Angeles, where he still lives. Bugs and Chris also found themselves settling in America. Chris became a successful record producer and later began designing record studios. He lives with his family in Oregon. Brian Jones went on to play with various bands, including Gary Glitter's Glitter Band, although reports that he played on 'You Know My Name (Look Up the Number)' on the B-side of the Beatles' 'Let It Be' are untrue – that was Brian Jones of the Rolling Stones. Geoff Nugent still appears on Merseyside, leading Geoff Nugent's Undertakers.

VAL Surname unknown. In a 1964 interview, Paul McCartney's brother, Mike, said that Val was the first girl that Paul ever liked. He was at a tender age at the time and began to notice Val on the school bus, staring at her long hair. 'Then one night word came along the grapevine that Val liked him,' said Mike. 'You should have seen the way he went on! He was completely knocked out! He took Val out once or twice – to the cinema, visiting friends, that sort of thing. Then the whole affair suddenly fizzled out.'

VAN EATON, Lon and Derek Brothers who were signed to Apple Records and had their album *Brother* issued by Apple on 9 February 1973. The LP was produced by Klaus Voormann, although George Harrison personally produced one track, 'Sweet Music'.

Derek suffered a heart attack in 1994 and to cover medical expenses they cut an album, *Dinosaurs*, on which Ringo Starr played drums.

VAN GELDER, Dick A Dutch promoter who brought the Beatles to the Netherlands in June 1964.

VARTAN, Sylvie Glamorous blonde French singer. At the time she co-starred with the Beatles and Trini Lopez at the Olympia, Paris, from 16 January to 4 February 1964, she was married to France's leading rock 'n' roll idol, Johnny Halliday.

VAUGHAN, Ivan A close friend of both John Lennon and Paul McCartney, who lived in Vale Street in the Woolton area of Liverpool with his widowed mother. Their rear garden backed on to Mendips, where John lived with his Aunt Mimi. They also lived close to Pete Shotton and Nigel Whalley and all four became a close-knit gang.

When he was six years old, Ivan went to Dovedale Primary School, as did John. Later John went to Quarry Bank School, while Ivan attended Liverpool Institute.

Ivan had the same madcap sense of humour as John and they both loved *The Goon Show*. When John invited him to join the Quarry Men on tea-chest bass, Ivan painted 'Ive the Jive, the Ace on the Bass' on his instrument, although he alternated with Nigel Whalley, until Len Garry replaced them both.

At the Institute Ivan was in the same class as Paul (they were both born on the same day).

Ivan's behaviour was eccentric, to say the least. One day when his mother wasn't home, he painted his name in letters three foot high right across the front of the house. Pupils at the Institute had to wear regulation black shoes, but one day Ivan arrived at school having coloured his shoes with thick dollops of canary yellow paint. Another time he left off his Institute uniform and entered Quarry Bank with John. Ivan said he was a new student and was given a set of textbooks and told to join the class. When the headmaster heard of it he reported the incident to the

Institute headmaster, who only mildly chastised him. Ivan also played truant quite often and would forge notes from his mother stating that he hadn't been able to attend because she couldn't afford to buy him new shoes!

Institute old boy Peter Sissons was to comment: 'John Lennon was a highly original character, but in my opinion, much of the outrageousness and unpredictability he displayed later in life came from Ivan Vaughan and not the other way round.'

One day Ivan asked Paul if he'd like to come along and watch his skiffle group play at a church fête. Paul wasn't particularly struck on the idea, but Ivan said that it would be a great place to pick up girls, so the two of them cycled along that afternoon. The date was 6 July 1957 and after the Quarry Men's first set Ivan took Paul into the Church Hall and introduced him to John.

He considered Paul to be talented and said: 'I only ever brought great fellows to meet John.'

A week later, when Paul was cycling to Ivan's house, he met Pete Shotton, who asked him if he'd like to join the group.

Over the years, Ivan kept in touch with his friends, particularly Paul and John. He was a Cambridge graduate and became a teacher and studied educational psychology.

He regularly visited them, travelled to America with them and was present at the time of the *Sgt Pepper* sessions. When Apple was launched, the Beatles suggested that Ivan and Jan, his schoolteacher wife, head the proposed Apple School. Ivan was given an advance payment of £10,000, but it was decided that the idea was premature and the scheme was dropped.

Sadly, during the 1970s Ivan contracted Parkinson's Disease, for which there is no known cure. Deciding not to simply accept the situation, he began to battle against the disease, using himself as a guinea pig for new drugs and mercilessly knocking his limbs against solid objects when they refused to respond.

Jonathan Miller heard of his remarkable and courageous struggle and produced a documentary, simply called *Ivan*, which was transmitted on BBC2 TV on 3 December 1984 as part of the *Horizon* series. Paul allowed his song 'Blackbird' to be played at the beginning and end of the programme free of charge. Paul invited Ivan to spend Christmas 1984 with the McCartneys at their home in Sussex and continued to keep in touch until Ivan's death.

Of the documentary, which centred on a day in his life, Ivan commented: 'I decided to make my illness my hobby. Not as something useful. Not to help thousands. Just selfishly, to find out all I could about it and its implications. I wanted to explore it, to play with it, and even to laugh about it.'

His book, *Ivan: Living with Parkinson's Disease*, was published in 1986. Tragically, Ivan died in 1994. His death touched Paul so deeply that he began to write poetry for the first time since he was a child.

VAUGHAN, Janet Wife of ex-Quarryman Ivan Vaughan. Janet taught French and when Paul McCartney was composing 'Michelle', he asked Janet if she could help him to write the French verses.

VERNONS GIRLS, The The Liverpool football company Vernons Pools sponsored a 70-strong girls' choir called the Vernons Girls for promotional purposes. This line-up was slimmed to a more manageable 16 and they began to appear on television shows such as *Oh Boy!* and recorded for Parlophone between 1958 and 1961, without success.

Various members of the vocal group split into solo and other acts, including Lynn Cornell, the Ladybirds, the Breakaways and the Two Tones.

The Breakaways appeared with the Beatles on the Little Richard show at the Empire Theatre, Liverpool, on Sunday 28 October 1962.

By 1962, the Vernons Girls were down to a trio comprising Maureen Kennedy, Jean Owen and Frances Lee. They signed to Decca Records and as the Vernon Girls Featuring Maureen reached No. 16 in the charts with 'Lover Please'. They also had minor hits with 'Funny All Over' and 'Do the Bird'.

It was this trio who featured with the Beatles on the TV show *Thank Your Lucky Stars* on Saturday 20 April 1963. Later that year they also appeared on the the first all-Merseyside edition of *Thank Your Lucky Stars* on 20 June. The Vernons Girls were part of the Beatles' autumn tour of Britain between 1 November and 13 December 1963 and were included on the *Pops Alive!* show at the Prince of Wales Theatre in London, when the Beatles topped the bill on Sunday 31 May 1964.

The trio were also booked to appear on the Beatles' Associated Re-diffusion television show *Around the Beatles*, first transmitted on 6 May 1964.

Lynn Cornell, a blonde girl who had lived quite close to Paul McCartney, married Alan White, the drummer who recorded with the Beatles at the Parlophone 'Love Me Do' and 'P.S. I Love You' sessions. She was still a member of the Vernons Girls when they recorded 'We Love the Beatles', a novelty record which didn't make the charts.

She did have some success with the similarly titled 'We Love You Beatles' in 1964. She recorded this number as a member of the Carefrees, whose other members were Barbara Kay, Johnny Evans, John Stevens and Don Riddell. The single was issued in America, where it reached No. 39 in the *Billboard* chart, becoming the biggest-selling Beatles novelty single ever released.

As a solo singer she was booked to appear with the Beatles on the all-British edition of the American pop show *Shindig*, recorded at the Granville Theatre, Fulham Broadway, London, on 3 October 1964.

VINCENT, Gene Seminal American rock 'n' roll star, born Eugene Vincent Craddock on 11 February 1935 in Norfolk, Virginia. An accident on a motorcycle caused him to spend several months in hospital and, as the bones in his broken leg didn't heal properly, he had to wear calipers.

His hits included 'Be-Bop-a-Lula' and 'Blue Jean Bop'. In 1959 he made his British debut, appearing there regularly for many years. He adopted a leather outfit, which may well have influenced the Beatles when they decided to buy leather clothes in Hamburg.

He was due to appear with Eddie Cochran in a concert at Liverpool Stadium, but an accident in which both were involved resulted in Cochran's death. Vincent appeared at the concert on 3 May 1960 and was supported by several Mersey groups.

The Beatles, who had featured several Vincent numbers in their repertoire, appeared with him at the Star Club in April 1962. When Sounds Incorporated asked Vincent what Hamburg was like, he told them: 'Oh, it's OK there. I had a nice band backing me up. They're called the Beatles.'

He appeared on the same bill as the Beatles at the Cavern on 1 July 1962 and during another visit to Liverpool in 1964 he told *Mersey Beat*: 'I sing rock 'n' roll because the kids always seem to have liked it – anyway, the stuff the Beatles sing is just rock 'n' roll, but a bit noisier.'

Vincent died on 12 October 1971 of a bleeding ulcer. He was 36 years old.

VINTON, Bobby American singer, managed by Allen Klein, who was knocked off the top spot in the American charts by the Beatles with 'I Wanna Hold Your Hand'. It heralded the virtual demise of the solo singer in the US charts for the next decade, although Vinton himself was to reach No. 1 again in 1964 with 'Mr Lonely'.

VISCOUNTS, The British male vocal group who appeared on the Chris Montez/ Tommy Roe tour with the Beatles in 1963.

VOORMANN, Klaus Son of a prominent Berlin physician, Klaus became a student in Hamburg, studying illustration at the Meister Schule. In 1958 he began going steady with a fellow student, Astrid Kirchherr, a pale, blonde girl who was studying photography. Klaus moved into a room in the house in Altona where Astrid and her mother lived.

In October 1960, the two had an argument, which led to Klaus wandering around the city centre, first going to the cinema and then finding himself in the Grosse Freiheit in the St Pauli district.

He was attracted by sounds coming from a club called the Kaiserkeller and went inside. On stage were a rock 'n' roll band from Liverpool called Rory Storm & the Hurricanes. The student was mesmerized by the appearance of the young musicians and the exciting sound they made on stage, but he was even more impressed by the band which followed them – the Beatles.

Klaus was completely captivated by the group and stayed in the club for hours, although he didn't pluck up the courage to speak to them. Back home he told Astrid about the group and asked her to come along and see them with him. She refused.

The next evening he returned to the Kaiserkeller, this time taking along with him a record cover he'd designed for a single called 'Walk Don't Run'. When the Beatles came off stage he approached John Lennon, whom he took to be their leader. In his halting English he explained that he liked to design album covers. John just pointed Stuart out to him and told him to show his work to Stu, as he was the artist. However, nervousness overtook Klaus again and he didn't approach Stu.

On the third visit he was accompanied by Astrid and Jurgen Vollmer, another student friend, and they were all fascinated by the visual appeal of the Beatles, particularly Stu, with his dark glasses and moody look. Astrid in particular was immediately attracted to the bass guitarist.

The three became regular visitors to watch the group and brought along other student friends. Soon the Beatles were joining their table and chatting to them. As a result Astrid asked Klaus if he could teach her some English.

Within a short time it proved obvious that Stu and Astrid were attracted to each other. She and Klaus had been sweethearts for two years, but within a fortnight Stu and Astrid had fallen in love. It was initially embarrassing for all concerned, but Klaus accepted the situation and Stu moved into the Kirchherr home.

The Beatles continued to prove a major influence on Klaus's life and he decided to become a bass guitarist, just like Stu. He moved to England, where he teamed up with two Liverpool musicians, Paddy Chambers and Gibson Kemp, in a band called Paddy, Klaus & Gibson.

They were managed by Tony Stratton-Smith, an author and journalist who had become enamoured of the music scene and also managed Liverpool artists the Kubas and Beryl Marsden. Unlike Epstein, Stratton-Smith really loved and was knowledgeable about the music and had specific plans to establish Paddy, Klaus & Gibson, beginning with a residency at the prestigious Pickwick Club in London's West End, which was frequented by celebrities like Paul McCartney and Jane Asher.

The Beatles mentioned Paddy, Klaus & Gibson to Epstein and he decided to make them a management offer. Despite Stratton-Smith's frustration, he reluctantly agreed to the management change. They signed with Epstein on 13 August 1965 and were soon to vanish into obscurity and then disband.

Arguably, they would have found success with Stratton-Smith, who went on to mastermind the success of Genesis and created the well-respected Charisma record label.

After the dissolution of the group, Klaus had the opportunity of joining one of several bands – the Hollies, John Mayall, the Moody Blues or Manfred Mann. He chose Manfred Mann, replacing Jack Bruce, and played on all the Manfred records featuring Mike D'Abo.

While in England, Klaus remained in close touch with the Beatles. Possibly remembering his first tentative approach to them in Hamburg with his design for a record sleeve, John Lennon phoned him up and gave him a free hand to design the *Revolver* album cover. It brought Klaus a Grammy award.

During the 1960s he married Christine Hargraves, a British actress who appeared on the popular Granada TV soap opera *Coronation Street*, and they settled in Hampstead. At one of their dinner parties, George Harrison noticed that Klaus had a pedal harmonium and started playing it, intrigued by the sounds it made. It possibly had some influence when he composed 'Within You, Without You'.

When Paul McCartney announced publicly that he was leaving the Beatles, John, George and Ringo considered replacing him with Klaus and continuing as a group using the name the Ladders.

Klaus was invited to discuss the plan with them at the Apple offices on 19 March 1971, only days after the High Court had granted Paul victory in the first round of his battle to dissolve the Beatles.

When Klaus spent days at George's Friar Park mansion, the music paper *Melody Maker* ran the headline: 'New Beatle Klaus Goes into Hiding'. On 20 March a story appeared in the *Daily Mirror* suggesting that Klaus was to be the new replacement for Paul. On 26 March Apple issued a statement denying that John, George and Ringo were to continue as a group with the addition of Klaus.

In some ways, it seemed as if Klaus had stepped into the shoes of the tragic Stu Sutcliffe – becoming a bass guitarist, designing a Beatles album sleeve and almost becoming a Beatle himself!

Despite the collapse of plans to have Klaus become the new Beatle, he was involved in numerous solo recordings by John, George and Ringo, initially becoming a member of the Plastic Ono Band, making records with John and appearing with the group in London and Toronto.

The singles by John on which Klaus played include 'Cold Turkey', 'Instant Karma', 'Power to the People', 'God Save Us', 'Listen the Snow is Falling' (the flipside of 'Happy Xmas') and 'Whatever Gets You Thru the Night'. The albums include *Plastic Ono Band – Live Peace in Toronto 1969*, *John Lennon/Plastic Ono Band*, *Imagine*, *Walls and Bridges* and *Rock 'n' Roll*.

The recordings that he made with George include singles such as 'My Sweet Lord' and the albums *All Things Must Pass*, *The Concert for Bangladesh*, *Living in the Material World*, *Dark Horse* and *Extra Texture (Read All About It)*.

With Ringo he recorded the singles 'It Don't Come Easy', 'Back off Boogaloo' and 'Photograph' and the albums *Sentimental Journey*, *Ringo* (packaged with a 24-page lyric book featuring ten lithographs by Klaus which illustrated each of the songs), *Goodnight Vienna* and *Ringo's Rotogravure*.

In the 1970s Klaus lived for a time on George Harrison's Friar Park estate, then moved to Los Angeles for eight years, playing on sessions for various artists, including Carly Simon, Billy Preston and Harry Nilsson.

He introduced Ringo to Harry Nilsson and co-composed a number with Ringo which was intended as the title song for the film *Blindman*, although it wasn't used in the final print.

Klaus also gained skill as a record producer and produced an album for Tony Sheridan called *World's End*.

In 1979 he decided to move back to Germany with his girlfriend and son. He became a record producer and one of his acts, Trio, had an international hit with 'Da Da Da'. In 1995 he was commissioned to design the covers for the "Anthology" series of CD releases.

WALKER, Cecil The registrar who conducted the wedding ceremony between John and Yoko at Gibraltar on 20 March 1969.

WALTERS, Lou Bass guitarist/vocalist with Rory Storm & the Hurricanes, his real name was Walter Eymond. Rory gave him the name when he selected stage names with a Western flavour for the members of his band.

Although Rory was the Hurricanes' lead singer, Lou, who was still referred to as Wally, was noted as one of the best vocalists on Merseyside and took the lead on several of the songs in the group's repertoire, including 'Mailman', 'Fever', 'Beautiful Dreamer', 'Let It Be Me' and 'Summertime'. Lou had been with the band since 1959, when they were known as the Raving Texans.

Rory Storm & the Hurricanes were a leading Liverpool group in 1960, with stronger pulling power than the lesser-known Beatles, and they were Allan Williams's original choice as the first Mersey group to appear in Hamburg, a stint which they turned down because they were booked for a season at Butlin's. However, Williams booked them to appear at the Kaiserkeller from October 1960, and they were once again billed above the Beatles.

Williams was in Hamburg to see the acts. He was present when Lou visited the Indra to watch the Beatles and got up on stage to sing several numbers with them. Williams was so impressed with Lou's voice that he wanted to make a record with him. He asked John, Paul and George to join them at the session. As Hurricanes drummer Ringo Starr was familiar with the numbers they were recording, he also joined the team.

The session, which took place on Saturday 18 October 1960 at the small Akustic studio at 57 Kirchenallee, near to Hamburg's Hauptbahnhof railway station, was a historic one, as the track 'Summertime' was the first recording to feature all four members of the group who were to become internationally known as the Beatles.

Other numbers recorded at the session were 'Fever' and 'September Song', on which Lou was backed by Ringo, Ty Brien and Johnny Guitar. The Beatles asked Williams if he would fork out some money for them to record more numbers, but he refused.

There were nine copies of the disc cut. Allan Williams lost his when he left it behind in a London pub in the 1970s. Rory Storm's copies were apparently lost when a number of his items were destroyed following his death. Wally's copy is possibly still in existence, in the hands of his estranged wife.

Lou left the Hurricanes briefly in 1962 to join the Seniors, but was soon back in Rory's group.

After Ringo had left them to join the Beatles, Lou was interviewed in a 1963 *Mersey Beat* feature, in which he discussed his reminiscences of Ringo:

I met Ringo during the old skiffle days. He was appearing at the Mardi Gras with Rory Storm and was dressed in a long black Teddy-boy suit. Later, I joined the group, which was then known as the Raving Texans, and we played numerous dates around the Liverpool area.

Ringo was not an exceptional drummer at the time, but as the group progressed he improved to such an extent that we realized he would be a very good drummer.

We had some good times when we made our first appearance at Butlin's Holiday Camp. Ringo was the lazy one of the group. In the morning he used to sleep late, and if woken would be very bad-tempered. The first signs of him waking took the form of one open eye which was staring round the chalet. Then it would be between one hour and one and a half hours before he'd stir properly, then he wouldn't speak for an hour or so. After that he'd revert to his normal self.

He was the life and soul of any party we went to and was well liked because of his sense of humour.

We had quite a laugh watching him taking swimming lessons off Ty. At one time he seemed to be doing fine until he realized that he was out of his depth and in the 12-footer. Then he just yelled and vanished from sight. It ended when three of us dived in and pulled him out – we had a good laugh about it afterwards.

Members of the group often went horse-riding, but Ringo only joined us once. The horse bit him and he ended up walking back to camp.

At that time he started to show some of his exceptional talent on drums and he also started singing. One of the numbers was 'Alley Oop', and the girls started to scream their applause. Ringo was born as a singer!

Following the season at Butlin's, we left for Germany. The audiences there liked him, but they also used to make him angry by asking him if he had dyed the streak in his hair. 'It's natural!' he used to scream back at them.

His popularity reached its peak when a girl became so excited that she had to be forcibly carried out of the club shrieking 'Ringo! Ringo!' at the top of her voice.

We then met Tony Sheridan who joined in sessions with us and he thought very highly of Ringo's ability. Before we left, Tony asked Ringo to join him, so he stayed in Germany for a few months.

On his return he rejoined the Hurricanes and we later returned for another season at Butlin's. Ringo now had a regular vocal spot in the group, and we all worked together as a team.

When Ringo left the group last year to join the Beatles, we felt we had lost a vital part of the group.

Now, Ringo is still one of our closest friends and we are all thrilled at his success, for now he is one of the most famous drummers in the country.

WATMOUGH, Harry Liverpool photographer, based in Moorfields, who specialized in publicity shots for local clubland artists. He provided the photographic coverage of clubland for *Mersey Beat*. When Brian Epstein moved his NEMS Enterprises from Whitechapel to Moorfields, he was in the same building, directly opposite Watmough, and commissioned the photographer to take a shoot in the studios of the Beatles with their new smartened-up image early in 1962.

WAYNE STEVENS & THE VIKINGS A group from Warrington who appeared with the Beatles at the Cavern on Tuesday 7 August 1962.

WEBB, Bernard Pseudonym used by Paul McCartney when he penned 'Woman' for Peter and Gordon. He wanted to see if he could write a hit record without the magic formula of the Lennon and McCartney name. The record reached No. 21.

WEBB, Sonny Liverpool vocalist, real name Ken Johnson, who began singing at the age of 16 during the skiffle boom. When the skiffle craze died he formed a C&W group, the Country Four, who appeared mainly at the Black Cat club and in social clubs. The group split up (later to re-form with Brian Newman) and Sonny joined the Wild Cats, who became Sonny Webb & the Cascades, and later the Hillsiders. Their line-up was John State (lead), Roger Williams (drums), Joe Butler (bass) and Sonny (vocals).

Sonny Webb & the Cascades appeared at a number of venues with the Beatles, including the Grafton Ballroom, West Derby Road, on Friday 2 August 1963 and the Cavern on Friday, 11 January 1963. The ordeal of appearing on the Grafton stage before the Beatles at a time when Beatlemania was growing in Britain caused Sonny to comment: 'It was awful to go on before the Beatles because the audience couldn't wait for us to get off!'

Sonny says that Brian Epstein wanted to sign the group up and let them have three unrecorded Lennon and McCartney numbers: 'Do You Want to Know a Secret?', 'Misery' and 'Tip of My Tongue'.

Before they had a chance to do anything, he gave 'Do You Want to Know a Secret?' to Billy J. Kramer. They recorded 'Misery', but were then approached by Beatles Fan Club secretary Freda Kelly, who also worked at NEMS, with a note from Epstein saying that they couldn't release it but would they be willing to record 'Tip of My Tongue'?

He then prevented them recording that too, so they lost interest in NEMS and signed with the Northern Variety Agency, changing their name to the Hillsiders and having some success as a live country music act.

WEISS, Nat American attorney whom Brian Epstein hired to represent him in America in 1964. He became a close friend of the Beatles' manager and the two decided to enter into an artists' management agreement the following year, forming a company called Nemperor Artists, managing a group called Cyrkle.

WEISS, Norman Man who organized the Beatles' first American tour. An executive of General Artists Corporation, a major American company, he first met the Beatles in Paris in January 1964, when he was representing Trini Lopez, who appeared on the Olympia bill with them.

WEISSLEDER, Manfred Imposingly tall, blond club-owner in the St Pauli district of Hamburg. Manfred owned several strip clubs and also produced lavish nudist films which were screened at his various venues.

His entrepreneurial skills were utilized when he decided to open Hamburg's biggest rock 'n' roll venue, the Star Club, which, with the passage of time, has become Germany's equivalent of the legendary Cavern club.

Unlike promoters such as Bruno Koschmider, who didn't particularly care about the well-being of bands, Manfred ensured that they were paid good money, installed in decent accommodation and were protected from being ripped off or mugged in the area by giving them a Star Club badge, which warned off any possible attackers. When Gene Vincent complained he'd been given a hard time by a taxi driver, Manfred took a group of waiters to the Reeperbahn, had Vincent point out the taxi driver and turned the cab upside-down in the street!

Groups were so appreciative of his approach that they dubbed the Star Club 'Manfred's Home for Wayward Scousers'.

He even bought a number of flats in the Grosse Freiheit for the bands to live in and allowed the Beatles to use the flats, telling them: 'I always want you should enjoy yourselves in the Star Club, but if you make shit I send you home.'

He took over the premises of the Stern Kino at 39 Grosse Freiheit and transformed it into a comfortable club, stripping out the cinema seats and replacing them with settee-style seating and tables. The ceiling of the entrance foyer was decorated with copies of *Mersey Beat* and the stage area had a colourful backdrop mural of the Manhattan skyline.

One of his first decisions was to appoint Horst Fascher as his assistant. He decided not only to book the best groups from Liverpool and other parts of the UK but also to nurture home-grown bands and to book the biggest names in American rock. As a result, appearing with the Mersey bands were their great heroes Little Richard, Jerry Lee Lewis, the Everly Brothers, Gene Vincent, Johnnie & the Hurricanes and Joey Dee & the Starliters.

Manfred also decided to bring in the top Liverpool names such as the Beatles, the Searchers, Kingsize Taylor & the Dominoes and the Big Three.

In January 1962, a few months before the club's official opening, he sent Horst and pianist Roy Young to Liverpool to book as many top Mersey bands as possible.

The astute Manfred had also instructed Horst to make sure there were exclusivity clauses in the contracts. When Horst met and negotiated a deal with Brian Epstein for the Beatles, the contract, which was signed on 22 January 1962, contained a clause which read: 'It is agreed that the band will not perform or accept other engagements in Germany from the date of this contract until the contract becomes effective.'

Peter Eckhorn of the Top Ten Club had offered Epstein 200 marks each per week for the Beatles. Horst had upped this to 350 marks and by the time they completed the negotiations the Beatles were to receive 500 marks each per week for their first Star Club engagement.

This took place from 13 April to 31 May 1962. The posters for the opening season read:

Die Note hat ein ENDE!
Die Zeit der Dörfmusik ist vorbei!
Am Freitag, dem 13 April, eröffnet
STAR CLUB
mit The Beatles, Tex Roberg, Roy Young,
The Graduates, The Bachelors.
Zusätzlich ab Mai: Tony Sheridan Quartet
und Gerry And The Pacemakers.
Eine Ballung der Spitzenklasse Europas
Hmb: St Pauli, Gr. freiheit 39.

The Beatles were required to play for four hours on one evening with a one-hour break between each set and for three hours on the following evening.

During their seven-week engagement they shared the bill with Little Richard and Gene Vincent.

Manfred raised the Beatles' fees to 600 marks each per week and booked them to appear from 1 to 14 November that same year. For their third and final Star Club season, from 18 to 31 December 1962, he paid them 750 marks.

Interested in building a major rock scene in Germany, he made arrangements to promote in other cities, to open further Star Club venues, to have his own Star Club label, to manage home-grown bands and to publish his own rock newspaper.

He invited me to move to Hamburg and run a rock newspaper, but I wished to remain in Liverpool with *Mersey Beat*, although I agreed to provide a regular column for Manfred's publication, the *Star Club News*.

Manfred hired Adrian Barber, former member of the Big Three, to become the club's stage manager and had him install a sound system to enable him to record groups live on stage.

Among the local groups he encouraged were the Rattles, promoted as 'Hamburg's Beatles'.

He was very conscious of the Liverpool–Hamburg relationship and encouraged it, arranging for Virginia and I to make several trips there to report on Star Club activities. He took colour transparencies of the Beatles exclusively for *Mersey Beat*, had exchange trips with the Cavern – sending groups such as the Rattles to play in Liverpool – and made various trips to Merseyside with Horst Fascher and Henry Henroid. He later employed Henry as Star Club manager.

Despite its popularity, the Star Club dream didn't last and Manfred closed it down in June 1964.

He died of cancer in 1980.

WELLS, Mary Detroit-born singer who topped the charts with 'My Guy' in 1964. The Beatles requested her appearance on their four-week autumn tour of Britain that year. She was also a guest on their *Around the Beatles* special and recorded an album, *Love Songs to the Beatles*. She died in August 1992.

WHALLEY, Nigel Neighbour of John Lennon, who became friendly with him from the age of five, nicknamed 'Whalloggs'.

Originally sharing the honours on tea-chest bass in the Quarry Men, he later became their manager for a time and even had business cards printed to promote the group.

While he served as an apprentice golf professional at Lee Park Golf Club, he arranged for them to perform at a club event and, through his contact with Dr Sytner, the Cavern owner's father, fixed up for them to appear at the cellar club on 7 August 1957.

Paul McCartney wasn't happy with Nigel receiving a split of their fee as manager, so his association with them came to an end.

It was Nigel who witnessed the death of Julia Lennon. On 15 July 1958 he was on his way to visit John and met Julia. They walked together for a while, then she continued on her way. He heard the squeal of brakes and turned to see her body tossed into the air by a car.

At the age of 18 he left Liverpool to become a golf professional at the Wrotham Heath Golf Club in Borough Green, Kent.

WHITAKER, Bob Australian photographer who took shots of Brian Epstein during the Beatles 'down under' tour in 1964. Epstein then hired him to become the group's official photographer from August 1964 to November 1966. During this time he documented their tours of America, Germany and Japan. His most famous photograph was that of the Beatles with parts of dolls' bodies and pieces of meat, originally to be used for their *Yesterday . . . and Today* American album cover. It was withdrawn due to controversy and is often referred to as the 'butcher cover'.

WHITE, Alan Drummer whom John Lennon recruited into the Plastic Ono Band while he was still a member of the Beatles. In addition to appearing on Plastic Ono Band singles such as 'Instant Karma', he travelled to Toronto with the group to play at a rock 'n' roll festival and was also a member of the Plastic Ono Supergroup which appeared at the Lyceum, London, in December 1969.

WHITE, Andy A session drummer who played on the Beatles' first single. Recording manager George Martin usually brought in various Musicians' Union drummers for studio sessions, including Ron Bowden, Jimmy Nicol, Bobbie Graham, Clem Cattini and Andy White.

Martin engaged White for the session on 11 September 1962. White was 32 years old at the time and played with the Vic Lewis Orchestra. He arrived at Abbey Road at seven that evening for the three-hour session, for which he was paid £5 15s.

Ringo hadn't known about the arrangement and immediately felt anxious when he arrived to discover White setting up his drums.

Ron Richards began recording the session and Martin arrived half-way through. Martin told them: 'I'm giving you a very good drummer, who's probably better than Ringo Starr, and that's who's going to play the drums.'

Ringo was showing signs of depression as the recording got under way, so he was asked to participate by playing maracas on 'P.S. I Love You'.

There were two versions of the A-side, 'Love Me Do', completed at the session, one with Andy playing drums and Ringo playing tambourine, the other with Ringo as drummer.

Despite Martin's preference for session drummers, the version of 'Love Me Do' initially released as a single featured Ringo on drums. The version with White was included on the *Please Please Me* album, then surfaced as a single issued with a black label when it was re-pressed in April 1963.

White was married to singer Lynn Cornell, a former member of the Vernons Girls. He was later to join the BBC Radio Orchestra in Glasgow, then moved to America, where he worked with a variety of artists including Louis Armstrong, Chuck Berry, Shirley Bassey and Marlene Dietrich. By 1992 he had settled in a two-room apartment in New York, where he worked as a part-time librarian and appeared as drum sergeant for the New York Police Band Drummers.

WHITE, Ron The man Brian Epstein initially approached in 1961 when he wanted EMI to sign the Beatles. White was general marketing manager with the company, met Epstein and approached all four of EMI's A&R men (George Martin was on holiday at the time) to see if they were interested. They all turned the group down and White was to write to Epstein with the bad news.

He later became managing director of EMI and died at the age of 67 on 18 September 1989.

WIGG, David Show-business writer for the *Daily Express* who interviewed the Beatles on a number of occasions. He also interviewed them for a series of *Scene & Heard* radio shows which were used for a Polydor double album, *The Beatles Tapes from the David Wigg Interviews*.

WILLIAMS, Allan Richard Gregarious Liverpool-Welsh club-owner, often mistakenly described as the Beatles' first manager, although this wasn't really the case. When he organized the Liverpool Stadium concert on 3 May 1960, in which he booked several local bands to appear with Gene Vincent, he didn't select the Beatles. At the time, John and Stu in particular used to hang around his coffee bar, the Jacaranda. Following the Stadium concert, impresario Larry Parnes asked Williams to organize some local groups to audition as backing bands to his acts, such as Billy Fury, Duffy Power and Johnny Gentle.

Williams asked several local groups to attend and some of them were booked by Parnes, including Derry & the Seniors, Cass & the Cassanovas and the Silver Beatles.

The Seniors turned professional and when their proposed tour for a Parnes artist fell through, a furious Howie Casey threatened Williams. As a result Allan drove the Seniors down to London and the 2 I's bar, where, by chance, Hamburg club-owner Bruno Koschmider was looking for groups. As a result he booked the Seniors on the spot and they became the first Mersey group to appear in Hamburg.

When Koschmider asked him for more bands Allan approached Rory Storm & the Hurricanes and Gerry & the Pacemakers. They turned him down and he decided on the Beatles as a last resort.

They were now playing in his Jacaranda coffee club and he'd also booked them for a series of gigs with Wallasey promoter Les Dodd at the Neston Institute and the Grosvenor Ballroom, Birkenhead, but for an agency percentage and not a management fee.

He decided to go over to Hamburg and consolidate an agreement with Koschmider, hoping to get an exclusive contract to book many other Liverpool bands over there. As he'd now booked the Beatles as the next band for Hamburg, he arranged for them to join him and his wife, brother-in-law and partner, Lord Woodbine, on the trip. He was involved in dealings with Koschmider to act as agent in booking various artists ranging from jazz bands to Cliff Richard for the Kaiserkeller, although these plans were abandoned.

Once in Hamburg he did no business for the Beatles and his association with them was over. They arranged a second trip with club-owner Peter Eckhorn themselves and had a dispute with Williams about paying an agency fee. His letter to them on 20 April 1961 makes it clear that he had acted for them in the capacity of agent only and not as manager.

It was once the Beatles had achieved their incredible fame that he claimed he was their first manager – something they always strenuously denied, although inexplicably Paul called him 'manager' in the *Anthology* TV series (a case of the Beatles themselves now beginning to believe in the myths which grew up around them).

Allan booked the Seniors for the Wyvern auditions and arranged for them to appear with Larry Parnes's artists. He took them down to London and planned their Hamburg season. He even had them open his new club, the Top Ten, in Liverpool – it burned down a few days later, destroying the Seniors' equipment and causing them to disband – yet he never claimed to be the Seniors' manager.

This is in no way meant to detract from Allan's genuine participation in the local scene in creating the opening for the Liverpool–Hamburg association or his position as a Liverpool club-owner, but he never assumed any management responsibilities for the Beatles, being mainly concerned with an agency percentage from a handful of bands over a period of 18 months. Mona Best assumed more management responsibilities for the band, and Sam Leach had aspirations to become their manager and knew the difference between being manager or agent.

Allan's book *The Man Who Gave the Beatles Away* (first published in 1975) was co-written with *Daily Mirror* journalist Bill Marshall and should be taken with a pinch of salt, as Marshall claims it owes more to his own imagination than to Allan's memories.

Allan opened his Jacaranda coffee club in September 1958 and next opened his most famous venue, the Blue Angel in Seel Street, in August 1960. His only attempt at a rock 'n' roll club, the Top Ten Club in Soho Street, was, as already mentioned, destroyed by fire in December 1960.

WILLIAMS, Danny Ballad singer born in Port Elizabeth, South Africa, on 7 January 1942. He made his recording debut with 'Tall a Tree' in 1959 and appeared regularly on the television show *Drumbeat* prior to reaching No. 1 in the British charts in 1961 with 'Moon River'.

On Friday 8 December 1961, Williams, then currently at No. 4 in the charts with 'Moon River', had been appearing for a week at Liverpool's Cabaret Club. He was added to the bill of a concert at the Tower Ballroom, New Brighton, which featured the Beatles.

Williams was also on the bill of the Beatles' first British nationwide tour, which was headed by Helen Shapiro. When Helen was ill on 26 and 27 February 1964, Williams topped the bill.

The 'velvet-voiced' singer had seven British chart hits between 1961 and 1963 and a major hit in America in 1964. He didn't enter the British charts again until 1977, with 'Dancin' Easy'. He continued to record for various labels, without success, and was signed to Prestige Records in 1991.

WILLIAMS, Larry Another of the Beatles' seminal influences, illustrating the range of American artists that inspired them. Williams' work also influenced numerous Mersey groups, dozens of whom performed his songs, including Howie Casey & the Seniors, the Swinging Bluejeans and the Escorts.

Williams had begun his musical career as a session pianist with Lloyd Price before branching out as a recording artist and composer in his own right.

The Beatles used many of his numbers in their early repertoire, including 'Bad Boy', 'Bony Moronie', 'Dizzy Miss Lizzie', 'Short Fat Fanny' and 'Slow Down'.

The Beatles were actually to record several of Williams's compositions. Their version of his 1959 release 'Bad Boy' was included on their *A Collection of Beatles' Oldies (but Goldies)* album in December 1966. His 1958 release 'Dizzy Miss Lizzie' was included on their *Help!* album and 'Slow Down', the flipside of Williams's 'Dizzy Miss Lizzie', was recorded by the Beatles and issued on their 'Long Tall Sally' EP.

John generally took lead vocal on their version of Williams's numbers and he was to record 'Bony Moronie' on his *Rock 'n' Roll* album.

Tragically, Williams took his own life on 2 January 1980.

WILSON, Sir Harold British politician, born in Yorkshire in 1916, who was elected leader of the Labour Party in 1963 and became Prime Minister in October 1964. On the eve of the election he received a telegram from Brian Epstein, which read: 'Hope your group is as much a success.'

The Beatles first met him on Thursday 19 March 1964, when he was still leader of the opposition. The occasion was the twelfth annual luncheon of the Variety Club of Great Britain. The event took place at noon at the Dorchester Hotel in Park Lane, London.

Wilson presented the Beatles with their award as Show Business Personalities of 1963.

When John Lennon got up to make his acceptance speech, he began, 'Mr Chief Barker ... ' he then looked at Wilson and added, ' ... and Mr Dobson'. This was a typical piece of Lennon humour, obscure to the population in general as he was referring to a Liverpool confectionery firm called Barker & Dobson.

Wilson, who was the MP for the Huyton district of Liverpool, recommended the Beatles for an MBE and he also officially reopened the Cavern club on 23 July 1966.

George Harrison was to harangue Wilson in his song 'Taxman', released in 1964.

Wilson died on 23 May 1995. The following evening, Paul McCartney was one of the celebrities to pay tribute to him on ITV's *London Tonight*. He said: 'He was very canny. The last time we met him, somebody from the press tried to put a microphone in his face and tried to get us to say something indiscreet with him. But he put the microphone in his pocket and just carried on puffing away on his pipe. I liked him a lot, he seemed like a nice man.'

WOODBINE, Lord Sobriquet used by this tall, lanky, Liverpool-based Trinidadian who steadfastly refuses to tell anyone what his real name is.

More commonly referred to as 'Woodie', he was originally given the name because of his habit of smoking Woodbines, a brand of cheap cigarette available at the time, which he chain smoked.

Local West Indians often adopted grandiose names and the steel band he was initially involved in called themselves the Royal Caribbean Steel Band.

When Woodie opened the New Colony Club in Berkley Street as a cellar shebeen, he booked the Silver Beatles for a couple of informal afternoon sessions in 1960. The entrepreneurial Woodie became involved in a number of ventures, some of them with Allan Williams. The two of them opened the New Cabaret Artistes Club in Upper Parliament Street in 1960. The street was in the heart of Liverpool's black area and rife with shebeens. They used the cellar of a Victorian house as an illicit strip club – strip-tease was banned in Liverpool at the time on the orders of the local Watch Committee.

When they booked a stripper called Janice for the venue, she insisted on live musicians to back her and the only musicians the duo could rustle up were the Silver Beatles, who received ten shillings each for playing two 20-minute spots a night.

Woodie was also part of the crew who set out on the Beatles' first trip to Hamburg. He travelled in the minivan with the Beatles, Beryl and Allan Williams and Barry Chang.

WOOLER, Bob A compère, stage manager and promoter, born in Liverpool on 19 January 1932. Immediately following his National Service, he began work as a clerk in the local railway dock office in 1952 and was based in the Garston area.

In 1957 Bob initially became involved in the music scene when he managed a skiffle group called the Kingstrums. They hailed from a tough area of Garston nicknamed 'Under the Bridge'.

Bob recalls entering the group in a skiffle contest at Gateacre Labour Club. The contest was won by the Mars Bars, who later evolved into Gerry & the Pacemakers. He says: 'At that Labour club I remember the Kingstrums coming into direct competition with John Lennon's skiffle group the Quarry Men. Because they came from posh places like Woolton and Aigburth, the Quarry Men were considered to be snobs "Under the Bridge"!'

When the Kingstrums disbanded, Bob began compèring shows locally for promoters such as Wally Hill of Peak Promotions, at venues such as Holyoake Hall in Smithdown Road. He also co-promoted dances at Hambleton Hall, Huyton, with Vic Anton.

Bob became one of the major figures on the Mersey scene and did much to help the various groups, and the Beatles in particular. He had a mellifluous voice, great wit and an extensive knowledge of the local scene. Bob was Liverpool's equivalent of Sam Goldwyn when it came to coining phrases which became established among the music fraternity – they were referred to as 'Woolerisms'. He called the Cavern 'the best of cellars', Brian Epstein was referred to as 'the Nemperor', he called Gerry Marsden 'Mr Personality', Rory Storm 'Mr Showmanship', Karl Terry 'The Sheik of Shake', Faron 'The Panda-Footed Prince of Prance', Bill Harry, 'The Boswell of Beat', Pete Best 'Mean, moody and magnificent' and referred to the soccer team the *Mersey Beat* XI as the 'Sock 'n' Sole Eleven'.

He contributed a column to *Mersey Beat*, 'The Roving I', in which readers would delight at his colourful, alliterative style of writing in which he described the Beatles as 'rhythmic revolutionaries' and shady agents as 'those characters from consville'.

Bob was particularly knowledgeable about the music the young Merseysiders wanted to hear and his record collection inspired a number of bands in their choice of repertoire. He also advised bands on their stage presentation and was probably the most efficient organizer of shows on Merseyside.

Inspired by the Top Ten Club in Hamburg, Allan Williams opened a rock 'n' roll club called the Top Ten at 100 Soho Street, Liverpool, in November 1960. Allan had talked the 28-year-old Wooler into giving up his job as a railway clerk to work full-time as disc jockey-compère at the new venue. At 11.30 p.m. on Tuesday 6 December, only eight days after it opened, the venue burned down.

All the equipment belonging to Derry & the Seniors was destroyed, so the group disbanded, but re-formed within weeks as Howie Casey & the Seniors. Williams was under-insured and only received £1,086 compensation, and Bob found himself out on a limb without a job.

He still had compère work to do for promoters such as Brian Kelly and he talked Kelly into booking the Beatles at Litherland Town Hall, the gig which brought them to the attention of Liverpool fans for the first time.

Fortunately, Ray McFall was changing his policy at the Cavern from a strictly jazz one and was now booking local groups. He employed Bob to become the Cavern's full-time compère. Bob's familiar, 'Hello, Cavern dwellers, welcome to the best of cellars,' was his trademark and it was Bob who began to organize lunchtime sessions. He recommended to Ray that they book the Beatles during lunchtime gigs as they didn't have any daytime jobs and would be readily available.

The group made their first lunchtime appearance on Tuesday 21 February 1961 and they continued to play there regularly until Saturday 3 August 1963.

Bob reckoned that the total number of occasions he introduced the group on stage at the Cavern was 274, but also believed that, counting all the other Mersey venues, the number of times he compèred their shows was nearer 400, an achievement which ensures his place in Beatlelore.

While Wooler was introducing them on stage at the Cavern once, John Lennon told the audience that Bob was his long-lost father, whom he hadn't seen for 15 years – and they believed him!

When Brian Epstein arranged for the Beatles to meet him at his NEMS offices to discuss his management proposals, they asked Bob to join them and to give his opinion. The date was Wednesday 3 December 1961 and Bob and the Beatles initially went to the Bridge pub for drinks to discuss strategy. They arrived late, which irked Epstein – particularly since Paul wasn't with them. Paul arrived half an hour later. When Epstein wanted to know who Bob was, Lennon said: 'This is me Dad.'

Bob was, indeed, a father figure for many groups and his knowledge and advice was to prove invaluable to Epstein.

When *Mersey Beat* was launched in July 1961, I gave Bob his own column 'The Roving I'. In his contribution to the 31 August 1961 issue, Bob proved prophetic when he wrote:

Why do you think the Beatles are so popular? Many people many times have asked me this question since that fantastic night (Tuesday 27 December 1960) at Litherland Town Hall, when the impact of the act was first felt on this side of the river. I consider myself privileged to have been associated with the launching of the group on that exciting occasion, and grateful for the opportunities of presenting them to fever-pitch audiences at practically all of the group's subsequent appearances prior to their last Hamburg trip.

Perhaps my close association with the group's activities, both earlier this year and since their recent reappearance on the Merseyside scene, persuades people to think that I can produce a blueprint of the Beatles Success Story. It figures, I suppose, and if, in attempting to explain the popularity of their act, the following analysis is at variance with other people's views, well that's just one of those things. The question is nevertheless thought-provoking.

Well, then how to answer it? First, some obvious observations. The Beatles are the biggest thing to have hit the Liverpool rock 'n' roll set-up in years. They were, and still are, the hottest local property any Rock promoter is likely to encounter.

I think the Beatles are No. 1 because they resurrected original style rock 'n' roll music, the origins of which are to be found in American negro singers. They hit the scene when it had been emasculated by figures like Cliff Richard and sounds like those electronic wonders, the Shadows, and their many imitators. Gone was the drive that inflamed the emotions. This was studio set jungle music purveyed skilfully in a chartwise direction by arrangement with the A&R men.

The Beatles, therefore, exploded on a jaded scene. And to those people on the verge of quitting teendom – those who had experienced during their most impressionable years the impact of rhythm 'n' blues music (raw rock 'n' roll) – this was an experience, a process of regaining and reliving a style of sounds and associated feelings identifiable with their era.

Here again in the Beatles was the stuff that screams are made of. Here was the excitement – both physical and aural – that symbolized the rebellion of youth in the ennuied mid-fifties. This was the real thing. Here they were, first five and then four human dynamos generating a beat which was irresistible. Turning back the rock clock. Pounding out items from Chuck Berry, Little Richard, Carl Perkins, the Coasters and the other great etceteras of the era. Here they were, unmindful of uniformity of dress. Unkempt-like long hair. Rugged yet romantic, appealing to both sexes. With calculated naivety and an ingenuous, throw-away approach to their music. Affecting indifference to audience response and yet always saying 'Thank you.' Reviving interest in, and commanding, enthusiasm for numbers which had descended the charts way back. Popularizing (more than any other group) flipside items – example, 'Boys'. Compelling attention and influencing, wittingly or unwittingly, other groups in the style, choice and presentation of songs.

Essentially a vocal act, hardly ever instrumental (at least not in this country), here they were, independently minded, playing what they liked for kicks, kudos and cash. Privileged in having gained prestige and experience from a residency at the Hamburg Top Ten Club, during the autumn and winter of last year. Musically authoritative and physically magnetic – example the mean, moody magnificence of drummer Pete Best, a sort of teenage Jeff Chandler. A remarkable variety of talented voices which song-wise sound distinctive, but when speaking, possess the same naivety of tone. Rhythmic revolutionaries. An act which from beginning to end is a succession of climaxes. A personality cult. Seemingly unambitious, yet fluctuating between the self-assured and the vulnerable. Truly a phenomenon – and also a predicament to promoters! Such are the fantastic Beatles. I don't think anything like them will happen again.

It is interesting to note that the only Beatle mentioned by name is Pete Best. Pete was undoubtedly the most popular member of the group in Liverpool at the time and it was Bob who made a suggestion for their St Valentine's Night appearance at Litherland Town Hall on 14 February 1961. He talked the group into taking the unusual step of placing Pete Best and his drums to the forefront of the band. This stratagem didn't work, as the fans immediately surged forward and dragged Pete from the stage!

In his column in issue No. 7 of *Mersey Beat*, Bob listed his Top Ten Mersey groups:

Well here it is then, my list of what I rate to be the ten most popular rock groups on Merseyside – excluding the Bluegenes, of course, they are beyond comparison. They are in a class of their own.

1   The Beatles
2   Gerry & the Pacemakers
3   Rory Storm & the Hurricanes
4   The Remo 4
5   The Strangers
6   Johnny Sandon & the Searchers
7   Karl Terry & the Cruisers
8   Mark Peters & the Cyclones
9   Ray & the Del Renas
10   The Big Three

Apart from his columns on *Mersey Beat*, Bob's ability as a wordsmith was evident in the number of classified advertisements he composed for the 'Jazz' columns of the *Liverpool Echo* for various promoters. One of his Hambleton Hall ads read:

Bob Wooler's Married!!
Yes Cats Mr 'Big Beat' Bob
Wooler Has Been Married To
The Best Rock Sessions In Liverpool.
See Him Only On Monday At
Hambleton Hall Page Moss – Huyton
3 Hours Non Stop Rock
Beatles and The Ravin' Ravens
On Friday And Saturday At Aintree Institute
And Every Lunchtime Session
Exclusively At the Cavern
Take Mr Big Beat's Advice And Go
To Only the Best In Rock!

Another read:

THE HIVE OF JIVE CLUB
Presents To-morrow (Sunday) 7.30 p.m.
John Lennon ('The Singing Rage')
Paul McCartney ('The Rockin' Riot')
George Harrison ('The Sheik Of Araby')
Pete Best ('The Bashful Beat')
In the Super, Colossal Presentation
THE BEATLES BEAT SHOW!
Co-starring these great attractions:
The Rockin' Climbers
Jimmy & The Midnighters
and The Panda-Footed Prince of Prance
Faron And The Flamingos
Staged and presented Only At
Hambleton Hall, Page Moss – Huyton.
If You Don't Feel Like Jiving, Come Along
To Watch. It's Still Great Fun! Be Early!
Next Wednesday: the Strangers.

A final, typical example of a Wooler advert reads:

To-morrow Night! Wednesday!
At the 'Hive of Jive'
Hambleton Hall Page Moss – Huyton
The Senior Weatherman (Derry)
Forecasts A Hot Time With a
Cool Storm (Rory Type), Hurricanes,
Tempests And Tornadoes.
And The Temperature Will Be Faron-Heit.
Take Note!!! There Will Also Be
An Invasion Of Boppin' Beatles.

A few days after the meeting between the Beatles and Brian Epstein, Wooler was able to reveal to Epstein that the group were indeed on the lookout for a manager.

When Brian set up his own NEMS promotions at venues such as the Tower Ballroom and the Queen's Hall, Widnes, he engaged Bob to organize and run them.

At one time Bob made a special trip to the *Mersey Beat* office to complain to me that I was including too much material about the Beatles in the paper. He said that lots of groups were becoming jealous and had begun calling the paper the *Mersey Beatle*. I then decided to include a special section called the 'Mersey Beatle' in each issue.

Although Bob was such a champion of the Beatles, he is perhaps unfairly more known because of an incident which took place at Paul McCartney's twenty-first birthday party on 18 June 1963. Bob made a remark to John which resulted in John giving him a beating. Lennon and Epstein had recently returned from a weekend in Spain and Wooler made a remark hinting at a homosexual relationship. John was to tell Cynthia: 'He called me a bloody queer so I bashed his ribs in.'

Bob had to be taken to hospital and Epstein immediately set out to repair the damage, ordering his solicitor Rex Makin to pay Bob £200 in damages. John refused to apologize, so Brian sent a telegram to Bob in John's name: 'Really sorry, Bob. Terribly sorry to realize what I had done. What more can I say?'

Daily Mirror showbiz correspondent Don Short picked up the story and ran a small item on the back page headed: 'Beatle in brawl says: Sorry I socked you.'

Bob remained at the Cavern until 1967. He compèred a radio show from the club and also managed a few local groups, such as the Carrolls.

He was to marry Brian Epstein's former secretary Beryl Adams.

At that particular time the Marine Offences Bill had put paid to the pirate stations and the BBC was in the process of setting up Radio 1. With the assistance of Henry Henroid, I had arranged for Bob to have an appointment with the head of Radio 1 with the opportunity of becoming one of the regular disc jockeys at the new station. Bob travelled to London, but failed to turn up for his appointment.

It semed that he wished to remain in Liverpool. His marriage ended and he became a bingo caller.

In succeeding years he continued to promote local events with Allan Williams, appeared regularly at the Liverpool-based Beatle conventions and often escorts visitors on special Beatles tours.

WRIGHT, Maggie   A young British actress who appeared in *Magical Mystery Tour* as Maggie, the Lovely Starlet, Paul's girlfriend.

WUMP & HIS WERBLES   In Tony Palmer's book *All You Need is Love*, he writes: 'Of the early Beatles – called variously the Quarry Men, Wump and the Werbles, the Rainbows, John and the Moondogs, and the Silver Beatles ... '

Wump & His Werbles weren't an early incarnation of the Beatles, although they did appear with them when the Beatles returned from their first trip to Hamburg.

They were formed in 1959 by Rod Punt, together with Dave Georgeson, Nev Humphries, John Cochrane and Jim Mellor.

Rod was appearing at Butlin's when Rory Storm talked him into entering a rock 'n' roll singing competition. Rod won – because the judges were his friends Rory and Ringo Starr.

Recalling their appearance with the Beatles at Lathom Hall, Seaforth, he says: 'We had just bought a new Selmer Truvoice Selectatape amplifier and they asked if they could borrow it. We lent it to them and they went on stage and started tuning up.

'John Lennon had his new Rickenbacker, played one chord and four strings broke all at once. He came off stage and we all helped him to restring it.

'They started playing and we watched from the wings. Paul was on rhythm guitar and we noticed that between numbers he would plug his guitar in and pluck a few notes, when the band started playing he would take the jack-plug out! We were convinced he wasn't playing at all.

'We then went out front to watch and, horror of horrors, Stuart Sutcliffe was playing bass guitar through our brand-new amp. It was bouncing all over the place. We never let anyone borrow our gear again!'

Rod changed his name to Steve Day and led Steve Day & the Drifters. The group appeared on several Beatles bills, including the Cavern on Wednesday 21 February, a Tower Ballroom promotion on 27 July and a further Tower Ballroom gig on Friday 1 December, all in 1962. They also supported the Beatles at 'The Beatle Club' night at the Thistle Café, West Kirby, on Thursday 1 February 1962. They appeared at Hamburg's Top Ten Club in 1963 and the group disbanded some months later.

In the 1970s Rod changed his name again to Rod McKenzie, became a comedian and won *Opportunity Knocks* in 1978.

YARDBIRDS, The London R&B band who formed in June 1963. The group replaced the Rolling Stones as resident band at the Crawdaddy Club in Richmond and also had a Friday night residency at the Marquee club in London.

The Yardbirds appeared at Liverpools' Cavern club and had a minor hit with 'Good Morning Little Schoolgirl' in November 1964.

The following month they were booked to appear at the Beatles' Christmas Show at the Hammersmith Odeon in west London, where they appeared in a ten-minute spot during the first half of the show, following Michael Haslam. Their line-up at this time comprised Eric Clapton (lead guitar), Paul Samwell-Smith (bass/vocals), Keith Relf (vocals/harp), Jim McCarty (drums) and Chris Dreja (rhythm).

The group were also to appear on the bill of the Beatles' final concert appearance in Britain, on 1 May 1966 at the Empire Pool, Wembley. Their line-up now comprised Jimmy Page (bass/lead guitar), Keith Relf, Jim McCarty, Chris Dreja and Jeff Beck (lead guitar).

Following their initial chart entry, they then had a succession of three Top 5 hits in a row: 'For Your Love', 'Heart Full of Soul' and 'Evil Hearted You.'

YEMM, Bryn Welsh singer who spent the day with the Beatles when they appeared at Abergavenny Town Hall on 23 June 1963. They gave him a signed copy of their album *Please Please Me*. Bryn was a local celebrity and was in the unique honour of staying with the boys backstage. He was to comment: 'At the time it did not really sink in and no one realized they would go on to greater things, because they were just another new band. At that time I was bigger in Abergavenny than they were!' Brian Epstein asked Bryn to travel to London and see him, but he never did. He had four albums in the chart in a single year, which earned him an entry in the *Guinness Book of Records*.

YOLLAND, Peter Man who was commissioned to devise, produce and direct the two Beatles Christmas shows. Yolland, who had previously produced pantomimes, made such a success of the initial show at the Finsbury Park Astoria that he was commissioned to produce a second at the Hammersmith Odeon, the following year. Plans were made for a third Christmas show, but were then scrapped.

YOUNG, Muriel Glamorous British radio and television presenter, born in County Durham in 1931, who was co-host of Associated Rediffusion's *Tuesday Rendezvous* when the Beatles appeared on a live broadcast on Tuesday 4 December 1962.

Muriel also co-hosted Radio Luxembourg's *Friday Spectacular*, on which the Beatles appeared three times. The transmission dates were 23 November 1962, 25 January 1963 and 15 March 1963.

Muriel, who was the first female announcer on commercial television when she started with Granada Television in 1955, found that her presentation altered after she'd had the Beatles on her shows.

She was to comment: 'The Beatles changed everything. Before them I used to do all my announcing in cocktail frocks and things, but after the Beatles you could wear any casual outfit you wanted. They got rid of all the stuffiness and many, many years of dressing up.'

In September 1965, Paul McCartney and Jane Asher visited Muriel at her holiday home in Portugal, where Paul discussed 'Michelle', the song he was working on.

Muriel's last television production commission was in 1987 and since that time she has moved back to County Durham, become a professional artist, working mainly in oils, and has had several exhibitions of her paintings.

ZAPPA, Frank   American musician, born in Baltimore on 21 December 1940. He formed his famous Mothers of Invention, whose debut album, *Freak Out*, was released in 1965. Zappa's album sleeve for *We're Only in It for the Money* in 1968 was a parody of the *St Pepper* cover.

Ringo was to feature as Zappa in the movie *200 Motels* in 1971, the same year in which John and Yoko appeared on stage with Zappa at the Filmore East in New York, John's first stage appearance since 1969.

He died in 1994.

ZEC, Donald   At the time of the Beatles' rise to national fame in Britain, the *Daily Mirror* was the newspaper with the world's largest circulation and its main show-business writer was Donald Zec.

Zec had conducted interviews with a range of world-famous stars, including Marilyn Monroe, at his home at 28 Maitland Court, Lancaster Terrace, London.

The *Melody Maker*, a music publication owned by the Mirror group, was due to announce that the Beatles had topped their reader's poll and Zec was commissioned to write a feature on them.

He first attended their concert at the Odeon, Dunstable Road, Luton, on 6 September 1963. Then he invited the group to his home for the interview, which appeared on Tuesday 10 September under the heading 'Four Frenzied Little Lord Fauntleroys Who are Making £5,000 Every Week'.